Questioning Causality

Questioning Causality

Scientific Explorations of Cause and Consequence across Social Contexts

Rom Harré and Fathali M. Moghaddam, Editors

An Imprint of ABC-CLIO, LLC
Santa Barbara, California • Denver, Colorado

Library of Congress Cataloging-in-Publication Data

Questioning causality : scientific explorations of cause and consequence across social contexts / Rom Harré and Fathali M. Moghaddam, editors.
    pages cm
Includes bibliographical references and index.
ISBN 978–1–4408–3178–2 (hardback)—ISBN 978–1–4408–3179–9 (ebook)
1. Social sciences–Research. 2. Research. 3. Causation. I. Moghaddam, Fathali M., editor.
II. Harré, Rom, editor.
H62.Q47   2016
300.72—dc23   2015031330

ISBN: 978–1–4408–3178–2
EISBN: 978–1–4408–3179–9

20 19 18 17 16   1 2 3 4 5

This book is also available on the World Wide Web as an eBook.
Visit www.abc-clio.com for details.

Praeger
An Imprint of ABC-CLIO, LLC

ABC-CLIO, LLC
130 Cremona Drive, P.O. Box 1911
Santa Barbara, California 93116-1911

This book is printed on acid-free paper ∞

Manufactured in the United States of America

Contents

PART THREE: CAUSAL CONCEPTS AND
LINGUISTIC TOPICS

PART FOUR: CAUSAL CONCEPTS AND
MEDICAL CONTEXTS

Acknowledgments

We are indebted to many colleagues and students at a number of universities, but want to particularly thank Ms. Nancy Swartz, Ms. Molly McGeady, Mr. Nazir Harb Michel (a.k.a., "be-Nazir"), and the Psychology Faculty at Georgetown University.

Introduction

Rom Harré and Fathali M. Moghaddam

Step into any introductory class or open any introductory text in the social sciences, health sciences, history, theology, literature, or law, the concept of causality is implicit in the exposition of almost every topic. Particularly when the discussion turns to research methodology, one way or another, causation is the core of most investigations, scientific, cultural, or lay. The goal of this volume is to present a multidisciplinary exploration of causation that is truly accessible and of interest to students and researchers in a wide range of academic studies, as well as a large circle of general readers. Each chapter includes a general description of the topics explored by researchers in a certain area and how causes and consequences are envisaged in this domain. Illustrative examples are used to bring the discussions to life.

As students learn in the course of their studies, the topic of causation has been discussed extensively since the time of Aristotle and causation continues to be an important topic in contemporary social science and philosophy of science (Beebee, Hitchcock, & Menzies, 2012; Machamer & Wolters, 2007; Psillos, 2002). That causation is something more than statistical regularity between events has been the core of the "realist" position (Cartwright, 1997; Harré & Madden, 1975). While some contemporary books continue to be on traditional philosophical topics, such as how to distinguish causation from mere long-run coincidence (Owens, 1992), others have tried to apply formal methods of analysis in old problematic areas, such as the predictive power of causal models (Pearl, 2009; Spirtes, Glymour, & Scheines, 2000). What is common to almost all of these texts is their highly technical and specialized nature, making them inaccessible to everyone except a small group of specialists, particularly in their use of probabilistic models of causal discourses.

We have taken steps to ensure that the text is "reader friendly." The chapters are written in a jargon-free style, and clear explanations are provided for all technical terms used. Research and applied examples are used to illustrate key points throughout the text.

This volume is in line with the multidisciplinary and multimethod approach in education. There is a growing trend toward multidisciplinary teaching and research, with a recognition that narrow specialization can have negative consequences (Moghaddam, 1997). Increasingly, people are looking across disciplines and reflecting back on their own specialized fields. This multidisciplinary examination inevitably leads to more critical interest in basic questions about the core concepts of different disciplines, including how causes and consequences are conceptualized. Second, and more specifically, there is now great enthusiasm for multimethod approaches in research and teaching. A basic question that arises in adopting this stance is the conceptualization of causes and consequences in making use of different research methods.

REFERENCES

Beebee, H., Hitchcock, C., & Menzies, P. (Eds.). (2012). *The Oxford handbook of causation.* Oxford: Oxford University Press.

Cartwright, N. (1997). Models: The blueprints for laws. *Philosophy of Science, 64,* S292–S303.

Harré, R., & Madden, E. H. (1975). *Causal powers.* Oxford: Blackwell.

Machamer, P., & Wolters, G. (Eds.). (2007). *Thinking about causes: From Greek philosophy to modern physics.* Pittsburgh, PA: University of Pittsburgh Press.

Moghaddam, F. M. (1997). *The specialized society: The plight of the individual in an age of individualism.* New York: Praeger.

Owens, D. J. (1992). *Causes and coincidences.* New York: Cambridge University Press.

Pearl, J. (2000). *Causality: Models, reasoning, and inference.* Cambridge, UK: Cambridge University Press.

Psillos, S. (2002). *Causation and explanation.* Montreal, QC: McGill-Queen's University Press.

Spirtes, P., Glymour, C., & Scheines, R. (2001). *Causation, prediction, and search* (2nd ed.). Cambridge, MA: MIT Press.

Part One

. . . .

The Concepts of Causation
as Developed by Philosophers

1

The Discourse Frame

Rom Harré

Most of the time things go rolling along pretty smoothly—the seasons proceed with their perennial march, people are cheerful and healthy, pine logs burn in the grate of the country cottage, the Metro runs on time, the car starts on demand, and the Bangladeshi garment factory floors sustain the workforce and their machines. But not always! Droughts, floods, and hurricanes disrupt seasonal expectations; people fall ill and some of them imagine they are hearing voices; the fire dies out; the train doors won't close; the car refuses to start; and the garment factory collapses. Here we have a common type of occasion when we resort to causal hypotheses. There must be something that accounts for the disruption of the orderliness we take for granted. However, we also try to manage the world so that our actions achieve the outcomes we want. This is also a common type of occasion for making use of causal hypotheses. Ideally the same body of knowledge should suffice both for plausible explanations of the untoward and for designing successful procedures to accomplish our projects. In both cases the focus is on the explanation and the management of change. Here we encounter the central role of causal discourses, stories and anecdotes, theories and explanations in the management of life.

Sight, sound, and touch, singly and together, present a conscious human being with a flux of ever-changing complexes of here and now experiences. We could call these "phenomena." Human beings are capable of maintaining records of what has been present and of foreseeing what the contents of the present that are yet to come might be. The contents of the present perish and new phenomena appear. We will call this "the flux." Looking "forward" and "backward" in remembering and forecasting, people build up stories, some of which are explanations of what has occurred and some predictions of what might occur. Change and endurance are key items in these stories. All such stories must be told in the present. "Past" and "future" are discursive categories that are organizational devices for storytelling. They are not ontological categories, that is, real-world locations in which events and other temporal items could exist. Only the present is such a domain. In Chapter 2 we will undertake a critical exploration of the links between time and causality.

As the studies presented here unfold, it will become clear that causal knowledge that results from disciplined enquiries both professional and lay is usually presented in what one might call a "causal format." For example, medical knowledge enables a clinician to diagnose the cause or part of the cause of a disease from various well-established tests. A clinician knows that a blood clot in the brain is the likely cause of the paralysis that is a symptom of a stroke. He uses an antibiotic to clear up an infection secure in his knowledge that this substance will kill the malignant bacteria. An experienced gardener knows that the cause of the rotten cores of his apples is an infestation of the Codlin moth. He uses derris dust to clear the white butterfly caterpillars from the cabbage patch secure in his knowledge that this compound kills them. Certain factors are picked out from the conditions antecedent to a change that someone hopes to bring about with respect to what is believed to be their relative efficacy in bringing about that change in the contents of the present. Elaborate theoretical constructions are developed to depict efficacious and productive mechanisms hypothesized to underlie observable phenomena. In this way, the forms of explanation are similar in the natural sciences, most "cultural" disciplines, and lay understanding of how new states of affairs come about as effects of causes. At the distal end of the alleged causal relation between causes and what they bring about, their effects, we find again a disparate catalog of candidates. Among effects are new beings, such as islands caused by volcanic eruptions; a material thing or stuff taking on new attributes, such as the coloring of the cloth from the dyeing vat; and, of course, events, such as the breaking of the legendary window pane as it is struck by the ball and the explosion that follows the ignition of a charge by the burning fuse.

I. THE CAUSAL VOCABULARY

"Causality" and "causation" are often used synonymously, but it is helpful to emphasize the distinction between a word for a causal process and a word for referring to such a process. We will use "causation" to refer to any *process* that is taken to be productive of changes in the world of the present. "Causality" will be reserved for describing such a process. So *causation* will refer to a real relation between particulars and *causality* will be the generic concept with which we refer to causal processes.

Causal discourses can refer to particular conditions and the specific antecedent events and local exercises of agency that are taken to be responsible for them. Causal talk can also be used to refer to relations between types of events or conditions. "I am tired because I have just run a mile" refers to what happened on a particular occasion, while "Exercise causes fatigue" links type with type. This person takes an aspirin each day to maintain a healthy heart and is acting in accord with the general adage that a daily aspirin promotes cardiac health.

Causal discourses can be used to describe several patterns in the flux of phenomena, including singular causes and singular effects, singular causes and multiple effects, multiple causes and singular effects, and multiple causes and multiple effects. Elaborated forms of these discourses use conjunctions or disjunctions of multiple causes or effects. We will study examples of patterns of both singular and multiple causes and effects.

Given that a study of the many ways that the concept of causality finds expression in a multitude of discourses reveals a variety of uses, it would be wise to be wary of presuming that there is a "conceptual essence" that defines what "causation" *really* is. The lesson that Wittgenstein (1953) teaches us is to acknowledge the existence of fields of family resemblances in the uses of prominent and important concepts and others of lesser moment without trying to pick out the essence of the phenomenon in question.

In this chapter we will present various concepts of causality that are used in descriptions of whatever is taken to be efficacious in the production of phenomena, that is, of changes in the contents of the present as the productive process begins to unfold. Our strategy will be to lay out a kind of "logical geography" of the uses of causal concepts in a wide variety of contexts. To initiate the study of concepts, we study the uses of words and other symbols for all the purposes implied by our subject matter, the description and explanation of change. Causal concepts are so central to the management of our daily practices that the analysis of the meaning of causal discourse has been a central topic for philosophers since antiquity. However, beginning in the eighteenth century the interpretations philosophers have placed on causal concepts have diverged more and more from lay understandings of causality. While dictionaries link causality to agents, individual things such as magnets, and substances such as wind and water, philosophers interpret the concept in terms of events.

We begin with considerations germane to causation in cases in which both causes and effects are individuals—singular causes linked to singular effects.

Causes as Agents

According to many dictionaries, a cause is an active agent that brings about a change. Intermediate between *enduring agents* such as acids and alkalis, charges and poles, and the fields associated with them and ephemeral events that trigger processes of change are *causal mechanisms*, such as a mechanical clock in which a wound spring changes the positions of the hands, via a nicely arranged train of gears.

Reports of human affairs rarely make use of the word "cause" itself in reporting noteworthy changes and innovations. However, a multitude of synonyms such as "produce," "generate," "bring about," and "make happen" leave no doubt as to the causal character of the discourses of everyday life both written and spoken. Here is an example from the London *Metro*: "A budding psychopath who murdered a friend after saying that listening to rap *made him* want to 'stab up someone's face' was convicted yesterday" Again from *London Times*: "The Iranian actress Leila Hatami *has outraged* conservatives at home by kissing the president of the Cannes Festival on the cheek—an act deemed insulting to the 'chastity' of women." These phrases clearly are meant to describe causal relations.

A popular online dictionary offers the following definitions:

> "Cause" as a noun: "A person or thing that gives rise to an action, phenomenon, or condition." Synonyms: source, root, origin, beginning (s), starting point, seed, genesis, agency, "cause" as a verb: "Make something . . . happen." Synonyms: bring about, give rise to, be the cause of, lead to, result in, create, begin, produce, originate, engender, spawn, occasion, effect, bring to pass, bring on, precipitate, prompt, provoke, kindle, trigger, make happen, spark off, touch off, stir up, whip up, induce, inspire, promote, foster, effectuate, occasion, etc.

This array of words is almost exclusively used to say something about the activity of agents accounting for change in all sorts of contexts. Unshackling an agent can also be a cause.

"Removing the support brought the roof down" is not likely to be challenged as an explanation of a disaster. It is linked to the proposition "Were the supports to be removed the roof would fall." Why do we believe these propositions? We presume that gravity would continue to be active in the imagined situation in which the supports are removed. Citing previous examples of support removal followed by a falling roof would have provided some grounds for the causal statement, but extending the instances into an imagined world, if accepted, gives much stronger grounds for the prediction of disaster and the explanation of the catastrophe than a summary of what has actually happened.

J. Pearl (2000) proposed a recipe for assembling a cluster of statements that would serve as a description of a causal mechanism. This calls for a representation of conditions extrinsic to the mechanism, a representation of conditions intrinsic to the mechanism, and an account of the components of the mechanism itself and how they interact. Thus, for a clockwork device to operate a switch on a bomb and therefore cause an explosion, the atmospheric and other environmental conditions must be right, the spring must be wound up, and the gears and cogs must mesh in the right ratios to smoothly transmit motion through the mechanism. A similar pattern of requirements would be needed to justify the claim that the heat in the oven caused the bread to rise, via the mechanism of fermentation. And so on. Though the analysis of the nature of causal processes as mechanisms has often been passed over in favor of the study of the logic of event sequences, nevertheless, in recent works such discourse recipes as Pearl's "causal models" do depend on recognizing such mechanisms and their role as agents of change.

Phenomena conceived as changes in the continuous flux of the present can count as causes only if they trigger the agentive powers of a productive or generative mechanism or release an agent, the activity of which has been blocked by some external feature of the environment (Cheng, 1997). We note that the internal workings of a mechanism are also causal, and at the heart of such a device, natural or contrived, there must be a source of activity: an agent. The pocket watch, which was my grandfather's pride and joy, incorporates a wound-up spring. Causal mechanisms structured in certain ways are collections of well-ordered parts together with a source of activity, an agent. For the most part the agents we encounter are not fundamental, but structures of parts, among which are yet more rudimentary agents. However, by repeated analyses we approach, step by step, the basic unanalyzable agents of the material universe: charges and their fields. In a similar way we eventually reach the basic unanalyzable agents of the social universe: human beings.

Looking at the matter from the point of view of the exploitation of natural phenomena for human purposes it seems that to cause something to happen is to bring into being an event or state of the desired type by creating a situation that it is known regularly precedes the desired effect. We also set about causing something to happen by releasing an existing power or capacity that has been blocked in some way. At most, both practices depend on the existence of a potent or efficacious agent. At least as a first impression it seems that in all the disciplines we admire as human studies, the concept of causation, implicit or explicit, refers to generative processes and causal powers and only indirectly to the regularities that the running of these processes produces. These are the regularities that alert us to the possibility that a causal mechanism, a power or an agency, is at work (Harré & Madden, 1972).

Causes as Events

When we turn to another popular source, but one influenced by the work of philosophers, Wikipedia, a very different interpretation is suggested: "Causality (also referred to as causation) is the relation between an event (the cause) and a second event (the effect)." Though the entry continues, "causes and effects are typically related to changes or events, candidates include objects, processes, variables, facts and states of affairs," most of the philosophical literature of the last 300 years has been focused on events as causes and effects. On this reading, causation is a link between events. So what causation can be is limited by what sort of links there can be between events.

According to many philosophers the most common category of beings supposedly linked by causal relations are events. Though this is the vaguest of terms, it has almost monopolized the attention of philosophers since Hume claimed to have eliminated all need for notions of real activity or agency from the discourse of the wise, reducing it to a mental state of expectation brought about by repetitions of like pairs of events.

In its most general sense, "event" refers to momentary changes in the states of things and substances that are correlated with later changes and so declared their causes. The analysis of the relations between events as happenings has become the main topic of the philosophy of "causation," the process, and "causality," the concept.

Causes as Facts

Hugh Mellor (1995) has suggested that we should think of causes and their effects as "facts." "The fact that the patient was given penicillin is the cause of the fact that he recovered." Mellor proposes the following: "Actual states of affairs corresponding to true statements, I shall call *facts*, like the fact that Don falls, which exists [if and only if] 'Don falls is true.' " Causal relations exist between particulars, this falling of Don and this breaking of bones. Facts are discursive entities and are in the same cognitive world as true statements, of which they are variants. We say, "The fact that the soufflé collapsed . . ." and whatever follows a "that" is propositional. There must be something else that serves as a truth-maker to the propositions of a causal account of some phenomenon, namely, a collapsed soufflé! Why would anyone develop such a strange account of causation? Mellor argues that his proposal comes from the need to admit that the correlative state of affairs to the true statement "C caused E" is a fact, the fact that C caused E. But the truth-maker of "C caused E" is something that exists in the material world.

II. THE EFFECTS OF VOCABULARY

The pattern of causation is always process to product. The methodological question is whether the products were constituents of the being on which the process was exercised and thus a certain kind of effect. Do we have analysis or genesis? To assume that processes directed toward targets always yield constituents is to fall into the "product-process" fallacy, or the mereological fallacy. A new and fruitful concept with which to manage these issues is the "affordance," developed from the perception theory proposed by J. J. Gibson (1986).

- Affordances as what can be accomplished in a certain set-up by an agent —for example, a still, mash, and fuel affords distillation to a moonshiner.
- Affordances as products, material stuff (distillation affords whiskey), or attributes (heating liquidity). In recent years two distinct concepts of "affordance" have appeared. A certain set-up affords a certain activity to an agent—a frozen lake affords walking to a wolf but not to an elk. We also say, in a second sense of "affordance," that a prism and white light suitably arranged afford spectra. That is a product of the use of the set-up by, say, Isaac Newton.

There is no doubt that effects as affordances are products of interactions between an agent and a target. However, some affordances are grounds for inferences as to the structure or other intrinsic characteristics of the targets, while others are not. Each case needs to be considered with respect to such matters as the plausibility of projecting what an interaction affords back onto the target that afforded it. Neglect of this philosophical precaution can lead to a mereological fallacy—taking the products of an interaction to be constituents of the target object, be it electrons in atoms or memories in brains.

III. THE MOST GENERAL CAUSAL CONCEPT

Is there any generic concept for referring to the production of change that emerges from this catalog of different uses loosely laid out as a field of family resemblances? We suggest that the most useful concept for thinking about the way changes occur in the content of "the flux" is that there must exist necessary and sufficient conditions for some change to occur. This is what we look for when we are searching for a cause, be it an agent, a mechanism, or an event or cluster of events. The list of necessary conditions comprises the factors in the absence of which the event of interest would not have occurred. The list of sufficient conditions comprises the factors that would bring about an effect of importance. The idea of a cause as the necessary and sufficient condition for a change to occur has been elaborated and refined by J. L. Mackie (1974). A cause, Hume proposed, could be identified as certain conditions obtaining among the antecedents of an event of interest. Two and a half centuries later, Mackie (p. 62) refers to something similar, namely, the INUS conditions on which he bases his analysis of causality in *The Cement of the Universe* (p. 36). He argues that an event is to be taken as causal when it occurs only when certain circumstances obtain in a field of relevant material conditions. He writes that a state or an event A is the cause or some part of the cause of an effect E if it is "an *insufficient* but *non-redundant* part of an *unnecessary* but *sufficient condition*" (Mackie, 1974, p. 62). A is not by itself sufficient to bring about E, but is required for the event to have occurred. But something else in the situation could have filled the prescription, so A is not a necessary condition for the occurrence of E. This yields the neat acronym "INUS conditions." There may be several sets of conditions sufficient to produce an effect, so no one of them is necessary, that is, without which the effect would not have occurred. However, among these conditions are some that are more relevant to a causal story than others. These are candidate causes. How the relative relevance of conditions is established in the absence of attention to causal mechanisms and natural agents is left mysterious.

Let us look at an example of this procedure. A medical research team wants to understand the occurrence of an acquired failure of the immune system in certain people. They belong to a minority cultural group and engage in activities that could serve to spread disease. Either seems to be strongly correlated with the advent of acquired immunity deficit syndrome (AIDS), so at this stage of the research we have a cluster of sufficient conditions. That either the cultural context or the minority activity could have been a necessary condition for the development of AIDS is challenged by the hypothesis that the condition is a consequence of depression as a result of membership of a minority group. However, this proposal is finally refuted by the discovery of a virus unique to the victims of AIDS, which now becomes the accepted cause of AIDS as its main effect on the human immune system. Not everyone who has been infected with the virus develops AIDS, and some people who are not members of the minority group display the syndrome of AIDS. Here we have a neat example of the INUS analysis of causality as the organizing concept of a medical discourse, which refers to the mechanism of the causation of the disease.

IV. NECESSITY AND PROBABILITY IN CAUSAL DISCOURSE

The "causes as events" view goes back to David Hume's famous discussion in the eighteenth century (Hume, 1739). Hume's event sequences were contingent in the sense that whatever we already knew about the world, an event of any kind could follow from the contents of the present. As he put it, there was no contradiction in conjoining a description of the cause event with the negation of a description of the usual event that had followed in the past. It was necessitarian only in the sense that long experiences of regular concomitances of certain event pairs created a feeling of expectation in the observer who comes to expect B on the occurrence of A. "Causal necessity" refers to a psychological phenomenon. But the expectation could just as easily be probabilistic as necessitarian.

No doubt the frequent appearances of an A together with a B suggest that A is the cause of B, after various other hypotheses have been disposed of. But this is the use of regularity as a criterion for the hypothesis that this is a causal process. In setting out his criteria for an event to be the cause of another event, Hume refers not only to observed cases of event of type E following one of type C but also to cases where in the absence of C, E does not occur. As a cause, C is not only a sufficient condition for E but also a necessary condition, "without which not." Mere juxtaposition in space and time is too weak as a reason for declaring that A has brought B about in any manner known to science or common sense. However, we might be inclined to think this if we had become convinced that all that could be known of the universe and of our own lives could be represented as sequences of independent events, as Hume argued. Here we encounter a long-running discussion concerning the hypothetical status of possible causal mechanisms in contrast with the certainty of our knowledge of observed patterns of sequences of events, culled from the flux of experience. We will return to this discussion from time to time in these chapters.

In setting out a methodological version of Hume's criteria, John Stuart Mill expressly presented causes as instances of phenomena, which are open to either an event or an active agent interpretation. However, he is also explicit about the point of the canons—they express criteria for finding causes, they are not analysis of the meaning of either the concept of causality or the nature of the process of causation. These rules are worth presenting in full because, though we do not often consult them explicitly, they have become a taken-for-granted methodology for conducting searches for causes. The canons are as follows:

- *Method of agreement:* If two or more instances of the phenomenon under investigation have only one circumstance in common, the circumstance in which alone all the instances agree is the cause (or effect) of the given phenomenon.
- *Method of difference:* If an instance in which the phenomenon under investigation occurs and an instance in which it does not occur have every circumstance in common save that one occurs only in the former, the circumstance in which alone the two instances differ is the effect, or the cause, or part of the cause, of the phenomenon.
- *Joint method of agreement and difference:* If two or more instances in which the phenomenon occurs have only one circumstance in common, while two or more instances in which it does not occur have nothing in common save the absence of that circumstance, the circumstance in which alone the two sets of instances differ is the effect, or the cause, or an indispensable part of the cause, of the phenomenon.
- *Method of residues:* Subduct from any phenomenon such a part as is known by previous inductions to be the effect of certain antecedents, and the residue of the phenomenon is the effect of the remaining antecedents.
- *Method of variation:* Whatever phenomenon varies in any manner whenever another phenomenon varies in some particular manner is either a cause or an effect of that phenomenon, or is connected with it through some fact of causation (Mill, 1996).
- A more subtle events-based interpretation of what it is to be a cause provides a further criterion for distinguishing correlations from genuine causal productions. Exploring this criterion will lead us to a richer notion of causation than that proposed by either Hume or Mill. This is the criterion of *counterfactual plausibility*. A rather different criterion for picking out causes from among the antecedent environment of an effect of interest is based on the logical concept of a counterfactual hypothesis usually expressed something like "If X were to be the case, then Y would be the case." Used as a criterion we would determine whether A is a cause of B by asking whether "A causes B" can be expanded into a true counterfactual statement or cluster of statements in an imagined context similar to that in which A has been known to cause B, for example, "If A had happened (though it did not) B would have happened (though it did not)." This context presupposes that it is possible to determine whether the counterfactual expansion from the real to an imagined world is true. According to one well-known account (Lewis, 1973), a counterfactual statement is true if the laws of

nature relevant to the actual known instances are preserved into the imagined environment and the parameters of the process that links A to B in the counterfactual environment are similar but not identical to those that link A to B in the actual environment.

Does the counterfactualist's faith in the preservation of the laws of nature in an imagined world refer to something more fundamental? The laws of nature are propositions describing processes, and whether they are preserved depends on whether we can imagine the same processes to be occurring and so the same causal mechanisms (agencies) to be acting in the imagined context. This is a realist grounding to counterfactualism at odds with the way that a metaphysics confined to events has been presumed by Lewis and many others. Using such phrases as "laws of nature" leaves the question of what it is they describe still open: the behavior of mechanisms. Or are they no more than a nomological form of universal affirmative propositions? As N. R. Campbell (1920) showed long ago, the existence of well-established laws of nature is compatible with a huge variety of real-world mechanisms. Only if there is an imagined and plausible mechanism are we entitled to assert the truth of a relevant counterfactual in circumstances that differ from the real world only in the states of affairs we imagine to obtain. Any cluster of general propositions purportedly serving as laws of nature at best describes the workings of some possible world, unless the existence of a definite and relevant mechanism can be established empirically. The explosive expansion of superheated steam that blew up Krakatoa is the same type of mechanism, an instance of which has so far not blown up Vesuvius this century, though it could. The subterranean circumstances, unknown to us, are different from those that led to the destruction of Pompeii, though the physics of superheated steam is the same.

Causes in the Context of Necessity

The fact that causal processes often do not turn out exactly as we anticipated they would on the basis of tidying up our observations of material processes would seem to undermine the principle that causal processes necessitate the appearance of the phenomena that are taken to be their effects. Setting fire to the kindling must ignite it, so we think. Sometimes the kindling does not light, and sometimes the antibiotic does not bring down the fever—but we do not give up our necessitarian presumptions—instead we add some selection of ceteris paribus (CP) clauses. The kindling must light unless interfered with by something, for example, the wood being wet. So "Matches not only will but must ignite kindling"; ceteris paribus, all else being equal. Swallowing what one believes to be two aspirin tablets do not cure one's headache. The principle behind taking aspirin can be preserved by adding any one of a number of possible CP clauses such as the tablets have deteriorated and it isn't really acetyl salicylic acid any more. Falling back on a CP clause ensures that we take the causal statement to be understood to be valid in near uniformity of conditions and sustained by a near-stable generative or productive process.

Causes in the Context of Probability

Associated with Hume's minimalist interpretation of causal concepts and rooted in the metaphysics of events as temporal entities is the proposal that a cause, A, is anything that raises the probability that B, a subsequent event, will occur. Probabilities are qualifications of events, so the probability interpretation is a refinement of the regularity interpretation. It has recently been proposed by several philosophers that we should define causes as those antecedents to a phenomenon that make that phenomenon more likely, that is, more probable in the circumstances. The range of phenomena to which this definition would apply can be very broad, from events, coming about of new stable states of matter or society, cures of diseases and the logic of clinical trials, to anticipating earthquakes and tsunamis. Before trying to assess the usefulness of this suggestion we must set out a viable account of the concept of probability. We will be following the suggestion of Bruno de Finetti that the probability of a phenomenon is the degree of belief that a reasonable person would have in the phenomenon occurring (Kyburg & Smokler, 1980).

For practical purposes the degree of belief that someone expresses should be well-grounded in the assessment rationale. There are two sources of support for such an assessment: a study of the frequency with which the event occurs in the relevant situation and reflection in the structure of the mechanism that is producing the event in question, be it a roulette wheel, horse race, or double slit. De Finetti proposed the rational betting quotient as the numerical measure of degree of belief in such an event occurring in this or that situation. The rational support from the two empirical sources is strong for coin tossing and weak for horse racing. The use of the word "probability" has spread from expressing the assessment of the likelihood of a certain event (or type of event occurring) to the expression of the degree of belief one should have in the truth of a proposition describing the event in question.

So there are two kinds of evidence a reasonable person would turn to, to make an informed judgment of the likelihood of a certain phenomenon occurring on the basis of his or her knowledge of the structure of mechanisms that are known to generate the phenomenon in question. For example, as soon as one realizes that the roulette wheels at Las Vegas have zero and double zero slots, one's ideas about what are reasonable odds would surely change. The other kind of evidence is the frequency with which the phenomenon of interest occurs in like situations relative to some stable past pattern. How often does a head turn up in a sequence of penny tosses? The former evidence is a priori or theoretical though it is derived from the actual structure of an event generator, while the latter is empirical in the simplest sense that it records observations unclouded by theory. Thus, a reasonable belief in the probability of heads turning up in a coin tossing activity is .5 because a coin has two faces modified by the statistics of actual tossings. Each corrects the other.

We turn now to the suggestion that the cause, or part of the cause of a phenomenon, is an epistemic proposal that makes the cause more likely. That is, the knowledge that it has occurred supports a greater degree of belief in the occurrence if the phenomenon in question were prior to its discovery. Thus, it is a contribution to the understanding of the concept of causality rather than of causation, that is, of the processes that bring the event about.

The belief that drinking alcohol increases the probability that the heart rate will rise is a contribution to the degree of belief a reasonable person would have on taking the pulses of drinkers at intervals. But finding the biochemical pathways to the neural mechanisms that regulate heart rate modifies, and in this case strengthens, the degree of belief readjusted by recording empirical observations.

A cause as phenomenon cannot be reduced to what makes a subsequent phenomenon more probable. Probability is part of the content of a *belief*. It is not a constituent of the world. It must act on the degree of belief that someone has, that is, on a psychological state. The custom of expressing the epistemic rule in algebraic terms conceals the slide from observations of phenomena to beliefs based on them.

V. MULTIPLE ANTECEDENTS AND RAMIFYING CONSEQUENCES

Presuming we have criteria for individuating causes and effects, there are at least the following patterns (the possibility of which has to be examined in concrete cases): We must bear in mind the distinction between the study of discourse patterns, the forms of causal talk, and the study of material patterns, the forms of causal processes that bring about changes in the contents of the flux. We must also take account of the distinction between cases in which the "other" cause or the "other" effect is imaginary, particularly when there are counterfactual conditional statements in the causal discourse. We hold that sorting out the components of a causal nexus is not a matter of the application of universal principles but a case-by-case analysis with practical matters in mind.

Singular Causes and Conjunctive Effects

The case in which a sequence of further effects stems from a single effect we take to be simply a case of the iteration of the simple one-to-one causal pattern.

When just one factor is cited as the cause of more than one effect that occurs more or less simultaneously, geneticists call this "pleiotropy." A sip of a fine tempranillo wine causes a delicate taste and a warm feeling at the same time. This concept is similar to the concept of "collateral damage" used to excuse unintended bad consequences of deliberate actions, and is linked to the principle discussed by philosophers as the law of double effect. This "law" supposedly licenses the claim that one is responsible only for the effects one's action is intended to bring about.

Singular Causes and Disjunctive Effects

A causal discourse expresses knowledge of the correlations of pairs not only of phenomena that occur in a certain significant way but also, by implication, phenomena that have not occurred but might have done. This event, "c1," *rather than* an alternative "c2" is causally linked to this effect, "e1," rather than "e2." Slowing the car rather than speeding it up is the result of pressing the brake pedal rather than changing down a gear. This elaboration of the traditional paired phenomena picture has been proposed by Schaffer (2005). Most cause-effect pairs can be expanded into at least one "rather than" dimension.

Adapting an example from Ballerin (2014) proposed originally by Sartorio (2006) we could ask how to apportion causal responsibility for the drowning of three incompetent swimmers, A, B, and C, who have all got into difficulties in the treacherous river. A passer-by, P, cannot decide to which swimmer he should throw the only life jacket on the bank. While he hesitates, they all drown. Ballerin argues that not only is this a case of causation by omission but also a case in which a singular cause has had a disjunctive effect, namely, that either A or B or C could have been saved. P did not save any of A or B or C, the disjunctive consequence of not throwing the life jacket. It is important to notice that the conclusion is based on a counterfactual move. Counterfactual propositions are true only if the conditions in which they are imagined to be meaningful are not too far from the conditions of the real word, and a similar causal mechanism is imagined to be operative in the imaginary world to the relevant mechanism in the real world, in this case the mechanism of death by drowning.

Conjunctive Causes and Singular Effects

- *Partial causes:* Two or more causes are proposed for an effect. Each is necessary but only in conjunction are they sufficient to bring about a change in the contents of the flux, that is, an effect.
- *Overdetermination:* What is to be said when two antecedent factors, each of which would have been sufficient to bring about an event or a new situation, occur simultaneously? The assassin's bullet destroys the brain of the dictator at the exact moment that he suffers a fatal heart attack. A is sufficient to cause C, the death of the tyrant, and B is also sufficient to cause C. They act simultaneously but should we say that together they bring about C?

Disjunctive Causes and Singular Effects

- *Preemption:* For our purposes the most important case is "preemption": A has occurred and causes C but if B had not been inhibited it would have caused C. There are two cases: A was brought about by some agency independent of the agency that inhibited B or it was the occurrence of A that inhibited B. In either case a certain effect is "guaranteed" (Paul & Hall, 2013, p. 98).

Which of these patterns is causal? Two tests have been proposed that echo the analysis we have been presenting. Does taking causality to refer to regularity of co-occurrence serve to answer questions about assignments of causal efficacy among the events presented in the set-up? Or is the claim that an event would not have occurred had a certain sequence of other events not occurred a clear criterion for deciding whether events in a certain pattern are related causally? Counterfactuals such as the above make sense only if causality is taken to refer to the action of an agent or a mechanism that is supposed to perform the causal act and it is only the circumstances that are imaginary or counterfactual. If these conditions are met we can make good judgments as to the truth of counterfactuals. The changing conditions must not be such as to make the mechanisms of production of effects unworkable—were my car to have a 5 liter engine it would go twice as fast (provided the earth's atmosphere and gravitational field and so on remain more or less the same).

There are several other possible patterns that we could analyze in detail. Thus, we have:

- *Conjunctive causes and conjunctive effects:* aiming correctly *and* firing the gun not only brings down the pheasant *but also* deafens the beaters.
- *Disjunctive causes and conjunctive effects:* taking *either* Panadol *or* aspirin brings down the temperature of the patient *and* deadens the pain of the wound.
- *Conjunctive causes and disjunctive effects:* playing the drum *and* marching excites the crowd or annoys them.
- *Disjunctive causes and disjunctive effects:* mowing the lawn or trimming the hedge makes one look hardworking or in need of an occupation.

These examples have illustrated a category of puzzles that philosophers have described as cases of redundant causes. From our point of view, we note that "redundant cause ambiguities" cannot be resolved if we have only Humean regularities to work with as the meaning of causal claims. This observation undermines the value of the regularity analysis of causation to provide an account of how the world works.

VI. A TAXONOMY OF VERNACULAR CAUSAL CONCEPTS

In his detailed presentation of a wide variety of accounts of the meaning of "cause" and "causes," John Losee (2011, p. 169) sums up his presentation in a rather oddly organized but illuminating table. This table displays a clear division of meanings that have been given to the process of causation and the

Table 1.1 Variety of Causal Concepts

Scheme One: Antecedents			
Events (Changes)		Conditions	
Regularity	Probabilistic	Strict	INUS

Scheme Two: Dispositions			
Active (Powers)		Passive (Liabilities)	
Capacities	Capabilities	Proneness	Tendency

Scheme Three: Mechanisms			
Self-Starting Operation		Require Activation	
Destroyed	Survive	Destroyed	Survive

logic of its descriptions. There are those that refer to regularities between the characteristics of sequences of events and there are those that refer to the activity of productive agents. Such agents are relevant to causation by virtue of their possession of capacities or powers to bring about changes in the world. Our analysis has shown that the "regularity of patterns of events" account is not an analysis of the meaning of causal claims but a criterion for recognizing situations in which it might be worthwhile to proceed further in search of the causal mechanisms and basic agents that bring about change in the contents of the present. We make use of the concept of causes as ephemeral events, prior members of similar pairs of events, echoing Hume (1739), and of causes as persisting agents capable of exercising causal powers, echoing Leibniz and Clarke (1992). Events are passive while agents are active.

The results of this exploration provide a causal field from which practical need and manipulative possibility together with personal or social interest enable someone to extract a cause. From our analyses of the many examples presented in this chapter we can lay out a conceptual scheme, something like the one depicted in Table 1.1.

We turn to this repertoire of concepts when we have some idea that there are necessary and sufficient conditions for the effect of interest to occur. Picking out a prior event of significance for the investigation opens up the search for agents and mechanisms, those enduring entities in which causal powers are located.

To find the causes of changes in the world of the present, we must explore the contents of the flux prior to the production of the effect in search of the necessary and sufficient conditions for the effect to be brought about. Sometimes we must be content only with Mackie's INUS conditions. To see some of these causal concepts at work, consider this minor domestic drama. Someone looks up—"See that damp patch on the ceiling, it wasn't there before." "Well, the water must have come from somewhere, maybe a leak." The handyman arrives—"Let's go up and try to trace the leak." "It seems to be coming from the gas boiler flue." They dismantle the flue and it's full of water that's slowly leaking into the ceiling below. "It must be blocked! How often have you cleaned the filter?" "What filter?" "Let's look—the filter is all choked up!" The burning gas produces water vapor and that is condensing on the inside of the flue. The final step is to identify a source—antecedent temporally because there is little doubt the leak started before the water reached the ceiling physically. The source of the water comes only at the end of the investigation—the condensate in the flue. In between is a mechanism consisting of running water that leaks into the veiling below. The handyman goes *up* to begin the investigation because he takes for granted that gravity is responsible for the movement of the water. Note also that the final resolution draws on another causal concept—the blocking of a natural process and the *removal* of the block bring about the draining of the condensate. Agency is invoked here and there—the cool flue condenses the water vapor, the burning gas produces the vapor, the leaking water dampens the ceiling, and so on.

We are now equipped with an arsenal of analytical procedures for investigating the meaning and plausibility of causal claims to be found in a discussion of a wide variety of topics in many and diverse circumstances. We have been able to distinguish criteria for making plausible causal claims from the metaphysics of causation as it is reflected in the way we use causal concepts in explanations of the becoming and perishing of phenomena in the flux of ever-present experience.

At the core of all causal explanations are causal mechanisms and the agencies that animate them. There are the gears in the mechanism of clock and the spring or battery that drives them. Unwound clocks and those with dead batteries are no longer capable of producing the effects we expect of them—the smooth continuum of the changing state of the clock face. Dividing the day into hours and the hours into seconds and so on offers a practical procedure for the management and measurement of the ever-present flux, but it runs into paradox if presented as the basic ontology of causation.

In further developing the insights and distinctions set forth so far, we explore the framing of causal talk within the grammars of temporal discourses in Chapter 2 and as essential components of explanatory discourses in Chapter 3.

In setting out the three main ways causality has been conceived, we have also revealed a very deep metaphysical chasm between meanings based on causes as events and meanings based on causes as agents. The former presuppose an "actualist" stance to the world, in which reality consists in what is manifest in the here and now, at base to the sensory systems of organisms and the reactions of instruments. The latter presupposes a "dispositionalist" stance to the world, in which reality consists in the relatively permanent dispositions, propensities, and powers that are constitutive of what there is (Mumford, 1992). The actualist stance reduces the world to the *ephemeral* and *occasional* manifestations of dispositions and powers, while the dispositionalist stance reduces the world to *permanent* and *enduring* dispositions and powers that are only occasionally manifested but which are constitutive of the world. We are sometimes justified in ascribing dispositions and powers to something that are never manifested in the life of that thing: the Intercontinental Ballistic Missile (ICBM) has the power to destroy a city but is dismantled without ever being launched, and the person who has the skill to sway millions by his/her golden tongue is never given the opportunity to speak. In analyzing the causal concepts that have been used in human studies, we will also try to locate the metaphysical foundations of the discourses in which they are used, actualist or dispositionalist.

REFERENCES

Ballerin, R. (2014). Disjunctive effects and the logic of causation. *British Journal for the Philosophy of Science, 65(1)*, 21–38. doi: 10.1093/bjps/axs040

Campbell, N. R. (1920). *Physics: The Elements*. Cambridge: Cambridge University Press; reissued as Foundations of Science, New York: Dover Publications, 1957.

Cheng, P. W. (1997). From covariation to causation: A causal power theory. *Psychological Review, 104(2)*, 367–405. doi: 10.1037//0033-295x.104.2.367

Gibson, J. J. (1986). *An Ecological Approach to Perception*. New York: Psychology Press.

Harré, R. & Madden, E. H. (1972). *Causal Powers*. Oxford: Blackwell.

Hume, D. (1739). *A Treatise of Human Nature* (2nd ed.). doi: 10.1093/oseo/instance.00046221

Kyburg, H. E. & Smokler, H. E. (1980). *Studies in Subjective Probability*. Huntington, NY: Krieger.

Leibniz, G. W. & Clarke, S. (1992 [1725]). *Correspondence*. R. Ariew (ed.). Indianapolis, IN: Hackett.

Lewis, D. K. (1973). *Counterfactuals*. Cambridge, MA: Harvard University Press.

Losee, J. (2011). *An Historical Introduction to the Philosophy of Science*. New York: Oxford University Press.

Mackie, J. L. (1974). *The Cement of the Universe: A Study of Causation*. Oxford: Clarendon Press.

Mellor, D. H. (1995). *The Facts of Causation*. London: Routledge.

Mill, J. S. (1996). *A System of Logic*. J. M. Robson (ed.). London: Routledge.

Mumford, S. (1992). *Dispositions*. Oxford: Oxford University Press.

Paul, L. A. & Hall, E. J. (2013). *Causation: A User's Guide* (1st ed.). Oxford: Oxford University Press.

Pearl, J. (2000). *Causality: Models, Reasoning, and Inference*. Cambridge, UK: Cambridge University Press.

Sartorio, C. (2006). Failures to act and failures of additivity. *Philosophical Perspectives, 20(1)*, 373–385. doi: 10.1111/j.1520-8583.2006.00111.x

Schaffer, J. (2005). Contrastive causation. *Philosophical Review, 114(3)*, 327–358. doi: 10.1215/00318108-114-3-327

Schaffer, J. (2014). "The metaphysics of causation." *The Stanford Encyclopedia of Philosophy* (summer 2014 ed.). Edward N. Zoltan (ed.).

Wittgenstein, L. (1953). *Philosophical Investigations*. Oxford: Blackwell.

2

The Temporal Frame

Rom Harré

Causal and temporal concepts have been linked in various ways by philosophers, to the extent that for some authors the cause-effect relation defines or at least largely determines what we mean by the "direction of time," from past to future, as if we were already clear as to what we use those concepts to express. Not only is the cause-effect relation temporal, but the "items" that it relates are also taken to be identifiable in temporal terms. In the philosophy of causality, events figure as individuals, with proper names and unique spatio-temporal coordinates. When all this is embedded in that metaphysical monster, that is, space-time, an enduring and rich source of confusion is laid. Causes and effects are assumed to be "events," that is, qualitatively distinct chunks of the temporal flux. But how do we accommodate the fact that the repertoire of events in any well-defined context may be distinctive and very different from that of any other?

There are two main topics of interest when we consider causality in relation to time. Given some account of temporal concepts, what is the temporal content of the concept of "event"? What processes have been proposed to link the members of those sequences of events we extract from the changing, flux-based understanding of cause-effect patterns? Here the other leading causal concept, agency, enters the discussion.

To examine the relation between causal and temporal concepts we need to have a clear understanding of the meanings of such words as "past," "present," and "future" as well as "before" and "after." We need to understand them as they are used in discourses recording the experience people have of the flux of events as well as in their role as ordering relations in temporal-historical discourses. The simplest but yet contestable way time and causation are interrelated is that a sequence of events, ordered as cause and effect, is just the temporal order of changes in the contents of the present from past to future.

The concept of temporal sequence is linked to various cause-effect relations conceptually by the representations of time by models of the temporal flux, the representations of the changing contents of the present. The main problems that trouble attempts to get clear about the grammar of descriptions of events are the result of treating a form of representation as if it were that which it represents. The contents of our memories consist of manifolds of representations. But memories, like all else, are among the contents of the present.

I. MODELS OR REPRESENTATIONS OF THE FLUX OF PHENOMENA

The study of the role of the concept of "causality" in the thinking, talking, and writing of people going about their lives begins with reflections on the several leading models with which the sequential contents of the present can be made intelligible.

Space as a Model for Time

The first misleading representational model to clear away is the idea of a temporal manifold of moments at which events occur parallel to the spatial manifold of places at which things occur. This is the spatialization of time. Locations in the spatial manifold are places at which things may or may not exist. The manifold of locations is independent of whether or not particular things exist, though it is constituted by abstraction from the array of things in general. If there were a temporal manifold of moments abstracted from the manifold of events that was modeled in every detail on the spatial manifold, there could be moments not occupied by events. If the causal succession of events as causes and effects is the source of the succession of moments as past, present, and future, then there is no sense to be made of the concept of "empty moments" in the flux. To examine this hypothesis we need to look more deeply into the metaphysics of the concept of "event."

Once we realize, with Saint Augustine, that nothing exists but the current state of the contents of the present, we see that treatises on the topic of "time" can be nothing but reflections on the phenomena of change and the discourses by which changes as sequences of present phenomena are described and their order examined. "Past," "present," and "future" are discursive concepts with which we order our representations of events.

Space is a manifold of locations that may or may not be occupied by things. Time is not a corresponding manifold of moments that may or may not be occupied by events. An empty time can only be a state of the one and only present when no changes are occurring, that is, where there is no flux and so no story to be told and where there is no time.

Time as Motion

Two versions of this interpretation have emerged in philosophical discussions of time. The first motion-model treats the passage of time as a journey. The sequence of scenes that we experience as the passage of time is already laid out and we are carried along the road by the temporal flow. Looking back down the track to where we have come from the view is clear at least for some distance. But looking ahead the scenery is more and more obscured the further we peer into the possibilities of events yet to come.

The second motion-model treats the passage of time as the motion of a sequence of events from future to past like a river the flotsam on which we witness from a point on the bank as items arrive from upstream and depart down river. We are not making a journey but the events of our lives pass by on the river of time. Though neither of these models survives critical analysis as the ultimate representation of time, each offers an insight into the cause-effect relation with which they are conceptually linked (Smart, 1955).

Time as Reservoir and Repository

There is another enticing picture that underlies many of the most elaborate accounts of the metaphysics of change. This is the core image of J. M. McTaggart's much-discussed analysis of temporal sequences into the A, B, and C series (1908). The A series is ordered by the concepts "past," "present," and "future." Past and future make sense only in relation to the present, that is, now. This series is indexical in that it incorporates the consciousness of the author of the story, his or her apprehension of this or that event not as remembered or foretold but as happening then and there. The B series of events is ordered by the relations "earlier than" and "later than" and these relations are independent of the present. At whatever position we choose to locate ourselves in the A series there will be points earlier and later than the arbitrarily chosen moment at which we pay attention to the contents of a position. McTaggart's proposal of the role of the concepts of past, present, and future in discourses descriptive of the flux offers a clear distinction between descriptions of the flux that are independent of an observer and those in which the order of the sequence of events depends on the consciousness of an observer or on some other way of picking out event after event as worthy of a special role in making sense of the A series. McTaggart's model rests on the intelligibility of a reservoir of *events* yet to come and a repository of events that have already passed. Conceiving of events as a C series is to think of the flux as independent of observer-based ordering relations. This series is not an empirical presentation to observers but a theoretical construct.

McTaggart also writes of a "series of *positions*" running from the far past through the near past to the present, and then from the present to the near future and the far future (McTaggart, 1908, p. 458). Presumably a "position" is a location in a temporal manifold at which an event can occur, but may not. Thus, locations and events are presented, perhaps inadvertently, as independent of one another, and it is contingent on whether there is an event at some position or not. This presumption can be safely ignored in our use of the A and B series grammars because it is events that these relations order.

McTaggart is best known for his argument that "time is unreal." An event, say the death of Queen Anne, at some moment after it has occurred is future, is present, and is past. But no event can have all three mutually exclusive attributes so the temporal manifold of positions cannot be a real feature of the universe. A resolution of the apparently startling conclusion of McTaggart's argument for the "unreality" of time is to suggest that "being past," "being present," and "being future" are not attributes of *events*, either qualitative or locative. They are attributes of the *representation of events* in here and now stories. In a story the assertion that an event is past and that it is now present is not a contradiction. However, if the temporal manifold is a grammatical device for the ordering of stories into chapters reflecting causal relations that do not change, then it is a human construction and, in a sense, unreal.

Causation must be grounded in something that does not change with the changes in the flux that appear as patterns of succession of current states of affairs in the one and only window we have on the world. One state of affairs perishes and another appears. We now turn to the explicit study of the grammar of temporal discourses and the pattern of family resemblances that displays the multiple meanings of "event."

II. A CONCEPTUAL MAP FOR "EVENT"

At least there seems to be change involved in what events are understood to be. Some items that were once among the contents of the present have perished but they are remembered in relation to our experiences of different items that have come to exist in the present. The juxtaposition of present memories and present experiences generates the sense of time. As we have seen in many philosophical discussions, the concept of cause and the concept of event are linked into a mutually defining pair. So even if this linkage is evident only in some cases, it can give us a starting point for examining the relation between the structure of temporal manifolds, for example, continuous or discrete, and that of cause-effect sequences.

Events are certainly linked through their criteria of identity with elements of some temporal manifold. To exist at a different moment in a temporal manifold is to be a different event. But that manifold might be continuous in the mathematical sense, a sequence of dimensionless points, or it might be a discrete manifold, a sequence of chronons, finite in contrast to infinitesimals of a continuous manifold. Should the flux be analyzed in terms of individual entities or moments be they infinitesimal or chunky, or should we think in terms of an unbroken stream of dynamic change? Are events to be chronons or are they abstracted from fluxions, to borrow a concept from Newton's physics?

Events that figure in causal relations are at least chunks of a temporal manifold. How these chunks are to be delimited has been a source of puzzlement since antiquity. Findlay (1963) laid the foundations for a resolution of these and other puzzles in his analysis of the mereology of events.

> Because it would be absurd to say of certain wholes—houses, mountains or libraries, for instance—they existed and were measurable though their parts were never together, we think it would be absurd to say the same

thing of happenings. But the fact that we shouldn't say that *some* of the things we call parts could constitute the things we call their wholes, unless they were present together, does not oblige us to say this in the case of other things we also call parts and wholes . . . we might say we were dealing with two totally different sorts of parts and wholes. (Findlay, 1963, p. 47)

There are two ways in which the flux can be partitioned into events. We can treat the flux as a continuum of changes, allowing for infinitesimal items, the present as a mathematical point in the continuum of changes. We can also treat the flux as a sequence of chronons, discrete happenings that could have temporal parts. Trouble comes only when we try to combine these analyses into a single scheme. We must acknowledge that there are "two totally different sorts of [temporal] parts and wholes."

The abstraction of various kinds of events is interest driven, context relative, and scale dependent so that, in one case, the result of the imposition of a mathematical continuum on the flux is a sequence of infinitesimal happenings and, in another, the result of chunking the flux into discrete chronons. The errors in the grammar of "event" ("happening" and so on) pointed out by Findlay and many others have led philosophers to treat events as entities in philosophical reflections on causation, arriving at two incompatible senses of "event." But if we return "event" to its vernacular home, there are no problems. "Event" is a word that encompasses a wide range of temporally diverse patterns of stasis and change, and so its meaning should be presented as a field of family resemblances rather than by laying out a strict and putatively fundamental definition of the essence of the concept.

This resolution was already prefigured in Saint Augustine's remarks on the "span" of events in relation to a continuum interpretation of change when that continuum is related to individual events by a manifold that included infinite divisibility (Saint Augustine, 397–398 [2006]). In Book 11, Chapters 15 and 16, he considers what it can mean to say that some times are long and others short—how might differences in the "length of time" be decided? A hundred years is a long time, but at the mid-century half of it has passed and so no longer exists and most of the other half has not yet occurred, so does not exist either. Now consider that mid-century year. The same analysis via days, hours, and so on leads to the conclusion that "if an instance of time be conceived, which cannot be divided into the smallest particles of moments, that alone is it which may be called present." Time present cannot be long, or short for that matter, but intervals can be if time can be compared with respect to duration. This can only be through the representation of the flux in the mind as memories; the present record of the past and anticipations from those times past are representations with respect to the present acts of foretelling of the future.

Saint Augustine's discussion involves reflections on the consequences of the imposition of a discrete manifold on a continuous flux, thus setting the analysis off in pursuit of the basic "event." But the indefinite divisibility of the flux tends toward dimensionless events that a fortiori can have no temporal properties, so are neither long nor short. Saint Augustine's analysis should convince us that "event" is an epistemological concept for recording what can be known of the flux, while ontologically there is only the flux where "flux" describes the continuous flow of the changing present, which we can partition as we like.

Saint Augustine's reflections help one to resolve the paradox that appears when we examine the result of refining the degree to which we chop up the flux into events. In the end, events seem to be instantaneous, but then how are we able to apprehend them one after the other? "If we consider an instant of time that cannot be divided further into the smallest particles of moments, it alone is that which may be called present. Yet it flies with such speed from future to past as not to be lengthened but 'with the least stay'. For if it is lengthened, it is divided into past and future. Thus the present has no 'space'" (Augustine, 397–398 [2006], §22). The seeming paradox can be resolved by attending to the mathematical character of two kinds of sequences. The first step suggests that the analysis of the temporal present should be applied to a continuous manifold. Yet, as Augustine rightly observes, the world as experienced is a manifold of discrete changes in the content of the present. Memory and anticipation, which provide the contents of the discursive regions of past and future, are always contemporary records of discrete changes. It is a fallacy to try to map them onto the "limit points" of a continuous manifold. Reflecting on how we experience the moment of the present, Saint Augustine observes that as we refine our discernment of the content of the present, it shrinks toward a dimensionless point that has no content. But we have moved from one kind of continuum to another. The procedure of division that allows for the retention of experiential content to a slice of the flux as experienced does not yield a continuum of dimensionless points.

To put this another way: the past and the future are created as psychologically distinct parts of a sequence of records of states of the present that no longer exist and anticipations of changes in the flux that also do not exist because they have yet to occur. But the contents of the present are not exhausted by reports, that is, by discursive entities. The experiential content of the present is not a member of either sequence. The present is not a cognitive construct and the flux of its contents is the only reality. Causation is a process that occurs in the real world of the changing state of the present—but "events" are not in the real world—they are present records of states of the flux, some of which exist and some of which do not. It is therefore a fundamental error in philosophy to analyze causation and interpret the concept of "causality" in terms of events.

The flux, as we presented it in Chapter 1, is digitalized for various purposes as a sequence of discrete events. Events are carved from a continuum of change. Would these "problems" have appeared if the ontological foundation of the conceptions of causation presupposed in these discussions had been continuously changing phenomena and agents exercising their causal powers instead of sequences of events? Analysis of philosophical error using Wittgenstein's method—identify the transfer of the mistaken grammar of certain concepts from vernacular uses to philosophy (of science)—in this case continuous change becomes sequences of events, so that events appear as material entities, though they are abstractions and their relations conceptual. Events are conceptual artifacts. Are they finite chunks or infinitesimal points? Reject the dichotomy, and then we are free to introduce other distinctions that will perhaps prove enlightening.

The mistake that most of the literature on causation incorporates is expressed in a defective analysis of the everyday grammar of "event," which is then used to characterize the generic character of "A caused B." This is hidden, so to say, in the use of such sentences as "event A caused event B" to set up the analysis of causation and the meaning of "causality," and in particular to lay out the puzzle cases. "Events" are changes in individuatable states of affairs, such as the acquisition of a quality by a substance, water coming to the boil or egg white becoming hard, paint becoming dry, skittles becoming disordered when struck by the bowl, and so on, abstracted from a temporal flux of continuous change. So long as we do not try to impose a continuous grid of infinitesimal temporal moments on sequences of events at least some problems that infect our thinking in terms of the "spans" of causes and their effects melt away.

The error in the philosophy of causation goes back to Hume's interpretation of causes and their effects as "objects," which soon became "events." But Augustine's paradox shows that they are arbitrary slices of a continuum of change. Causation is the process of change and should not be represented as a digital atomic sequence of independent events for any purpose other than expository purposes, such as the writing of histories.

III. CAUSES AND EFFECTS AS REPEATED SEQUENCES OF EVENTS

Hume's influential and long-standing analysis of the use of the concept of "causality" ties the cause-effect relation to a certain relation between pairs of events of a certain kind. Though Hume wrote of "objects," such a juxtaposition is regularly repeated among the impressions we have of our world (1739–1740). This very general specification of the metaphysical category of causes and effects allows us to include substances, things, qualities, and relations among the effects of causal processes without making further qualifications.

Hume's first formulation of his "regularity account" interprets cause-effect relations as repeated patterns of similar events and causal necessity as the reflection of a psychological tendency to expect such regularities to continue. "A CAUSE is an object precedent and contiguous to another, and so united with it, that the idea of the one determines the mind to form the idea of the other, and the impression of the one to form a more lively idea of the other" (Hume, 1739–1740, p. 170). Hume remarks that in each single instance, one of the "objects" is precedent and contiguous to the other, and in considering several instances, "like objects are placed in like relations of succession and contiguity."

Furthermore, this relation between "objects" cannot be a matter of a priori reasoning. It can "never operate upon the mind, but by means of custom, which determines the imagination to make a transition from the idea of one object to that of its usual attendant, and from the impression of the one to a more lively idea of the other" (Hume, 1739–1740, p. 170).

According to Hume (1739–1740, p. 171), "Tis the constant conjunction of objects, along with the determination of the mind, which constitutes a physical necessity." By the same line of argument, "the distinction, which we often make betwixt power and the exercise of it, is equally without foundation."

Given that the relation between cause and effect is not logically necessary, it follows that "anything may produce anything" (Hume, 1739–1740, p. 173). Summing up the analysis in terms of the rules for determining whether to judge a relation among events is causal. Hume offers the following:

- Cause and effect must be contiguous in space and time.
- The cause must be prior to the effect.
- There must be a constant union betwixt cause and effect.
- The same cause always produces the same effect, and "the same effect never arises but from the same cause."

While Rules 1 and 3 could apply to either things or events, and to Hume's "objects," Rule 2 seems to restrict causes to events. It is easy to dispute all four of these "rules" in the light of the way the concept of cause-as-event is used in practice. We often identify the cause of an event as something that happened in the past and led to the effect through a chain of intermediaries. Similarly, we often allow a chain of spatially distributed intermediate states between a cause and its effect. Sometimes we take a cause to be simultaneous with its effect, or coexisting with it. The constant union condition is highly idealized since, for the most part, we offer causal laws with *ceteris paribus* qualifications. Of course, one might read the Humean Rule 4 as a tautology—that *such and such* effect is a constant conjunct of just *this* precedent event as cause.

Commenting on the possibility that the same effect might be conjoined with different causes, Hume (1739–1740, p. 174) says, "where several objects produce the same effect it must be by means of some quality, which we discover as common amongst them."

Some 30 years later, Hume returned to the concept of causation (Hume, 1777, pp. 63–79). Though his later account is very similar, there is an important difference of emphasis. The treatment that follows is grounded explicitly on a thesis concerning the very nature of experience: all our ideas are copies of impressions we receive from the external or internal senses.

However, when we examine real cases, we find that there is a simple way in which the past and the future can be linked materially so that causes do indeed produce their effects—this is the existence of entities that exist unchanged in the present, while other contents of the present emerge and perish. Among such beings are agents, persistently active while events come and go, and causal mechanisms, which, though consisting of persisting parts, display sequential states of the changing present as their internal relations change. Only if we accept the Humean presumption of the world as events are we stuck with the apparent impossibility of real causation. Hume and Kant both leave us with only "causality" as a concept. Whatever lies behind, beyond events as moments in the one and only present, is noumenal, beyond all possible experience for Kant, or illusory, a consequence of the effect of repetition on expectation, or a sort of conditioning, according to Hume.

In this chapter and in the commentaries on all that follow, we will adopt Saint Augustine's masterly and succinct analysis of temporal concepts, as set out in his *Confessions* of 397–398. In §23 he says,

> [I]f past and future exist, I would like to know where they are. Even as I cannot know them, yet I know wherever they are, they are not there as future, or past, but as present. Yet if they are in the present and also of the future, they are not yet there in the present. On the other hand, if they are also in the present as the past, they are also no longer there. Thus, whatever exists, it is only as being in the present. When past facts are related, we draw out of the memory not the things themselves, which are past, but words that are stimulated by images of the things that in passing have through the senses have been left as traces in the mind.

IV. CAUSALITY AS A SYNTHETIC A PRIORI PRINCIPLE

Hume explained the meaning of the causal necessity we ascribe to certain relations between events as the result of the empirical fact of the repetition of event correlations. Kant offered a cognitive account of the source of the experience of causation in which the conditionality of the relation between a cause-event and its expected effect-event is a structure imposed on the unordered flux of mere phenomena by the synthesizing powers of the mind. Causation is not read off experience a posteriori but is imposed on experience a priori. Kant found the source of intelligibility of organized experience in the basic logical laws of all intelligible discourses. Certain synthetic a priori principles have their source in a definitive list of the categories with which knowledge is created. Applied as schemata to the unordered flux of human experience, they produce an intelligible material and mental empirical reality. The appearance of causal order came from schematizing experience according to the principle of conditionality—"if X then Y"—not from abstraction from it. Kant argues that we do not extract a principle of causality from our experience of the world, but impose a causal structure on the flux of sensations. The phenomenal world and its representation in individual minds are brought into being as spatial and temporal manifolds by a more fundamental a priori synthesis, which he explains in the Transcendental Analytic (Kant, 1787, part 1, section 2). The source of the experience of the flux of events as time is different from the synthesis of phenomena into the flow of cause and effect. Though causation is imposed on the flux of change, it is not an acquired habit. It is rather an a priori form derived ultimately from the list of categories that must be realized in discourse to maintain intelligibility. Kant's account of the origin of causation is set out in the Second Analogy in the *Critique of Pure Reason* (Kant, 1787).

V. TEMPORALLY REGRESSIVE CAUSATION?

Effects are always contemporaneous with or later than their causes. Is this rule a matter of fact of great generality or is it a rule of grammar recording a conceptual relation? Can we imagine cases in which it would make sense to say that a cause came after its effects? If causal relations and temporal relations are conceptually linked, such a proposal would be incoherent. What it is to be the effect of a cause is at least to occur later than the item identified as a cause. The possibility of imagining cases in which an item could properly be identified as a cause of an event that had preceded it has been debated in response to Michael Dummett's amusing and deep speculations on the question of whether our conceptual resources admit of intelligible claims that at least some causes come after their effects (Dummett, 1954). Recent revivals of this debate have been discussed by Jan Faye (2010).

Dummett sets out the conditions that a case of quasi-causation would have to satisfy if it were to count as an instance of the causation of an effect "e" by a temporally later event "c."

- No other explanation can be found for the occurrence of "e."
- The earlier event "e" is not construable as the cause of the later event "c."
- The later event "c" is casually accounted for without reference to the earlier event "e."

Flew (1954, p. 52ff) argues that the conditions set out could find an application to an actual observable phenomenon and so make sense of the idea of backward causation only if we are thinking in terms of Humean regularities and so take on the "standpoint of the meditative observer" rather than that of the experimentalist. Backward causation seems plausible only if we accept Hume's event-correlation account as the grammar of the story of passively observed events. In our relationship with the world, we actively do experiments and make use of causal mechanisms and causal powers to bring about events in the flux. We cannot do that after the event as the effect has already occurred. To suppose otherwise is to assume that we can activate a current causal mechanism to generate a past state of affairs. To suppose that it might have come about without the activation of a mechanism or the efficacious action of a causal power is to presume the simplest version of the Humean account.

VI. SUMMARY

Both Hume and Kant identify causal relations among events, taken as individuatable temporal items, by virtue of a certain formal property of causal discourses. Hume argues that the property he takes to be definitive, namely, the sense of necessity that accompanies the perception of regular concomitances between events of the cause type and those of the effect type, is psychological in origin, no more than a habit of expectation induced by the human experience of that very same regularity. Kant argues that the source of the causal organization of experience is psychological but not an acquired habit. Rather it is the consequence of the schematism of the flux of undifferentiated experience by the imposition of an a priori form expressing one of the foundational requirements for the possibility of intelligible experience. In the constitution of the empirical world, in accordance with the categories, the causal schematism is the realization of the propositional form "if . . . then . . . ."

Our analysis has shown that the result of the analysis of the flux into a pattern of sequential contents of the present is independent and has a distinct existence. There can be nothing real that ties together materially or symbolically both members of the pairs of phenomena that are presented in the sequence. Whatever happens always happens *now*. Causation as a productive relation can exist only now. The past is a cognitive construction, and records in the present, the only moment, former and extinguished contents of that present. All that survives this analysis is the results of repetitions of like pairs of events on human expectations. Yet something drives the changing contents of the present. Once we have seen that the "dimensions" of the present are not the infinitesimal instances that pursuing Augustine's analysis of the measure of time into paradox suggests, we can understand how the present can be rich in content. In the next chapter we will turn to a study of the role of agents and their causal powers as the source of the world as the ever-changing flux.

REFERENCES

Augustine, St. (397–398 [2006]). *Confessions*. Trans. E. Bouverie. London: Watkins.

Dummett, M. (1954). Can an effect precede its cause? *Proceedings of the Aristotelian Society: Supplementary Volume*, 27–44.

Faye, J. (2010). Backwards causation. In E. N. Zelta (ed.). *Stanford Encyclopedia of Philosophy*. Retrieved from: http://plato.stanford.edu/archives/spr2010/entries/causation-backwards/

Findlay, J. N. (1963). Time: A treatment of some puzzles. In A. G. N. Flew (ed.). *Logic and Language, Series One*. Oxford: Blackwell.

Flew, A. G. N. (1954). Can an effect precede its cause? *Proceedings of the Aristotelian Society: Supplementary Volume*, 45–55.

Hume, D. (1739–1740 [1963]). *A Treatise of Human Nature*. London: Fontana.

Hume, D. (1777 [1951]). *Enquiries Concerning the Human Understanding and the Principles of Morals*. Oxford: Clarendon Press.

Kant, I. (1950 [1787]). *Critique of Pure Reason*. Trans. J. M. D. Meiklejohn. London: Dent.

McTaggart, J. E. (1908). The unreality of time. *Mind 17*, 457–474.

Smart, J. J. C. (1955). Spatialising time. *Mind 68*, 239–241.

3

The Explanation Frame

Rom Harré

Phenomena are only of cultural significance insofar as they have meanings for the people among whom they occur. In many contexts giving an explanation is synonymous with suggesting a cause. Sometimes this commonsense practice is supplemented by another explanatory framework. Some sequences and patterns of meanings are not related by causality but by semantic and other conventions, some of which are local, some panhuman (Wierzbicka, 1992). In certain circumstances a causal pattern among phenomena is the best one to look for. Sometimes the greater insight comes from looking for patterns of meanings and rules and conventions according to which they appear to be managed. Keeping these methodologies distinct is an important part of skilled research techniques in many human studies, for example, cognitive psychology.

I. THE LOGIC OF CAUSAL REASONING

How are the rules for the use of causal principles represented in logic, the formal principles of reasoning? Considering causal concepts in a framework of logic becomes important not only when the question of the validity of cause-effect inferences are at issue but also when we assess the modality of causal claims, that is, how concepts like "necessity," "possibility," and "probability" appear in causal discourses. Does the effect follow the cause of necessity? Expressing this question as a matter of the relations of propositions becomes the question of whether an inference from the description of a cause to a description of its usual effect is logically valid. It may be valid but it does not seem to be logically necessary; that is, the principle of inference seems to be a supposed matter of fact, which could have been otherwise. As Hume pointed out, other outcomes than those we have learned to expect of a causal process are conceivable. Nevertheless, we also take for granted that the expected effect must occur *ceteris paribus*, that is, all else being equal in some sense or another. If the anticipated effect does not occur, we look around among the conditions that comprise the causal antecedents of productive process, such as the composition of the material components of the system, for a significant and causally relevant variation of the usual conditions. If the doorbell doesn't ring, there is likely to be a fault in the circuit, a flat battery, and so on. If the dough does not rise, the yeast we used was degraded and out of date. The logical character of the relations between propositions describing events taken to be causes and those describing their expected effects are neither pure happenstance nor logically necessary. Can we work out a formal pattern that would express "natural necessity"?

There are also patterns of causal reasoning that involve probabilistic notions. Given a certain effect, what was the probable cause? Given a certain cause, what would be its likely effects? Again, we can ask whether it is possible to give a formal analysis of the validity or at least the plausibility of modes of reasoning involving probabilities. Is there any limit to the possible effects of a causal event and how would it be settled?

Causality as a logical relation is tied up with causality as an explanatory category. The simplest explanation format, as we shall see, is also the simplest logical pattern that governs a pattern of propositions that emulates causal relations, among whatever items on critical analysis they turn out to be.

II. THE FORM OF THE SIMPLEST CAUSAL EXPLANATION

Russellian logic defines the rules for valid inferences among propositions when the only issue is "truth preservation." The ultimate logical sin is the deduction of a false proposition from one or more truths. The formal analysis of propositional reasoning introduces the *material conditional* as the core logical relation, expressed in the formula "if p then q" or "p $\rightarrow$ q." Expressed in terms of "truth functions," the formal definition of this relation could be displayed in a truth table.

Suppose "p" is a proposition describing an event taken to be the cause of a subsequent event described by the proposition "q," "p" and "q" can be either true or false. There are four possibilities: "p" and "q" are both true, "p" and "q" are both false, "p" is false and "q" is true, and finally "p" is true and "q" is false. In the Russellian logic of propositional reasoning, only the last combination is false. We must rule out drawing a false conclusion from true premises.

Drawing a true conclusion from true premises is surely intuitively acceptable. The remaining possibilities in the above catalog portray inferences that are formally valid though they proceed from false premises to conclusions that are assigned a value of "true" or of "false." This may seem counterintuitive, but it does no harm to our beliefs and makes the consistent interdefinitions of "and" and "or" as truth functions. For example, "the faucet leak caused the bath to overflow" is valid if the faucet did leak and the bath did overflow. It is invalid if the faucet leaked and the bath did not overflow—the leak was not the cause of the overflow. Maybe it was the blocked drain. If the faucet did not leak we can say what we like on the basis of that fact alone.

The limitations of Russellian logic in representing the bare bones of causal reasoning are obvious. The formal truth-functional presentation of causal hypotheses is schematic—we would need to move on to ask what is the *connection* between leaking faucets and overflowing baths. This step leads to a much stronger logical relation, namely, that between general and particular propositions. If we could defend the claim that leaking faucets always lead to overflowing baths, *ceteris paribus*, we would have usable knowledge. It might be defended by a study of the hydrography of domestic water supplies, and some elementary physics, together with an assumption of the conservation of quantities of water. Just assembling cases where leaking faucets were followed by overflowing baths could have been a report of long-running coincidence and the causes have lain elsewhere. Rendering "X causes Y" in the formal algebra of quantifiers looks like this: $((Ax) X \rightarrow Y)$. Even so "For all X, if X then Y" is not adequate as a representation of causal knowledge. We need to know a great deal about the situations presumed to surround such generalizations before we can use such formulas in causal inferences. Some of what we need to know to achieve a rich and intuitively satisfactory explanation was already prefigured in the writings of Aristotle.

III. ARISTOTELIAN ORIGINS

In a very fine recent paper, James Grice (2014) proposes returning to Aristotle to be our guide in trying to make sense of patterns of change in human affairs.

In *Physics* II.3 Aristotle sets out a schema for establishing a complete explanation of all changes, natural, social, and symbolic, including coming into existence and passing away. All four of the formal, material, efficient, and final "causes" should be looked for as the components of a full scientific explanation of patterns in the natural and the social world. The Greek word he uses is *aition*. The usual translation is "cause," though the pattern of uses of the English word has drifted some way from those of *aition*, at least as Aristotle understood it. The contemporary meaning of the word "cause" in English is very much narrower. At best, both the Greek *aition* and the Latin *causa* refer to aspects of the situations in which things come about.

Using as an example the bronze out of which a statue has been made, Aristotle identifies one sense of *aition* as the stuff out of which the object has been made. This is the "material cause."

To explain how the octave difference in musical pitch comes about, he cites the ratio of the lengths of the string that produce this difference, namely, 2 to 1. This is cause as "form" or "pattern," which is another sense of *aition*.

Something must initiate a process of change. This is the "efficient cause," exemplified by the person who advises someone to undertake a certain course of action, or the father as the progenitor of a child.

The "final cause" is the purpose of the thing, such as health as the purpose or reason for adopting a certain medical regime.

In short, if someone were to ask, "How and why did this come about?," be it event, state, process, or thing, a full answer requires specifying all four "causes."

Philosophers, perhaps under the spell of Hume's positivist reduction of the "cause-effect" relation to "regularity of concomitance," have tended to focus on efficient cause. And, in the same vein, they have mainly taken efficient causes to be events, antecedent triggers to change rather than substances or structures or final outcomes. Imperceptibly the emphasis in philosophy shifted from the whole pattern of explanation to just one factor: the efficient *aition* as "the cause."

While restoring Aristotle's account of the components of a complete explanation (the four *aitia*) as a basic scheme for proposing and answering research questions, Grice interprets and illustrates these discourse components in terms of physical causality as we understand it, rather than as explanations of historical and cultural matters where rules and conventions tend to be cited to account for the way regularities in phenomena are brought about. How would we map discursive-cultural psychology on to Aristotle's scheme in such a way that the completed explanation format for any topic is laid out in terms of norms rather than causes? Here is a suggestion:

- *Efficient causes*: people.
- *Material causes*: sounds, sights, feelings, environments, and so on.
- *Formal causes*: rules, conventions, customs, habits, and so on.
- *Final causes*: intentions, plans, projects, and so on.

When did it become the custom to translate the word *aition* into the Latin *causus*? What did "cause" mean in the thirteenth century when translations began, and what does it mean in the twenty-first-century academic English? We can usefully contrast "causal law" with "normative convention" in setting up contrasting modes of explanation relevant to recovering Aristotle's explanation schema as a fundamental research format. But what is the difference?

- Causes are either agencies acting out their intrinsic natures or generative mechanisms. Causes often include events that, in appropriate conditions, release the powers of agents or activate causal mechanisms. Nature is complex, so there are always processes other than those in our focus of interest going on—and we deal with that by appending, usually implicitly, ceteris paribus conditions to any "law."
- Norms are striven for, adhered to, or ignored and shape actions of human beings in a noncausal way. We do not deal with disparities between what people do and the norms that are acknowledged in a community by adding a ceteris paribus clause. A person can be criticized or even punished for not keeping up with the norms, adhering to the rules, and so on, particularly when that person is supposed to know what he or she is supposed to do! We need umpires, referees, and "sin bins" even for

games. Knowledge of the norms of some social practice is not a necessary and sufficient condition for someone to act correctly or some social state of affairs to come to be, ceteris paribus.

Returning to our attempt to follow Grice's suggestion and recruit Aristotle to our authorities, we note that many secondary sources are not content simply to present Aristotle's examples of each of the four *aitia*, but offer interpretations of the philosophy of the Latin West, using words like "cause" and "essence." Even the admirable *Stanford Encyclopedia of Philosophy* advertises its treatment of this part of philosophy as "Aristotle on Causality"—though as the article develops, it becomes clear that the author is actually presenting "Aristotle on Explanatory Discourse Formats." The English philosophical lexicon has adopted "causa" rendered as "cause." But Latin dictionaries for rendering original meanings into contemporary European languages provide huge fields of family-resembling uses for "causa." They include "cause" (whatever that is assumed to be in English!), "reason," "motive," "responsibility," "symptom," "occasion," "plea," "position," trial, "law suit," "process," and "stipulation"—so the word ranges over moral contexts and the related legal meta-discourse as well as its use in a predominantly psychological sense. We propose to drop the Latin and return to talking of a study of *aitia* as a field of family resemblances guiding our intuitions with Aristotle's own examples and any others we can glean from the ancient literature. This chapter begins with Aristotle's format for a complete explanation and those cases where it makes sense to ask for such a thing—notably the human world. Its richness stands in sharp contrast to the regularity analysis suggested by Hume, which we discussed in Chapter 2.

We propose to map cultural-discursive psychology, an important core of the range of human studies we examine in this book, onto the Aristotelian format as suggested by Grice (2012), but to avoid the misleading implications of the modern usage of "cause" in English. We take the "four causes" scheme to be realized in the assembly of a complete or ideal explanatory *discourse*. And so we can promote the Aristotelian methodology, as Grice wants us to do, as the proper format for finding the components of the mechanisms of change and writing out explanations not only for material patterns of change but also for social and psychological phenomena and processes by filling its slots.

It would be appropriate to describe this fourfold scheme as the layout of a complete explanation of something that occurs in the world. A statue is made, a man becomes healthy, a child is born, a governor is elected, and a couple becomes an item, and so on.

By picking possible modern equivalents for the four *aitia*, we can set out a useful explanatory scheme for our own time. The formal and material *aitia* become standing conditions for the phenomena to be produced, and so to be cited in explanations. Following a suggestion by Ernest Nagel, the final cause can be interpreted as a present representation of a possible outcome for the causal process initiated and maybe maintained by the causal power of an efficient *aitia* (Nagel, 1979).

IV. CONTEMPORARY PATTERNS OF CAUSAL DISCOURSES

Examining the patterns of human practices shows that they exhibit charac-teristic forms and distinctive contents. These aspects are relatively indepen-dent of one another. This fact should appear in the analysis of causal discourses, with the same pattern being filled out with various contents. C. G. Hempel (1965) proposed a much-discussed schema for setting out explanations that stands at the opposite extreme from that of Aristotle. It makes the least possible use of matters of content that would typify a scien-tific, and thus a causal, explanation. Hempel intended it to be of very wide application, and it has appeared in discussions of theorizing in economics and other human sciences as well as theories in physics and engineering.

According to Hempel, the form of a deductive-nomological explanation includes three components:

- A law or law-like premise that is taken to be naturally necessary, that is, in the circumstances, admits of only one meaning and only one truth assessment
- A number of other premises that describe the conditions under which the law is to be applied in a deductive inference from these premises and the law-like premise
- The item to be explained

Among the premises described in (2), one could select a statement describ-ing a cause, on the basis of its relevance to some inquiry that was afoot, from which with the help of the law-like premise, one could deduce a description of a possible or actual effect. Hempel weakened this very strong demand when it came to describing actual scientific practice.

There is a serious problem with this explanation format, namely, that the requirement that the main premise should be law-like or nomological. How do we know whether a suggested premise is nomological? There are several possibil-ities, including linking it to the description of a mechanism or the hypothesis refers to the capability, capacity, or efficacy of a "powerful particular," an agent capable of bringing about the effect on the occurrence of the cause. We discuss these in the next section; effectively, they bear the burden of establishing the extra strength of the nomological premise over and above a mere generalization.

V. DEDUCTIVE-NOMOLOGICAL SCHEMATA

What must an explanatory discourse include beyond the bare bones of a formal logical schema? Mechanisms are at the core of a wide variety of explanation discourses. A mechanism is a stable structure of parts within which processes occur that lead from an initiating state, picked out as the cause, to a final state as the effect, selected from the various final states of the mechanism at some arbitrary or more usually interest-relative moment. Sometimes the initiating state is an external imposition. Sometimes it is the continuous action of an internal component, the unspooling spring in an old mechanical clock, for instance.

We recall from Chapter 1 that Judea Pearl (2000) defines a causal *model* as a discursive or cognitive object with three components, U, V, and E. U is a set of exogenous variables, the values of which are determined by conditions outside the system, for example, the state of the environment; V is a set of endogenous variables whose values are determined by factors inside the system; and E is a set of structural equations that express the values of each endogenous variable in terms of the other variables in V and U. If the conditions "outside" and "inside" the system are material states of affairs, then that of which they are outside or inside must also be something material, a mechanism perhaps. Sets of variables and equations cannot be analogues of anything but other sets of variables and equations. Pearl's (U, V, E) assembly cannot be a *model* of a causal mechanism. It must be a *description* of a causal mechanism supposed to be an analogue of the mechanism that it is being used to represent, and it must include a description of the conditions under which it runs. Bohr's electron model of the atom is an imagined entity that bears certain analogies to whatever are the constituents of atoms. It can be described in terms of sets of variables and structural equations, but it is not those variables and equations that are the Bohr model. Why does this matter? Because the all-important question of the constraints that may or must be exercised on the formation and development of a model are material and metaphysical—not formal and mathematical.

No doubt artifacts are important causal mechanisms to be considered in human studies, but the erosion of riverbanks, the melting of the ice caps, and the warming of the surface of the earth are also mechanisms or parts of mechanisms that are of relevance to human affairs. It is also useful to think of some institutional or political arrangements as mechanisms—what is the mechanism for choosing a new head of the department, or current talk of the market as a mechanism?

The defining aspects of a system as a mechanism include the requirement that it should consist of a number of interacting parts that retain their integrity when it is working, and certain relations among them. Their interactions constitute a process that eventuates in some new state of affairs. To justify drawing on the causal mechanism format the components would have to be identified, their relations discovered (or in some social contexts created), and their manner of working investigated. Wittgenstein's caveat about making too quick and superficial assumptions about the future state of a machine should be kept in mind (Wittgenstein, 1953).

VI. DESCRIPTIONS OF GENERATIVE AND PRODUCTIVE AGENCIES

At the core of a causal mechanism there must be a relatively ungrounded source of energy that maintains the activity of the device. We are familiar with the powers of nature in such phenomena as the pull of gravity—a power of the earth and all other material things to exert mutual attractions. In physics we discover the power of magnets to draw iron objects toward them, and we learn of the electromagnetic powers of electrons. These are native powers, belonging to the very natures of these beings. We also recognize acquired powers as we hear the crash of glass as the ill-struck baseball reaches the window of the adjoining house with sufficient impetus to smash it. Basic powers, be they native or acquired, are ascribed to the grounding objects of the field of phenomena we are studying. Persons are the grounding objects of psychology, and it is to them that we ascribe certain native and acquired powers. It is by virtue of their possession of these powers that persons are the grounding agents of psychological phenomena and social phenomena from personal decision making to judicial judgments and parliamentary edicts. We note that in some regimes the management of society is a matter of personal decision making by the tyrant. In such circumstances a different psychology must be turned to for suggesting explanations of social events from those we are familiar with in democracies. Psychological phenomena are the result of the exercise of native and acquired powers by people, shaped and sometimes restricted by the powers of environmental agencies.

To exercise a power is to act as an agent. In simple cases of agency in the material world, an agent can initiate a process or a linked series of events without itself being acted upon, and in some cases an agent can sustain such a process when initiated. However initiating and sustaining a process may require different agents.

The ontology of the natural sciences, as they are actually practiced, rests on the concept of a natural agent, that is, a material being endowed with certain causal powers for which no further explanation is forthcoming. We will begin by examining the concept of natural agency in detail, using the results of this study as a model for the analysis of various concepts of human agency. Human agency is a matter of the exercise of human powers. The generic concept of "power" seems to involve two root ideas, "spontaneity" and "efficacy." The field potentials of an electric charge do not require anything to bring them into being. Furthermore, they are displayed when constraints on motion are removed or absent.

Attributions of causal status to events make sense only on the presumption of an underlying agent causality (Harré & Madden, 1972). There are material beings with powers to bring about various kinds of changes, events, and new states of affairs, as primary and secondary agents, that is, causal mechanisms that are efficacious but at the core of which is a basic source of energy.

Causal efficacy is ascribed to a "powerful particular" in the language of dispositions: "If such and such conditions are fulfilled, then such and such an effect will (is likely to) occur." A dispositional ascription links two empirical concepts. One representing the conditions under which a change occurs, and the other the event picked out for various reasons as the effect. However, to answer the question, "Why does this or that entity or stuff display such and such a disposition?," we need to invoke causal powers. Causal powers are theoretical properties that account for the manifestation of observable phenomena, but they are not themselves observable. Causal powers are attributes of material entities, such as a plasmodium or a magnet, an engine or a force field. Some powerful particulars are observable, some are not. But in none of them are their powers observable except in how they are manifested—say in the motion of a body in a gravitational field.

The causal powers of natural agents usually persist in time. There are two patterns of persistence. The fact that this stuff in the bottle has the power to alleviate pain is true now, but lasts only until the analgesic is metabolized. The fact that this elementary charge has the power to repel some elementary charges and attract others is true now and it persists through a great many interactions in which this entity plays a part.

Causal powers are identified but not fully individuated in terms of their effects. For example, "Aspirin has the power to reduce pain; that is, it is an analgesic." Codeine too has the power to reduce pain; that is, they display the same dispositional property just as blood and stop signs are both red. Powers are attributes in just the way that "red" is an attribute of flags and noses. However, the differentia of powerful particulars, the agents that have such powers, include the chemical structure of the molecules of each type of particular and the active route by which each brings about its effect.

According to Purvis, Cranefield, and Ward (1998, p. 4),

There are two basic aspects of a causal agent model:

- The nature or structure of the agent itself.
- The architecture of the system in which the agent operates.

The first basic aspect covers two very different cases. A simple agent may possess the power to act in a certain way, as its defining (or one of its defining) attributes. The question, by virtue of what internal structure does an electron have a unit charge, had no place in physics, but it may turn out that an electron is not a simple agent. A complex agent may possess its powers as emergent properties of a more basic structure. Here is an example of the use of the concept "causal agent" from medicine. According to the *CDC Medical Dictionary* (2005), the causal agents of malaria are blood parasites whose power to cause malaria is an emergent property of their anatomical/physiological structure; this plays an essential role in the causation of the symptoms in the appropriate circumstances. To what sort of beings can powers be ascribed?

Table 3.1 Hierarchical Catalogue of Causal Agents

	Causal Agent		
Entity		Substance	
Simple	Complex	Observable	Unobservable
(*electron*)	(*plasmodium*)	(*acid*)	(*energy*)

The taxonomic tree depicted in Table 3.1 sums up my example-driven intuitions.

The powers severally ascribed to such beings include the power to repel positively charged bodies, the power to cause the symptoms of malaria, the power to etch metal, and the power to do mechanical work.

The endurance requirement on causal powers leads to the quest for an account of how a powerful particular can properly be said to have a power when not exercising it. In chemistry this quest leads to a hierarchy of structural hypotheses, which are taken to be the ontological basis for the powers of complex beings as emergent properties (Stemwedel, 2003). Acidity is an emergent property of some chemical substances that yield H ions in a solution. These ions continue to exist whether or not the acidity of hydrochloric acid is being exercised on anything, for example, a sample of zinc. If no reductive analysis of "causal power" into something else seems likely to be successful, then the presumption that there are causal powers of active agents underlying those sequences of phenomena we identify as causal chains must be reckoned a Wittgensteinian "hinge"—a presumption on which much of science turns, particularly chemistry and physics. With human beings as the powerful particulars at the heart of the causal patterns of human life, the very same hinge underlies human thought and action, both individual and collective.

Hiddleston (2005, p. 42) expands the analysis to include "preventative power." Roughly a preventative power "is [expressed in] the probability that P prevents generative cause C from producing E." What then is P? It might be a platform on which a cannon ball rests. It might be an antibody in the bloodstream; it might be a mosquito net in Panama; and so on. Each of these entities has the relevant causal powers by virtue of their material nature. Each answers the relevant "Why?" question, such as "Why doesn't the cannon ball fall?" I go to the pharmacy. "I need something to stop my flea bites itching." "Here you are," says the pharmacist, "a nice drop of Betnovate!"

VII. HUMAN AGENCY

Causal chains in nature regress indefinitely. This is made manageable in the special sciences by local decisions as to the salience of one or a few among myriad antecedent conditions. Is human agency an exception to this pattern? In the midst of the myriad conditions surrounding some sequence of events in the human world, do we not find a human decision as the starting point of such a sequence and a human actor as the source of the causal efficacy that brings about the effect in question? Put otherwise, "The buck stops here!," or as Wittgenstein (1953, §217) remarked, "[t]his is simply what I do!"

The authors of *Complete Psychology* (sic) offer this definition of motivation: "Motivation is that which gives the impetus to behavior by arousing, sustaining and directing it towards the successful attainment of goals. So motivation energizes people to act and moves them from a resting state to an active state" (Davey, 2004, p. 464). On the contrary, discursive psychologists argue that motivations are what people offer by way of explanations for what they are doing. Motive talk does not report prior causes of action but is a sense-making practice, with all kinds of cultural variations. Persons are the agents, not their constituents, nor many of their collective associations. We must enter an important caveat at this point: A great deal of confusion has been created in philosophy of the human sciences by claiming that social structures are causally efficacious. Social structures are not, and indeed cannot be, efficacious causes. Of course, as discursive patterns in human interpersonal interactions, they are among the conditions that shape the outcome of human agentive acts and so produced by them. In Aristotelian terms, they may be formal causes but they can never be efficient causes.

VIII. ARGUMENTS FOR ABANDONING AGENTIVE CAUSALITY

Lay folk, lawyers, physicists, and almost everyone else are so accustomed to ordering their lives and thoughts with agentive concepts that efforts by philosophers to dislodge the concept may seem very odd. The arguments against the usefulness of concepts of agency turn on the meaningfulness of agentive concepts. The core concept of this group is that of "power" or "efficacy." If one were to hold that only those words that have observable referents are meaningful, then one might be tempted, after failing to observe the exercise of agency other than in its prior conditions and its apparent effects, to declare the concept, and its family of related concepts, incoherent. This is the core of Hume's famous argument and the positivistic line of thought that flowed from it.

Another promising line of argument against taking the concept of a causal power seriously begins with the apparent ease with which people are aware of their own efforts in bringing about various states of affairs. It is then suggested that the concept, now rendered meaningful in the empiricist way, can be displaced by a simile or metaphor onto other contexts, particularly those comprehended by the sciences of physics and chemistry. Skeptics declare either that the metaphor is weak, being no more than a dubious anthropomorphism, or that the personal experience on which it is based is an illusion—the individual simply being unaware of the forces that have led the action he or she believes they have initiated.

More telling is the *virtus dormativa* objection. If the identifying criterion for a power of a certain kind is uniquely tied to the effect that it has when the corresponding disposition is activated, then there is a vicious circularity between powers and their manifestations. In principle, there would be a power for every disposition. Opium has the power to put someone to sleep—a *virtus dormativa*. But there is no independent criterion for the ascription of this power. Moreover, if by the work of biochemists we are now able to give a chemical account of why opium makes people sleepy, we have eliminated the "power" term from the explanation in favor of the occurrent chemical properties of "poppy juice." Is this a fatal flaw in explanatory regresses that terminates in powers, be they attributes of powerful particulars or ultimate beings?

Finally, in this catalog of doubts of the viability of the concept of agency, some philosophers, again and notably David Hume, have linked power, agency, and causal efficacy with necessity, as if active causes necessitated their effects. Hume argued that there could never be a contradiction in supposing that though the antecedent causal conditions had been satisfied, the usual effect did not occur. On this view there is no substantial link between causes and their effects. The only "link" is mere statistical regularity.

The *virtus dormativa* objection undercuts the use of the concept of "power" in scientific theorizing in a much more serious way. It poses a dilemma that forces us to pay close attention to the criteria of identity, both numerical and qualitative, of causal powers, whether they are attributes of powerful particulars or individual substance—the foundations of the material world.

IX. CONDITIONALIZED ATTRIBUTES

Powers invoke the idea of agency, as sketched above, while liabilities invoke the idea of passivity. Beings with powers act and beings with liabilities are acted upon. Something may properly be said to have a power to initiate a chain of events, even when quiescent. Similarly, something may be said to have a liability to be affected in a certain way by an outside influence, even when nothing is affecting it. Gilbert Ryle's (1949) distinction between occurrent and dispositional properties is an essential element in the analysis of the concepts of "power" and "liability." An occurrent property is properly ascribed to a person, an animal, or a suitably sensitive instrument at the time that it displayed. A dispositional property is manifested only when certain conditions are fulfilled—conditions that occur only occasionally. Typically we express the content of a dispositional attribution in conditional form: "If conditions C are (were to be, had been etc.) realized, then phenomenon P will (would, would have etc.) occur(ed)." Since powers are not always exercised and liabilities not always revealed, powers and liabilities can be ascribed to certain beings even when they are not displaying the relevant behavior or activity.

Conditionalized properties, in general, are empirical. Both the clauses of the conditional formulation of the content of the attribution of such properties are observables. In the statement "If it rains the picnic will be called off," "rain" and "calling off the picnic" are observables. The same epistemic character is a feature of powers and liabilities. "This magnet has the power to attract iron" when spelled out goes something like this—"If a piece of iron is near a magnet it will be drawn towards it"—and both "iron near magnet" and "iron being drawn" are observables.

Ryle set about showing that the best analysis of the predicates used to ascribe mental attributes to people is conditional. That is, mental attributes such as "knowing," "believing," and so on are dispositions. "She knows the way home" is analyzed as "If asked to lead the party she successfully brings us home." This scheme worked very well for cognitive attributes such as knowledge and belief. However, another important class of words in this context is the "mongrel categoricals," such as "ready," "careful," "intelligent," and "resolute" (Ryle, 1949, p. 47). Instead of taking "he drove carefully" to refer to two activities, driving and being careful, there is just one activity performed in a certain way. These words are semi-dispositional (i.e., conditionalized attributes) and semi-episodic (i.e., descriptive of something occurrent). "He solved the problem brilliantly" is an occurrent performance displaying brilliance. But his "brilliance" like her "intelligence" is a dispositional attribute, true of each of them even when they are not solving problems—to act resolutely, intelligently, diligently, and so on is the exercise of personal power. These features of human action don't just happen.

Where do "tendencies," "dispositions," and "propensities" appear on this grammatical map? They are certainly conditionalized attributes, but they do not carry necessary implications of agency. Rather the contrary, in that to remark that he has a tendency to slice the ball when driving off the tee suggests that this defect is outside his control or that she has a kindly disposition it was something intrinsic to the person and not a deliberate pose.

The notion of a power as an emergent property of a complex being does no more than mimic a genuine power attribution because the "no further back" condition is violated. In science we do not rest content with secondary powerful particulars, but try to account for them by searching for primary powerful particulars as part of the grounding conditions of their efficacy, that is, their dispositions to display in various ways, as observable properties, as deriving forces for various kinds of change, and so on. Clearly, this inaugurates regresses. To manage this feature of scientific thinking we need to attend to the difference between homogeneous and heterogeneous regresses as originally formulated by Stroll (1994, p. 196).

In a homogeneous regress each level that is reached as the regress progresses from macro-wholes to micro-parts and from micro-parts as micro-wholes to nano-parts and so on. The ontological category of the beings at each successive level is the same. A traffic jam consists of cars, each of which is an ordered collection of material parts; each of these parts is an assemblage of yet smaller parts. This is a very strong mereological principle. Even in chemistry, the regress from material stuffs to molecular constituents, to their atomic components, to their subatomic particle makeup, to the realm of quarks raises all kinds of metaphysical problems about the relative metaphysical status of the beings at each level. For example, it is far from clear that the criteria of identity effective at the "upper levels" hold good at the deeper levels. How do we decide it is the "same electron"? Certainly not according to the criteria we use for determining it is the "same boulder."

In a heterogeneous regress, a temporary halt is reached when the beings of the lowest level are singularities in the ontology that defines identity in the whole scheme. However, by various linking devices, a second regress can be constructed to support that first. For example, to take a case from discursive psychology, we make use of rule-regresses in psychological explanations, and these soon run out. As Wittgenstein (1953, §217) famously quipped, "my spade is turned." Of course, we can always turn to cultural and historical studies to account for the existence of particular rule-systems. Driving on the right defines one possible motoring culture, but that rule is explicable by reference to anti-Royalist sentiment in eighteenth-century France and the United States.

We can now make sense of the idea that the emergent powers of structured beings are not fundamental. As we build an explanatory regress, we reach a point at which the constituents of the being with emergent powers do not have these powers as individuals. The possibility of one or more heterogeneous regress(es) now opens up the possibility of terminating in singular beings, ultimate powerful particulars that are elementary causal powers.

X. POWERS AS ATTRIBUTES

As the argument unfolds, we might become convinced that the concept of a causal power is ineliminable from intelligible discourse be it concerning human affairs or the material world. At this point the concept of causal power appears to refer to an attribute—the salient attribute of this or that kind of powerful particular, be it human agent or electric charge. We can ask what sort of beings have causal powers, and what is it about their natures that so endows them.

Identity Criteria for Causal Powers

By resting content with associated dispositions as the basis of criteria for the identity of either secondary or primary powers, we have no defense against the *virtus dormativa* objection to the entire project of developing an analysis of science as the working out of the application of a metaphysics of casual powers to natural and social phenomena. If there is a power for every observable disposition, then the powers concepts do no work at all in the discourse of the sciences. Of course, observable dispositions are involved in the semantic content of distinctive powers, but so are the natures or constituent structures of the material beings in question, be they particulars like electrons or mass substances like rivers.

The problem is easily resolved for secondary or derived powers, which are manifested as emergent properties of complex particulars. The same essential nature characterizing a powerful particular stands in an explanatory role to a variety of dispositions insofar as this variety is explicable by reference to the conditions under which they are displayed. Petrol can be a solvent in one condition and an explosive in another. These distinctive dispositions are the expression of distinctive causal powers that are grounded in a common structure of carbon and hydrogen atoms. However, the serious "powers" devotee wants to go further. The elementary beings of the material universe and of the social worlds of people are singularities—active beings with no internal complexity and the bearers of simple powers. Emergent or secondary powers are the result of the structural forms of congeries of simple powers. What is the sense of "same power" in such an observation as "The same power is manifested in several different dispositions"? If the "sameness" concept is numerical identity, then the claim depends on the *persistence over time* of a powerful particular as an individual being, *the real essence of which is stable* within a certain set of parameters. This principle holds good whether the power is emergent and secondary or native and primary. However, if the "sameness" of the power is a matter of qualitative identity, then, though the powerful particulars that have this power are numerically distinct, the similarity of composition (e.g., the structure of elementary powers) is a sufficient condition for an identity claim for a power as an attribute.

The situation is just a little more complex than presented here. In many cases the typical disposition that is animated by a causal power is involved in the identification of the power as a power of this or that kind. The complexity is made tolerable by the way that an environmental condition is a necessary element in the criteria for "same power" but not a sufficient condition—that requires the nature or constitution of the relevant powerful particular.

XI. CAUSATION AMONG UNIQUE PARTICULARS

Finally, can we make sense of the idea of a causal process that links unique individuals in a productive way using the concepts and discourse structures we have already examined? We certainly talk as if there were one-off cases of some agent, event or situation, which is like no other, bringing about an effect that is like no other. The long-running debate about the origins of World War I has been reopened on the hundredth anniversary of that conflict's beginnings. In psychology and sociology, just as in cosmology, we may have to recognize and try to make sense of unique sequences of one-off events. These can be understood as individuals and states of affairs linked productively by one-off mechanisms and cognitive as well as, perhaps, neurological processes that have their day and vanish forever.

At least we can rule out the Humean account of causation as a repeated and repeatable sequence of events to provide concepts for understanding and recording unique patterns of phenomena. By hypothesis, the cases we would want to deal with are unique, so there are no previous examples of any of them, and there will be no subsequent ones. There is nothing like a unique event, situation, or entity either before or after its appearance as the unrepeatable content of the one and only present time.

However, by turning to the role of causal mechanisms in the whole range of natural and social sciences, as well as human studies in general, we can make some headway in setting out a schema for making sense of unique causal processes. We have little reason to doubt that the biological evolution of human beings is a unique process, but every step of the way from hominids to *homo sapiens* can be explained on each change in form and function of the hominid body and brain, and of its cultural activities, by a combination of genetics and environmental changes overlaid by a kind of cultural selection process. So far as we know, the universe came into being only once, though from the moment the big bang had happened, its evolution thereafter was driven by known causal mechanisms, though seemingly these have changed over time. The reign of the Tudor dynasty in Britain, and that of the Stuarts who succeeded it, is a unique sequence of moments the unique outcome of which was the hybrid state of Great Britain. Such a process, we all believe, could not happen again—why? Though every step along the way is explicable in some loosely causal mode, the running together of so many streams of change in so many diverse ramifying and converging sequences of situations is unrepeatable.

As we decompose such complex and unrepeatable patterns, we do not come across unheard-of causal processes, nor do we believe that, on a grand scale, there are unheard-of causal processes either. Piecemeal analysis and explanation is all we can accomplish.

XII. SUMMARY

Having laid out a structure for the related concepts of "disposition," "power," and "agency," can we show that in the discourses of human studies and in everyday life this conceptual pattern is inevitable and ineliminable? This may be too ambitious a project, but we certainly display the power of this way of thinking to make sense of a great many of the ways that people behave. What we have brought out in the analysis of the concept of "causal power" is the way that it includes two root concepts, namely, dispositions to respond to external conditions and radical agency or spontaneity.

Dispositions are properties possessed permanently but that are displayed only occasionally, if at all. What is the justification for ascribing these properties to an entity when they are not being displayed? In short, what grounds dispositions? It should be a permanent occurrent property of the being in question—for example, chemical composition, repertoires of knowledge or belief, inherited and learned character traits, and so on. However, such properties cannot be an exhaustive analysis of any disposition since the latter includes an external aspect, the conditions under which the disposition is displayed (Mumford, 1992). Spontaneity catches the idea that the causal activity or efficacy of a basic powerful particular is not brought into being by the prior activity of some other particular. A primary powerful particular is a being that is efficacious not as the result of internal processes within the particular itself. A secondary powerful particular acts by virtue of some process or structure or both internal to the being in question. Sometimes this "nature" is the source of the identity of the being in question; that is, it is its intrinsic nature or part of its intrinsic nature. Without this cluster of occurrent properties, that entity in question would not be of the type or species or chemical kind that it is thought to be.

Hiddleston (2005) invokes the idea of an active route between cause event and effect event, which is contrary to the mere juxtaposition of events at the heart of the Humean account of causation. To turn to the last act of Tosca, the moving executioner's bullet is the basis of an "active route between the cause-event and the effect-event," or in this case the state, the being dead of the victim. Similarly, in the case of someone who ducks out of the way of a falling boulder in one scenario, but might not have done so in another, both counterfactuals are supported by the boulder as persisting causal agent—a status the boulder has whether or not the hiker ducked. The moving boulder is there as an active agent in both scenarios. The hiker is dead, and we say, "had he ducked he would have survived." The hiker is alive, and we say, "had he not ducked he would be dead." Of all the goings-on in the vicinity of the hiker, why is the boulder so important? It is the "powerful particular" required to make sense of either situation.

REFERENCES

Aristotle. (c. 350 BCE [1994]). *Posterior Analytics*. Trans. Jonathan Barnes. Oxford: Oxford University Press.

Davey, G. & Sterlig, C. (2004) *Complete Psychology*. London: Routledge.

Grice, J. W. (2014). Observation oriented modeling: Preparing students for research in the 21st century. *Innovative Teaching*, 3–30.

Harré, R., & Madden, E. H. (1972). *Causal Powers*. Oxford: Blackwell.

Hempel, C. G. (1965). *Aspects of Scientific Explanation*. New York: Free Press.

Hiddleston, E. (2005). Causal powers. *British Journal for the Philosophy of Science*, 56(1), 27–59.

Mumford, S. (1992). *Dispositions*. Oxford: Oxford University Press.

Mumford, S., & Arjan, R. L. (2011). *Getting Causes from Powers*. Oxford: Oxford University Press.

Nagel, E. (1979). *Teleology Revisited and Other Essays in the Philosophy of Science*. New York: Columbia University Press.

Purvis, M., Cranefield, S., & Ward, R. (1998). *Distributed software systems: From objects to agents*. Proceedings of the International Conference on Software Engineering. Los Alamitos, CA: IEEE Press.

Ryle, G. (1949). *The Concept of Mind*. London: Hutchinson.

Wierzbicka, A. (1992). *Semantics, Culture and Cognition*. Oxford: Oxford University Press.

Wittgenstein, L. (1953). *Philosophical Investigations*. Oxford: Blackwell.

Part Two

....

Causal Concepts and Research Methods

4

Causation in Introductory Psychology Texts

Raven Dunstan and Fathali M. Moghaddam

In order to better understand the role of causation in traditional psychology, we examined 15 widely used general psychology texts, published between 2006 and 2015. These texts are displayed in Table 4.1.

There are important reasons for giving attention to general psychology texts. Approximately 1.5 million students take an introductory psychology course each year in the United States (Information about education, 2014). Some texts have played an important role in shaping the future direction of the field. Two early examples are William Wundt's *Principles of Physiological Psychology* (1874), which spread the use of introspection in experimental contexts to study subjective experiences. William James's *Principles of Psychology* (1890) was an early exponent of a biosocial approach in psychology. Entry-level psychology classes influence the future of the field through teaching a specific conception of psychology to the next generation of psychologists (and nonpsychologists).

It may appear that by including only North American texts, we have limited the generalizability of our findings. However, the United States has been the lone superpower of psychology for the past half century (Moghaddam, 1987). Psychological knowledge is exported from the United States to the rest of the world (Moghaddam & Lee, 2006). Traditional psychology reflects reductionism, individualism, and other characteristics of American culture, but is "verified" as universal through a process of double reification "involving the exportation and propagation of cultural phenomena from one nation to another, and the later harvesting of the outcomes of this exportation through so-called international research, as validation of universalization" (Moghaddam & Lee, 2006, p. 164). The influence of traditional American psychology is reflected, for example, in course descriptions for introductory-level psychology classes in India, where Euro-American psychology is given priority (Syllabus for Delhi University, 2014). Thus, because of the global dominance of traditional American psychology, we believe that American psychology texts help to shape the minds of psychology students around the world.

Table 4.1 Fifteen Texts

Name	Author	Edition	Year Published
Introduction to Psychology	James W. Kalat	Tenth	2014
Psychology Around Us	Ronald Comer, Elizabeth Gould	Second	2013
Psychology and Life	Richard J. Gerrig	Twentieth	2013
Psychology in Action	Karen Huffman	Tenth	2012
Psychology	Douglas A. Bernstein, Louis A. Penner, Alison Clark	Seventh	2006
Psychology	Henry Gleitman, Daniel Reisberg, James Gross	Seventh	2007
Psychology in Your Life	Sarah Grison, Todd F. Heatherton, Michael S. Gazzaniga	First	2015
The Science of Psychology	Laura A. King	Second	2011
Psychology	Peter Gray	Fifth	2007
Psychology	Saundra K. Ciccarelli, Glenn E. Meyer	First	2006
Psychology	Lester M. Sdorow, Cheryl A. Rickabaugh	Sixth	2006
Psychology: An Introduction	Benjamin B. Lahey	Ninth	2007
Psychology: Making Connections	Gregory J. Feist, Erika L. Rosenberg	First	2010
Psychology: The Science of Behavior	Neil R. Carlson, C. Donald Heth, Harold Miller, John W. Donahoe, William Buskist, G. Neil Martin	Sixth	2007
Understanding Psychology	Robert S. Feldman	Tenth	2011

I. INTRODUCING PSYCHOLOGY THROUGH CAUSATION

We gave particular attention to the first two chapters of each of the 15 texts, because it is in these early chapters that the role of causation in psychology is discussed most explicitly. Our primary concern was with the manner in which, rather than the frequency with which, causation is discussed. We focused on discussions of the following terms within the introduction and research methods chapters: manipulation, cause, effect, scientific method, determination, free will, experimentation, alternative methods of study, independent variable, and dependent variable.

The Goals of Psychology

Why is psychology a useful research field and what does it seek to accomplish? These questions are central to the manner in which the authors frame psychology in the minds of new students. Psychology attempts to answer specific research questions about human behavior utilizing a variety of data. Gerrig (2013) asserts that the role of psychologists is to "inquire about the how, what, when, and why of human behavior and about the causes and consequences of behaviors you observe in yourself, in other people, and in animals" (p. 2). By asking questions and collecting information, psychologists are trying to explain our behavioral and mental processes. "Explanation" as used in psychology holds one goal. According to Gray (2007), to explain "is to identify causes" (p. 9). Standard definitions of psychology claim that psychology tries to discover the causes for how humans act and think using the scientific method.

II. METHODS FOR FINDING CAUSES

Psychology employs a variety of methods, including surveys, case studies, naturalistic observation, descriptive research, quasi-experimentation, correlational studies, and experimentation. The authors of introductory psychology textbooks examine the efficacy of each of these research methods in terms of causation. Psychologists evaluate the utility of each methodology based on their definition of causation, which focuses primarily on efficient causation. If the method fails to localize the cause, then it is ultimately rejected.

The survey questionnaire is used to assess attitudes on a wide range of topics, from political opinions to perceived happiness. Huffman (2012) dismisses this procedure as an inadequate method to fulfill the purpose of psychology. She asserts "survey techniques cannot, of course, be used to explain *causes* of behavior" (p. 28). Likewise, the case study method fails to isolate one factor as causal. Sdorow and Rickabaugh (2006) maintain that "because a person's behavior is affected by many variables, the case study method cannot determine the particular variables that caused the behavior being studied" (p. 35).

Discussions in psychology texts often include warnings about the complexity of identifying causes. For example, in a discussion of family relationships, Bernstein, Penner, Clarke-Stewart, and Roy (2006) discuss a possible connection between the activation of specific genes and the appearance of certain mental disorders, such as schizophrenia. These authors note that merely the simultaneous existence of these activated genes and the disorder fails to prove causation, adding that "the appearance of similar disorders in close relatives might be due to environmental factors instead of, or in addition to, genetic ones. After all, close relatives tend to share environments as well as genes" (Bernstein et al., 2006, p. 47).

Naturalistic observation is another method employed by researchers. For example, several psychology textbooks point to Jane Goodall's study of chimpanzees, which involved no intervention into their daily routines

(Kalat, 2014, p. 43). Feldman (2011) admits that "[a]lthough the advantage of naturalistic observation is obvious—we get a sample of what people do in their 'natural habitat'—there is also an important drawback: the inability to control any of the factors of interest" (p. 38). The lack of an adequate capacity to manipulate elements within the environment renders the method unsuitable for singling out one causal factor for an action or event.

Descriptive research methods face a similar issue. This entails simply providing details about the result of an action, such as what happens after a child watches violent television. Does the child act more aggressively? King (2011) emphasizes that "[d]escriptive research allows researchers to get a sense of a subject of interest, but it cannot answer questions about how and why things are the way they are" (p. 31). Since we have operationalized explaining as identifying causes, descriptive research fails to identify the driving force behind an action.

Correlational study is defined in the majority of these texts as a "[r]esearch method in which variables are observed or measured (without directly manipulating) to identify relationships between them" (Huffman, 2012, p. 29). Correlation is given much attention in the textbooks. Bernstein et al. (2006) provide the correlational example of "[t]he number of drownings in the United States rises and falls during the year, along with the amount of ice cream sold each month" (p. 39). However, to claim that the number of drownings per month is caused by ice cream sales would clearly be a ridiculous conclusion. Instead, a third factor is involved, such as the summer season that would permit swimming and boating, during which more ice cream is consumed. For this reason, the authors of psychology texts qualify the "relationship between variables" established by correlational studies. Gerrig (2013) asserts that "[a] strong correlation indicates only that two sets of data are related in a systemic way; the correlation does not ensure that one causes the other" (p. 28).

Another method, quasi-experimentation, "makes use of naturally occurring groups rather than randomly assigning subjects to groups" (Feist & Rosenberg, 2010, p. 71). Feist and Rosenberg (2010) provide the following example of a quasi-experiment: "[F]indings suggest that musical training can change the brain, but because the researchers relied on naturally occurring groups and the groups were not matched, the results are correlational but *not* causal" (p. 71).

Twin studies are described as more promising, but not a widely applicable method, for proving causal relationships between variables. Gray (2007) argues that "[i]f identical twins, who share all their genes with one another, are much more similar in jealously than are same-sex non-identical twins, who are no more closely related than other siblings, that would indicate that much of the variation among people in sexual jealousy is caused by variation in genes" (p. 11). Bernstein et al. (2006) fortify this argument that "much" but not all of the variation can be attributed to genetics. These authors point to the fact that "[c]ases in which identical twins who have been separated at birth are found to have similar interests, personality traits, and mental abilities suggest that these characteristics have a significant genetic component" (Bernstein et al., 2006, p. 48). But only a limited number of questions can be addressed using the twin method.

Since none of the widely applicable methods discussed so far identify causes, according to the texts they are not fulfilling the main purpose of psychology. If psychology relied merely on these methods, it would not be considered a science in the traditional sense. Only a method that identifies causes qualifies as science: "Experimental research is the most powerful research method because it allows experimenters to manipulate, isolate, and control chosen variables, and thereby determine *cause and effect*" (Huffman, 2012, p. 21). Experimental psychology has remained reductionist, attempting to locate causes in the smallest units possible, on the basis of an assumption explained in the mid-twentieth century by Jessor (1958): "Obviously an inherent attraction of reductive explanation is its implications for possible ways of unifying the separate scientific disciplines" (p. 170).

III. WHAT IS EXPERIMENTATION?

What is it about experimentation that (supposedly) permits the identification of cause-effect relationships? Huffman (2012) claims that "[o]nly through an experiment can researchers isolate a single factor and examine the effect of that factor alone on a particular behavior" (p. 21). The "factors" in this assertion are also known as independent and dependent variables. Feldman (2011) emphasizes the importance of these two variables. He believes that "[c]rucial to every experiment is the dependent variable, the variable that is measured and is expected to change as a result of changes caused by the experimenter's manipulation of the independent variable" (p. 42). Gray (2007) offers a nearly identical definition with an emphasis on the principle of causation pointing out that in an experiment the variable that is hypothesized to cause some effect on another variable is called the independent variable, and the variable that is hypothesized to be affected is called the dependent variable. Huffman (2012) highlights that every experiment "is designed to answer essentially the same question: Does the independent variable (IV) *cause* the predicted change in the dependent variable (DV)?" (p. 22). Feldman (2011) fortifies this point by boldly claiming that "[a]ll true experiments in psychology fit this straightforward model" (p. 42).

Authors of introductory-level texts also present numerous examples to elucidate the use of experimentation in psychology. Gerrig (2013) explains,

> Imagine, for example, that you wished to test the hypothesis we considered earlier: that children who view a lot of violence on television will engage in more aggressive acts toward their peers. To test that hypothesis, you might devise an experiment in which you manipulated the amount of violence each participant viewed. That factor you manipulate

would be the independent variable; it functions as the causal part of the relationship. For each level of violence viewed, you could then assess how much aggression each participant displayed. Aggression is the effect part of the cause-effect relationship; it is the dependent variable, which is what the experimenter measures. If researchers' claims about cause and effect are correct, the value of the dependent variable will depend on the value of the independent variable. (p. 23)

Carlson et al. (2007) add, "Each variable must be *operationally defined*, and the independent variable must be controlled so that only it, and no other variable, is responsible for any changes in the dependent variable" (p. 28).

It is telling that in discussing independent and dependent variables, examples in introductory psychology texts are drawn from the fields of medicine, the biological sciences, and the physical sciences. Feist and Rosenberg (2010) discuss trial treatments in this way, "Remember: the response, or dependent variable (DV), depends on the treatment. It is the treatment, or independent variable (IV), that the researcher manipulates" (p. 53). Feldman (2011) offers the following example to clarify the importance of the control group:

For example, consider a medical researcher who thinks he has invented a medicine that cures the common cold. To test his claim, he gives the medicine one day to a group of 20 people who have colds and finds that 10 days later all of them are cured. Eureka? Not so fast. An observer viewing this flawed study might reasonably argue that the people would have gotten better even without the medicine. What the researcher obviously needed was a control group consisting of people with colds who *don't* get the medicine and whose health is also checked 10 days later. (p. 41)

Feldman (2011) adds, "Through the use of control groups, then, researchers can isolate specific causes for their findings and draw cause-and-effect inferences" (p. 41). By presenting these terms within the first two chapters, the authors reinforce their definition of psychology as a science focused on discovering causes in thought and action.

IV. COMPARISON TO OTHER SCIENCES

Introductory texts position psychology as, first, different from "pseudopsychologies," defined by Ciccarelli and Meyer (2006) as "systems of explaining human behavior that are not based on scientific evidence and that have no real value other than being entertaining" (p. 34). Examples of pseudopsychologies are astrology and palm reading. Second, introductory texts position psychology as similar to "real sciences" such as chemistry.

Comparison to the Natural Sciences

Through subtle but repeated comparisons, the texts present psychology as similar to the natural sciences. Feist and Rosenberg (2010) describe how "in the mid-to late 1800s, many German universities were starting laboratories in physics, chemistry, and medicine. In the 1870s they opened the first laboratories in psychology" (p. 16). Besides a shared history, psychology claims to share methods with the other sciences. Sdorow and Rickabaugh (2006) claim that "[s]ciences are 'scientific' because they share a common method, not because they share a common subject matter. Physics, chemistry, biology, and psychology differ in what they study, yet each uses the scientific method" (p. 2). According to these authors, this shared method begins with the first step of observation. Carlson et al. (2007) make this point:

> For example, people described mountains, volcanoes, canyons, plains, and the multitude of rocks and minerals found in these locations long before they attempted to understand their formation. Thus, observation and classification of the landscape and its contents began long before the development of the science of geology. (p. 30)

Ciccarelli and Meyer (2006) assert that "every science has goals. In physics, the goals concern learning how the physical world works. In astronomy, the goals are to chart the universe and understand both how it came to be and what it is becoming. In psychology, there are four goals that aim at uncovering the mysteries of human and animal behavior: description, explanation, prediction, and control" (p. 4).

In addition to the shared features among all sciences, the authors of these introductory-level texts draw connections between psychology and one specific natural science. Feist and Rosenberg (2010) study the close relationship between psychophysics and physics: "[I]f physicists study the physical properties of light and sound, psychophysicists study human perception of light and sound" (p. 16). They also claim that physics aided psychology's transition from a branch of philosophy to a science: "With the work of these pioneers, psychophysics took the first steps toward establishing psychology as a science" (p. 17). Kalat (2014) affirms this relationship with the following comparison between the two fields: "[J]ust as physicists could study gravity by dropping any object in any location, many psychologists in the mid-1900s thought that they could learn all about behavior by studying rats in mazes" (p. 19). Another contributor to psychology's status as a science that Feist and Rosenberg (2010) acknowledge is William Wundt. Wundt (1999) helped psychology to gain independence from both philosophy and physiology, by applying the research methods of physiology to questions arising out of philosophy.

Another commonly compared natural science to psychology is chemistry. Kalat (2014) presents the following thought experiment for introductory-level psychology students: "Imagine a chemist adding one clear liquid to another.

Suddenly the first mixture turns green and explodes. We would conclude cause and effect, as we have no reason to expect that the first liquid was about to turn green and explode on its own" (p. 44). Chemistry is heavily discussed in the structuralism section of introductory-level psychology textbooks. Feist and Rosenberg (2010) highlight the key component of structuralism: "Wundt, the chief proponent of structuralism, wanted to describe human experience in terms of the elements that combined to produce it" (p. 18). Huffman (2012) offers a pertinent example of a commonly made comparison between psychology and chemistry:

> Titchener was a type of mental chemist who sought to identify the basic building blocks, or *structures*, of the mind. Titchener's approach later came to be known as *structuralism*, of the mind. Just as the elements of hydrogen and oxygen combine to form the compound water, it was believed the "elements" of conscious experience combined to form the "compounds" of the mind. Structuralists sought to identify the elements of thought through introspection and then to determine how these elements combined to form the whole of experience. (p. 10)

Equating the division of compounds into basic elements to the separation of the mind into components functions to compare the subjects of each study and serve as another similarity that the two fields share.

V. LEGITIMIZING PSYCHOLOGY AS A SCIENCE

After raising the question "What is a science?," the authors defend psychology as having the status of a science. Feist and Rosenberg (2010) claim that "not only is psychology a science, but it is also considered a core science, along with medicine, earth science, chemistry, physics, and math" (p. 7). Carlson et al. (2007) provides the following example:

> Weber, an anatomist and physiologist, found that people's ability to distinguish between two similar stimuli—such as the brightness of two lights, the heaviness of two objects, or the loudness of two tones— followed orderly laws. This regularity suggested to Weber and his followers that perceptual phenomena could be studied scientifically as physics or biology. (p. 14)

Carlson et al. (2007) affirm that "[p]sychology as a science must be based on the assumption that behavior is strictly subject to physical laws, just as any other natural phenomenon" (p. 14). The ultimate goal of psychology and the role of causation is "to discover general laws about human behavior" (Grison, Heatherton, & Gazzaniga, 2015, p. 34). Most recently, cognitive neuroscience has attempted to localize the causes of specific actions to specific brain activity. Bernstein et al. (2006) explain that researchers in this branch of psychology "are trying to discover the building blocks of cognition and to determine how these components produce complex behaviors such as remembering a fact, naming an object[,] writing a word, or making a decision" (p. 22). Thus, the claim by Comer and Gould (2013) that as a "meteorologist relies on physical laws to describe and predict the force and path of hurricanes … psychologists seek out laws to describe and predict mental processes and behaviors" does not seem to hold weight (p. 37).

If we accept Comer and Gould's (2013) logic that "[t]he universe operates according to certain natural laws. Scientists believe that things happen in and around us in some kind of orderly fashion that can be described using rules or laws," (p. 37) then we are confronted by questions concerning moral responsibility. If the universe is controlling the actions of the actors living within its boundaries, then we must accept the principle of determinism. Gerrig (2013) asserts that "[a]t the common core of most psychological theories is the assumption of determinism, the idea that all events—physical, mental, and behavioral—are the result of, or determined by, specific causal factors" (p. 22). Feldman (2011) emphasizes the nature of causality: "The notion of free will stands in contrast to determinism, which sees behavior as caused or determined, by things beyond a person's control" (p. 20). If the mechanisms driving the actions of humans are not within their power to influence, then a lack of accountability follows.

The assumption of causation and thereby determinism has major implications for accountability and legal responsibility. If a person can claim that he or she did not perform an action under free will, can we hold the person accountable under the justice system? If human beings are to be compared to basic elements, such as molecules or atoms, what role does free will actually play in the world? Locke and several other British empiricists "argued that thoughts are not products of free will, but reflections of one's experiences in the physical and social environment" (Gray, 2007, p. 6). But how can the justice system work if we do not assume some measure of free will? Some of the psychology texts attempt to at least raise this complexity by also giving attention to the humanistic approach, which focuses on the free will and potential for self-actualization of each individual (Maslow, 1970). This viewpoint means we can continue to hold humans accountable for their actions (King, 2011, p. 12). Kalat (2014) offers a key distinction: "When a ball bounces down a hill, its motion depends on the shape of the hill. When you run down a hill, you could change direction if you saw a car coming toward you, or a snake lying in your path. The ball could not" (p. 5). This seems to separate the study of psychology from that of physics—but the implication for a science that searches for causal accounts of human behavior is not clarified.

VI. CONCLUDING COMMENTS

In *What Counts as an Experiment?: A Transdisciplinary Analysis of Textbooks, 1930–1970*, Winston and Blais (1996) examine 10 introductory psychology texts and find 9 utilized the words "independent variable" and "dependent variable." All 10 of these texts operationalized experiment through the manipulation of the dependent variable and control of all other factors (also see Moghaddam & Allen, 2013). By focusing on this methodology, traditional psychologists strive to distinguish psychology from pseudopsychologies and thereby draw the field closer to the natural sciences (Winston & Blais, 1996). In our study of 15 traditional psychology texts, we found that authors attempt to position psychology next to chemistry, physics, and other "real" sciences. The assumption among authors has been that "real" sciences are reductionist and positivist in their outlook. At the same time, the 15 textbooks also report studies and concepts that clearly show how human beings, the subjects of psychology, are singular and self-reflecting. One example of a "universal law" derived from psychology is the Hawthorne effect: "Being observed can lead participants to change their behavior, because people often act in particular ways to make positive impressions" (Grison et al., 2015, p. 27). The confounding variable related to the presence of the researchers or societal standards prevents the isolation of one variable from directly causing another.

Traditional psychology texts assume that only by adopting a causal account of behavior can psychology become a science. At the same time, some of the same texts recognize that the subject matter of psychology, human thought and action, is fundamentally different from the subject matter of chemistry, physics, and other "real" sciences. Various solutions have been proposed to solve this dilemma, such as distinguishing between thinking and action that can be explained using "causal" accounts, and thinking and action that is better explained using "normative" accounts (Moghaddam, 2013, ch. 2). Such solutions have not yet made their way into traditional psychology texts.

REFERENCES

Bernstein, D. A., Penner, L. A., Clarke-Stewart, A., & Roy, E. J. (2006). *Psychology* (7th ed.). Boston: Houghton Mifflin Company.

Carlson, N. R., Heth, C. D., Miller, H., Donahoe, J. W., Buskist, W., & Martin, G. N. (2007). *Psychology: The Science of Behavior* (6th ed.). Boston: Pearson Education, Inc.

Ciccarelli, S. K., & Meyer, G. E. (2006). *Psychology*. Upper Saddle River, NJ: Pearson Education, Inc.

Comer, R., & Gould, E. (2013). *Psychology around Us* (2nd ed.). Chichester: John Wiley & Sons, Inc.

Feist, G. J., & Rosenberg E. L. (2010). *Psychology: Making Connections*. New York: McGraw Hill.

Feldman, R. S. (2011). *Understanding Psychology* (10th ed.). New York: McGraw Hill.

Gerrig, R. J. (2013). *Psychology and Life* (20th ed.). Upper Saddle River, NJ: Pearson Education Inc.

Gleitman, H., Reisberg, D., & Gross, J. (2007). *Psychology* (7th ed.). New York: W.W. Norton & Company.

Gray, P. (2007). *Psychology* (5th ed.). New York: Worth Publishers.

Grison, S., Heatherton, T. F., & Gazzaniga, M. S. (2015). *Psychology in Your Life*. New York: W.W. Norton & Company.

Huffman, K. (2012). *Psychology in Action* (10th ed.). New York: John Wiley & Sons, Inc.

Information about education and the psychology educational pipeline. (2014). Retrieved October 16, 2014, from http://www.apa.org/workforce/about/faq.aspx

James, W. (1890). *The Principles of Psychology*. New York: Henry Holt and Company.

Jessor, R. (1958). The problem of reductionism in psychology. *Psychological Review, 65*, 170–178.

Kalat, J. W. (2014). *Introduction to Psychology* (10th ed.). Belmont: Cengage Learning.

King, L. A. (2011). *The Science of Psychology* (2nd ed.). New York: McGraw Hill.

Maslow, A. H. (1970). *Motivation and Personality* (3rd ed.). New York: Harper & Row.

Moghaddam, F. M. (1987). Psychology in the three worlds: As reflected by the "crisis" in social psychology and the move towards indigenous third world psychology. *American Psychologist, 47*, 912–920.

Moghaddam, F. M. (2013). *The Psychology of Dictatorship*. Washington, DC: American Psychological Association Press.

Moghaddam, F. M., & Allen, K. F. (2013). Representations of friendship, enmity, conflict resolution, and peace keeping in introductory psychology textbooks. In R. Harré & F. M. Moghaddam (Eds.), *The Psychology of Friendship and Enmity: Relationships in Love, Work, Politics, and War* (p. 24). Santa Barbara, CA: Praeger.

Moghaddam, F. M., & Lee, N. (2006). Double reification: The process of universalizing psychology in the three worlds. In A. C. Brock (Ed.), *Internationalizing the History of Psychology* (pp. 164–165). New York City: NYU Press.

Sdorow, L. M., & Rickabaugh, C. A. (2006). *Psychology* (6th ed.). Cincinnati, OH: Atomic Dog Publishing.

Syllabus for Delhi University. Retrieved October 16, 2014, from http://www.ipi.org.in/texts/courses/syllabus-delhi.php

Winston, A. S., & Blais, D. J. (1996). What counts as an experiment?: A transdisciplinary analysis of textbooks, 1930–1970. *The American Journal of Psychology, 109*, 599–616.

Wozniak, R. H. (1999). Introduction to grundzüge der physiologischen psychologie wilhelm wundt (1874). Retrieved from http://psychclassics .yorku.ca/Wundt/Physio/wozniak

EDITORS' COMMENTARY

The examination of causation in psychology by Dunstan and Moghaddam is limited to 15 American general psychology textbooks. They justify this limitation by pointing out the global dominance of American psychology, as well as the enormous influence of American general psychology textbooks both within and outside the United States. Millions of students annually take courses based on these textbooks, and many non-Western countries use translations of these books. Consequently, the treatment of causation in American textbooks has widespread international consequences.

The first thing that is striking is the adoption of causal language in all of the textbooks. This is justified by the textbook authors in two main steps. First, science is explained as concerning the discovery of cause-effect relations. Second, it is claimed that the science of psychology must necessarily focus on discovering cause-effect relationships in human behavior. Arguments in support of this position are made using examples from, and references to, the "real" sciences, particularly chemistry and physics. Thus, the American textbooks studied by Dunstan and Moghaddam make a serious effort to position psychology as a "real" science that, like physics and chemistry, adopts the goal of discovering cause-effect relations.

A second striking feature of the coverage of causation in the 15 textbooks is how the interpretation of causation remains very limited. As discussed in earlier chapters, particularly Chapter 3 by Harré, there are different types of causation. For example, Aristotle discussed material, form or pattern, efficient, and final causes. Among these, it is final cause, concerned with the purpose or meaning of things, that is the most important in human thinking and actions. Human experience is characterized by the collaborative construction of meaning, and the continuous negotiation of meanings in social interactions. Human behavior is purposive and intentional, in the sense that humans construct narratives about why and how they behave. Of course, such narratives are not necessarily objectively accurate, but nevertheless, they serve as the "reason why" people behave as they do.

It is remarkable that the 15 texts are not at all about final causation and that they give almost no attention to the question of meaning making and intentionality. In the research methods section of these texts, all the different methodologies that could serve to explore meaning making are dismissed. For example, interviews and observational studies are dismissed as unscientific. The only research method identified by these texts as suitable for psychological science is the laboratory experiment, because this is the method that is viewed as identifying "cause-effect" relations. The laboratory experiment is presented as the only really "scientific" method, because it is the method that best isolates the independent and dependent variables, or the assumed "causes" and "effects" in causation. Of course, the "causation" the texts have in mind is not the final cause. At most, the texts have efficient cause in mind.

The overall impression one gets from the discussions of causation in these 15 textbooks is that traditional psychology has remained extremely insular. There is no coverage in these texts of "alternative" research methods, including the varieties of qualitative methods, that treat causation more broadly and include final causation. Consequently, there is almost no coverage in these texts of processes involving interpersonal and intergroup interactions. Such processes are longer term, certainly longer than the one-hour laboratory experiment allows, and involve meaning making, that is, final causation.

5

Rerum Cognoscere Causas: Dependent and Independent Variables in Psychology

Adrian Furnham

Psychologists are somewhat unique with respect to the concepts of cause and consequence because they are interested both in the "actual" cause of a wide variety of phenomena—from depression to dyslexia, suicide to school results —and also in how ordinary people "think" about cause. There is an extensive literature in clinical, experimental, and social psychology concerning *attribution theory*, which is concerned with how people assign causality to events that affect them and others. This literature celebrates the biases and "errors" that people make in their understanding of causal powers. There is, however, less work on how psychologists themselves fall into various "traps" when trying to assign the cause and consequence to various psychological phenomena.

Often different academic disciplines attempt to give causal accounts of the same phenomena. Thus, anthropologists, psychologists, and sociologists may all try to explain the same issue such as the rise and fall of delinquency, or failed marriages or educational achievement. Each has preferred variables and explanatory concepts. Thus, while psychologists are interested and surprised by people "following the lead" of others and have theories of conformity and obedience, sociologists are more interested in those people who do not conform and hence have theories about deviance.

The problem, such as it, for the different disciplines occurs where a large and longitudinal data set is available that provides variables of interest to different disciplines. Thus, a sociologist might be interested in parental social class and a psychologist in childhood IQ in trying to predict later adult outcomes like educational or career success.

An example of this is the work of Cheng and Furnham (2012, 2013), where they have re-analyzed a publically available data set that traces people over time. It is in many ways the almost ideal data set for the social scientist: a large population (>5,000), which has been tested soon after birth and then at very regular intervals for over 50 years, providing different sorts of data— self-report, observational, and test data. So there is everything from childhood intelligence and illnesses to later educational achievement and income. The researchers have all done increasingly complicated and sophisticated multivariate statistics to interrogate the data to show how statistically X measured at time A relates directly (and/or indirectly) to Y at time B suggesting its causal power.

There are various themes to psychological thinking and work concerning the concept of cause. *First*, one of the most repeated message to any undergraduate social science methodology course is "correlation is not causation" (Mueller & Coon, 2013). Much psychological data are temporally cross-sectional in the sense that data are collected about different types of behavior *at the same time* (and by the same data collection method) and relationships examined. Students are castigated for their causal inferences when the data are only correlational. Things may be related but we cannot and should not infer that those relationships are causal.

Second, related to this is the design of studies that are very particularly mandated to ensure that causal explanations can be correctly attributed. There are many psychological concepts like the "Hawthorne effect," the "Placebo effect," and "Spontaneous remission" that alert researchers to making "correct" causal inferences. Hence, the obsession with particular experimental paradigms like the famous "randomized, controlled, double-blind" methods that try to eliminate or control various factors that may "cause" the result. This will be discussed later.

Third, there is the issue of ideology just below the surface in much psychological research and debate. It has been argued that patient, passive, and presuppositionless enquiry is a methodological myth. That is, psychology researchers have powerful biases that affect the design and interpretation of their studies. This is particularly the case when looking at issues like intelligence or sex differences and where the nature-nurture issues cause great consternation.

Fourth, there is always the problem of multiple causation in the sense that there are often many distal and proximal factors involved. Further some of these factors may not be the "province" of psychologists. Thus, parental social class may be considered a "sociological variable" and therefore underrepresented in psychological studies. Psychologists are also acutely aware of moderator and mediator factors that "come between" two other variables and better explain the causal relationship. It is often the case that psychological concepts and processes are complexly multidetermined.

Fifth, there is the ever-present problem of tautology where explanations are little more than tautological descriptions. This is most present in the research on personality where people report in questionnaires that they are outgoing and confident and later told by psychologists that they are extraverts who are outgoing and confident. There are various themes to psychological thinking and work concerning the concept of cause, which will be covered in this chapter.

I. CAUSE AND CORRELATION

Critics of various branches of psychology (but less so experimental psychology) point out that much of it is simply correlational. Worse, there is often method invariance in the sense that researchers may correlate the results of two questionnaires together. Psychologists are used to differentiating between self-report data, observational data, and test data and know that correlations are always higher when they stay within one area. Further, there are moderator and mediator variables that can and do make the simple interpretation of the relationship between two variables very tricky.

Students are told to adopt a multitrait multimethod approach. This, in effect, means that different (but usually related) variables are measured at the same time but using different methods. The aim is to escape or limit spurious effects that inflate results. Psychologists often favor experimental designs that attempt to show that by "manipulating" variable A, variable B responds accordingly. Thus, if you increase a person's state anxiety (experimentally and ethically), he or she would be more likely to seek out friends. Change one variable and you see a corresponding change in the other. This is usually and acceptably described and explained in causal language though the mechanisms and processes are often poorly understood.

A crucial issue is what would constitute a real causal explanation between two phenomena. Psychologists are usually happy to use advanced statistics to "infer causality" showing for instance that X at time 1 is statistically beyond chance related to Y at time 2. However, statistical correlations are unable to describe or explain the process whereby they are causally related. Usually psychological researchers resort to plausible, but untested, explanations for that causal process which is inferred from the statistical finding. In physics and branches of medicine, "this would not do" and be considered to be evidence of causality.

More than that, it is apparent that some groups seem opposed to the very idea of trying to find causal explanations for phenomena they are interested in. This is particularly the case with different cures and therapies, where practitioners for a variety of reasons seem strongly opposed to those investigating how, when, why, and whether their "causal account" of the process is indeed true.

Lilienfeld, Rotschel, Lynn, Cautin, and Latzman (2013) suggest six major causes of practitioner resistance to investigations of therapeutic efficacy.

Naïve Realism

Naïve realism is the idea that the world is just as we see it, that we are not hampered or constrained by preconceptions, biases, and blind spots. Practitioners believe that they can rely on their own intuitions. They don't see that a change in a person following therapy/training is not because of it (the post hoc, ergo propter hoc fallacy).

There are well-known causes of spurious effectiveness evidence. In other words, people do change, not as a result of the therapy/training, but rather because of such well-known factors as placebo effect (people improve as a result of the *expectation* of improvement), spontaneous remission (people get better on their own over time), regression to the mean (extremes of all sort become less so over time), effort justification (people justify their commitment to the training regime by saying they are better), and multiple treatment interference (other things they are doing are working, not the therapy/training).

Myths about Human Nature

There are lots of myths about human nature, such as myths about recovered memories and the role of early experience. People hold passionate beliefs based on theories that have been demonstrated to be wrong. These beliefs can encourage people to dismiss or ignore the efficacy evidence because it goes against some deeply held (and unjustifiable) belief system.

The Application of Group Findings to Individuals

Another major cause of practitioner resistance is generalizing from single case studies to groups, but refusing to apply group probabilities to individuals. "Aah," the coach says, "everyone is different," which is often a let-out.

Reversal of the Onus of Proof

Surely it is up to practitioners to show (beyond all reasonable doubt) that their training works rather than for the critics to amass sufficient good evidence that their claims are invalid. So the trainers attack the skeptics' evidence rather than providing their own. There is all the difference between an invalidated and an unvalidated theory: the former has been found not to work, and the latter has not been subjected to rigorous enquiry.

The Mischaracterization of What (Causal) Proof Is All About

The defensive practitioners put up all sorts of arguments to allow them off the hook. All this scientific evidence requirement stifles innovation; leads to a "one-size-fits-all" approach; does not generalize to all individuals; neglects other (special) evidence; or, worst of all, because (real, subtle, meaningful) changes cannot be quantified and human behavior is impossible to predict with any certainty.

Pragmatic Objections

Here, the argument is that while it is desirable to obtain proof of efficacy, it is difficult/impossible because of constraints of time; investigators need to become fully acquainted with the training materials; it requires an understanding of complex statistics; and, ultimately, such research is a nice, but pointless ivory tower activity.

This means that people can carry on peddling interventions that really do not work at all, or not in the way they say they do. The medics, by and large, have embraced the evidence-based approach. That is why we see no more bloodletting, leeching, or prefrontal lobotomies.

The trouble is that there is too much at stake here as those who attack alternative practitioners with these arguments have found. Proof that some coaching or training does not work threatens the livelihood of individuals and whole companies who (quite naturally) resist, screaming and shouting, the very idea that disinterested, evidence-based, causally descriptive research is rather a good thing.

Thus, within the psychological community there are those who seem happy to rely on sophisticated statistical modeling to "reveal causal patterns," those who struggle to design studies that examine the relationship between a limited number of variables to investigate very specific causal processes, and those who dismiss the whole empirical project as time wasting and pointless.

II. "BOGUS EFFECTS" AND INAPPROPRIATE CAUSAL INFLUENCES

Some famous psychological studies are so well known that concepts like the Hawthorne effect are almost common knowledge (Furnham, 2010). The word comes from a particular factor where in the 1920s ergonomists were experimenting with working conditions like lighting. They were good experimentalists and had a control group. Yet, their initial results puzzled them: When they increased lighting intensity, productivity went up, but when they did the opposite, it stayed up. The same happened when they varied other factors like breaks. They discovered that it was not what they did to the environment but rather how they treated people in the experimental group. It was suggested that the productivity gain occurred due to the impact of the motivational effect on the workers as a result of the interest being shown in them. That is, it had nothing to do with the experimental manipulation. The simple causal inferences of the "time-and-motion" approach were erroneous. The effect has also been associated with behavior changes as a function of people being aware of the fact that they were being observed.

Yet more famous and perhaps more import is the equally well-known placebo effect. Placebo means "to please." Modern research on the topic is usually attributed to a paper written in the *American Dental Association* journal by Henry Beecher, who claimed that placebo procedures like giving sugar pills or even sympathetically physically examining the patient lead to an improvement in 30 percent of patients' welfare and health.

Indeed it has been estimated that between a half to three quarters of patients with all sorts of problems from asthma to Parkinson's show real lasting improvements from a range of essentially placebo treatments. Many people believe placebo effects are more effective for psychological rather than physical illnesses, though it is difficult to untangle the two. Placebos administered in an orthodox medical context have been shown to induce relief from symptoms in a wide array of illnesses, including allergies, angina pectoris, asthma, cancer, cerebral infarction, depression, diabetes, enuresis, epilepsy, insomnia, Menière's disease, migraine, multiple sclerosis, neurosis, ocular pathology, Parkinsonism, prostatic hyperplasia, schizophrenia, skin diseases, ulcers, and warts.

Although a placebo is simply defined as a preparation with no medicinal value and no pharmacological effects, active placebo is one that mimics the side effects of the drug under investigation but lacks its specific, assumed therapeutic effect. In other words, the power of the intervention to change behavior has essentially nothing to do with its physical or pharmaceutical effects. The effect, such as it is, is actually caused by some "psychological factor," though it is not always easy to separate the two processes.

Pain is the commonest symptom giving rise to a medical consultation. It has also been the commonest outcome measure in studies of the placebo effect, though other measures have included blood pressure, lung function, postoperative swelling, and gastric motility.

Adverse effects of placebo administration have also been noted. These include dependence, symptom worsening (the nocebo effect), and a multitude of side effects, both subjective (headache, concentration difficulties, nausea, etc.) and objectively visible (skin rashes, sweating, vomiting. etc.). Differences between placebo responders and nonresponders have long been of interest. Attempts to spot such differences on sociodemographic characteristics (age, gender, ethnicity, educational level) have generally yielded weak and inconclusive findings other studies have looked at possible individual differences in intelligence and personality. Any patient may benefit from the placebo effect, not just a gullible minority.

One question often asked is what type of placebo "works best" and why. The color and size of capsules and pills have been subject to experimental manipulation, but with little reliable impact. Some suggest that for a placebo to be maximally effective, it should be very large and either brown or purple or very small and either bright red or yellow. Indeed "major" or invasive procedures do appear to have stronger placebo effects.

Injections per se appear to have a greater impact than pills, and even placebo surgery (where people are cut open and sewn up with little or nothing done) has yielded high positive response rates.

The style of treatment administration and other qualities of the therapist appear to contribute substantially to the impact of the treatment itself. Those therapists who also exhibit *greater interest in/concern for their patients, greater confidence in their treatments, and higher professional status* all appear to promote stronger placebo effects in their patients.

There are many ideas and theories as to how the placebo process works. Various concepts have been proposed including operant conditioning, classical conditioning, guilt reduction, transference, suggestion, persuasion, role demands, faith, hope, labeling, selective symptom monitoring, misattribution, cognitive dissonance reduction, control theory, anxiety reduction, expectancy effects, and endorphin release. Yet there exists no accepted single account that seems to explain and predict placebo effects. The explanations, such as they are, of how cognitive psychological processes that are the result of the treatment have an effect on observable behavior.

The well-established problems of Hawthorne, placebo, and other effects have lead researchers to try to design studies that show "real causal relations." The gold standard in medicine, particularly pharmacology, is the *randomized, double-blind, controlled trial*. People in the study have to be *randomly* sent to different groups, some of which are *control* groups having no treatment, alternative treatment, or placebo treatment. Further, *neither* the doctor/scientist/ therapist *nor* the client/patient *knows which treatment* they are providing or receiving.

The first randomized controlled trial took place soon after the war. Patients were randomized to a treated or control group, by consulting sealed envelopes held at a central location. Bias in allocation was therefore hopefully avoided. The entry criteria were strict and determined prior to the allocation. Great care was taken to avoid bias from any source. There was no placebo control though, as it would have meant giving four painful intramuscular injections every day for four months; treated patients were simply compared with untreated patients. However, the clinical assessment was carried out by independent observers who had no knowledge of the patient's allocation. The trial also marked the first attempt to grapple with the ethical issues involved in controlled trials, in that the committee considered it would be unethical not to attempt a speedy, formal evaluation of a potentially fatal disease, presumably as opposed to waiting for an accumulation of clinical experience.

It was not until 20 years ago that "blinded" studies were introduced. It was recognized that psychological factors may affect the response to treatment; patients may be kept "blind" to the nature of the treatment they got. Psychological factors may also affect the clinicians giving the treatment; they may unknowingly communicate their beliefs to the patient, thus biasing the result of the trial. Where both the patient and the clinician are unaware of the nature of the treatment (drug versus placebo, for instance), the trial is referred to as *double blind*. Where the clinician is unaware, but the patient is not, the trial is called *single blind*. A further important refinement, crucial when blinding the patient or clinician, is that the assessment is carried out by an independent observer who is unaware of the treatment allocation.

Yet the placebo controlled randomized double-blind approach does have its problems: *First*, problems may arise because people randomized to different treatment groups may meet and discuss their treatment. Assignment to natural groups (e.g., comparison to two schools or two geographical regions) may be preferable to randomization. *Second*, blinding may not be feasible for some treatments. While neither the doctor nor the patient may be able to distinguish a real tablet from a sugar pill, placebo tablet, there are no clear equivalents to placebo drugs for some treatments. *Third*, participation in a study may affect the behavior of people taking part. Simply being monitored and assessed regularly may have a beneficial effect.

Fourth, participants agreeing to take part in a trial may not be typical of the general population of patients with that particular problem. An entry criterion to a trial needs to be strict to ensure comparability between groups and give the best chance of showing a treatment benefit. A *fifth* problem is the reduced compliance with treatment because of the possibility of receiving placebo treatment. If patients are told that they might be taking a placebo, they might be more inclined to give up on the treatment if there are no immediate effects.

Sixth, using standard treatment in the trial may be artificial and have little relevance to the clinical practice. This may inhibit a more flexible patient-centered approach. The trial may therefore not be a true test of the therapy as used in clinical practice, and the needs of the patient may conflict with the requirements of research. *Seventh*, individual variations in response are often ignored in an analysis that considers only average group responses. Patients who are made worse by the treatment may not be given enough attention in the reports, unless they suffered particularly obvious side effects.

Ethical problems may arise in a variety of contexts, particularly where placebo treatments are involved or the patient or clinician has a marked preference for one treatment option over another. *Eighth*, the main outcome measure, based on clinical assessment and objective tests, may not reflect the patients' perspective of what constitutes an important and beneficial change. Patients may be more concerned with the quality of their lives, which may not be closely linked with changes in biochemical parameters or other disease indicators. *Ninth*, the concern with *eliminating* the placebo effect when assessing a treatment in relation to a comparable placebo may mean that important psychological variables are neglected. Therapist characteristics and the attitude of the patient to treatment are seldom examined in a medical context, and yet may be important determinants to the patient's compliance with treatment and attitude toward illness.

There are probably other objections to the famous gold-standard approach. Most, however, argue that like democracy and peer review in science, it may be a problematic system, but it is the best we have.

III. IDEOLOGY: MEN AND WOMEN, NATURE AND NURTURE

All scientists like to think they are disinterested and that personal ideology and bias play no part in their endeavors (Furnham, 2010). Whereas scientist ideology may play less a role in geology and microbiology, it often plays a very large part in psychology and psychiatry. This is partly because of the consequences of psychological theories with various causal assumptions. To discuss, believe in, and attempt to explain the differences between any groups of human beings soon becomes ideological. It inevitably appears associated with ideas of nature-nurture, which is then associated with left- vs. right-wing politics. Over the past century there have been periods where both the "difference" and the "nondifference" view occurred. The growth of environmentalism and feminism from the 1960s onward perpetuated the idea that any observable differences between the sexes were the result of socialization. Further, the differences were iniquitous and could and should be changed. However, the pendulum from the 1990s onward swung the other way toward a more biological and evolutionary perspective that recognized and "explained" sex difference.

There really are recognized sex differences at all stages of life. We know that in infancy boys are more active and spend more time awake, whereas girls are more physically developed and coordinated; girls show R-hand preference at five months (not boys); girls have better hearing and are more vocal; and girls make more eye contact and show more interest in social and emotional stimuli, whereas boys are more interested in things and systems.

In the preschool period, we know, boys are more interested in block building and vehicles, while girls prefer doll play, artwork, and domestic activities; boys like rough and tumble play, while girls are more sensitive and sedentary; and boys show narrow interests, while girls a wider range, including boy-typical activities (asymmetrical sex typing). Gender segregation (same-sex playgroups) appears for both boys and girls. Boys groups are larger and more concerned with dominance issues; girls play in groups of two to three and are more sharing—concerned with fairness. There are noticeable differences particularly in language. Girls acquire language earlier than boys and remain more fluent throughout life; girls develop larger vocabularies, use more complex linguistic constructions, and enunciate and read better. Boys are less communicative and use language instrumentally (to get what they want). Brain localization of language is more bilateral for females than males (MRI and lesion studies). Males suffer from bilingual development (e.g., memory deficit), while females seem unimpaired.

If you give girls and boys at primary school different tests, you will see clear differences. Boys can draw bicycles better than girls, who in turn are more fluent with words. Boys are better at mathematical reasoning, dart throwing, and rotating objects. Girls are better at remembering displaced objects, recalling stories, and precision tasks calling for good motor coordination.

Over the years various different "positions" have been taken when it comes to explaining sex differences in intelligence. They are essentially as follows:

1. Intelligence cannot be accurately measured, and therefore, it is difficult to prove or disprove the existence of sex difference. This view is perpetuated by educators, journalists, or politicians who are ideologically opposed to testing of any sort. They refuse to take part in a debate.
2. There are no differences at all for one of two reasons. First, there are no good evolutionary or environmental theories or reasons to suppose there

are. Second, the early tests were developed specifically to show no difference. That is, subtests were included and excluded so that neither sex was advantaged or disadvantaged.

3. There are no mean or average differences between the sexes, but there are differences at the extremes. Thus, men tend to be overrepresented at both the extremes of the Bell Curve. The most brilliant, and so the most challenged, are men, meaning the average is the same but the distribution is wider for men. Overall there is no sex difference in intelligence.

4. There are numerous, demonstrable and replicable, sex differences in a whole range of abilities that make up overall intelligence. This is probably the most commonly accepted position, but the debate heats up with respect to how many and how big these differences are. Thus, some argue that there are "big differences" (i.e., 5–10 IQ points) on spatial intelligence (and possibly mathematical/computational intelligence) favoring men while others dispute the size of the difference.

5. Sex differences that do emerge are not real and essentially occur for three reasons. First, girls are taught humility and boys hubris; this social message leads them to approach tests differently. That is, where it can be shown, sex differences are explained by test-taking attitude not the underlying ability. Second, it is less of a social requirement (particularly in mate selection) for girls to be intelligent, so they invest less in education and skill development. Third, females are less emotionally stable than males and thus anxiety reflects that in test performance. So any differences that emerge do not reflect the underlying reality.

6. There are real differences between the sexes, with males having a 4–8-point advantage, which become noticeable after the age of 15. Before adolescence, females in fact have an advantage. The difference between the sexes is greatest for spatial intelligence. This difference is reflected in the difference in brain size (corrected for body size) between men and women. Further, this "real" difference "explains" male superiority in arts, business, education, and science.

There are those now who say that sex difference in intelligence is important and real. They tend to opt for five arguments: *First,* similar differences are observed across time, culture, and species (hence unlikely to be learned). *Second,* specific differences are predictable on the basis of evolutionary specialization (hunter/warrior vs. gatherer/nurse/educator).*Third,* brain differences are established by prenatal sex hormones; later on, hormones affect ability profiles (e.g., spatial suppressed by estrogen; HRT maintains verbal memory). *Fourth,* sex-typed activity appears before gender-role awareness. At age 2, girls talk better, while boys are better at construction tasks. This is not learned. *Fifth,* environmental affects (e.g., expectations, experience training) are minimal. They may exaggerate (or perhaps reduce) differences.

Psychologists are, however, aware of the issue of having to explain how, when, or why sex differences in IQ have a direct effect on any outcome variable like specific exam success or promotion at work. Again, this is statistical effect, and an actuarial rather than a scientific approach. Equally, psychologists accept that these are population statistics and cannot say anything about specific individuals.

Those interested in intelligence, particularly the nature/nurture debate, were excited and frustrated by what has come to be known as the Flynn effect. James Flynn noticed two things when he inspected famous and respected IQ tests manuals. First, that every so often the norms that describe typical scores for different age, sex, and race groups had to change. Every few years scores in the same age group differences were growing. It looked as if people were doing better over time and becoming smarter. The tests seemed to be getting easier, or we were, as a species, getting brighter, or both.

The first thing was to check that this effect was true of many countries and many tests. Data from well over 20 countries have now been examined, including the United States, Australia, and Austria to Belgium, Brazil, and Britain. Furthermore, it was true over different types of test: tests of fluid or problem-solving intelligence as well as knowledge-based vocabulary tests of crystallized intelligence. One rich data source was that kept by armies who measured the IQ of conscripts to see whether they should or could become fighter pilots or submariners, cooks, or military police. The graph of the average IQ of many thousands of young men in the same country appears to move steadily and remorselessly upward.

There seemed to be impressive evidence of "massive IQ gains." But the central question became, Why? Are we really becoming more intelligent? This of course led to the more fundamental question of whether these tests are really measuring intelligence or something else related to intelligence. Flynn never questioned the reliability, validity, and usefulness of IQ tests in educational and occupational settings.

At first it was suggested there may be two reasons why IQ scores were rising but the actual IQ was not: over time it was clever people who were tested. People were just getting better at taking tests because they were more used to test-taking at school: evidence of a practice effect.

The Flynn effect is in search of a causal explanation. At least five causes have been proposed:

1. *Education*: In most countries, with every generation people are spending longer at school, and with better facilities. Schooling has become compulsory, and people from all backgrounds have become used to learning and being tested. Intelligence is related to learning, so as education gets better and more widespread, scores get higher.
2. *Nutrition*: People are now better nourished particularly in childhood, which reduces the incidence of "backwardness" in the population. There are fewer people who had poor nutrition in youth, so the bottom end of the distribution is removed, which means the average score goes up.

3. *Social trends:* We are all now much more used to timed tests and performing against the clock. People are familiar with tests and testing and so do better overall.
4. *Parental involvement:* The idea is that parents provide richer home environments for their children and express a great interest in their education than they used to. They have higher expectations and get involved more. The trend to have smaller families where parents invest more in their children may also be an important factor.
5. *Social environment:* The world has become more complex and stimulating. Modernization and new technology means people have to manipulate abstract concepts more, which is essentially what intelligence tests measure.

The Flynn effect suggests environmental rather than genetic causes of change in intelligence. While it is perfectly conceivable to argue that brighter people seek out more simulating environments for themselves and their children, which further increases their IQ, it raises the old arguments about nature and nurture. Thus, for the Flynn effect to work, environmental effects can work both ways. Therefore, in a rich environment and with sustained effort, IQs can increase. On the other hand, in poor polluted environments and with people with little interest in personal development, the opposite effect occurs.

Other questions have arisen about whether the Flynn effect has begun to taper off: that is, whether there is now a decline in the increase in IQ. This means the next generation will not score higher than this generation. Indeed, there is increasing skepticism as reports emerge from countries where IQ scores are on the decline or from teachers who say there is no evidence whatsoever that children are getting brighter despite their increased exam results.

In essence, it could be argued that as one ideology "creeps in," people are happy to accept certain causal-type explanations without actually investigating them. This would require complex evolving-over-time, population effect computer modeling based on a very specific theory. This is usually dismissed as too expensive and complex, particularly if a preferred "causal explanation" may be found wanting.

IV. THE DANGERS OF TAUTOLOGY

The field of personality and individual differences has endured for over 100 years. The early work was taxomonic, and after bitter fighting there is considerable agreement about the structure of personality. This is called the Five Factor Model though there are of course those who want a Six or Seven or Nine Factor Model. Yet taxominisation is only the first step. The second and more complicated activity is to explain and describe the process. How do these hypothetical concepts inside the person (traits) determine and cause social behavior?

Rerum Cognoscere Causas: *Dependent and Independent Variables in Psychology*   79

Cynics and skeptics have suggested that the following are essentially where this whole endeavor has got:

1. People possess something (traits) that causes/predisposes them to behave in certain ways in "something-evoking situations": situations relevant to that trait.
2. We describe clusters of behaviors as indicative of someone who possesses an amount of something (the strength of a trait) that causes/predisposes them to behave in certain ways. The more they have, the more likely they are to act. That is the sum total of the explanatory reasoning.
3. We classify the behaviors as "typical" of a person who possesses an amount of a particular trait. The classifications can take many forms, from a single-trait, to 2-trait, 5-trait, or even 16-trait model.
4. The "trait theorist" now has to decide whether to say a trait causes each of these relatively homogeneous behavioral clusters or has to begin differentiating between a facet and a "trait."
5. Furthermore, the trait theorist also has to confront equifinality, where the same behaviors considered to be caused by a single trait can be envisaged as being caused by two or more alternative processes. For example, you are conscientious because you take pleasure in being so, but you may also be conscientious because you fear the perceived social cost of not engaging in "conscientious" behaviors. The fact that the outcome remains the same negates the statement "Conscientiousness is a trait that causes conscientiousness behaviors."

The "jumping through hoops" that a trait theorist has to do to maintain the perception of coherence for a claim that "traits cause behaviors" is why some argue that modern trait theory is a mess.

For example, if a trait theorist cannot answer a simple question such as *How does a single trait of conscientiousness cause those behaviors we describe as typical of a conscientious person?*, then what exactly is the evidence that supports the validity of the claim that conscientiousness is a trait that causes behaviors we label as descriptive of a conscientious person?

Many psychologists are not content to state "people vary in how we would describe them as being Conscientious, Sensation Seekers, Ambitious, Impulsive, Aggressive, Agreeable, Guilt-prone, Dutiful, Timid or Tough Minded." Personality psychologists then collapse or aggregate these descriptive terms into useful taxonomies and seek consequential associations between these attributes and various kinds of outcomes.

Years ago the tautology in personality tests was observed whereby people reported their behavior in certain situations and then *told they were an X or Y, which was defined as how people behaved in those situations.* However, Eysenck (1981) argued for nearly 50 years for a biophysical model of personality, which attempted to describe and explain the process that accounted for individual differences, hence, the arousal model of extraversion and the quasi-physiological model of neuroticism. There has been, and continues to be, a major research effort to identify the physiologically process of traits that escapes the tautology and offers a clear causal model for behavior. That research effort continues despite lack of success.

In essence, there is all the difference between describing and summarizing observable phenomena, however perspicaciously and succinctly, and offering a (causal) explanation for the process. Deriving a robust taxonomy is the first step, offering an explanation for the process is the second. Psychologists have mastered the first, but certainly not the second.

V. CONCLUSION

The motto of the LSE (London School of Economics) is the title of this chapter. It means, "To know the cause of things." In many senses it is the quest of all academic disciplines. An understanding of cause implies an understanding of the mechanisms and processes that lead to events, phenomena, and objects coming into being. However, as this chapter has attempted to show, the research into the cause of psychological phenomena is far from simple, in part because of the complexity of the things being discovered.

The central question is whether aggregated and statistical techniques can do any more than "hint at" possible causal patterns on an aggregated issue. It is possible that all that early teaching in Psychology 101 on dependent and independent variables gives psychologists a specious confidence that they are doing a form of "human physics" and which yields data that both describe and explain behavior. Most of the issues that interest psychologists are highly complex and multidetermined and not really amenable to such simple explanations.

Further, this does not even touch on the difference between deterministic and probabilistic concepts of cause. It is the hope of many psychologists that progress on two fronts, namely, vast increases in statistical power and tools and technological advances in brain science, will "uncover" the complexities of causal patterns much more clearly. That remains to be seen.

REFERENCES

Cheng, H., & Furnham, A. (2012). Childhood cognitive ability, education, and personality predict attainment in adult occupational prestige in 17 years. *Journal of Vocational Behavior, 81*, 218–226.

Cheng, H., & Furnham, A. (2013). The associations between parental socio-economic conditions, childhood intelligence, adult personality traits, social status and mental wellbeing. *Social Indicators Research, 117*, 653–664.

Eysenck, H. (1981). *A Model for Personality*. New York: Springer-Verlag.

Furnham, A. (2010). *50 Psychology Ideas You Really Need to Know*. London: Quercus.

Lilienfeld, S., Rotschel, L., Lynn, S., Cautin, R., & Latzman, R. (2013). Why many clinical psychologists are resistant to evidence-based practice: Root causes and constructive remedies. *Clinical Psychology Review, 33*, 883–900.

Mueller, J., & Coon, H. (2013). Undergraduates' ability to recognize correlational and causal language before and after explicit instruction. *Teaching of Psychology, 40,* 288–293.

Vincent, A., & Furnham, A. (1997). *Complementary Medicine: A Research Perspective.* Chichester: Wiley.

EDITORS' COMMENTARY

Furnham provides a sweeping review of how causation is assumed and used in modern psychology. This commentary will focus on two of the many insights in Furnham's discussions: the first concerns the confusion about probabilistic and deterministic explanations, and the second is about the need to test the efficacy of different therapies and practices.

Psychologists have turned to increasingly powerful inferential statistical procedures as a path to identifying causal connections between different variables. The classic laboratory experiment with one or a few independent variables and one or a few dependent variables is still commonly used, but the new trend is the analysis of "big data." An advantage of big data is that a lot of it is readily available in areas such as education and health, and now we have available computers powerful enough to process very large data sets. The statistical procedures used provide probability estimates, which researchers use as a basis for making statements about "causation" between variables with different levels of confidence. The probabilistic model is not an exact fit with a deterministic model: gravity does not work with "95% or 99% or 99.9% probability"; its effect is 100 percent certain.

"Big data" has, for the most part, consisted of quantitative information, such as the school test scores and demographic characteristics of tens of thousands of children. The search for probabilistic estimates of causal relations in a quantitative study is typically not trying to get at meaning. However, the same powerful statistical procedures are now being turned to the analysis of narratives, and here the claim of researchers is that they are getting at meaning—in the aggregate, at least.

A second interesting insight discussed by Furnham concerns "causation" in the realm of evaluation: testing the efficacy of different psychological treatments and practices. There is an enormous gap between the claims of psychologists to have discovered "causes" in their research and the ability of psychologists to actually demonstrate causation in the practical arenas. This is true in both the "established" areas of psychological practice, such as educational programs and mental health, and in the newer domains of psychological practice, such as peace building. Evaluation is extremely weak and seldom carried out effectively, with the result that we have very little idea of the causes of the success and failure of different applied psychological programs. Thus, weakness is largely an outcome of the confused assumptions and use of "causation" in the psychological research that serves as a basis for the applied psychological programs.

6

On the Concept of "Effects" in Contemporary Psychological Experimentation: A Case Study in the Need for Conceptual Clarity and Discursive Precision

James T. Lamiell

More than 135 years have now passed since, in 1879, Wilhelm Wundt (1832–1920) opened the first experimental psychology laboratory at the University of Leipzig in Germany. Over that span of time, psychology has become a vast and sprawling field, so much so that already by 1985 Sigmund Koch (1917–1996) had found himself compelled to doubt that psychology could continue to be regarded as anything remotely approximating a unitary, coherent scientific discipline (Koch, 1985).

Yet despite this disjointedness, there has long been a widely accepted methodological canon for psychological experimentation across the discipline's various content areas (cognitive, social, developmental, personality, abnormal, etc.). The present chapter discusses the historical foundations and conceptual commitments of that canon, paying particular attention to the way in which the term "effects" has come to be used and understood within its framework.

Contemporary textbooks are usually clear enough on the *methodological/ statistical* meaning of the term "effect." In presentations of the basic and widely used data analysis procedure known as "analysis of variance" (ANOVA), for example, students are taught to speak of a "main effect" for some independent variable (IV) if the analysis reveals a statistically significant relationship between that IV and the dependent variable (DV). Our quest here, however, is for something deeper. We want to know how knowledge of such statistical "effects" is understood by psychologists to advance the basic explanatory objectives of psychological science. We begin with a brief discussion of the contemporary canon's historical emergence.

I. WHENCE THE CURRENTLY PREVAILING CANON?

The Ascendance of a Positivistic/Empiricistic Conception of Explanation

A scant 15 years after Wundt had formally established his laboratory, the philosopher Wilhelm Dilthey (1833–1911) leveled a pointed critique of the new science's agenda. He launched his critique as follows:

> The explanatory psychology, to which today so much interest and work is being devoted, sets up a causal framework which would claim to make all manifestations of mental life comprehensible *(begreiflich)*. It proposes to explain the composition of the psychological world in terms of its components, powers, and laws in just the same way that physics and chemistry explain the physical world. An explanatory science entails the notion that all of the relevant phenomena can be subsumed under a limited number of clearly identified elements, i.e., components of the larger whole. . . . Thus will the explanatory psychology subsume the phenomena of psychological life under a causal network by means of a limited number of clearly determined elements? (Dilthey, 1894, p. 139)

Dilthey did not believe that a psychology pursuing *explanatory* knowledge objectives on the model of the *natural* sciences *(die Naturwissenschaften)*—in particular, physics and chemistry—could possibly do justice to the complexities and nuances of human "doings" (a word I propose to use to cover the variety of specifics with which psychologists might concern themselves, including sensations, perceptions, judgments, cognitions, memories, emotions, behaviors, etc.). Accordingly, Dilthey called instead for a discipline that would be modeled on the *human* sciences *(die Geisteswissenschaften)*—disciplines such as history, anthropology, and literary studies—and would seek knowledge that would provide an *understanding* of those doings. Such understanding would be achieved through the careful discernment of the meaningful relationships between various particulars (cognitions, behaviors, social practices, etc.) and the larger historical and cultural practices within which those particulars are embedded. In a fashion, actually much more consonant with Wundt's *cultural* psychology *(die Völkerpsychologie*; cf. Wundt, 1912) than with his experimental psychology, Dilthey argued:

> It is precisely through the fact that, in consciousness, we live in terms of the coherent wholeness of the entirety that it is possible for us to understand a single sentence, gesture, or behavior. All psychological thought has this characteristic: that it is the grasping of the whole that makes possible and determines the interpretation of the singular event or happening. (Dilthey, 1894, p. 172)

Dilthey's (1894) core conviction was that "[t]he experienced coherence is primary, the distinction between isolated components of that experience is secondary" (p. 144). For him, then, it would be futile to attempt to build up explanations for experience through the study of the putative elements of mental life and the mechanisms by which the causal powers presumed to be contained within those elements issued in their effects.

This, then, was Dilthey's rationale for his pithy claim that "nature is something we *explain* (*erklären*); mental life is something we *understand* (*verstehen*)" (p. 144).

The most forceful and public response to Dilthey's arguments did come, not from Wundt, but instead from Hermann Ebbinghaus (1850–1909), who, a decade earlier, had published groundbreaking experimental work on the psychology of memory (Ebbinghaus, 1885). In an article published two years after Dilthey's critique of mainstream thinking had appeared, Ebbinghaus (1896) defended the explanatory psychology modeled on the natural sciences. In doing this, however, Ebbinghaus did not argue that the causal/explanatory knowledge objectives that Dilthey had attributed to experimental psychology were achievable. He argued instead that those knowledge objectives could no longer properly be attributed *either* to the explanatory psychology *or* to the natural sciences on which that psychology was being modeled.

In developing his argument, Ebbinghaus (1896) began by recapitulating Dilthey's central thesis:

> According to Dilthey, the currently dominant psychology is pursuing a false ideal. It seeks to be an explanatory psychology on the model of physics or chemistry. That is, it seeks to subsume its phenomena under a limited number of clearly defined elements ... [in accordance with] the general presumption of strict causality in psychological life, following the principle *causa aequat effectum—causes contain their effects*. (Ebbinghaus, 1896, pp. 161–162)

Ebbinghaus then claimed that in characterizing scientific psychology's explanatory objectives as he had, Dilthey had attacked a straw man. Ebbinghaus conceded that the conception of explanation that Dilthey had attributed to psychology might have been championed decades earlier by the likes of the German educator Johann Friedrich Herbart (1776–1841). But apart from Herbart, Ebbinghaus (1896) asked rhetorically, "to whom else could Dilthey's claim apply? With reference to modern association psychology, his claim is empty" (p. 185).

In an especially telling passage, Ebbinghaus went on to argue as follows:

> It may be that most natural scientists hold to the assumption that the external world can be explained in mechanistic fashion, but the scientific status of their work is not dependent on this idea ... One should recall the writings of E. Mach [1836–1916] who never tired in his efforts to [establish that] the mechanical explanation of things is not a necessary component of genuine and truly scientific investigations. Rather,

when such occurs at all, it is a supererogatory matter, so to say. (Ebbinghaus, 1896, pp. 185–186)

The E. Mach to whom Ebbinghaus referred here was, of course, Ernst Mach (1838–1916), the physicist-turned-philosopher who was one of the early spokespersons for a philosophy of science that would later come to be known as positivism. Through his invocation of Mach, then, Ebbinghaus was quite explicitly and deliberately advocating a psychology that endorsed an essentially positivistic conception of cause-effect relationships. He elaborated:

> To see [how Mach's ideas apply in psychology], one need look no further than to the law of association . . . Psychologists see a causal relationship in the co-occurrence of two sensations based on the fact that, over a series of instances, the mental image of one produces the other. No one claims on the basis of such a relationship that the effect must somehow be contained within the cause, or that there must be some sort of quantitative equivalence between the two. Indeed, however one might construe the process, it is difficult to understand what might be meant by such a claim. [A]ccordingly, we must see that it is unfair [of Dilthey] to criticize psychology for failing to accomplish something that it is not trying to accomplish in the first place. (Ebbinghaus, 1896, p. 186)

As experimental psychology moved into and through the twentieth century, its embrace of an essentially positivistic view of causal explanation both broadened and deepened, and the gradual emergence of a positivistic *cum* empiricistic conception has maintained its hold on mainstream thinking to the present. One especially vivid example of this can be found in the defense of trait-based explanations for behavior published by McCrae and P. T. Costa Jr. (1995), who emphasized quite pointedly their conviction that "explanations need not specify causal mechanisms" (p. 246) and that "as scientists we understand . . . that a real understanding of causes is evident in some level of prediction and control" (pp. 248–249).

More recently, R. E. Costa (not to be confused with the above-mentioned P. T. Costa Jr.) and C. P. Shimp reported the results of their study of a number of currently prominent research methods textbooks in psychology. The study yields evidence that mainstream pedagogy in the field continues to advocate a decidedly positivistic/empiricistic conception of explanation in the interpretation of psychological research findings; that conception is rarely explicitly acknowledged (Costa & Shimp, 2011). So, even if few contemporary researchers—and the students they are indoctrinating—are awake to the historical roots of the canon they are teaching and being taught, respectively, the view being espoused is, at its core, the one so enthusiastically advocated by Ebbinghaus (1896) in his critique of Dilthey (1894) well over a century ago.

This is one extremely important thread in the history of contemporary mainstream thinking on the matter of "causes and consequences." There is, however, a second, crucially important thread in that history that must be recognized as well.

From N = 1 to N = Many

At its inception, experimental psychology was what might be characterized in contemporary parlance as an "N = 1" investigative discipline. This means that experimental results were fully definable for and linked to specific individuals. The famous "forgetting curve" discovered by Ebbinghaus in the experiments on memory mentioned above (Ebbinghaus, 1885) provides a vivid example of this point.

The reason that the original experimental psychologists proceeded in this manner is to be found in their shared conviction that the phenomena of relevance to a psychological science would somehow have to be manifested in the doings of *individuals*. Nor was there anything at all about this approach that would have been seen by the original experimental psychologists as somehow at cross-purposes with the search for *general* lawfulness. Quite the contrary, their understanding was that the sought-after lawfulness would be *general* in the sense of "common to all" individuals, and if that understanding of "general" dictated that investigations eventually be completed on many individual subjects, it also mandated that those investigations be executed in their entirety *one individual subject at a time*. The obvious fact that investigating *all* individuals in this fashion would be impossible for mere mortals did not blind Wundt or Ebbinghaus or their contemporaries to the fact that such evidence as could be adduced *in favor* of generality would nevertheless demand the subject-by-subject approach just described.

For reasons that cannot be reviewed here (but see Danziger, 1987, 1990), the first several decades of the twentieth century witnessed a widespread migration of experimental psychologists away from the original "Wundtian" model in favor of a quite different model for experimentation that Danziger (1990) labeled "neo-Galtonian." As its name suggests, that model emerged as a variation on an investigative procedure that was developed and employed extensively by Francis Galton (1822–1911) and, in turn, his student Karl Pearson (1857–1936). That procedure was designed and first implemented well prior to the opening of Wundt's laboratory in Leipzig and, indeed, without any particular regard for questions of the sort that would center the interests of the late-nineteenth-century experimental psychologists. The Galtonian model was developed instead to enable the systematic examination of statistical relationships between *variables* demarcating individual and group *differences* within *populations* (with greatest emphasis on the variable of intelligence; Fancher, 1985).

Psychologists' interest in the Galtonian investigative methods took root in their desire to make their research practically useful in addressing problems that arose outside of psychology's experimental laboratories in domains such as schools, business and industry, and the military, where Wundtian investigative methods seemed to be of no use (see, e.g., Münsterberg, 1913; Stern, 1914). To be sure, the increasingly widespread adoption by psychologists of those methods did facilitate the movement of their discipline in a more applied direction (Danziger, 1990). However, there was a price to be paid. After all, Galtonian inquiry was—and remains—essentially *correlational* in nature, and, as is still preached today to students of research methods in psychology, *correlation does not by itself establish causation*. So to the extent that psychology forsook Wundtian experimental methods in favor of Galtonian investigative procedures, the discipline seemed to be compromising its valued status as a basic science capable of revealing cause-effect relationships, however much it might also have been enhancing its status as an applied science able to generate knowledge of practical use in addressing problems outside the laboratory.

As Danziger (1987, 1990) has explained, psychology found its solution to this dilemma by embracing the so-called *treatment group* method of experimentation. This method retained its Galtonian features in that its essence was still the detection of statistical relationships between variables marking differences between groups of individuals. In treatment group studies, however, the groups would be defined not on the basis of characteristics with reference to which individuals could be categorized whether a research investigation was being conducted or not (characteristics such as sex, race, age, and intelligence), but instead in terms of differential treatments defined and imposed by an investigator for the specific purpose(s) of the study in question.

It is because this new approach to psychological experimentation retained its Galtonian emphasis on the statistical analysis of variables defined for groups of individuals within populations that Danziger (1990) labeled it "neo-Galtonian." It rose to prominence within psychology during the first third of the twentieth century and, in its simplest form, is recognizable today as the method for experimentation now widely referred to as the "randomized group" method. As virtually any contemporary research methods textbook will confirm, psychologists continue to rely heavily on this form of experimentation, seeing its great advantage over straightforward "Galtonian" (correlational) studies in its power to reveal cause-effect relationships involving the variables that have been singled out for investigation (see, e.g., Myers & Hansen, 2012). This power is seen to accrue to the random assignment of research subjects to the different treatment conditions. Meanwhile, Wundtian-style experimentation has all but entirely disappeared from psychology.

Now precisely because the population-level statistical considerations that play such a prominent role in neo-Galtonian/treatment group experimentation played no role at all in the original Wundtian model, the influx and rise to hegemony of such considerations profoundly altered the nature of the empirical grounds on which psychologists came to stake their knowledge claims. To the best of the present author's knowledge, however, that change was not accompanied by, nor in the ensuing decades has it ever been followed by, any explicit and thoroughgoing discussion of the question of *whether*—and, if so, exactly *how*—the new neo-Galtonian model for experimentation could serve adequately as a means of pursuing the same knowledge objectives as the original Wundtian model. Instead, generations of psychology students have simply been taught to accept that the answer to the *whether* part of the question just identified is "yes"; that is, neo-Galtonian experimentation *is* formally well suited to scientific psychology's original quest for knowledge of *general* laws (or law-like empirical regularities) in terms of which to explain *individual* "doings" across the various substantive domains of psychological investigation. Yet in my examinations of countless contemporary research methods and statistics texts, I have yet to encounter a text that directly addresses the "exactly *how*" part of the above-identified question. It is to this matter that the following discussion is directed.

A Simple Illustration

Let us consider the following example taken from a current research methods textbook (Graziano & Raulin, 2013, pp. 281–287). In that text, the authors discuss a hypothetical experiment in which the participants were 40 children (age not specified), all of whom were known to be fearful of the dark. Using heart rate as the dependent variable (DV) to indicate fear level, the experiment was designed to investigate the "effects" of two independent variables (IVs): (1) the viewing of photographic images known to be either fear-inducing or neutral and (2) the presence or absence of lighting in the room in which those photographic images would be viewed. The investigation thus conformed to a standard 2×2 factorial design—one of the most frequently used designs in contemporary psychological experiments.

Each of the 40 children who participated in the experiment was assigned at random to one of the four treatment conditions under which he or she would view 10 photographic images: lighted room/fearful images, lighted room/neutral images, darkened room/fearful images, and darkened room/neutral images. The reader is asked to imagine that the maximum heart rate achieved by a given child during his/her experimental session, expressed in beats per minute, was as displayed in Table 6.1 (with the respective treatment group means shown in the lower right portion of each panel). Figure 6.1 displays the treatment group means graphically, and Table 6.2 presents the results of the two-way factorial ANOVA conducted on the heartbeat data.

As can be seen in the column of Table 6.2 designated "p," the long-standing and widely accepted criterion for achieving statistical significance, that is, $p < .05$, was achieved in this analysis for each of the two main factors, room illumination and photographic content of the photos, and for their interaction. An investigator discussing these results in the traditional fashion would thus state that each of the two independent variables exerted an "effect" on the average heart rate of the subjects in the respective experimental conditions both alone and in interaction with the other.

In the case of factor A, these experimental results would be taken to indicate that, without regard for the fearfulness of the presented photographs, the "effect" of viewing those photographs in a lighted room was to *lower* the average heart rate among the 20 children so treated by 4.375 heartbeats

Table 6.1 Maximum Heart Rate in Beats per Minute Recorded for Each Child Across the Four Experimental Conditions

		A Room Illumination		
		Lighted (a_1)		Darkened (a_2)
		80		121
		95		110
		101		113
		99		112
	Fearful (b_1)	112		131
		106		125
		97		111
		92		103
		102		99
Photographic		99	$M_{11} = 98.3$	116	$M_{11} = 114.1$
Content		80		90
		90		92
		100		95
		98		95
	Neutral (b_2)	115		119
		110		112
		97		95
		83		91
		105		107
		103	$M_{21} = 98.1$	102	$M_{21} = 99.8$

Grand mean: 102.58
Total variance: 132.14

Source: Adapted from Graziano and Raulin (2013).

per minute, from the initial overall average of 102.575 down to an average of 98.2. Conversely, the "effect" of viewing the photographs in a darkened room was to *raise* the average heart rate among the 20 children so treated by 4.375 heartbeats per minute, from the initial overall average of 102.575 up to an average of 106.95 beats per minute.

As can be seen from the ANOVA summary depicted in Table 6.2, the sum of squares attributable to factor A in this hypothetical experiment, SS_A, is equal to 765.625, which amounts to 14% of the total sum of squares, SS_{TOT}, for the entire experiment, 5285.78. In this sense, factor A, level of room illumination, may be said to "explain" 14% of the total variance in the heart rate data.

Turning to factor B, the results of the statistical analysis of the data would be seen as evidence that, without regard for the illumination level in the experimental room, the "effect" of viewing neutral photographs was to *lower*

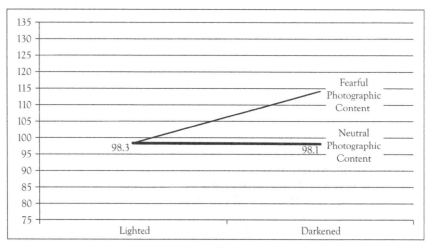

Room Illumination

Figure 6.1 Plot of Four Treatment Condition Means (Adapted from Graziano & Raulin, 2013)

the average heart rate among the 20 children exposed only to those photos by 3.625 heartbeats per minute, from the initial overall average of 102.575 down to an average of 98.95, while the "effect" of viewing the fearful photos seems to have *raised* the overall average heart rate among the 20 children exposed only to those photos by 3.625 heartbeats per minute, from 102.575 up to an average of 106.2.

As done in the case of factor A, it can be seen from the ANOVA summary in Table 6.2 that the sum of squares attributable to factor B in this hypothetical experiment, SS_B, is equal to 525.625, or 10% of the total sum of squares, SS_{TOT}, for the entire experiment, 5285.78. Factor B, fearfulness of the photographs, would thus be said to "explain" 14% of the total variance in the heart rate data.

Over and above the two so-called main effects discovered in this experiment, a glance at the graphic display in Figure 6.1 of the mean heart rates obtained in the four treatment conditions indicates that it was the

Table 6.2 ANOVA Summary Table

Source	Sum of Squares	d.f.	Mean Square	F	p	Percent Variance
A (room illumination)	765.625		765.625	7.88	<.05	0.14
B (photographic content)	525.625		525.625	5.41	<.05	0.10
A × B	457.025		457.025	5.19	<.05	0.09
Error	3457.500		97.15			
Total	5285.788	36				

combination of fearful photographs with a darkened room that exerted the most powerful "effect." The average heart rate among the 10 children exposed to that treatment combination was 114.1—fully 11.525 beats per minute above the initial overall average of 102.575. Each of the other three treatment group means was slightly lower than the overall average by 4.275, 4.475, and 2.775 heartbeats per minute for the lighted/fearful, lighted/neutral, and darkened/neutral conditions, respectively. It is the disproportionate influence of the darkened room/fearful photos treatment combination relative to the other three treatment combinations that brought about the statistically significant A × B interaction "effect" statistically documented in Figure 6.1.

Following the pattern established above, we can see from the ANOVA summary depicted in Table 6.2 that the sum of squares attributable to the A × B interaction in this hypothetical experiment, $SS_{A\times B}$, is equal to 457.025, which is 9% of the total sum of squares (SS_{TOT}) for the entire experiment, 5285.78. The A × B interaction may thus be said to "explain" approximately 9% of the total variance in the heart rate data.

II. THE CONCEPTUAL PROBLEMS

Throughout the above discussion, I have sought to illustrate how the term "effect" is commonly used and understood in a sense that is strictly *methodological/statistical* or, to coin a term, "methodistical." In mainstream practices, it is always the establishment of a statistically significant ($p < .05$) relationship between variables that is used to warrant an investigator's claim to knowledge of an "effect." Moreover, the nature of the putative "effect" is typically elaborated in terms of the juxtaposition of group means, and the strength or magnitude of that "effect" is typically understood in terms of some index of its power or usefulness in explaining dependent variable/criterion variance.

As stated at the outset of this chapter, however, our objective is not, and cannot be, realized by mere "methodistical" considerations. Our objective is to understand how the experimental production of statistical "effects" in the fashion illustrated above is supposed to advance the overarching goal of scientific psychology: to identify laws or law-like empirical regularities that are *generally* valid as explanations for *individual* "doings"—where, again, the term "doings" is being used to cover a wide variety of psychological phenomena, including sensations, perceptions, judgments, thoughts, memories, emotions, and behavior. It is here that we find the need for the conceptual clarity and discursive precision that is so sorely lacking in the mainstream canonical literature.

Latent Positivism/Empiricism in Psychologists' Thinking about the Nature of "Effects"

Observations made over three decades ago by Harré (1981) in a critical discussion of the traditional mainstream research practices illustrated above point to what is problematic here:

It is easy to see how adherence to a degenerate Humean theory of causality leads directly to the mindless empiricism of much psychological experimentation. If there could be causation in the mere juxtaposition of [variables], no role is left over for an agent or powerful particular in a theory of production of effects. As a positivist one is counseled to study the confidence levels of correlations between types of treatments and types of effects through examining numbers of cases. By adopting this advice, one can avoid the deep study of the internal processes and activities of agents which bring these effects about. *But causal processes occur only in individual human beings, since mechanisms of actions, even when we act as members of collectives, must be realized in particular persons.* (Harré, 1981, p. 14; emphasis added)

The reader should have no difficulty seeing the historical and conceptual connection between Harré's dim view of the statistical juxtaposition of variables as the sole basis for psychologists' claims to knowledge of cause-effect relationships and the discussion earlier in this chapter of the reply by Hermann Ebbinghaus (1896) to the critique of the mainstream "explanatory" psychology made by Dilthey (1894). In each case, we encounter the notion, endorsed by Harré (1981) but dismissed as "supererogatory" by Ebbinghaus (1896), that a satisfactory account of cause-effect relationships requires the scientist to go beyond the mere establishment of statistical covariations between variables and into a theoretical elaboration of the dynamics that could possibly be producing those statistical covariations.

Knowing that mainstream psychology endorsed Ebbinghaus's views on this matter makes it is easier to understand why contemporary research methods textbooks are universally silent on the question of how students of the canon should understand, *as psychologists*, the nature of the "effects" putatively revealed by their statistical analyses. After all, why should precious pages of text be devoted to what is merely "supererogatory"? The end result of this pedagogical practice could scarcely be other than the latent positivism/empiricism that saturates the "textbook science" served up in the "tourist brochures" still being used by contemporary instructors to train cohort after cohort of psychology researchers (Costa & Shimp, 2011).

III. IMPLICIT ASSUMPTIONS CONCERNING THE LOCUS OF THE "EFFECTS" REVEALED BY PSYCHOLOGICAL RESEARCH

Even if psychological researchers continue to abide by Ebbinghaus's (1896) claim that a full explication of what Harré called "mechanisms of action" in discussions of the "effects" putatively revealed by statistical analyses is "supererogatory" in scientific work, there is an additional and, arguably, even more serious conceptual problem in canonical thinking that for decades has escaped the attention and/or concern of its disciples. It lurks in the implicit assumption that whatever the exact nature of the causal mechanisms producing a given statistical "effect" might be, that "effect" is realized in *each one* of the individuals to whom the treatment condition or personal attribute producing that "effect" applies.

If the explicit formulation of this implicit assumption surprises advocates and practitioners of currently dominant mainstream research practices, that is due to the very lack of conceptual clarity and discursive precision of concern here, and this is exactly why the assumption merits close and careful consideration.

Beginning at a relatively superficial level, we may note the conformity between the "each one" assumption just asserted and the computations used in ANOVA to determine independent variable "effects" on dependent variables. Consider factor A in the hypothetical experiment discussed above. In the case of treatment a_1, the "effect" of maintaining light in the room where the subjects viewed the photos is determined quantitatively by calculating the squared difference between the mean maximum heart rate among the subjects exposed to that treatment and the overall average heart rate within the design as a whole, and then multiplying that squared difference by 20, that is, once for each one of the 20 subjects who was, in fact, exposed to that treatment. Similarly in the case of treatment a_2, the effect of the eliminating light from the room in which the photos were viewed is determined quantitatively by calculating the squared difference between the mean maximum heart rate among the subjects exposed to that treatment and the overall average heart rate within the design as a whole, and then multiplying that squared difference by 20, that is, once for each one of the 20 subjects who was, in fact, exposed to that treatment.

Of course, the "effects" of treatments b_1 and b_2 are indexed in directly analogous fashion, and the same considerations hold for indexing the "effects" of each of the four A × B combinations, a_1b_1, a_1b_2, a_2b_1, *and* a_2b_2, noting that the squared difference between each of those four treatment group means and the overall mean within the design as a whole is multiplied not by 20 but by 10, since 10 is the number of subjects exposed to each A × B treatment combination.

Thus, do we see that the computations proper to ANOVA formally reflect the assumption that each "effect" revealed by the statistical analysis is realized in each one of the individuals to whom the treatment condition, or personal attribute that has presumably generated the "effect," applies? But be this as it may, the most decisive considerations lie still deeper.

To see this, it is helpful to consider the implications of relaxing the "each one" assumption. Doing so would be tantamount to acknowledging that the "effect" under consideration might not have been realized in some given individual subject. But if that could be the case, then it could just as well be the case that the "effect" in question might not have been realized in some other given individual subject.

The end result of this line of thinking is readily apparent: if the statistical "effects" generated by neo-Galtonian inquiry really cannot warrant claims to knowledge of what is regulating the "doings" of each individual, then it cannot possibly warrant claims to knowledge of what is regulating the "doings" of the individuals *in general*—certainly not if "general" is to be understood in the sense of *allen gemein*, or *common to all*, intended by psychology's original experimentalists. The "effects" revealed by such inquiry would thus have to be understood as warranting—at best—claims to knowledge of regularities in the "doings" of the experimental subjects *in the aggregate*, or "in general" *only* in the sense of *on average*.

This latter meaning of "general" is emphatically *not* the one understood by the discipline's original experimentalists, and the fact that this is so is why a further and more precise explication of the tenets of the contemporary research methods canon is needed. That explication might proceed along one of two lines. One would clearly acknowledge that the abandonment of the Wundtian model of experimentation, where $N = 1$, in favor of the neo-Galtonian/treatment group model of experimentation, where $N =$ many (see discussion above), brought with it a fundamental change in the knowledge objectives of scientific psychology. The other line of explication would unambiguously insist that neo-Galtonian experimentation *is* suited, albeit in a way different from Wundtian experimentation, to the same knowledge objectives as the latter, that is, to the generation of knowledge of laws or law-like regularities governing the "doings" of individuals in general (in the sense of "common to all").

To exercise the first of these two options would be to concede that scientific psychology is now (and for decades has been) oriented toward the generation of law-like regularities in the "doings" of individuals *on average* within *populations*—not in the "doings" of individuals in general in the sense of "common to all"—and hence that the discipline has long since become, de facto, a species of demography. It is the other of the two alternatives stated above, that is, the insistence that neo-Galtonian inquiry really does yield knowledge of laws or law-like regularities pertaining to the "doings" of individuals *in general* and not merely in the aggregate, that logically requires the "each one" assumption stipulated above. Assuming, for now, that it is this latter alternative that contemporary mainstream thinkers have implicitly endorsed and with which they would prefer to continue to identify themselves, the question that begs answering is: what, if anything, warrants the "each one" assumption?

If a clear answer to this crucial question is ever forthcoming, it will inevitably appeal to some version of the notion that knowledge of statistical relationships between variables of the sort that can be discovered through neo-Galtonian experimentation enables the estimation or prediction of individual-level outcomes (under relevant circumstances) with a level of accuracy greater than that achievable without knowledge of those statistical relationships. Of course, such an appeal would entail no presumption that perfectly accurate predictions will ever be achievable in practice. On the contrary, it is well understood that individual outcomes can be—and for all practical purposes perhaps always will be—affected by factors other than those that have been brought under investigation. There will therefore always remain some degree of unpredictability in individual outcomes. What mainstream thinking does demand, however, is the understanding that those "other" factors, whatever they might be, operate in addition to, in opposition to, or perhaps in complex interaction with—*but not instead of*—the factors that have been investigated.

This is precisely the understanding embedded in the oft-invoked mantra *ceteris paribus*, that is, the notion of "all other things being equal." Of course, all other things never are equal. But *if* they ever were, the thinking goes, the validity of the "each one" proviso would manifest itself empirically in the exact correspondence between actual individual outcomes and the outcomes that would have been estimated or predicted given knowledge of the statistical relationships that the empirical research has now revealed. Meanwhile, and just because *ceteris paribus* is never, in fact, realized empirically, the "each one" proviso entailed by the line of thinking being explicated here can be stipulated while ever remaining immune from empirical challenge.

It is only by sanctioning this understanding of the statistical findings revealed by neo-Galtonian experimentation that the prevailing canon can *both* incorporate the "each one" proviso *and* accommodate the ubiquitous empirical reality of outcome differences between subjects who would otherwise be expected to manifest identical outcomes. It is just such outcome differences that are aggregated into the "error" term in the ANOVA summary tables illustrated in Table 6.2, and ubiquitous throughout the mainstream research literature. Moreover, it is precisely the above-described way of thinking that lies behind the notion, usually left implicit but once stated explicitly by Dar and Serlin (1990), that, "as our theory and measurement get continually better, the errors of prediction will approach zero *for each individual*" (Dar & Serlin, 1990, p. 198, emphasis added).

IV. THE FLY IN THE OINTMENT

Within the mainstream canon, the standard by which the "continual betterment of theory and measurement" is gauged is the proportion of DV variance explained (or some proxy for it), and by this standard, the utterly basic problem with the above assertion by Dar and Serlin (1990) is that it is simply *not true*. Elsewhere (Lamiell, 2003, see especially Chapter 7), the reader can find a detailed empirical illustration of this point. In the limited space available here, the following brief exercise will have to suffice.

In the hypothetical experiment discussed above, the DV was defined in terms of the maximum heart rate (beats per minute) reached by the various children across the different experimental sessions. In this illustrative case, the overall mean maximum heart rate among the 40 children who participated in the experiment, calculated across all experimental conditions, was 102.58 beats per minute. Knowing this and nothing else, and then asked to blindly estimate, case by case, the maximum heart rate achieved by each child in the experiment, one's best guess, statistically speaking, would be that mean value, 102.58, in each case. That guess would be "best" in the "least squares" sense, that is, in the sense that the average of the resulting squared differences between the 40 actual results and that repetitive guess, 102.58, would be lower than it would be if any other guessing strategy were employed.

The reader interested to do so can verify that for the present hypothetical experiment, this value, that is, the average of the squared differences between the 40 actual outcomes and 102.58, was 132.14. Note that this quantity denotes the total DV variance in the design (see Table 6.1). Prior to the determination of any IV "effects," this total variance is all unexplained or "error" variance, and, expressed in statistical language, psychologists see the challenge to them as researchers as that of reducing "error" variance by identifying variables in terms of which to explain as much of that initially unexplained variance as possible.

Now as we saw earlier, each of the IVs in this hypothetical experiment, A, B, and A × B, was found to exert a statistically significant "effect." Further, it was determined that factor A accounted for 14% of the total variance, factor B accounted for an additional 10% of the total variance, and the A × B interaction accounted for an additional 9% of the total variance. Together, then, some 33% of the total variance could be explained by the experimental factors investigated, and thus could no longer be regarded as "error" variance. "Error" variance was thus reduced to 67% of what it had been prior to the experiment.

Knowing these results, and now asked once again to estimate the DV outcome for each of the 40 children, the best (least squares) estimate in each case would no longer be the overall mean, 102.58 as before, but would instead be the mean DV outcome obtained for the particular treatment condition to which the individual child under consideration had been exposed, that is, either 98.3 or 98.1 or 114.1 or 99.8, as the case may be. Using these latter means would exploit the knowledge gained through the statistical analysis of the DV outcomes.

The question at this point is: does the decrease in *aggregate*-level error variance in the DV outcomes documented by the results of the ANOVA warrant the inference that the inaccuracies of case-by-case estimates of *individual* DV outcomes will likewise have been reduced? To answer this question, the reader is invited to try the following exercise: Step 1—calculate, for each of the 40 children in the experiment, the absolute difference between his/her actual DV outcome, Y, and the "best" guess of that outcome, Y′, knowing nothing other than the overall mean, 102.58, a value we may symbolize as Y′. In other words, calculate for each of the 40 children the value Y − 102.58. Step 2— repeat this exercise, but specify Y′ in each case not as the overall mean regardless of a given child's experimental treatment condition, as in Step 1, but instead as the mean for the particular treatment condition to which that child had been exposed. Note that in each step of this exercise, the calculated absolute differences between actual outcomes, Y, and estimated outcomes, Y′, represent errors of estimate in individual cases.

The reader who carries out this exercise will discover that in 26 of the 40 cases, the inaccuracy of the estimate, $Y - Y'$, in Step 2, where the results of the statistical analysis (ANOVA) have been exploited in formulating the estimates, is less than the corresponding inaccuracy of the estimate in the first step, where the results of the ANOVA were not yet taken into consideration. This pattern of results conforms exactly with what would be expected on the basis of the claim by Dar and Serlin (1990), quoted above.

However, the reader who carries out the above exercise will also find that in 14 of the 40 cases, the inaccuracy of the estimate at Step 2 was actually *greater* than at Step 1, despite the reduction in aggregate error variance reflected in the ANOVA results. In those 14 cases, then, the outcome runs directly *counter* to Dar and Serlin's (1990) bold claim. This shows that reductions in aggregate error variance are *not necessarily* accompanied by improvements in the accuracy of DV outcome estimates in individual cases. Sometimes accuracy is improved, sometimes it is not. Moreover, and what is most important, this just *means* that in order to know what has transpired in any given individual case, it is necessary to look at the outcome for that individual case.

In fact, therefore, and coming full circle to the considerations that led into this exercise, there is nothing established by the statistical regularities revealed through neo-Galtonian experimentation that can properly be said to warrant the "each one" assumption discussed earlier. The long-received view on this matter is demonstrably incorrect.

To further underscore this point, the reader may find it worthwhile to consider what it would mean if knowledge of the overall degree of error in DV outcome estimates or predictions, as reflected in "error" variance, actually did justify claims to knowledge of the inaccuracies of *individual* DV outcome estimates/predictions. Were that the case, an investigator would have at hand all that would be necessary to eliminate *completely* the inaccuracies in his/her individual-level DV estimates/predictions! She/he could simply adjust each individual DV estimate/prediction by the putatively known error contained within it, and the resulting estimates/predictions would always be perfectly accurate!

This last consideration points to the *only* condition under which knowledge of aggregate-level error variance would be, ipso facto, knowledge of the inaccuracy of each and every individual-level DV estimate/prediction. That condition would be met if the statistical relationship used as the basis for formulating the DV estimates were *perfect*. Under that condition, error variance would, by definition, have been reduced to zero, and this would logically guarantee that the discrepancy between actual individual DV outcomes and their corresponding estimates/predictions would likewise be zero in each and every individual case.

However, under *all* other circumstances, which is to say under all circumstances ever realized empirically in psychological research, error variance will not be zero, and the inaccuracy of individual DV estimates/predictions will be unknown and unknowable without investigating each case individually. This is the inescapable reality that eluded Dar and Serlin (1990) in their formulation of the passage quoted above, and that, alas, seems to have eluded the overwhelming majority of mainstream psychological researchers as well. By the same token, these considerations offer yet another angle from which to see the complete unsuitability of aggregate statistical regularities as empirical grounds for *any* claims to knowledge of general lawfulness in individual-level "doings" when the intended meaning of "general" is "common to all."

V. CONCLUDING COMMENTS

In his 1913 essay, *Die Psychologie im Kampf ums Dasein*, and in *Psychology's Struggle for Existence* (2013), Wundt warned that were psychology to sever its ties with philosophy, psychology would be undermining its own long-term intellectual health by compromising its facility with conceptual matters so vital to any scientific discipline in conjunction with its empirical pursuits. While a relative handful of Wundt's contemporaries agreed with him in this regard (e.g., Stern, 1935), the great majority did not, and this was especially true in the United States (cf. Lamiell, 2013). Eventually, the divorce against which Wundt warned was effectively achieved, and there are now, a century on, some clear indications that the untoward consequences for psychology that he forecast have come to pass (Lamiell, 2013; Machado & Silva, 2007). In this light, it seems not implausible to suggest that the lack of conceptual clarity and discursive precision surrounding the concept of "effects" in psychological experimentation is one very vivid example of the problem that Wundt foresaw.

In any case, it is to be hoped that the discussion in this chapter has helped bring to light the pressing need for much greater clarity than may currently be said to exist with respect to the concept of "effects" in psychological experimentation. A purely "methodistical" understanding of the concept is not nearly adequate. On the contrary, if the field as a whole is resolved to remain true to the overarching knowledge objectives of the discipline's original experimentalists, then what is needed is a conceptually coherent and precise statement of how the statistical "effects" revealed through neo-Galtonian experimentation advance the quest for knowledge of the laws or law-like regularities governing the psychological "doings" of individuals. On the other hand, if fidelity to the knowledge objectives of the original experimentalists is no longer to be regarded as psychology's overarching scientific mission, then a clear and forceful statement to that effect is what is necessary.

Meanwhile, it is the view of the present author that, intellectually speaking, the status quo within mainstream psychology with regard to questions regarding causes and consequences is decidedly unhealthy.

REFERENCES

Costa, R. E., & Shimp, C. P. (2011). Methods courses and texts in psychology: "Textbook science" and "tourist brochures." *Journal of Theoretical and Philosophical Psychology, 31*, 25–43.

Danziger, K. (1987). Statistical method and the historical development of research practice in American psychology. In L. Krueger, G. Gigerenzer, & M. S. Morgan (Eds.). *The probabilistic revolution, Vol. 2: Ideas in the sciences*, pp. 35–47. Cambridge: MIT Press.

Danziger, K. (1990). *Constructing the subject: Historical origins of psychological research*. New York: Cambridge University Press.

Dar, R., & Serlin, R. C. (1990). For whom the bell curve toils: Universality in individual differences research. In D. N. Robinson & L. P. Mos (Eds.). *Annals of theoretical psychology*, Vol. 6, pp. 193–199. New York: Plenum.

Dilthey, W. (1894). Ideen über eine beschreibende und zergliedernde psychologie [Toward a descriptive and analytical psychology]. *Sitzungsberichte der Akademie der Wissenschaften zu Berlin:* zweiter Halbband, 1309–1407.

Ebbinghaus, H. (1885). *Über das Gedächtnis* [On memory]. Leipzig: Duncker & Humblot.

Ebbinghaus, H. (1896). Über erklärende und beschreibende Psychologie [On explanatory and descriptive psychology]. *Zeitschrift für Psychologie und Physiologie der Sinnesorgana*, 9, 161–205.

Fancher, R. E. (1985). *The intelligence men: Makers of the IQ controversy*. New York: W. W. Norton.

Graziano, A. M., & Raulin, M. L. (2013). *Research methods: A process of inquiry* (8th ed.). New York: Pearson.

Harré, R. (1981). The positivist-empiricist approach and its alternative. In P. Reason & J. Rowan (Eds.). *Human inquiry*, pp. 3–17. New York: Wiley.

Koch, S. (1985). Foreword: Wundt's creature at age zero – and as Centenarian: Some aspects of the institutionalization of the "New Psychology." In S. Koch & D. E. Leary (Eds.). *A century of psychology as science*, pp. 7–35. New York: McGraw Hill.

Lamiell, J. T. (1990). Explanation in the psychology of personality. In D. N. Robinson & L. P. Mos (Eds). *Annals of theoretical psychology*, Vol. 6, pp. 219–231. New York: Plenum.

Lamiell, J. T. (2003). *Beyond individual and group differences: Human individuality, scientific psychology, and William Stern's critical personalism*. Thousand Oaks, CA: Sage Publications.

Lamiell, J. T. (2010). *William Stern (1871–1938): A brief introduction to his life and works*. Lengerich, Germany: Pabst Science Publishers.

Lamiell, J. T. (2013). On psychology's struggle for existence: Some reflections on Wundt's 1913 essay a century on. *Journal of Theoretical and Philosophical Psychology*, 33, 205–215. doi: 10.1037/a0033460

Machado, A., & Silva, F. J. (2007). Toward a richer view of the scientific method: The role of conceptual analysis. *American Psychologist*, 62, 671–681. doi: 10.1037/0003-066X.62.7.671

McCrae, R. R., & Costa, P. T., Jr. (1995). Trait explanations in personality psychology. *European Journal of Personality*, 9, 231–252.

Münsterberg, H. (1913). *Psychology and industrial efficiency*. Boston and New York: Houghton-Mifflin.

Myers, A., & Hansen, K.C. (2012). *Experimental psychology* (7th ed.). Belmont, CA: Wadsworth Cengage Learning.

Stern, W. (1914). Psychologie [Psychology]. In D. Sarason (Ed.). *Das Jahr 1913: Ein Gesamtbild der Kulturentwicklung.* Leipzig: Teubner.

Stern, W. (1935). *Allgemeine Psychologie auf personalistischer Grundlage (General Psychology from the Personalistic Standpoint).* The Hague: Nijhoff.

Wundt, W. (1912). *Elemente der Völkerpsychologie* [Elements of Cultural Psychology]. Leipzig: Alfred Kröner Verlag.

Wundt, W. (1913). *Die Psychologie im Kampf ums Dasein [Psychology's struggle for existence]* (2nd ed.). Leipzig, Germany: Kröner.

Wundt, W. (2013). Psychology's struggle for existence (J. T. Lamiell, Trans.). *History of Psychology, 16,* 197–211. doi: 10.1037/a0032319

EDITORS' COMMENTARY

The insights discussed by Lamiell lead to a rethinking of how the term "causation" has been used in traditional psychology since the pioneering research of Wundt in the nineteenth century. This commentary will focus on two points. First, in addition to laboratory research, Wundt dedicated several decades to what today would be called "cultural psychology." This is cultural research as published in the journal *Culture & Psychology* rather than the *Journal of Cross-Cultural Psychology.* Second, the laboratory method pioneered by Wundt involved idiographic rather than nomothetic research, focusing on one participant at a time rather than examining aggregate trends. The implication is that the pioneering research of Wundt, celebrated in the standard psychology textbooks as having introduced the laboratory method to psychology, had an approach to causation that differs from how causation is conceived in traditional twenty-first-century psychology.

Lamiell's criticisms suggest that we should abandon the traditional causal model in psychological research. An alternative is to study individuals and collectivities through a normative approach. The assumption here is that human behavior is regulated or "patterned" by normative systems integral to culture. This is a probabilistic approach. Most people, most of the time, behave in ways that are normative and seen as "correct" according to the local culture. Thus, with high probability, we can make predictions about how individuals and groups will behave in different contexts. However, this does not match efficient causation, because some people do not behave in a normative manner; they do what in local terms is seen to be the "wrong thing"—they behave incorrectly. This includes a wide range of behavior, from crime to fashion—some people break the rules.

But these are types of causation, discussed from the time of Aristotle, that do match a normative psychology. In particular, formal cause, to do with meanings and purpose, is a good match with normative psychology. Human beings are intentional or "purposive" agents, and they construct and seek meanings in their lives. Rather than seeing human behavior as "causally determined" by factors inside their heads (e.g., cognitive mechanisms) or in their environments (e.g., stimuli), normative psychology leads us to see human behavior as patterned through the meaning making individuals and groups engage in. An important point made by Lamiell is that to understand the meaning making engaged in by an individual, it is not enough to study the aggregate of the group to which the individual belongs.

7

Legislating Causal Logic: Scientifically Based Educational Research in the United States

Naomi Lee and Alissa Blair

I. INTRODUCTION

This chapter aims to clarify how causes and consequences are conceived of in educational research through a critical examination of the scientifically based research (SBR) movement in the United States. The educational research community is marked by diversity if not disunity. Born of the need to address practical issues in public education, educational research has been concerned with causal inference insofar as such knowledge can inform policy-making and pedagogical practice. The debate on SBR in education offers an especially intriguing case study in how notions of causality, and scientific inquiry more broadly, are shaped by the forces at play in scientific communities. The SBR debate has attracted diverse voices that extend the "paradigm dialogues" of the 1970s and 1980s. Using Bakhtin's notions of "official" and "unofficial" forces, we map the contours of the SBR debate that has raged since the U.S. federal government legislated an "official" definition of scientific research in the No Child Left Behind Act of 2001 (NCLB, 2001). We examine how causal inference is conceptualized by both official and unofficial voices as they stake out positions on the question of what kind of inquiry is scientifically legitimate and who should decide.

II. SCIENTIFIC EVIDENCE DEFINED

The SBR movement in education, which posits randomized controlled trials as the "gold standard" of educational research, has gripped educational researchers and policy-makers in debate for more than a decade. Sparking this controversy was the passing of federal legislation in the early 2000s that inscribed into law a particular definition of scientific inquiry. Scholars cite the NCLB Act of 2001 and the ubiquitous appearance of the term "scientifically-based research" as evidence of a federally mandated push for defining and requiring educational practice to be based on a view of high-quality research that places a premium on randomized experiments (Borman, 2002; Feuer, Towne, & Shavelson, 2002; Olson & Viadero, 2002).

The first official definition of SBR, which appeared in NCLB, involves the application of "rigorous, systematic, and objective procedures to obtain reliable and valid knowledge relevant to educational activities and programs" and

> [i]s evaluated using experimental or quasiexperimental designs in which individuals, entities, programs, or activities are assigned to different conditions and with appropriate controls to evaluate the effects of the condition of interest, with a preference for random-assignment experiments, or other designs to the extent that those designs contain within-condition or across-condition controls. (NCLB, 2001, Section 9101)

By this account of SBR, research questions and designs that examine causal relationships, established using prescribed methods, are the most valuable to educational reform. While the NCLB definition does not discount other forms of scholarship or models of causality, "random-assignment experiments" or other designs that contain "with-in condition or across-condition controls" are preferred for testing causal claims. Under this legislation, only interventions and programs that are consistent with the government-sanctioned definition of SBR qualify for federal funding (Eisenhart & Towne, 2003). The NCLB definition of SBR continues to represent the current and official stance on scientific research in education given that this piece of legislation has not been subsequently revised and ratified by Congress.

The controversy over defining scientific evidence, in part, reflects the multidisciplinary origins and subsequent disunity of educational research (Lagemann, 2002). In comparison with the natural sciences, education as a discipline is unique for the historic role of values, democracy, and diversity of students and teachers (National Research Council [NRC], 2002) as well as the variability of instruction and governance across educational settings that shape systematic study using randomized controlled trials (Borman, 2002; Slavin, 2003). Labaree (1998) describes the variegation of educational research as a blessing and a curse: a blessing because the various methodologies and perspectives create a rich and democratic discourse about what matters in education and a curse because this diversity is perceived as contradictory and confusing. The educational historian Lagemann (2002) sums up the negative consequences of multidisciplinarity for education this way:

> Neither singular in focus nor uniform in methods of investigation, education research grew out of various combinations of philosophy, psychology, and the social sciences, including statistics. The variety that has characterized educational scholarship from the first, combined with the field's failure to develop a strong, self-regulating professional

community, has meant that the field has never developed a high degree of internal coherence. (p. ix)

With Lagemann's insights in mind, the SBR debate can be understood as an important phase in the history of educational research when a disjointed professional community attempts to self-regulate its members, and in so doing exposes the deep fissures that have existed since the formation of the discipline.

The SBR debate is important for the purposes of this chapter because it serves as a focal event through which to understand how the concept of causality is handled in the field of education. Lagemann's historical analysis suggests that a history of the causality concept in educational research could be told only by observing the evolution of causality through the mother disciplines that together comprise educational research. Tracing the relative contributions of philosophy, psychology, and statistics to current understandings of causality in educational research is a worthy endeavor but beyond the scope of our chapter. Instead, with the space afforded to us, we would like to offer our analysis of how the current SBR debate casts light on how the concept of causality is approached by different subcommunities within educational research. Naturally, the positions that emerge in the debate on SBR carry remnants of past debates, and in a historical interlude, we will briefly highlight the historical intertextuality of the debate.

III. BAKHTINIAN VOICES

In our analysis of the SBR debate, we find Bakhtin's notions of official and unofficial forces to be particularly useful tools for mapping the positions of participants to the SBR debate. Bakhtin viewed the cultural world as subject to "official" and "unofficial" forces. As Bakhtinian scholars Morson and Emerson (1990) put it, "The former seek to impose order on an essentially heterogeneous and messy world; the latter either purposefully or *for no particular reason* continually disrupt that order" (p. 30). They go on to explain that unofficial forces may have nothing more in common than their divergence from the "official." They are not a galvanized opposition. For example, Stalinist propaganda and coercion operated in Bakhtin's time as official forces that served the interests of the dictatorship, while a variety of not-necessarily-allied opposition groups countered the dictatorship as unofficial forces. Official and unofficial forces also do not stand in immutable relation to each other, as they are "themselves subject to the centrifuge" (Morson & Emerson, 1990, p. 30). The nuanced and dynamic approach to the cultural world that Bakhtinian theory offers is well suited to mapping the contours of a complex, multilayered, multivocal debate that is not over. In this chapter we will examine the discourses that have circulated in the U.S. debate on SBR, discuss what these debates imply about the concept of causality in educational research, and conclude with some comments about official and unofficial forces in scientific communities.

IV. CONFLATING QUALITY AND CAUSALITY IN EDUCATIONAL RESEARCH: A CASE CONCERNED WITH "WHAT WORKS"

"Official voices" consistent with and contributing to the government's position and "unofficial voices" comprised of scholars of diverse epistemological commitments, have brought a scholarly debate to the public arena and raised deeper questions as to the meaning of quality research in education and who should have the power to define quality research (Erickson, 2005; Pellegrino & Goldman, 2002). Supporters of the definition of science promoted by the SBR movement (Slavin, 2002, 2003) praise experimental research for advancing the fields of medicine, agriculture, engineering, and technology, and contend that educational practice and public decision-making would similarly benefit from research that is "systematic" and "evidence-based"—terms that have referred to research findings that are obtained through randomized controlled experiments (Feuer et al., 2002; NRC, 2002). Some scholars who question experimental research as the preferred scientific method oppose the implicit hierarchization of methodologies and associated epistemologies (Berliner, 2002; Erickson & Gutiérrez, 2002; St. Pierre, 2002). Others focus their critique on the federal government's involvement in evaluating scientific methods (Laitsch, Heilman, & Shaker, 2002; Lather, 2004; Olson & Viadero, 2002).

"Official Voices"

Table 7.1 displays a time line of key events in the SBR movement. Prior to NCLB, a series of significant events gave rise to the conditions and momentum for federally defined and mandated research (Denzin, 2009; Walters, Lareau, & Ranis, 2008). Motivated by President Johnson's "War on Poverty," the Elementary and Secondary Education Act (ESEA) of 1965 set a precedent for federal involvement in education, which had hitherto been state controlled (Halperin, 1975). ESEA was the first law of its kind to require annual effectiveness evaluations of a federal educational program (Borman, 2002). Revisions to ESEA during the 1980s and 1990s focused on raising student achievement (Billig, 1997). These revisions reflected angst that U.S. students were not internationally competitive and the nation's position as a global superpower was at stake. Fueling this perception was President Reagan's commissioned report, *A Nation at Risk* (1983), which publicized evidence of U.S. students' underachievement on national and international scales. Soon thereafter, the first instance of a federally funded program to reference "research-based evidence" was the 1988 Reading Excellence Act (Eisenhart & Towne, 2003; Feuer et al., 2002), which coincided with unprecedented legislation appropriating $150 million to schools to adopt "proven, comprehensive reform models" (Slavin, 2002, p. 15, citing U.S. Department of Education, 1999). Subsequent policy initiatives have employed similar rhetoric including the Comprehensive School Reform Demonstration Act of 1997 (Eisenhart & Towne, 2003; Feuer et al., 2002). Thus, prior to NCLB, federal education programs and legislation explicitly referenced research-based evidence for effectiveness. Yet at that time, no specific methods for collecting such evidence were promoted by the federal government.

NCLB is the 2001 reauthorization of the ESEA of 1965. NCLB marked a definitive shift to the federal sanctioning of randomized controlled trials as the "gold standard" of educational research. This legislation was proposed by George W. Bush and written by a small bipartisan committee. States are held accountable for student achievement and progress in reading/English language arts, math, and science. If students do not make adequate yearly progress on standardized assessments in those content areas, districts and schools face, in the most severe cases, punitive measures and corrective actions, such as replacing staff or changing the curriculum (Esch et al., 2004). This outcomes-based

Table 7.1 Seminal Events in the U.S. Scientifically Based Research Movement in Education

1965	The **Elementary and Secondary Education (ESEA) Act** was signed into law as part of Lyndon B. Johnson's "Great Society Program" and set a precedent for federal involvement in education, which hitherto had been state controlled.
1983	The report **"A Nation at Risk"** was published by Ronald Regan's National Commission on Excellence in Education, declaring the extent of the nation's academic underachievement at national and international levels.
2001	In **No Child Left Behind**, the 2001 reauthorization of ESEA, a definition of "scientifically based research" was inscribed into law.
2002	The National Research Council (NRC) published **"Scientific Research in Education,"** which details general principles that apply to all scientific inquiry, including in education.
2002	The **Education Sciences Reform Act of 2002** was founded and created the **Institute of Education Sciences (IES)**, a premier funding source for educational research that manifests a preference for randomized controlled trials.
2005	The National Research Council (NRC) published **"Advancing Scientific Research in Education"** that makes recommendations for improving scientific research in education.

legislation demands evidence of student progress through benchmark setting, assessments, and annual accountability reporting, yet the legislation does not mandate what interventions—instructional, programmatic, or otherwise—an educational entity should deploy to meet benchmarks (Riley, 1995). Hence, schools and districts exercise a great deal of autonomy in selecting from among myriad educational programs and practices that make effectiveness claims. For better or worse, one consequence of NCLB is that educational policy-makers and educational entities now have definitive federal guidance on how to distinguish between weaker and stronger evidence of effectiveness.

As signaled earlier, NCLB put forth the first official definition of SBR, which grants superior status to randomized controlled trials for developing and evaluating instructional initiatives eligible for federal funding (Eisenhart & Towne, 2003). This is illustrated by the following excerpt: "The Secretary shall evaluate the demonstration projects supported under this title [Title I], using rigorous methodological designs and techniques, including control groups and random assignment, to the extent feasible, to produce reliable evidence of effectiveness" (Section 1502). NCLB encourages the use of experimental research designs to demonstrate the "effectiveness" of adopted instructional initiatives, which under Title I alone impacts school-wide and targeted assistance programs for disadvantaged populations including early reading interventions, family literacy programs, and services for English language learners.

The federal government is not alone in favoring a particular definition of scientific research. Private research organizations, scholars, and policy-makers support the government's official voice by also promoting experimental or quasi-experimental designs as preferred methods of scientific inquiry and establishing causality in educational research. Scholars serving on the NRC have been particularly vocal in their support of SBR. The NRC is a nonprofit research entity organized by the National Academy of Sciences to coordinate the community of science and technology toward furthering knowledge and advising the federal government. At the request of the federal government, the NRC issued two influential publications that elaborated the context and rationale for SBR. The book *Scientific Research in Education* (NRC, 2002) has at its stated aim "to examine and clarify the nature of scientific inquiry in education and how the federal government can best foster and support it" (p. 1). This book is often cited for what it posits are "six guiding principles that underlie all scientific inquiry, including education research" (NRC, 2002, p. 2). Here the merits of so-called "descriptive research" are neither overlooked nor overtly praised, as exemplified by the following statement: "These examples of descriptive work meet the principles of science, and have clearly contributed important insights to the base of scientific knowledge. If research is to be used to answer questions about 'what works,' however, it must advance to other levels of scientific investigation such as those considered next," which are those that establish cause-and-effect relationships (NRC, 2002, p. 108). The second NRC publication, *Advancing*

Scientific Research in Education (NRC, 2005), builds on the previously outlined principles of scientific inquiry with the potent aim of "spur[ing] actions that will advance scientific research in education" (p. 1). Thus, the NRC creates a bright line of separation between research methods that describe phenomena and those purportedly more advanced methods that test for causal relationships.

The "official" definition of scientific inquiry has also been supported through policy initiatives that have reshaped how federal education research dollars are awarded. The Education Sciences Reform Act of 2002 created the Institute of Education Sciences (IES) as the research arm of the U.S. Department of Education whose stated aim is to improve federal education research and dissemination. The year of its founding, 100 percent of all IES-funded projects addressed causal claims, and 74 percent used random assignment designs, an outcome consistent with the funding priorities of the Department of Strategic Planning during the same period (Eisenhart & Towne, 2003). In 2002 the IES extended its influence over education research and the practice of education by initiating and funding the What Works Clearinghouse (WWC), a "central and trusted source" for disseminating "what works" in education. Only those studies employing randomized controlled trial, quasi-experimental, regression discontinuity, and, since 2012, single-case study designs are eligible for review and disseminated through the WWC Web-based publications. To date, the WWC has reviewed 10,331 research studies, which are based on criteria that exemplify a "narrow NCLB-type definition" (Eisenhart & Towne, 2003). The WWC also proffers judgments of the effectiveness of specific educational programs, products, policies, and practices.

In sum, the official voices in the SBR movement have shared a quite consistent, unified position on the question of what research questions and designs are most able to improve how students in the United States are educated. The most salient question is, "What works?," and the most powerful research designs are randomized experiments or at least those that use within-condition and across-condition controls. It is difficult to discern whether the official voices we have discussed (federal bureaucrats, scholars in public and private organizations) are "principals," "authors," "animators," or some combination thereof (Goffman, 1981). What is clear is that supporting and exercising the official definition of SBR means occupying a privileged position with regard to accessing federal research dollars and receiving the esteem proffered by such entities as the NRC and the WWC.

"Unofficial Voices"

Given the origins of educational research discussed earlier, it is not surprising that the official voice of SBR has been met with opposition from within the education research community. Many scholars criticize the federal government's involvement in judging research as more or less scientific (Laitsch et al., 2002;

Lather, 2004; Olson & Viadero, 2002). Others challenge the superiority of randomized controlled trials as the "gold standard" of educational research on the grounds that a broad range of rigorous qualitative and quantitative research methods are equally scientific, whether they address causal questions or not (Erickson & Gutiérrez, 2002; Rudolph, 2014). Additionally, the official definition of SBR is criticized as placing an "overtrust" in one epistemological perspective (Berliner, 2002), while marginalizing alternatives (St. Pierre, 2002). Although any introductory social sciences research methods textbook would support the claim that experimental and quasi-experimental designs under ideal conditions allow for a sound basis on which to evaluate causal claims, this commonplace does not preclude the possibility that other methods can reveal causal relations. In our literature review, we found that two nonexperimental approaches to causal inquiry were not included in the federally sanctioned view of SBR: nonexperimental quantitative research and the use of qualitative data for causal inference.

Among the nonexperimental quantitative approaches to causal inquiry, the causal comparative method, which is not often heard of outside of educational research (Johnson, 2001), involves statistical analysis of independent variables on naturally occurring phenomena. A more popular method, especially in education policy research, is the structural approach, which was imported from economics. This method relies on complex statistical modeling of specific, albeit hypothetical, counterfactuals that offer insight into how an intervention might work under a different scenario (Kapplan, 2009). Although these techniques do not involve manipulation or random assignment to conditions, they do provide information about the strength and direction of associated variables. These methods are valued in educational research since so many independent variables cannot be manipulated (e.g., educational spending, class size) (Johnson, 2001), and some policy questions are not suited to experimental designs (Kapplan, 2009).

Cogent arguments have also been made for using qualitative inquiry to answer causal questions, though the concept of causality espoused departs from the Humean or regulatory perspective (Donmoyer, 2012; Maxwell, 2012). Causation in the Humean sense is rejected because of its (1) association with the positivist view of knowing reality objectively, (2) incompatibility with an interpretivist account of human agency, (3) denying of the importance of context, and (4) exclusion of process. Instead, a realist, generative, or process-oriented approach, developed in philosophy (Bhaskar, 1978, 1989; Salmon, 1984, 1989, 1998) and in social science (Mohr, 1982), is preferred. The alternative approach abandons the Humean understanding of causation in favor of causal explanation as a matter of identifying "actual processes that resulted in a specific outcome in a specific context" (Maxwell, 2012, p. 655, citing Little, 2010; Pawson & Tilley, 1997; Sayer, 1992). Represented as an equation, mechanism + context = outcomes. By this view, causal processes can be directly observed, even in single cases (Maxwell, 2004; Scriven, 2008), without the need for comparison or quantitative measurement

(Cartwright, 2000; Salmon, 1998). The role of context is also central to this view. Beliefs, values, intentions, and meanings, as well as objects and events both in the immediate situation and in broader social and cultural contexts, make up the causal context involved in the outcome of that process (Maxwell, 2012). Donmoyer (2012) refutes the notion that qualitative researchers, individually or collectively, are categorically prohibited from investigating cause and effect within a constructivist paradigm. In response to the provocative question and title of the 2012 article "Can Qualitative Researchers Answer Policymakers' 'What Works' Question?," Donmoyer contends that "incommensurability" does not mean "logically incompatible" and resolves that "any researcher who hopes her or his work will be used in the policymaking process is virtually required to speak and write in the language of causes and effects" (p. 666).

Interestingly, even those who are deeply committed to randomized controlled trials for answering policy questions warn that a successful trial in one context is just one piece of evidence to support the claim that the intervention will produce similar effects elsewhere (Cartwright & Hardie, 2012). Cartwright and Hardie (2012) encourage the use of systematic reviews, econometrics, and process analysis as additional sources of evidence to be weighed when asking, "What will work here?"

In some ways, the debates about SBR are a continuation of the paradigm dialogues of the 1980s and 1990s, a time in the social sciences when a number of "alternative" theoretical paradigms began to challenge the "Old Guard" that operated under post-positivist assumptions, such as the dichotomizing of objectivity/subjectivity and the privileging of experimental methods over other forms of scientific inquiry (Denzin, 2009). Both the SBR debate and the paradigm dialogues have challenged a disparate community to wrestle with internal differences in theoretical commitments and preferred research methods. During the paradigm dialogues, critical theorists, constructivists, feminists, queer theorists, action researchers, and others argued for the merits of their diverse perspectives. These developments were not the quiet murmurings of isolated dissenters. As Denzin (2009) comments, the "Alternative Paradigms Conference" held in 1989 under the sponsorship of Phi Delta Kappa International and the Indiana School of Education (Guba, 1990) exemplifies the depth of engagement that occurred across theoretical and disciplinary lines during this time. The paradigm dialogues had lasting effects in education and other disciplines, having spurred the establishment of alternative professional groups, journals, textbooks, handbooks, and dissertation awards (Denzin, 2009). For instance, within the American Educational Research Association, the largest and oldest professional society in the field of education, the Qualitative Research SIG was founded in 1987 to bring methodological diversity to educational research. During the same period, the *International Journal of Qualitative Studies in Education* (1988) and *Qualitative Inquiry* (1995) were founded.

Yet, also during this period, randomized controlled trials became more firmly entrenched as the method of choice by private research firms and government agencies for evaluating educational initiatives (Walters et al., 2008). This sector of education research became even more removed from university-based educational research, since most researchers conducting randomized controlled trials in education are trained in fields outside of education, such as economics and psychology, and do not necessarily share the same model of scientific inquiry (e.g., ontologies, epistemologies, methodologies) as those in traditional departments of education (Borman, 2002). In the 1990s, mixed-methods approaches that used qualitative data yet adopted post-positivist assumptions also gained increasing popularity (Denzin, 2009).

It could be argued that because alternative paradigms became so firmly established in universities, they are able to operate quite independently of each other (separate journals, separate professional societies, and physical separation) and without significant interaction with traditional paradigms. This insularism may partly be the reason that alternative paradigms have not constituted a galvanizing force that challenges status quo definitions of scientific research in education. The dissenters to SBR have not organized an alternative to the NRC. Nor have they collectively advanced a competing definition of scientific research to counter the NRC reports' claims in "Scientific Research in Education" and "Advancing Scientific Research in Education." In this way, we find Bakhtin's notion of "unofficial voices" especially suited to our analysis. While official voices are unified and attempt to impose order, unofficial voices are multivocal and attempt to disrupt that order (Morson & Emerson, 1990). Unofficial voices bring disorder and even chaos.

V. CONCLUSION

The debate over scientific evidence and underlying causal assumptions has important implications for scholarship, in particular the acceptance and visibility of various forms of educational research. The extent of these differences is evident in graduate programs of education, funding sources, and scholarly journals (Denzin, 2009; Laitsch et al., 2002; Lather, 2004). As previously analyzed, the definition and scope of SBR in legislation and related policy initiatives favor experimental research designs on the basis of their effectiveness in demonstrating "what works." We are concerned that a method's applicability to answering causal questions has become synonymous with quality and rigor. The exclusion of a wide range of research designs high in rigor though not directly concerned with establishing causality impacts their credibility and visibility. In the words of Erickson (2005), exclusion "silences implicitly through omission as well as what it says explicitly" (p. 8). Research reports such as those by the WWC that synthesize research without including ethnographic and other qualitative research findings lead to an "artificial narrowing of the literature" (Laitsch et al., 2002, quoting Darling-Hammond, 2001). As a result, an even greater burden is placed on researchers who ask noncausal questions to defend their research as high quality (Alexander, 2006).

Access to funding streams is a matter of practicality and prestige in making certain forms of research visible and viable. Sound research is timely and expensive (NRC, 2002), and the underfunding of educational research compared with other fields is well known (Borman, 2002; Burkhardt & Schoenfeld, 2003; NRC, 2002; Slavin, 2002). A dated but telling statistic revels that in 1998 the United States spent $300 billion on education but only $300 million (less than 0.01 percent) on educational research. This statistic differs dramatically from other fields such as medicine and agriculture, which devote 5–15 percent of expenditures on research and development (Burkhardt & Schoenfeld, 2003, citing U.S. House Committee, 1998). The diminishing availability of research funds coupled with the IES funding priority for experimental designs discussed earlier greatly reduces the share of federally funded research for nonexperimental research.

The potential for informing policy is also at stake in this debate. In view of the previously described policy drivers of scientific inquiry, Lather (2004) asks whether the push for SBR is "science for policy or policy for science?" Berliner (2002) contends that "improving the quality of practice" requires attention to the "complexity and messiness of practice-in-context" rather than a narrow preoccupation with "what works" (p. 19). In defense of the value of interpretive research, Lather (2004) declares that the "loss" of paradigmatic pluralism is borne by children, teachers, and schools (p. 768). Demerath (2006) characterizes the types of responses to the SBR movement into a typology of pathways by which educational scholars, qualitative researchers in particular, may take to make their research more impactful: (a) from a critical stance, inquiring into the SBR accounts of research; (b) instructive, educating peers and policy-makers about value of qualitative research; (c) elucidative, striving for greater transparency in all educational research, including the development of inferences and theory; (d) pragmatic, employing mixed-methods approaches; and € making research more accessible and public.

Bakhtin theorized that "centrifugal forces" created by unofficial voices conflict with the "centripetal forces" created by official voices and that this conflict gives rise to "heteroglossia" (Morson & Emerson, 1990) or change. Just how much change can we expect from the SBR debates with regard to the federally legislated definition of scientific research? From our perspective, the debates on SBR have only scratched the surface of current thinking on causal inference. Disciplinary "boundary crossing" (Moss et al., 2009) by educational researchers and philosophers of science would be one promising way to enrich the debate over what legitimate scientific inquiry is in educational research. In our review of literature following the SBR movement and paradigm wars, it is clear that differing assumptions about the purposes of education research, treatments of the concept of causality, and specialist terminology pose potential threats to advancing the debate. By making causal concepts from the philosophy of science more accessible to a multidisciplinary community such as education researchers, volumes such as this can function as resources for a scientific community so that internal debates drive innovation rather than insularism.

Moss et al. (2009) contend that it is more fruitful to propose "principles, practices, social structures, and initiatives that ensure a vivacious educative dialogue" (p. 514). As an example of the very approach they advocate, the 2009 article was co-authored by six scholars representing disparate views of quality in educational research. Through jointly and individually written sections, this article embraces consensus and ideological pluralism. This arguably heteroglossic approach embodies the spirit of what they consider to be other successful instances of scholarly dialogue that enhances mutual understanding. These include journal volumes dedicated to the SBR movement that appear in *Educational Researcher, Teacher's College Record,* and *Qualitative Inquiry* and handbooks on complimentary research methods among other edited volumes. Several points can be distilled from Moss et al. (2009) for what to keep in mind when collaborating in interdisciplinary environments: (a) scholars set up key issues often using discipline-specific assumptions and terminology; (b) different paradigms have different foci, questions of interest, units of study, constructs, and distinctions, but these are not necessarily oppositional or always applicable to other paradigms; (c) no paradigm is necessarily "wrong" or "superior" since these judgments can be made only from within a particular paradigmatic stance. Keeping these points in mind while engaging in collaborative endeavors doesn't diminish the differences in aims and perspectives on quality in education; rather, these differences serve as natural resources for learning.

REFERENCES

Alexander, H. A. (2006). A view from somewhere: Explaining the paradigms of educational research. *Journal of Philosophy of Education, 40*(2), 205–221.

Berliner, D. C. (2002). Comment: Educational research: The hardest science of all. *Educational Researcher, 31*(8), 18–20. doi: 10.3102/0013189X031008018

Bhaskar, R. (1978). *A realist theory of science* (2nd ed.). Brighton, UK: Harvester.

Bhaskar, R. (1989). *Reclaiming reality: A critical introduction to contemporary philosophy.* London: Verso.

Billig, S. H. (1997). Title I of the Improving America's Schools Act: What it looks like in practice. *Journal of Education for Students Placed at Risk (JESPAR), 2*(4), 329–343. doi: 10.1207/s15327671espr0204_3

Borman, G. D. (2002). Experiments for educational evaluation and improvement. *Peabody Journal of Education, 77*(4), 7–27.

Burkhardt, H., & Schoenfeld, A. H. (2003). Improving educational research: Toward a more useful, more influential, and better-funded enterprise. *Educational Researcher, 32*(9), 3–14. doi: 10.2307/3700019

Cartwright, N. (2000). An empiricist defense of singular causes. In R. Teichmann (Ed.), *Logic, cause, and action: Essays in honor of Elizabeth Anscombe* (pp. 47–58). Cambridge, UK: Cambridge University Press.

Cartwright, N., & Hardie, J. (2012). *Evidence-based policy: A practical guide to doing it better.* New York, NY: Oxford University Press.

Demerath, P. (2006). The science of context: Modes of response for qualitative researchers in education. *International Journal of Qualitative Studies in Education, 19*(1), 97–113. doi: 10.1080/09518390500450201

Denzin, N. K. (2009). *Qualitative inquiry under fire: Toward a new paradigm dialogue.* San Francisco, CA: Left Coast Press.

Donmoyer, R. (2012). Can qualitative researchers answer policymakers' "what works" question. *Qualitative Inquiry, 18*(8), 662–673.

Eisenhart, M., & Towne, L. (2003). Contestation and change in national policy on "scientifically based" education research. *Educational Researcher, 32*(7), 31–38. doi: 10.3102/0013189X032007031

Erickson, F. D. (2005). Arts, humanities, and sciences in educational research and social engineering in federal education policy. *The Teachers College Record, 107*(1), 4–9.

Erickson, F. D. (1992). Why the clinical trial doesn't work as a metaphor for educational research: A response to Schrag. *Educational Researcher, 21*(5), 9–11.

Erickson, F. D., & Gutiérrez, K. (2002). Comment: Culture, rigor, and science in educational research. *Educational Researcher, 31*(8), 21–24. doi: 10.3102/0013189X031008021

Esch, C., Lash, A., Padilla, C., Woodworth, K., Laguarda, K. G., & Winter, N. (2004). *Evaluation of Title I accountability systems and school improvement efforts (TASSIE): First-year findings.* U.S. Department of Education, Office of the Under Secretary, Policy and Program Studies Service.

Feuer, M. J., Towne, L., & Shavelson, R. J. (2002). Scientific culture and educational research. *Educational Researcher, 31*(8), 4–14. doi: 10.3102/0013189X031008004

Goffman, E. (1981). *Forms of talk.* Philadelphia: University of Pennsylvania Press.

Guba, E. G. (Ed.). (1990). *The paradigm dialog.* Thousand Oaks, CA: Sage Publications.

Halperin, S. (1975). ESEA ten years later. *Educational Researcher, 4*(8), 5–9. doi: 10.3102/0013189X004008005

Johnson, B. (2001). Toward a new classification of non-experimental quantitative research. *Educational Researcher, 30*(2), 3–13.

Kapplan, D. (2009). Causal inference in non-experimental educational policy research. In G. Sykes, B. Schneider, & D. N. Plank (Eds.), *Handbook of education policy research* (pp. 139–153). New York, NY: Routledge.

Labaree, D. F. (1998). Educational researchers: Living with a lesser form of knowledge. *Educational Researcher, 27*(8), 4–12.

Lagemann, E. C. (2002). *An elusive science: The troubling history of education research.* Chicago, IL: University of Chicago Press.

Laitsch, D. A., Heilman, E. E., & Shaker, P. (2002). Teacher education, promarket policy and advocacy research. *Teaching Education, 13*(3), 251–271. doi: 10.1080/1047621022000023253

Lather, P. A. (2004). Scientific research in education: A critical perspective. *British Educational Research Journal, 30*(6), 759–772. doi: 10.1080/0141192042000279486

Maxwell, J. A. (2004). Causal explanation, qualitative research, and scientific inquiry in education. *Educational Researcher, 33*(2), 3–11. doi: 10.3102/0013189X033002003

Maxwell, J. A. (2012). The importance of qualitative research for causal explanation in education. *Qualitative Inquiry, 18*(8), 655–661.

Mohr, L. B. (1982). *Explaining organizational behavior.* San Francisco, CA: Jossey-Bass.

Morson, G. S., & Emerson, C. (1990). *Mikhail Bakhtin: Creation of a prosaic.* Palo Alto, CA: Stanford University Press.

Moss, P. A., Phillips, D. C., Erickson, F. D., Floden, R. E., Lather, P. A., & Schneider, B. L. (2009). Learning from our differences: A dialogue across perspectives on quality in education research. *Educational Researcher, 38*(7), 501–517. doi: 10.3102/0013189X09348351

National Research Council. (2002). *Scientific research in education.* Washington, DC: National Academy Press.

National Research Council. (2005). *Advancing scientific research in education.* Washington, DC: The National Academies Press. Retrieved from http://www.nap.edu/openbook.php?record_id=11112

No Child Left Behind Act of 2001, 20 U.S.C.

Olson, L., & Viadero, D. (2002). Law mandates scientific base for research. *Education Week, 21*(20), 1–6.

Pellegrino, J. W., & Goldman, S. R. (2002). Comment: Be careful what you wish for—you may get it: Educational research in the spotlight. *Educational Researcher, 31*(8), 15–17. doi: 10.3102/0013189X031008015

Riley, R. W. (1995). Improving America's Schools Act and elementary and secondary education reform. *The Journal of Law & Education, 24*, 513–566.

Rudolph, J. L. (2014). Why understanding science matters: The IES research guidelines as a case in point. *Educational Researcher, 43*(1), 15–18. doi: 10.3102/0013189X13520292

Salmon, W. C. (1984). *Scientific explanation and the causal structure of the world.* Princeton, NJ: Princeton University Press.

Salmon, W. C. (1989). Four decades of scientific explanation. In P. Kitcher & W. C. Salmon (Eds.), *Scientific explanation* (pp. 3–219). Minneapolis: University of Minnesota Press.

Salmon, W. C. (1998). *Causality and explanation.* New York, NY: Oxford University Press.

Scriven, M. (2008). A summative evaluation of RCT methodology: An alternative approach to causal research. *Journal of Multidisciplinary Evaluation, 5*(9), 11–24.

Slavin, R. E. (2002). Evidence-based education policies: Transforming educational practice and research. *Educational Researcher, 31*(7), 15–21. doi: 10.3102/0013189X031007015

Slavin, R. E. (2003). A reader's guide to scientifically based research. *Educational Leadership, 60*(5), 12–16.

St. Pierre, E. A. S. (2002). Comment: "Science" rejects postmodernism. *Educational Researcher, 31*(8), 25–27. doi: 10.3102/0013189X031008025

Walters, P. B., Lareau, A., & Ranis, S. (2008). *Education research on trial: Policy reform and the call for scientific rigor.* New York, NY: Routledge.

EDITORS' COMMENTARY

There is competition in society between groups with different approaches to defining and studying causation. The groups involved in this competition have different levels of resources and influence. Their motivation is ultimately political, because how cause and effect are conceived influences the picture of the world we arrive at, and also has implications for the actions we need to take. For example, if we come to the conclusion that poor school test scores are "caused by lazy and incompetent teachers," the implication for action is clear: target teachers as the "cause" of the problem (the policy already adopted in some states). If the "inborn low intelligence of some children" is assumed to be the cause of low test scores, then the argument can be (and has been) put forward that the government should not invest in educational enrichment programs and better prepared teachers, because such investments will not change the abilities of "low intelligence children." On the other hand, if the assumption is that test scores in large part reflect environmental conditions, then government investments to improve community and educational environments seem logical. But there is also a relationship between the cause-effect relations assumed and the methodology used to assess causal relations.

The analysis by Lee and Blair lays bare the relationship between different assumptions about causation and the established power groups who get to define causation as it is used in mainstream education and technology. The federal U.S. government has intervened in the debate about causation and determined that only certain cause-effect relations should be researched and only certain research practices are effective at identifying these "valued" cause-effect relations. Because the federal government controls much of the funding for research, the perspective it adopts has enormous impact on educational research and practice.

Perhaps most surprising is the narrowness of the position taken by the federal government on the issue of causation in education. Only a certain type of research is acceptable, a position that assumes that there is complete agreement in the research community about how to proceed. As Lee and Blair discuss, an "unofficial" position is occupied by numerous but disorganized "unofficial" voices, but these are dismissed by the federal government as unscientific and unable to locate causes. Obviously there are dangers when the federal government enters into scientific debates and takes sides in favor of one particular perspective.

Part Three

· ·

Causal Concepts and Linguistic Topics

8

Triggers and Their Consequences for Language Acquisition[1]

David W. Lightfoot

I. INTRODUCTION

Like many elements of cognition, a person's mature language emerges from an interplay of nature and nurture. Genetically determined properties common to the species interact with environmental factors resulting from being raised in a particular speech community or in a community using a signed system. What is striking about work on language is that scientists can tease out information that needs to be postulated for the human linguistic genotype. This genotypical information is distinct from information that comes from experiencing the ambient language encountered in the first few years of life, before the genetic system closes down after the expiration of various sensitive periods. In some areas, precise and resilient hypotheses have been developed.

The fact that children become speakers of Chinese or Chichewa, depending on the community where they are raised, makes it clear that a person's language development cannot be entirely a matter of biological endowment. Furthermore, a newborn child of Chichewa-speaking parents, if taken immediately from her birth family into a Chinese-speaking household in Beijing, will develop like a child of the Chinese parents next door and very differently from children raised by Chichewa speakers in Malawi. It is also true that a mature language system cannot arise entirely by experience, unaided by species-specific biological properties, despite strenuous efforts to develop such scenarios (e.g., raising chimpanzees among humans using a signed language). This is because a person's mature system goes far beyond what they experience as children, a fundamental point that we shall illustrate in detail.

---

[1]Most readers of this book will not be linguists, and they owe a great debt to Betty Tuller and Ali Moghaddam, who made me aware of the needs of psychologists and philosophers in thinking about the miracle of language acquisition.

The logical problem of language acquisition, as it is called (Baker & McCarthy, 1981), distinguishes what is learned from what is not learned and is part of what Bertrand Russell characterized as Plato's Problem: "How comes it that human beings, whose contacts with the world are brief and personal and limited, are nevertheless able to know as much as they do know?" (Russell, 1948, p. 5). Plato argued that there is much that we know that does not result from environmental experiences or learning (Chomsky, 1986; Lightfoot, 2005). In the *Meno*, his Socrates, a self-described midwife, famously elicited knowledge of basic properties of Euclidian geometry from an uneducated slave boy and argued that this reflected intrinsic knowledge. For Plato, this intrinsic knowledge was attained in a previous life and rendered subconscious, when the soul drank from the River Lethe, the river of forgetting, just before birth; modern psychologists view this as "pre-wiring."

Similarly in the mid-nineteenth century, Gregor Mendel teased out invariant properties of pea plants, which were not affected by environmental variation, and postulated internal "factors," or genes, to explain them. Many properties of pea plants resulted from internal factors, he argued, notably the universal 3:1 ratio in which properties occurred (e.g., leaves distributed along the branch in some plants versus those clustering at the branch's end in others). The shaping effects of the environment were quite limited, although he didn't know how his "factors" might be biologically instantiated.

Modern linguists have followed this classical, Platonic, Mendelian reasoning, seeking to separate the contributions of nature and nurture and identifying information that must be available independent of experience in order for a natural language system to emerge in a child. Like Mendel, we don't know how this information is encoded biochemically in the genome or whether it results from epigenetic, developmental properties of the organism; it is, in any case, native. As a shorthand device for these native properties, I write of the linguistic genotype, the part of our genetic endowment that is relevant for our linguistic development. Each individual's linguistic genotype (what linguists call "universal grammar," or UG) is uniform across the species (apart from pathological cases). That is, linguistically we all have the same potential for functional adaptations, the same pre-wiring. Any of us may grow up to be a speaker of Chinese or Chichewa, depending entirely on our circumstances and not at all on variation in our genetic makeup.

We will identify what children need to hear in order for their mature language system to develop, the triggers. What is distinctive about what I sketch here is that I postulate specific triggers for specific aspects of an individual's mature linguistic competence. This differs from standard approaches that evaluate systems globally, rating their overall success in generating a target set of expressions (Chomsky, 1965) and postulating no specific causes for particular elements of mature systems. Following standard practice since the work of Konrad Lorenz, Nikolaas Tinbergen, and Karl von Frisch, joint winners of the 1973 Nobel Prize in Physiology or Medicine and founders of ethology as a distinct area of biology, I use the term "trigger" to refer to the environmental experiences that elicit aspects of the mature system. Those triggers are the "causes" of the title of this volume and what they trigger are the "consequences."

II. SOME THINGS THAT ARE INNATE

Everybody's mature language system, whether ranging over Chinese, Chichewa, or Chinook, has general properties that are not learned but must be part of an innate endowment for language, the pre-wiring. For example, the mature system is represented in the brain, but there is an infinite number of things one can say and understand. Everybody's language, regardless of where they were raised, has devices (often called recursive) that permit sentences, in principle, to go on indefinitely, much as the number system allows an indefinite range of numbers. For each of 1–3 below, the reader may add another clause, or two or three, to make it more complex, just as one may add one or two or three to any large number. And, of course, all three of the recursive devices may be used in any single expression.

1. *Relative clauses:* This is the cow [that kicked the dog [that chased the cat [that killed the rat [that caught the mouse [that nibbled the cheese [that lay in the house [that Jack built]]]]]]].
2. *Complement clauses:* Ray said [that Kay said [that Jay thought [that Fay said [that Gay told me [that Clay reported [that there was hay on the way]]]]]].
3. *Coordination:* Ray and Kay went home and Jay and Fay to the store, while Gay and May and Clay worked where Shay and Jack were playing, but Zach and Mack slept.

If sentences may, in principle, go on indefinitely, then there is an infinite number of possible sentences. That infinite capacity links to something fundamental: most of what we say and hear is novel. It may be quite banal, *I think that this year's Perseid meteor show will rock*, but we say it because we want to express that thought, not because we heard somebody else say it some time ago. In that way, the language capacity is infinitely creative and that makes human communication different from that of other animals.

This isn't learned: no child hears a sentence of indefinite length; sentences all end and therefore what children experience is not rich enough to determine the infinity of language. We overcome the poverty of the stimulus by postulating intrinsic properties of the native human language capacity, in this case the three recursive devices that we see in all languages.

Another thing that isn't learned, which must be built into the system, is that everybody's language is compositional; it consists of meaningful units that consist of smaller units, structures, substructures, and sub-substructures. In the expression *I saw a man with curly hair*, the words "man with curly hair" constitute a unit (a noun phrase), "with curly hair" is a prepositional phrase, but the words "man with" are not a unit. The units undergo the computational operations of the system, for example, the deletion operations to be discussed in the next section. Again what children hear is not rich enough by itself to determine the nature of the units and subunits unaided; intrinsic properties must be playing a role.

Recursiveness and compositionality are two fundamental properties of the human language capacity. But remarkably, people are not aware of these properties and there was no evidence for them in their childhood experience. This reveals details of the genetic component of language through what are called poverty-of-stimulus arguments.[2] The central question is: how do we develop such a complex competence when the stimuli, the specific expressions we hear in our environment, reflect the general nature of the system but contain so little evidence for its properties. The general answer is that humans must be genetically endowed with information that encompasses the fundamental properties of languages. Furthermore, as children we are sensitive to certain aspects of what we hear as we acquire language-specific properties of the mature system, that is, how we develop our mature capacity, how we learn. Discovering how something is acquired may reveal the nature of what is acquired.

III. INNATE PROPERTIES ARE NOT ENOUGH

So we need to postulate intrinsic, innate properties but that is not enough: all language-specific properties must be learned, that is, shaped by external drivers. For example, a property specific to English is that people say *Kim is taller* or *Kim's taller*, with *is* reduced. One can think of this as an operation *is becomes 's'*. Children hear both the full and reduced forms and therefore can learn the operation on exposure to external data. However, the poverty-of-stimulus problem here, the first of five that we will explore, is that the operation sometimes may not apply: in 4 the underlined *is* never reduces and nobody says **Kim's taller than Jim's* (the asterisk indicates a non-occurring sentence).

4. Kim's taller than Jim is.

The experiences that children have do not convey this kind of information, often referred to as negative evidence, data about what does not occur. Children hear things but they are not ordinarily instructed about what does not occur, and therefore they do not learn the exception. Helicopter parents may try to correct the occasional *goed* or *taked*, usually unsuccessfully, but they don't tell children that a reduced *is* does not occur in 4. That is partly because they don't know and partly because children do not misuse the reduced forms,

---

[2]*The Linguistic Review* devoted an issue to distorted discussion of poverty-of-stimulus arguments, but the lead article restricted discussion to defective data and oddly excluded cases where there was an *absence* of relevant data (Pullum & Scholtz, 2002, pp. 14–17), setting aside the clear cases and focusing attention on unclear cases. The cases discussed here all involve absence of relevant data.

so there is nothing to correct—much ingenious experimental work has shown how rich children's language systems are (Crain & Thornton, 1998).

This is no longer mysterious. Children are exposed to simple speech, what linguists call "primary linguistic data." That is part of external language (E-language), language out there, which acts as triggering experience. The initial genetic inheritance, the linguistic genotype, blossoms into a specific internalized, individual system (I-language), depending on whether the children are raised in Tromsø or Tokyo; for the distinction between internal and external language, see Chomsky (1986).[3] Linguists distinguish internal and external factors, contributions of the invariant genetic inheritance and contributions of environmental factors. Both are needed to account for the very complex competence that all children develop, the pre-wiring provided by the genotype and the learned elements of a particular mature I-language.

Consider a second poverty-of-stimulus problem, again illustrating that language acquisition is shaped by both internal factors and external triggers. English embedded clauses (the words in the square brackets of 5 and 6) may start with a sentence introducer (a "complementizer"), a word like *that*, as shown in 5. Those words may be omitted, perhaps due to an operation *Delete that*. This is specific to the I-languages of speakers of forms of English; French and Dutch children do not hear equivalent forms with an empty complementizer and do not acquire any comparable deletion operation, because it is never triggered (*Je crois il fait chaud*, *Ik denk het warm is* ["I think it is warm"]). The operation is learnable from experience: English-speaking children hear both the full forms and the forms without *that*.

> 5. a. Peter said [~~that~~ Kay left].
>   b. The book [~~that~~ Kay wrote arrived].
>   c. It was obvious [~~that~~ Kay left].

Here is the poverty-of-stimulus problem: sometimes the operation *Delete that* may not apply. English speakers would not say the forms without *that* in 6 (the undeletable *that* is boldface, indicating that the deletion does not occur).

> 6. a. *Ray said yesterday in Chicago [**that** Kay had left].
>   b. *The book arrived yesterday [**that** Kay wrote].
>   c. *Fay believes, but Kay doesn't, [**that** Ray is smart].
>   d. *[**that** Kay left] was obvious to all of us.

Again, children have no direct evidence for this limitation in what they hear. They sometimes hear forms with *that*, sometimes without *that*, but they

---

[3]Chomsky echoes von Humboldt (1836), who distinguished the language of individual citizens and the language of a nation, and Paul (1880), for whom "Wir müssen eigentlich so viele Sprachen unterscheiden als es Individuen gibt" ("we must in fact distinguish as many languages as there are individuals"; p. 31).

are not explicitly told that the forms of 6 without *that* do not exist. Somehow they deduce that limitation without conscious awareness, using both learned and intrinsic knowledge of language. Thus, deletion is subject to constraints, which are pre-wired, part of the innate, linguistic genotype. The phenomena illustrated in 5 and 6 may be due to a simple genotypical principle, which can be formulated as 7.[4]

7. A language-specific deletion operation may delete a constituent if that constituent is (in) the complement of an adjacent, overt word.

In the simple forms of 5, the clause introduced by *that* completes the meaning of *said*, *book*, and *was obvious* and is, therefore, the complement of those words. *That* is adjacent to those words, is in the complement, and may therefore be deleted by the *Delete that* I-language operation that is triggered in English speakers. However, the bracketed clauses of 6 do not complete the meaning of the adjacent *Chicago*, *yesterday*, or *doesn't* and therefore are not their complement, and therefore *that* isn't in their complement. And in 6d there is nothing preceding *that*. Therefore, in 6 *that* may not be deleted. That simple principle of our linguistic genotype 7 is quite general, holds of all I-languages, solves this poverty-of-stimulus problem, and accounts for other things in the I-languages of speakers of forms of English, as we shall illustrate. Other languages manifest the principle in other ways. Put differently, in 5 *said*, *book*, and *was obvious* "license" the adjacent deletion site, but in 6 the potential deletion site is not adjacent and therefore deletion is not licensed.

English-speaking children hear expressions like those of 5, which trigger the *Delete that* operation in their I-languages. However, the general, genotypical principle of 7 prevents the operation from affecting a *that* which is not adjacent to its complement-taking licensor in 6, *said*, *book*, *believe*. We see the interplay of the intrinsic, unlearned principle 7 with the I-language operation *Delete that* triggered by the E-language expressions *Peter said Kay left*, *The book Kay wrote arrived*, and *It was obvious Kay left* in 5. Together they correctly account for where *that* may be deleted.

Consider now a third learned, I-language operation, *Gap V*, whereby the second of two identical verbs may be omitted or "gapped." There may be an understood, empty verb in the second clause, indicated as $_\text{v}$e in 8c ("e" for empty). So alongside sentences like 8a, children hear 8b, perfectly normal, comprehensible speech, which has a representation with an empty verb 8c. The gapping operation is learnable, triggered by exposure to E-language expressions like 8a and b.

8. a. Jay introduced Kay to Ray and Jim introduced Kim to Tim.
   b. Jay introduced Kay to Ray and Jim Kim to Tim.
   c. Jay introduced Kay to Ray and Jim $_\text{v}$e Kim to Tim.

---

[4]For a detailed discussion of this aspect of pre-wiring, see Lightfoot (2006b).

9a is another example of a gapped verb. But we do not gap a verb and delete the sentence introducer *that* in 9b, which would have the representation 9c. Again our principle 7 has the explanation: *that* may not delete at the front of its clause, if it is not (in) the complement of an adjacent, overt verb. Here the verb is not overt and not pronounced, and the deletion is not licensed.

9. a. Fay said Ray left and Tim that Jim stayed.
   b. *Fay said Ray left and Tim Jim stayed.
   c. Fay said Ray left and Tim ᵥe [**that** Jim stayed].

A fourth example: from a sentence like *Jay saw Ray*, English speakers form questions by copying an interrogative word *who* at the front of its clause and deleting the original element in the position where it is understood; English speakers have in their I-languages an operation *Copy and delete wh-*. The simple expression *Who did Jay see?*, where *who* is understood as the complement of *see*, has a representation in which *who* is copied to the front of the clause and the original *who* is deleted: who did Jay see ~~who~~? The deleted *who* is the complement of *see* and the deletion conforms to our principle. However, we do not find sentences like 10a, which would have the structure 10b, where the boldface *who* may not delete, because there is no adjacent overt, pronounced verb. Such a sentence is a logical possibility and we know what it would mean, but it is not a biological possibility, given that principle 7 is part of our biology, and the sentence does not occur.

10. a. *Who did Jay introduce to Ray and who (did) Jim to Tim?
    b. Who did Jay introduce ~~who~~ to Ray and who (did) Jim ᵥe ~~who~~ to Tim.

And now a fifth and final poverty-of-stimulus problem: English allows deleted verb phrases (VPs), and children have much evidence to that effect, for example, *Max left for Rio and Mary did as well*, with the structure 11a. In 11a the deleted VP is the complement of *did*. In fact, there must be an overt, adjacent complement-taking word to license the deleted VP, suggesting that deleted VPs occur only where they are licensed, like deleted complementizers and deleted *wh-* constituents; they are subject to principle 7. A deleted VP may occur in many structures: in a subordinate clause to the right in 11b (*Max left for Rio, although Mary didn't*) and to the left in 11c, in a separate sentence from the referent in 11d, or within a complex determiner phrase (DP) in 11e, when its referent is contained in a complex DP in 11f, or even without any overt referent in 11g. But a deleted VP must be the complement of an overt word immediately to the left. Where that is not the case, there is no deletion, as indicated by the contrasts of 11h, i, j, and k. In the non-occurring structures of 11i and k the deleted VP is separated from its potential licensor, *had*, hence failure to delete, hence boldface and the sentence does not occur.

11. a. Max left for Rio and Mary did ᵥₚ~~leave for Rio~~ as well.
    b. Max left for Rio, although Mary didn't ᵥₚ~~leave for Rio~~.
    c. Although Max couldn't ᵥₚ~~leave for Rio~~, Mary was able to leave for Rio.

d. Susan went to Rio. Yes, but Jane didn't ~~vpleave for Rio~~.
e. The man who speaks French knows ~~DP~~[the woman who doesn't ~~vpspeak French~~].
f. ~~DP~~[People who appear to support mavericks] generally don't ~~vpsupport mavericks~~.
g. Don't ~~vptickle me!~~
h. They denied reading it, although they all had ~~vpread it~~.
i. *They denied reading it, although they had all ~~vpread it~~.
j. They denied reading it, although they often/certainly had ~~vpread it~~.
k. *They denied reading it, although they had often/certainly ~~vpread it~~.

We now return to our first example 4 and see that the same deletion principle 7 accounts for the distinctions noted. A reduced *is* is not only reduced but also absorbed into the preceding word, becoming an integral part of it (a "clitic"). It is pronounced differently, depending on the last segment of the word it attaches to, as a voiceless "s" in *Pat's*, as a voiced "z" in *Doug's*, and as an extra syllable in *Alice's* in 12.

12. Pat's happy, Doug's happy, and Alice's here.

Now we can see why we don't reduce *is* in certain contexts in 1. Example 13a has a representation 13b, where *tall* is deleted, adjacent to the verb *is*, of which it is the complement (hence an operation *Delete adjective*). However, 13c does not exist: the representation would be 13d, where the reduced *is* has been absorbed into *Tim* and therefore is no longer a separate word that may license the deletion of *tall*; after the absorption of *'s*, *tall* isn't the complement of anything, therefore not deletable.

13. a. Kim is taller than Tim is.
    b. Kim is taller [than Tim is tall].
    c. *Kim is taller than Tim's.
    d. Kim is taller [than Tim's **tall**].

We are beginning to see the vast complexity of our language capacity, how every surface generalization has exceptions and why. Principle 7 interacts with many learned generalizations to account for the limitations observed but nothing complex is learned by children. One's language is a complex system but the complexity can be understood in terms of an interaction between simple principles at the genetic level such as 7 and simple generalizations that are triggered in children's I-languages by exposure to the speech around them (14). Principle 7 accounts for a vast range of facts in the language systems of the world, of which we have given a few sample illustrations here for speakers of forms of English.

In short, we have sketched six different operations (or four instances of a single deletion operation), each learnable by children on exposure to the relevant sentence type (italicized in 14). They result in a deleted complementizer, a deleted adjective, a deleted *wh-* phrase, a gapped verb, a deleted VP, and reduced (cliticized) instances of *is*, *am*, and so on. The italicized expressions are the triggers for the operations to the left, hence the causes of those operations in the I-languages emerging in children.

14. Delete *that*   *Peter said Kay left.*
    Delete adjective   *Peter is taller than Mary is.*
    Copy and delete *wh-*   *Who did Jay see?*
    Gap V   *Jay saw Ray and Jim Kim.*
    Delete VP   *Kim didn't.*
    Cliticize *is*   *Kim's happy.*

The interplay between intrinsic and learned elements captures the immense complexity of a person's mature language competence, revealing distinctions that most people are unaware of.

Corresponding to the operations of 14, we say that children identify structures, like an empty complementizer in sentences without *that* (*Peter said Kay left* [5]). Other examples of structures are a *wh*-phrase copied at the front of its clausal phrase, $_v$[e] for a gapped verb, or [NP+'s] for a cliticized verb. These abstract structures are part of the child's I-language, but they are expressed by E-language sentences such as those italicized. That is, *Peter said Kay left*, meaning what it means (e.g., with *[Kay left]* as the complement of *said*), can be analyzed only with an empty complementizer in the child's internal system, that is, a missing *that*. Similarly, *Jay saw Ray and Jim Kim* requires an analysis with an empty verb, that is, the $_v$e structure. In that sense the triggers cause the abstract structures and their consequence, along with the general, native principle 7, is the complex range of data discussed in this section.

This is to say that the italicized material of 14 is part of unanalyzed, amorphous E-language, but when we hear and understand such expressions, they now exist in our minds and have an internal I-language analysis with the abstract structures.

Under this view of acquisition and given that children are endowed with the information of the linguistic genotype, for example, 7, they need to hear particular kinds of things in order to acquire central properties of the I-languages of English speakers. That is, specific experiences, the italicized sentences in 14, trigger or cause the I-language operations to their left and, therefore, the corresponding structures.

IV. LEARNING FROM ONLY SIMPLE DATA

There is good reason to believe that children learn only from simple expressions: they only need to hear simple expressions, because there is nothing new to be learned from complex expressions. This is the idea of "degree-0 learnability" (Lightfoot, 1989), which hypothesizes that children need access only to unembedded material.[5] Such a restriction would explain why it is that many

---

[5]Specifically to unembedded binding domains, but we don't need technicalities here.

languages manifest computational operations in simple, unembedded clauses, which do not appear in embedded clauses (e.g., English subject-inversion sentences like *Has Kim visited Washington?* but not comparable embedded clauses **I wonder whether has Kim visited Washington*), but no language manifests operations that appear only in embedded clauses and not in matrix clauses. This impressive asymmetry requires explanation and our explanation is that children do not learn from embedded domains. Therefore, much that children hear has no consequences for the developing I-language and causes nothing to emerge in I-languages; nothing complex triggers any aspect of I-languages.[6]

If successful language acquisition is triggered on exposure to simple data, then we are not surprised that children exposed under exceptional circumstances only to very restricted data nonetheless acquire normal mature systems. A great deal of interesting work has examined this in recent years, focusing on the acquisition of signed systems. A striking fact is that 90 percent of deaf children are born to hearing parents, who normally are not experienced in using signed systems and often learn a primitive kind of pidgin to permit some communication. In such contexts, children surpass their models readily and dramatically and develop a more or less normal kind of mature capacity, despite the limitations of their parents' capacities. See Hudson Kam and Newport (2005) and Singleton and Newport (2004).

Indeed a remarkable recent event has cast new light on these matters: the birth of a new language in Nicaragua. The Samoza dictatorship regarded the deaf as subhuman and prevented them from congregating. Consequently, deaf children were raised almost entirely at home, had no exposure to fluent signers, were isolated from each other, and had access only to home signs and gestures. The Sandinistas took over the government in 1979 and provided a school where the deaf could congregate in an area of Managua, Villa Libertad, soon to have 400 deaf children enrolled. Initially the goal was to have them learn spoken Spanish through lip reading and finger spelling, but this was not successful. Instead, the schoolyard, streets, and school buses provided good vehicles for communication and the students combined gestures and home signs to create first a pidgin-like system and then a kind of productive creole, and eventually their own language, Nicaraguan Sign Language. This took place quickly, over just a few decades.

This may be the first time that linguists have witnessed the birth of a new language, and they were able to analyze it and its development in detail. Kegl, Senghas, and Coppola (1998) provide a good general account, and Senghas, Kita, and Özyürek (2004) examine one striking development, whereby certain signs proved to be unacquirable by children, not conforming to demands of the genotype, and were eliminated from the emerging language. Sandler, Meir, Padden, and Aronoff (2005) discuss the birth of another sign language among the Bedouin community, which has arisen in ways similar to the emergence of

---

[6]Just as children learn only from simple, unembedded domains, it is worth noting that principle 7 forces children to delete material only in "prominent" positions, as the complement of an adjacent, overt head. This restriction may have a functional basis.

Nicaraguan Sign Language and was discovered at about the same time. These two remarkable discoveries have provided natural laboratories to study the capacity of children exposed to unusually limited linguistic experience to go far beyond their models and to attain more or less normal mature I-languages.

V. LANGUAGE CHANGE

Language change provides another laboratory to examine our general approach to language acquisition, caused by exposure to specific events that trigger particular elements of I-languages in young children.

This cause-and-effect view of the language capacity and its development in children obliges us to think about change in a certain way, which turns out to illuminate mysteries about how particular languages have developed over time. Children acquire their I-language under the influence of their biology and their environment. The environment means language out there, the kinds of simple, unanalyzed expressions that children hear readily, and certain aspects of what children hear may trigger certain aspects of their I-languages within the limits of the linguistic genotype. Sometimes the ambient speech may shift a little, yielding new primary data so that some children hear different things. That may yield a phase transition, a new I-language. Changed E-language sometimes triggers new I-languages, with far-reaching consequences, as we shall see in this section.

Language change of this kind is an instance of the "punctuated equilibrium" of evolutionary biologists: things may be fairly stable for long periods but then are punctuated by major structural shifts, when many phenomena change in rapid succession.

We noted earlier that people's speech is individual and unique; people may have slightly different systems and furthermore they use their systems differently. For example, people differ in how they use "tag questions" like *It is raining, isn't it?* or in how they use the "topic" constructions favored by sports commentators: *Taylor, he throws the ball down the middle.* People's use of their system varies, sometimes randomly and sometimes with statistical tendencies that can be identified, with certain construction types coming to be used more or less frequently.

Even in relatively homogeneous language communities, children have different experiences and hear different things around them with different frequencies. It is those experiences of external language, language out there, that trigger the development of a child's internal language. Since no two children have exactly the same experiences, there is always the possibility of new I-languages emerging. Once that happens and some children have new I-languages, E-language changes further, because the new I-language entails that people speak differently. This happens quickly in a small number of children. As a result, the new I-language may propagate through the population rather quickly and the spread of changes can be studied through the methods of population biology (Lightfoot, 2006a). The spread through the speech community, of course, takes longer than the few years in which one child grows its new I-language and the spread depends on the complexity of the speech community: some languages have millions of speakers dispersed over

a wide area, whereas Nicaraguan Sign Language has just a few hundred, con-
centrated mostly in Managua.

I will illustrate language change with a well-understood example from the
history of English, the kind of structural shift that has made Shakespeare
sometimes difficult for modern Londoners to understand, Chaucer still harder
without special training, and *Beowulf* as incomprehensible as German.

The linguistic genotype provides the structures available for people's I-
languages and children select from what is on offer. Sometimes we see changes
in these structures over time and thereby learn about the structures themselves
and about what triggers them in children. This yields domino effects, where a
change in one aspect of internal systems leads to another; for example,
changes in morphology often lead to changes in syntax (Lightfoot, 2002).

Beginning in the northeast of England, Middle English underwent a massive simplification of morphology. In Old English, spoken until about 1150,
verbs had different inflectional forms depending on tense and agreement (person and number). So with a first-person subject, *I*, a verb might be *fremme*
(meaning "do"), but a second- or third-person singular subject (*you* or *she*)
would require the forms *fremst* or *fremþ*, and third-person plural *they* would
require *fremmaþ*. Another verb was *rīde, rītst, rītt, rīdaþ* ("ride"), and the past
tense forms were *rād, ride, rād, ridon*. This is just a fraction of the complexity;
there were strong verbs, weak verbs, and verbs of many inflectional classes.
Most of this disappeared under the influence of intermarriage with
Scandinavians (Lightfoot, 2006a, pp. 137–138). Specifically, the bewildering
range of endings on different classes of verbs reduced to just one ending in
the present tense, *-s* in the third-person singular. This had consequences.

In Old English the verbs *can, could, may, might, must, will, would, shall,* and
should belonged to a particular inflectional class, so-called preterit presents.
What was distinctive about this class was that, unlike all other classes of verb,
there was no *-eth* or *-s* ending for the third-person singular present tense forms.
Verbs like *can, may,* and *must* never had the *-s* ending (**She cans lift 50 kilos*).
When there were many kinds of inflectional classes, as just described, this was just
one fact among hundreds. However, once the morphological system had eroded,
the presence of an *-s* ending for the third-person singular became the single, general, defining property of English verb morphology, and these verbs lacked it.

In general, children determine which category words belong to on the basis of
formal and distributional properties: words with the same forms and the same distribution are assigned to the same category. As a result, verbs with no *-s* ending
became distinctive, and evidence shows that they were assigned to a new category, were no longer treated as verbs, and became what traditional grammarians
call modal auxiliaries and what we call inflection elements.[7] We turn now to
that evidence.

---

[7]There was another distinctive property: the past tense forms *could, might, would,* and *should*
did not usually carry the standard past time meaning. I ignore this here in order to keep the
exposition simple.

Speakers of present-day English use lexical verbs like *understand* with a perfective marker *have* (15a) but not modal auxiliaries like *can* (15b). Sentences like 15b do not occur, although it is clear what it might mean: he has been able to understand chapter 4 but now cannot. Not only is it clear what it would mean, but equivalent forms with a perfective marker occur in many languages closely related to English, which have not undergone the equivalent change.

15. a. He has understood chapter four.
    b. *He **has could** understand chapter four.

Lexical verbs also occur in an infinitival *to* form (16a) but not modal auxiliaries (16b). Likewise, a lexical verb like *try* may occur with a modal auxiliary (17a), but a modal auxiliary does not occur with another modal auxiliary (17b).

16. a. He wanted to understand.
    b. *He wanted **to can** understand.
17. a. He will try to understand.
    b. *He **will can** understand.

This is true of modern English but not of English up to the early sixteenth century. The (b) forms of 15–17 appear in historical texts, where we find combinations of modal verbs. Sir Thomas More was the last writer to use such combinations (18a), a modal verb in a *to* infinitive (18b), and with a perfective marker (18c).

18. a. I fear that the emperor will depart thence, before my letters **shall may** come unto your grace's hands (1532, Cranmer, *Letters*).
    b. That appeared at the fyrste **to mow** stande the realm in grete stede (1533, More, *Works* 885 C1), "appeared at first to be able to stand the realm in good stead."
    c. If wee **had mought** convenient come togyther, ye woulde rather haue chosin to haue harde my minde of mine owne mouthe (1528, More, *Works* 107 H6), "If we had been able to come together conveniently, ..."

The loss of expressions like 18 reflected a single change in people's I-languages. In Middle English all verbs could be copied to a higher inflection position, I (with the original item deleted—it is in the complement VP of the adjacent overt verb in I), as illustrated by 19a and b. However, by the early sixteenth century all speakers of English had classified words like *can, must, shall,* and *may* no longer as verbs (they lacked the formal properties of verbs) but as a new inflectional category, and they were no longer copied from a lower verb position (19c); the structure of 19a was replaced by 19c and that was the single change in I-languages. Children had developed a new I-language, and from that single fact about people's I-languages, it follows that each of the 15–17b forms did not exist any longer, thereby changing the ambient E-language further.[8] The simultaneity of the loss of 15–17b followed from the singularity of the change in I-languages.

19. a. ₁can ᵥₚ[ᵥcan see stars]
    b. ₁see ᵥₚ[ᵥsee stars]
    c. ₁can ᵥₚ[see stars]

There were two sets of observable changes: First, the morphology of verbs was simplified with the loss of almost all suffixes, which entailed new E-language for young children. Second, expressions like 15b, 16b, and 17b dropped out of the language, reflecting the change in I-languages affecting the category membership of *can*, *must*, *shall*, and *may* and changing E-language still further, that is, what children heard.

We can also identify a plausible reason for the shift in I-languages, and we see that language change has domino effects. The change in category membership, hence the new structures of 19c, was due to prior morphological changes, changes in E-language that had the effect of singling out the new modal auxiliaries from other verbs.

Furthermore, our explanation is contingent: related European languages underwent no such parallel changes, because the morphological changes that they underwent did not single out a new class in the same way. So the structural shift took place in the I-languages of English speakers at a particular time because of specific properties of the language at that time.

The new behavior of modal auxiliaries is one feature of Early Modern English, one way in which Shakespeare's language differed from that of Chaucer. And Shakespeare's language also differed from Jane Austen's because of other structural shifts, phase transitions in the history of English that gave rise to yet newer forms, a topic for another occasion. Meanwhile, our account of language acquisition explains why and how I-languages changed in English and what caused that change. Work on language change has proven to be a productive laboratory for understanding what kinds of structures are acquired by children and how and which structures cease to be acquired under certain circumstances.

VI. CONCLUSION

I have sketched a cause-and-effect model of language acquisition, identifying particular E-language triggers for particular aspects of people's I-languages and thereby identifying causes of people's mature language systems. The linguistic genotype interacts with the learned operations of people's I-languages, and that interplay explains the immense complexity of language at a phenomenological

---

[8]This is because an inflection element can no longer occur to the right of a perfective marker in VP, hence 15b, and there can be only one inflection element in any clause, hence the non-occurrence of 16b and 17b.

level. In addition, E-language is in constant flux but sometimes there are changes that trigger a new I-language, which then spreads through a speech community and explains big structural changes that languages may undergo from one generation to another—changes like the emergence of inflection elements and the resulting loss of expressions like 18.

Triggers for elements of I-languages are to be found only in simple, unembedded domains; therefore, much of what a child hears has no effect on the emerging I-language, and children may acquire features of their mature system even when exposed only to limited data. A little goes a long way and children attain normal mature systems, even when exposed to abnormally restricted data, and we understand why. Linguists have developed rich accounts of language acquisition and cognitive scientists can look to work on language to enrich accounts of the development of other aspects of cognition.

REFERENCES

Baker, C. L., & McCarthy, J. (Eds.). (1981). *The logical problem of language acquisition*. Cambridge, MA: MIT Press.

Chomsky, N. (1965). *Aspects of the theory of syntax*. Cambridge, MA: MIT Press.

Chomsky, N. (1986). *Knowledge of language: Its nature, origin and use*. New York: Praeger.

Crain, S., & Thornton, R. (1998). *Investigations in Universal Grammar: A guide to experiments on the acquisition of syntax and semantics*. Cambridge, MA: MIT Press.

Hudson Kam, C., & Newport, E. L. (2005). Regularizing unpredictable variation: The roles of adult and child learners in language formation and change. *Language Learning and Development 1*(2), 151–195.

Humboldt, W. von. (1836). *Über die Verschiedenheit des menschlichen Sprachbaues und ihren Einfluss auf die geistige Entwicklung des Menschengeschlechts*. Royal Academy of Sciences of Berlin [Linguistic variability and intellectual development, transl. G. C. Buck & F. A. Raven 1971. Philadelphia: University of Pennsylvania Press].

Kegl, J., Senghas, A., & Coppola, M. (1998). Creation through contact: Sign language emergence and sign language change in Nicaragua. In M. DeGraff (Ed.), *Language creation and change: Creolization, diachrony and development* (pp. 179–237). Cambridge, MA: MIT Press.

Lightfoot, D. W. (1989). The child's trigger experience: Degree-0 learnability. *Behavioral and Brain Sciences 12*, 321–334.

Lightfoot, D. W. (Ed.). (2002). *Syntactic effects of morphological change*. Oxford: Oxford University Press.

Lightfoot, D. W. (2005). Plato's problem, UG and the language organ. In J. McGilvray (Ed.), *The Cambridge companion to Chomsky* (pp. 42–59). Cambridge: Cambridge University Press.

Lightfoot, D. W. (2006a). *How new languages emerge*. Cambridge: Cambridge University Press.

Lightfoot, D. W. (2006b). Minimizing government: Deletion as cliticization. *The Linguistic Review* 23(2), 97–126.

Paul, H. (1880). *Prinzipien der Sprachgeschichte*. Tübingen: Niemeyer.

Pullum, G. K., & Scholtz, B. (2002). Empirical assessment of stimulus poverty arguments. *The Linguistic Review* 19, 9–50.

Russell, B. (1948). *Human knowledge: Its scope and limits*. New York: Simon & Schuster.

Sandler, W., Meir, I., Padden, C., & Aronoff, M. (2005). The emergence of grammar: Systematic structure in a new language. *Proceedings of the National Academy of Sciences 102*, 2661–2665.

Senghas, A., Kita, S., & Özyürek, A. (2004). Children creating core properties of language: Evidence from an emerging sign language in Nicaragua. *Science 305*, 1779–1782.

Singleton, J. L., & Newport, E. L. (2004). When learners surpass their models: The acquisition of American Sign Language from inconsistent input. *Cognitive Psychology 49*, 370–407.

EDITORS' COMMENTARY

Lightfoot's discussion of "triggers," environmental experiences that elicit aspects of mature human linguistic competence, illuminates how "causes" are conceptualized by scholars of language acquisition. Second, Lightfoot's discussion is extremely helpful because he makes explicit the kinds of assumptions that influence other fields of research, but often remain implicit.

A central focus of Lightfoot's discussion is "poverty-of-stimulus" arguments, which are central to how causation is assumed in language acquisition. The logic of these arguments is as follows: (1) human language capacity has certain fundamental properties, such as recursiveness and compositionality; (2) there is no clear evidence of these properties in childhood experiences; (3) people are not self-aware of these properties; and (4) the source of these properties must be genetic. The same poverty-of-stimulus argument is implicit in a great deal of both policy and research regarding human behavior, but is seldom brought out into the open for discussion. This includes explanations in highly controversial areas such as terrorism: the environmental conditions of individual X does not explain why he has traveled from France to Syria to join and fight for Islamic State. Therefore, it must be something inherent in individual X that explains his terrorist actions.

Of course, in making the poverty-of-stimulus argument explicit in linguistics, Lightfoot has also suggested the possibility that we have not looked hard enough for the appropriate environmental stimuli.

Lightfoot's discussion of language change and the link he makes to punctuated equilibrium is particularly valuable. Monitoring change in language is very useful, because, in many respects, language change reflects culture change, but far more precisely than many other indicators of culture change (see also Mühlhäusler's discussion of language death, Chapter 9 in this volume). Linking this to punctuated equilibrium, it is useful to introduce the distinction between *first-order*, within-system, and *second-order*, between-system, change discussed by the so-called Palo-Alto group of therapists. First-order change is incremental and does not bring about a change in the larger system; second-order change brings shifts from one system to another—this is the relatively rapid and major structural shift.

First-order change in language is probably "triggered" by incremental environmental shifts, whereas second-order language change is more likely to be caused by sudden and major changes in the environment—such as invasions, wars, natural disasters, and other events that result in the movements and coming into contact of large numbers of people using different mature languages. Globalization and the massive movement of large numbers of immigrants, refugees, and temporary workers is an important twenty-first-century factor contributing to changes in languages. Thus, at least with respect to language, we would expect punctuated equilibrium to involve shorter time intervals between each major change.

9

Causes of Language Death

Peter Mühlhäusler

I. INTRODUCTION

It is estimated that between 80 percent and 90 percent of the world's languages will disappear within a couple of generations. Importantly, it is not the loss of language as such for languages have come and gone in the history of humankind—Walsh, for instance, demonstrates convincingly that the number of languages that disappeared in Australia during 50,000 years of Aboriginal occupation must have amounted to several hundred thousands (Walsh, 1997), whereas by the time of European colonization there were probably only about 500 Aboriginal languages spoken. Rather, it is the mismatch between language birth and language loss that is at issue. Far more languages are on the way out nowadays than newly emerge.

The topic of language loss has been widely debated among linguists, and a vast number of books and papers dealing with the disappearance of the world's linguistic diversity have been published over the last couple of decades, including several by the author (Mühlhäusler, 1996, 2002, 2005a, 2005b, 2012).

There is no shortage of suggestions as to the cause of language loss nor is there a shortage of suggested remedies. Remedies are needed, it is argued, as there are excellent reasons why linguistic diversity is desirable. Arguments in favor of such diversity include:

- Moral arguments;
- Economic arguments;
- Scientific arguments; and
- Aesthetic arguments.

These same arguments employed in the discourses about the natural environment (see Harré, Brockmeier & Mühlhäusler, 1998) are also encountered in the discourses about other big issues (e.g., AIDS, asylum seekers). To what extent such discourses lead to action is not always clear, and in the worst case, they simply become substitutes for action.

Two of the above discourses, the moral and the scientific one, figure prominently in Australia's National Indigenous Languages Survey (NILS Survey
Report, 2005), which resulted in increased public awareness, substantial funding, and much action in the form of language centers, school programs, and so
on. Nine years after the first NILS (2005), a second NILS (Marmion, Dough,
Kazuko, & Troy, 2014) indicates that a number of languages have disappeared
in the last decade and that the state of indigenous languages is worse than it
was then:

> The findings in NILS2 show a complicated picture with ongoing decline
> but also some definite signs of recovery. The previous NILS1 survey
> found that of over 250 Australian Indigenous languages about 145 were
> still spoken, with about 110 severely or critically endangered and that
> about 18 languages were strong, still spoken by all age groups and being
> passed on to children.

Examination of the NILS2 data allows us to make the assessment that there
are now only around 120 languages still spoken. Of these about 13 can be considered strong, which is five fewer than in NILS1. These five are now in the
moderately endangered group, while some languages from that group have
moved into the severely/critically endangered category.

There appear to now be around 100 languages that can be described as
severely or critically endangered, but at the same time a fair number of languages in this category, perhaps 30 or more, are seeing significant increases
in levels of use as a result of language programs.

Again, Marmion et al. (2014) appeal to scientific and moral arguments and
make no mention of the economic ones such as those discussed in a detailed
report to the same body that funded NILS2.

Before presenting the substance of my arguments, I have to make it clear to
my readers that I am not a neutral observer, but that I have been very active in
trying to reverse the decline and loss of languages in Australia and the adjacent Pacific; that I currently am the manager of a Mobile Language Team,
set up to preserve the languages of South Australia; and that I have been playing a central role in reviving the Norf'k language, spoken by the descendants
of the Bounty Mutineers on Norfolk Island in the South Pacific.

II. THE NOTION OF LANGUAGE

The notion of language that emerged in Western Europe from the seventeenth century is based on powerful metaphors, prominent among them
the reification metaphor: this metaphor converts situated ways of speaking
(an activity) into an abstract object "language" characterized by having well-
defined structural and geographical boundaries, a closed system of grammatical
rules, and a well-defined lexicon. It is a fixed code, which lends itself to being
represented in a written form.

This myth, as Harris (1980) calls it, ignores the fact that what is referred to as a "language" by linguists, politicians, and educated Westerners as well as Western-educated non-Westerners is the consequence of deliberate language making. Linguists continue to speak about "natural languages" and the grammar of "natural languages" in spite of the fact that such languages inevitably turn out to be human artifacts brought into being by linguists, missionaries, administrators, anthropologists, and other language makers; in a paper about the ontology of language spoken in the colonial sphere read at the Bremen Conference on Colonial Linguistics (2013; see appendix), I argued that languages such as Hindi, Bahasa Indonesia, Ewe (Togo), Kâte (PNG), and Pitjantjatjara (Western Desert, Australia) are the outcome of deliberate human choices and agency, not labels for natural kinds discovered and described by objective linguists.

My argument consequently is that to portray language loss or death as the disappearance of well-defined language species is misguided. In preliterate societies, the notion of a language is an inadequate descriptor. Attempts to count and catalog languages are popular and are given respectability by the compilers of the *Ethnologue* and other language lists. However, as I have tried to show for the languages of PNG (Mühlhäusler, 2006), language inventories are highly inconsistent, arbitrary, and often at odds with their speakers' own metalinguistic judgments: it is noted that the majority of language names found in language catalogs have been invented by outside language makers.

Whereas it seems relatively unproblematic to refer to the death of a natural life form such as the extinction of the dodo or the Norfolk Island bat, it is less easy to speak of languages as natural kinds. There is, of course, a long tradition in linguistics that has done precisely that, beginning with Max Müller (1855) and has been growing in popularity in recent years through Chomsky's characterization of human language as a "mental organ." Unsurprisingly, when equating human languages with biological species, appeal to neo-Darwinian ideas regarding the survival of the fittest (Mufwene, 2001; reviewed by Mühlhäusler, 2005c) makes an appearance. In the past, many arguments have been put forward to the effect that not only are the small number of European natural languages inherently fitter than other languages, but the loss of other languages is highly desirable. As Swiggers (1990) has shown, for instance, the superiority of French was established by the discourses of a number of seventeenth-century French scholars such as Father Lamay and Louis le Laboureur (1669), who argued (p. 118) that "in all our utterances we follow exactly the order of thinking which is the order of nature." He also argued that "the Romans thought exactly as the French do, but they chose to speak differently against the order of thinking much to their own inconvenience" (Swiggers, 1990, p. 119). The superiority of the Aryan languages over the Semitic and Turanian ones was argued by Max Müller (1855), and the superiority of a number of European national languages over other languages was argued in a vast body of writings concerned with the topic of primitive languages and language fitness (Mühlhäusler, 1996).

The acceptance by a small number of European governments of the superiority of a small number of European national languages is one of the reasons for massive language loss in their colonies, as it was accompanied by deliberate measures to reduce linguistic diversity including:

- Forced assimilation;
- Killing off populations of speakers; and
- Massive displacement of indigenous populations.

Similar policies have also been put in practice by other powers. The record of Mandarin-speaking Chinese, the Japanese, the Malayans, Indonesians, and the rulers of many modern African countries is not that different from that of European colonizers: it matters little whether such colonization is external or internal. Once national languages were imposed, all other forms of speaking became a target and the ideologies of the powerful over time became internalized by those colonized.

The growing power differential between language speakers in modern times thus must be seen as the prime cause in the decline and death of the majority of the world's languages.

III. WAYS OF SPEAKING: LANGUAGE ECOLOGIES

It needs to be remembered that the notion of language is a metaphor, precisely an instance of the reification metaphor that many branches of inquiry employ. "Behavior" and "attitude" in psychology, "virtue" in moral philosophy, or "demand" in economics, like the notion of "language" in linguistics, ignore that it is human activities, not abstract objects, that ultimately need to be understood and explained. The ways people communicate and their ways of speaking change and disappear. Different speaker groups can have very different agendas for using verbal signals. As Malinowski (1935) has shown, communicating new information is of little importance in low-information societies such as Kiriwina of the Trobriands, where most knowledge is shared by all members of the community. In this case, phatic communication, using verbal signals to indicate the communication channel is open, is the primary function of Kiriwina language. The wish to preserve ways of speaking to insiders only is a powerful motif in many esoteric speech communities. Thus, Anêm speakers of West New Britain (Thurston, 1987) have developed linguistic complexities that render the language very difficult to penetrate for outsiders. Teaching the language to outsiders attracted severe penalties, as did the teaching of Japanese and Chinese to European visitors in past centuries. One of the recurrent problems encountered in reviving Australian Aboriginal languages is "who is entitled to speak the language?," and associated with this view, "is it better for a language to disappear than to be spoken by people with the wrong background?"

Note that keeping a particular way of speaking for insider use only does not preclude communication with outsiders: for that purpose a number of solutions were adopted in the past including:

- *The development of intergroup pidgins that served to facilitate communication about matters of shared interest such as trade or periodic shared ceremonies*: These pidgins lacked the expressive power to discuss other topics and their use was at times highly restricted: women and children, for instance, were not allowed to speak the Hiri Trade languages spoken in the Gulf of Papua (Dutton, 1983).
- *Sign pidgins that straddled the boundaries of verbal ways of communication*: A particularly developed system of sign languages is found in many parts of Aboriginal Australia (Kendon, 1988).
- *Distinguishing an endo- and exo-lexicon*: Speakers of the so-called Western Desert languages of Australia communicate over a wide area in spite of many differences in the speech forms they produce. What enabled them to do this is that for each lexical item actively used they also had a much larger passive lexicon that enabled them to recognize words produced by outsiders; up to 10 synonyms can be found in some instances (Hansen, 1984). In such societies, the endo-vocabulary is used as an index of the speaker's identity, whereas the exo-lexicon enables communication with members of many other groups.

IV. DUAL LINGUALISM

The distinction between active and passive understanding need not be restricted to the lexicon but can involve entire languages (Lincoln, 1975). Note that in the case of the Solomon Islands described by Lincoln and in many other situations, dual lingualism is not a transitional phenomenon such as is the case with language death, where members of the younger generation only passively understand their elders but speak a different language with other people.

V. SOCIETAL MULTILINGUALISM

Many societies in the past have been highly multilingual, be it that multilingual skills were associated with power as in the New Guinea Highlands (Salisbury, 1972) or with the metalinguistic belief that each language could be used only in a very restricted area, or to discuss a certain topic, or to speak with a particular social or gender group within the society. Multilingualism remains statistically normal, but for reasons discussed here, it is a disappearing phenomenon.

The repertoire of ways of speaking found in different parts of the world is best characterized as an ecological phenomenon in the sense that different ways of speaking are chosen in response to different external/ecological parameters. They include both the social ecology, for example, how to speak with different addressees or different social settings, and natural ones, for example, which language is needed or tied to a particular place (Sutton, 1991). There is a reciprocal relationship between ways of speaking and the wider ecology in which these ways are embedded. Speaking brings into being and sustains social practices, the management of natural resources, and views about the world. Conversely, such practices and the world around languages sustain ways of speaking. It is of utmost importance, when talking about the question of language death, to investigate the nature of the different ecological support systems that sustain certain ways of speaking. As can easily be seen, these support systems can vary greatly and what sustains one language, for example, literacy, language testing, or a language academy, may be irrelevant or even detrimental to sustaining other ways of speaking. It is therefore of utmost importance when talking about the question of language death to ask "what is the ecological support system that sustains certain ways of speaking?"

The standard explanations given for language death typically underestimate the complexity of the ecological systems and tend to overemphasize generalities to the virtual exclusion of singular facts.

VI. THE PROBLEM REDEFINED

The problem of language death is not the loss, within two generations, of 50 percent, 60 percent, or 90 percent of the languages cataloged and named by linguists in problematic inventories such as *Ethnologue*, an encyclopedic reference work cataloging all of the world's 7,105 known living languages. Rather, linguists need to address the following problems:

- The ecological support systems that underpin a structural diversity of ways of speaking are disappearing in the wake of colonization, modernization, and globalization.
- Languages qua named entities may continue to exist but in a modified and changed form. Typically, traditional semantactic patterns become heavily Westernized; languages become standard average European (SAE) languages.
- The rate at which language ecologies disappear and languages become semantactically colonized is far greater than the emergence of new ways of speaking.

Neither the question of the ecological support system nor that of identity of languages over time has figured prominently in discourses about language death, and there are linguists who tell us that there is nothing to worry about, as does Matisoff (1991, pp. 221–222):

All in all, however, I do not find reason to be overly gloomy about the possible loss of linguistic diversity in Southeast Asia. Though some languages are dying, others are just being discovered! New forms of speech are being spawned all the time, or at least are just coming to the attention of linguists. We can only thrust that the forces of renewal are in the long run just as powerful as the forces of decline.

In what follows I shall provide details on both the reasons why languages and ways of speaking come into being and why they disappear.

VII. CAUSES FOR LANGUAGES/WAYS OF SPEAKING

The question why there are so many human languages has over the years received a great deal of attention not just from linguists but also from philosophers, psychologists, and historians, as Steiner (1975) has shown. There is little agreement whether we are dealing with a natural or deliberately human-made phenomenon; there is also insufficient understanding of the causes of linguistic diversity. Understanding what brings languages into being, what leads to their diversification, growth, and decline, is the requisite for understanding language death and its causes. I shall employ Aristotle's distinction between four different causes (material, formal, effective, and final), which I will use as tools to obtain answers. Let me hasten to point out that this is very much a pre-theoretical project and that I continue to struggle with the large number of parameters involved. Like philosophy, linguistics provides very little certainty and the key concepts of the title of this chapter "language" remains very much disputed.

The *material cause* refers to what things are made from. In our particular case, ways of speaking and languages are not material things but processes or activities. Ways of speaking are social practices shared by a community of speakers. They are enabled both by biological factors such as the nature of the human brain or the speech tract and ear and by biological constraints on cognition. They are also sustained by cultural and historical factors: the latter are in constant flux and little can be said about the indefinitely large number of sociocultural parameters that effect ways of speaking.

At this point it would seem to be necessary to say a few more words about the intrinsic causes of language death, that is, whether certain ways of speaking or types of languages are more prone to disappear than others. It is important to avoid crude neo-Darwinian explanations in terms of survival of the fittest as were made frequently in the context of European nationalism and colonization. Such explanations focused on structural properties rather than on patterns of language use or sociocultural factors, though the latter are better candidates when it comes to explaining why languages are no longer passed on to the next generation of speakers.

As regards structural properties, the amount of conscious language learning needed, as opposed to simple acquisition, varies considerably across languages as does the role of children in their creation and transmission (Hockett, 1950). Young languages such as creoles came into being when a community of children created a new full language out of the restricted pidgin language spoken by their parents as an auxiliary means of communication. Creoles have been characterized as being more natural and hence easier to acquire than old languages with a complex history. However, ease of acquisition and learning in itself does not protect a language. For instance, Tok Pisin, the Melanesian pidgin/creole of Papua New Guinea, in spite of its rise as the language of inter-communication throughout this nation and in spite of its recognition as an official status, is in danger of becoming replaced by English. Like other creoles of the Pacific area (Ehrhart & Mühlhäusler, 2007), Tok Pisin's low social status outweighs its many other advantages. At the other end of the naturalness–ab-naturalness scale, there are a number of structurally and lexically highly complex esoteric languages (Markey, 1987) whose successful transmission from one generation to the next depends on social institutions such as extensive language tuition as part of initiation, monitoring of younger speakers by older ones, and a high degree of metalinguistic awareness. Fluency in such languages is achieved only once speakers are in their mid-twenties.

Ways of speaking are converted by abstraction and a range of similar professional practices into entities named languages. It is such abstractions that are represented in books titled *The French Language*, *The Grammar of English*, and the like. The criteria for abstracting named languages from ways of speaking are inconsistent and arbitrary, as are the criteria for establishing dialects and other named "subvarieties" of languages. Haugen (1972), for instance, characterizes the languages of Scandinavia as "cultural artefacts" brought into being by the establishment of nation-states such as Norway and by discursive practices. Linguists may appeal to structural criteria, lexical differences, or intelligibility when attempting to identify distinct languages, but ultimately there are no reliable methods to establish the number of languages spoken in any area. The fact that Bosnian, Serbian, Croatian, and Montenegrin are recognized languages is not based on any reliable linguistic criteria but on the consequence of historical contingencies. The listing of 42 named Australian Aboriginal languages for South Australia similarly is the outcome of problematic practices by anthropologists and linguists. How many of them have died or are highly endangered is not possible to determine either by linguistic criteria or by asking their speakers. Languages as referred to in the discourse of language death and endangerment are not entities out there, discoverable by objective observers, but constructions. To speak of English or Hindi or Pitjantjatjara as "natural languages" or species is unwarranted.

The *effective causes* of the large diversity of ways of speaking are numerous. Conventionally, geographical isolation, splits and mergers of user groups, and deliberate human-made changes for taboo reasons or for signaling separate identity have been portrayed as the principal causes. More recently, Nettle (1998) has proposed a significant correlation between biological and linguistic diversity. Inasmuch as languages function as management tools for particular ecologies, ecologically diverse regions such as tropical rainforests favor linguistic diversification.

The effective causes of named languages are far fewer. These are brought into being by language makers such as linguists (Harris, 1980), politicians, missionaries, administrators, and interest groups of all kinds.

The *final causes* for ways of speaking or indeed languages that have emerged in the evolution of humanity are unknown, other than they emerged as a means of sharing meanings. There have been many attempts to explain the origin of human language. They include enabling collaborative activities (e.g., hunting or tool making), communicating nonshared information, facilitating rumor as a means of sustaining social groups, and numerous others.

The final causes of individual languages include the wish to have a means of signaling separate identity. Le Page and Tabouret-Keller (1985), for instance, argue that they are brought into being by acts of identity. Other final causes are social control, carving up people's space, and managing change. Languages typically are in part the result of deliberate planning and language making.

VIII. CAUSES OF LANGUAGE DEATH

The *material causes* for the disappearance of ways of speaking, qua cultural and political artifacts, need to be distinguished from the causes for the disappearance of languages. Ways of speaking are embedded in or part of the social and natural ecologies that sustain their use. When the sustaining ecology disappears, ways of speaking become first weakened and then obsolete.

Because languages are constructs, the material cause of their disappearance is reconstruction or changes in the conventions for constructing them. Languages may lose importance or disappear, for instance, because linguists have changed their mind. I have tried to show with the example of PNG that the ways linguists have classified and counted languages have not led to reliable answers (Mühlhäusler, 2006). The fact that a language listed in an older source no longer appears in recent accounts is not necessarily a reflection of the loss of any language but can simply be the result of different linguistic naming practices or of changed conventions for distinguishing between languages and dialects. Similarly, the statement that Yankunyjatjara of the Western Desert of Australia is a strong language may reflect, among other things, that communities that were previously listed as separate, such as the Antikirrinya, have now been grouped together by linguists as Yankunyjatjara. Yankunyjatjara in turn is a much weaker language than Pitjantjatjara. Speakers who identify with it do not wish to be classified as Pitjantjatjara speakers although the linguistic differences between Pitjantjatjara and Yankunyjatjara are not greater than those between Montenegrin and Serbian. It is anybody's guess how many Western Desert languages there are, how many have been lost, and how many are weak or strong. Again, the small number of languages listed for Germany would seem to reflect the discursive practices of politicians and linguists who refer to Bavarian and Alemanic not as languages but as dialects, unlike in Spain, where Asturian, Galician, and

Catalan are recognized as languages. Whether Valencian or Mallorcan are languages separate from Catalan remains disputed.

From the perspective of *formal cause*, language death is best understood as the disappearance of ways of speaking around the world at a rate much faster than the rate of emergence of new ways of speaking. It is also manifested in the disappearance of non-inter-translatable languages and the growing semantactic similarity between these various ways of speaking.

It is further manifested in the increase in inter-translatability and semantactic similarity between these various ways of speaking in the wake of globalization, shared educational practices, and communication technology.

The many *efficient causes* of the disappearance of numerous ways of speaking are that the ecological factors that sustain language variety or ways of speaking have become weakened or destroyed. This can be a consequence of deliberate human policies, for instance, the spread of Mandarin and the disappearance of other varieties of Chinese in Singapore, or the numerous language policies aimed at reducing variation (Mühlhäusler, 1996). It can also be invisible hand processes such as the unintended consequences of new technology, urbanization, migration policies, universal education, and disappearance of traditional marriages. As regards the latter, the vast majority of Australian Aboriginal people wish to see their languages passed on and to remain strong. However, with 80 percent of Aboriginal people in Australia no longer marrying spouses from traditional communities, the patterns of multilingualism found in precolonial families have all but disappeared. Whatever the views of the parents and older relatives are, in such families the children shape the implicit family language policies (Næssan, 2007), which, in the vast majority of instances, results in their abandoning the use of their parents' language and the loss of even passive understanding in subsequent generations. Researchers concerned with revitalizing endangered languages increasingly focus on factors that could motivate children to continue using their parents' languages. The role of technology and social change is experienced worldwide and continues to erode the ecological support systems needed to sustain the former diversity of ways of speaking (Mühlhäusler, 2005b).

As regards the *final cause*, ever since the days of the enlightenment and the creation of a French national language, those in power have subscribed to streamlining policies of language planning and the ideology of economies of scale. Their aim has been to have a single language for each political unit, state, or colony; to optimize communication within such a unit; and to have a symbol of national identity and power and the remaining ways of speaking that were a perceived threat to political unity and consequently were marginalized and denigrated. Postcolonial states have adapted and adopted the policies of their colonial masters: Bahasa Indonesia, originally developed by the Dutch as an administrative language for colonial purposes, has become a national language and arguably much more destructive of the numerous small languages spoken throughout the Indonesian archipelago.

IX. CONCLUSIONS

The causes of the rapid decline of the linguistic diversity of the world are both deliberately human-made and uncontrolled and unintended consequences of human actions. As regards the former, some of the most damaging deliberate decisions can be unmade. Spain and France, once ardent proponents of linguistic homogeneity, have begun to recognize languages other than Spanish and French, respectively, and put in place programs to strengthen them. While well intentioned, such recognition has not necessarily arrested the trend toward mono-lingualism in a single national language. Again, positive policies and growing support for the Aboriginal languages of Australia have not prevented the disappearance of an increasing number of Aboriginal languages nor weakened the status of English. Still changes in official attitudes toward minority languages can do some good as long as language maintenance and revitalization is carried out in close collaboration with the minority groups concerned. Inasmuch as most language revival is focused on single languages, however, and not on the (re)construction of a viable language ecology that can sustain linguistic diversity, the long-term results of the new policies are likely to be disappointing. The erosion of the language ecology sustaining diversity by technological and economic change is regrettably largely uncontrolled and irreparable. The concept of "linguistic impact assessment," pioneered by Wales, is not recognized in other parts of the world where all kinds of developments impact on language ecologies and consequently ways of speaking will continue to disappear. The languages of fishing people, for instance, will disappear as habitual fishing grounds are depleted, as fishing villages become swamped by tourism, as parts of the coast are reclaimed, and as the world's big lakes become polluted and drained. GPS removes the need for naming fishing grounds. In some instances this affects only some dialects such as Cockney; in other situations contact languages such as the Basque Icelandic Fishermen's Pidgin are abandoned; in others whole language communities such as the Kristang community of Singapore disappear; and in yet others the central domain of discourse disappears such as the Whalers' and Fishermen's discourses of Norf'k (Norfolk Island, South Pacific).

Change is inevitable and the disappearance of the many ways of speaking is equally inevitable. However, as in the case of the disappearance of the world's natural species, it is possible to lessen the impact of such change.

What I have suggested in this chapter is that the principal tasks for those involved in preventing or turning around the loss of the world's linguistic diversity are:

- To identify those factors that sustain linguistic diversity in particular language ecologies;
- To identify possible new ecological support systems for endangered ways of speaking;

- To understand what structural and sociohistorical properties make some languages more vulnerable than others; and
- To create awareness and appreciation of the importance of linguistic diversity.

Understanding the causes of language diversity and the causes of language death is a precondition for changing the current situation.

REFERENCES

Australian Institute of Aboriginal and Torres Strait Islander Studies and Federation of Aboriginal and Torres Strait Islander Languages, (2005). *National Indigenous Languages Survey Report*. Canberra: Department of Communications, Information Technology and the Arts (DCITA).

Crystal, D. (2000). *Language Death*. Cambridge: Cambridge University Press.

Dutton, T. (1983). Birds of a feather: A pair of rare pidgins from the Gulf of Papua. In E. Woolford & W. Washabaugh (eds.), *The Social Context of Creolization*, pp. 77–105. Ann Arbor: Karoma.

Ehrhart, S., & Mühlhäusler, P. (2007). Pidgins and creoles in the context of language endangerment in the pacific. In O. Miyaoka, O. Sakiyama, & M. E. Krauss (eds.), *The Vanishing Languages of the Pacific Rim*, pp. 118–143. Oxford: Oxford University Press.

Grin, F. (1989). The economic approach to minority languages. *Fourth International Conference on Minority Languages, General Papers*. Vol. 1, pp. 153–173. Genève: Université de Genève.

Hansen, K. C. (1984). Communicability of some Western Desert communi-lects. In J. Hudson & N. Pym (eds.), *Language Survey*, Work Papers of SIL/AAB, B-11. Darwin: Summer Institute of Linguistics.

Harré, R., Brockmeier, J., & Mühlhäusler, P. (1998). *Greenspeak*. Thousand Oaks: Sage.

Harris, R. (1980). *The Language Makers*. Duckworth: London.

Haugen, E. I. (1972). The Scandinavian languages as cultural artifacts. In *The Ecology of Language*. California: Stanford University Press.

Hinton, L., & Hale, K. (eds.). (2001). *The Green Book of Language Revitalization in Practice*. San Diego: Academic Press.

Hockett, C. F. (1950). Age-grading and linguistic continuity. *Language*, 26, 449–457.

Kendon, A. (1988). *Sign Languages of Aboriginal Australia: Cultural, Semiotic and Communicative Perspectives*. New York: Cambridge University Press.

Le Laboureur, L. (1669). *Avantages de la langue françoise sur la langue latine*. Paris: G. de Luyne.

Le Page, R. B., & Tabouret-Keller, A. (1985). *Acts of Identity: Creole-based Approaches to Language and Ethnicity*. Cambridge: Cambridge University Press.

Lincoln, P. C. (1975). *Acknowledging Dual-Lingualism*. Honolulu: University of Hawaii.

Malinowski, B. (1935). *Coral Gardens and their Magic*. London: George Allen & Unwin.

Markey, T. L. (1987). When minor is minor and major is major: Language expansion, contraction and death. In G.M. Eoin et al. (eds.), *Third International Conference on Minority Languages, General Papers*, pp. 3–31. Clevedon: Multilingual Matters.

Marmion, D., Kazuko, O., & Troy, J. (2014). *Community, Identity, Wellbeing: The Report of the Second National Indigenous Languages Survey*. Canberra: Australian Institute of Aboriginal and Torres Strait Islander Studies.

Matisoff, J. A. (1991). Endangered languages of Mainland Southeast Asia. In Robins & Uhlenbeck (eds.), *Endangered Languages*, pp. 189–228.

Mufwene, S. S. (2001). *The Ecology of language Evolution*. Cambridge: CUP.

Mufwene, S. S. (2004). Language birth and death. *Annual Review Anthropology 33*, 201–222.

Mühlhäusler, P. (1996). *Language Ecology: Linguistic Imperialism and Language Change in the Pacific Region*. London: Routledge.

Mühlhäusler, P. (2002). Why one cannot preserve languages (but can preserve language ecologies. In D. Bradley & M. Bradley (eds.), *Language Endangerment and Language Maintenance*, pp. 34–39. London: Routledge Curzon.

Mühlhäusler, P. (2005a). Linguistic communities. In F. Marti, P. Ortega, I. Idiazabal, A. Barrefia, P. Juaristi, C. Junyent, B. Uranga, & E. Amorrortu (eds.), *Words and Worlds: World Languages Review*, pp. 10–45. Clevedon: Multilingual Matters.

Mühlhäusler, P. (2005b). Information society: Reduction of linguistic and cultural diversity. In G. Berthoud, A. Kundig, & B. Sitter-Liver (eds.), *Informationsgesellschaft Geschichten und Wirklichkeit: Société de l'information, Récits et réalité*, pp. 3–28. Freiburg: Academic Press.

Mühlhäusler, P. (2005c). Review of Salikoko Mufwene *The Ecology of Language Evolution*. *Language*, 8(1), 265–268.

Mühlhäusler, P. (2006). Naming languages, drawing language boundaries and maintaining languages with special reference to the linguistic situation in Papua New Guinea. In D. Cunningham, D. E. Ingram, & K. Sumbuk (eds.), *Language Diversity in the Pacific-Endangerment and Survival*, pp. 24–39. Clevedon: Multilingual Matters.

Mühlhäusler, P. (2012). Prologue. In A. Idström & E. Piirainen (eds.), *Endangered Metaphors*, pp. 1–15. Amsterdam: John Benjamins.

Mühlhäusler, P., & Damania, R. (2004). *Economic Costs and Benefits of Australian Indigenous Languages*. Department of Communications, Information Technology and the Arts, Canberra.

Müller, F. M. (1855). *The Languages of the Seat of War in the East: With a Survey of the Three Families of Language, Semitic, Arian, and Turanian*. London: Williams & Norgate.

Müller, F. M. (1871). *Lectures on the Science of Languages*. London: Longmans Green.

Næssan, P. (2007). Results from a random sampling in three South Australian localities concerning family transmission of Indigenous languages. Manuscript. Department of Linguistics, University of Adelaide.

Nettle, D. (1998). Explaining global patterns of language diversity. *Journal of Anthropological Archaeology, 17*, 354–374.

Nettle, D., & Romaine S. (2000). *Vanishing Voices: The Extinction of the World's Languages*. Oxford: Oxford University Press.

NILS Survey Report. (2005). arts.gov.au/sites/default/files/pdfs/nils-report -2005.pdf

Salisbury, R. F. (1972). Notes on bilingualism and linguistic change in New Guinea. In J. B. Pride & J. Holm (eds.), *Sociolinguistics*, pp. 52–64. Harmondsworth: Penguin.

Steiner, G. (1975). *After Babel: Aspects of Language and Translation*. Oxford & New York: Oxford University Press.

Sutton, P. (1991). Language in Aboriginal Australia: Social dialects in a geographic idiom. In S. Romaine (ed.) *Language in Australia*. Cambridge: Cambridge University Press.

Swiggers, P. (1990). Ideology and the "clarity" of French. In J. E. Joseph & T. J. Taylor (eds.), *Ideologies of Language*, pp. 112–130. London: Routledge.

Thurston, W. R. (1987). *Process of Changes in the Language of North-Western New Britain*. Canberra: Pacific Linguistics 1399.

Walsh, M. (1997). How many Australian languages were there? In D. Tryon & M. Walsh (eds.), *Boundary Rider: Essays in Honour of Geoffrey O'Grady*, C-136, pp. 393–412. Canberra: Pacific Linguistics. …www .eryrinpa.gov.uk/_data/…/lingustic_impact_assessment_eng.pdf

APPENDIX

2013 Bremen Conference on Colonial Linguistics
Colonial language descriptions and language policies from the perspective of sausage manufacture

The American poet John Godfrey Saxe (*Daily Cleveland Herald* 29:3:1869) once observed: "Laws, like sausages, cease to inspire respect in proportion as we know how they are made." I shall argue that very much the same applies to most colonial language descriptions and language policies.

Progress in linguistics as in scholarly inquiry in general is enabled by applying heuristic metaphors to illuminate the nature of poorly understood phenomena. "Language family," "language drift," "communication conduit," and "bio-computer" have all contributed to progress in linguistics, as have the metaphors of "sink," "Gaia," and "plant community" in environmental studies. As metaphors are tools and not iconic images of any reality, their usefulness or otherwise can only be determined by the work they do.

This paper equates the processes of describing and policy making to with sausage making and the products, descriptions and policies, to sausages. Particular attention will be given to the creation of Hindi (Hindustani), Bahasa Indonesia, Ewe, Kâte and Mota and to colonial language policies in German New Guinea.

Aspects of the sausage metaphor that will be considered include:

- Introduction of a product not previously known in the colonies;
- Different sausage making traditions of German, English, and Dutch producers;
- The cheapness of sausages;
- The mix of natural and man-made ingredients;
- Non-transparency of ingredients;
- Cultural adaptation;
- Ad hoc ingredients;
- Competition between sausage makers;
- The difficulties of comparing sausages to determine the typological properties of a natural category "sausage";
- Applications and limitations of the metaphor.

EDITORS' COMMENTARY

Peter Mühlhäusler sets his discussion of the concepts of cause in language studies in the context of ways of understanding the appearance and disappearance of ways of speaking. Languages, he points out, are cultural constructions. "Ways of speaking," he argues, "are converted by abstraction and a range of similar professional practices into entities named languages." So the question of the causes of the disappearance of ways of speaking and the causes of the disappearance/appearance of languages are distinct. The question of the causes of the disappearance of a way of speaking is not independent of the causes of the disappearance of the ecological support system of that way of speaking.

Languages are constructions created by human beings on the basis of knowledge and experience of ways of talking (and writing). So if we were to ask what brought the French language into being, as a causal question, the answer is certain people, namely, French grammarians, the Academie Francaise, and so on. It is quite a different sort of answer from that of the question as to what brought the ways of speaking of the people who have lived and now live in the territories of France into being. We must also note the fact that what is to count as "France" is dependent, in part, on what ways of speaking are mutually intelligible to some population.

There are two main distinctions that shape Mühlhäusler's discussion of contexts in which causal concepts seem to be the natural resource of the researcher. There is the distinction between languages and ways of speaking, and there is the distinction between ways of speaking and the ecologies they create and also reflect. Before we turn to examine his uses of causal concepts, we should note Mühlhäusler's important comment that languages may exist that have lost their link to ways of speaking.

One genre of explanatory theories to account for the decline of some ways of speaking and the survival of others is based on the idea of fitness relative to the cultural purposes and living environment of those who speak this way. Here we encounter a sort of teleological explanation, drawing on the point or outcome of a way of talking, and this can be reflected in the abstractions created by the scholars who act as "language makers."

Proposals of causes for the decline and extinction of ways of speaking and the abstract versions of these in "languages" have suggested ways in which the process of decline might be halted and even reversed.

Mühlhäusler sets out various aspects of that which brings about linguistic decline in the light of the distinction between "language" and "way of speaking." He turns to the Aristotelian pattern of explanation, the four *aitia*. The material cause of language decline is the neglect of the lexicons and grammar books in which "languages" are realized. The material cause of the decline and extinction of a way of speaking is the disappearance of the ecology that it expressed and shaped.

Formal causes of language death involve the phenomenon of inter-translatability. If a language is inter-translatable with another of higher status or technical sophistication, the latter will destroy the former. And the same goes for ways of speaking, so we have extinction through the formation of pidgins and creoles.

The efficient causes of the disappearance of ways of speaking may be deliberate language policies adopted for many reasons, some practical and some political and some even religious. However, there may be cultural and economic shifts in practices, particularly novel ways of living and working that bring with them distinctive vocabularies and grammatical constructions. Even though the new jargon is provided with neologisms in the "home" language, the universality of English in particular swamps the intuitive convenience of using neologisms.

The final causes of the extinctions of both ways of speaking and their abstract doppelgangers, languages, are to be seen in the way certain states have implemented language policies to try to delineate political boundaries and to promote ease of communication within a linguistically homogenized national state.

It is striking how neatly the main lines of Mühlhäusler's discussion and his many examples of the death of ways of speaking and of languages can be mapped onto the Aristotelian scheme of the four *aitia*. Is this because our linguistic capacities and the core of our social interactions and constructions are mediated by words?

This chapter illustrates a more general feature of the analysis of human practices and the institutions they make possible—the way it is easy to slip into taking a certain picture for granted. How important it is to be wary of this tendency is illustrated in this chapter by the great importance of the distinc-tion between ways of speaking, the concrete activities of people in distinct cultural historical and material environments, and the abstractions that are set down by scholars as "languages." How does the death or survival of the one influence the death or survival of the other?

10

A Picture Is Worth a Thousand Words: On Causes, Reasons, and Images

Jens Brockmeier

Sigmund Freud was a frequent traveler to Rome, a city he loved like no other place. He loved it for its beauty, its light, its Mediterranean colors. It appeared to him as a counter-vision to what he saw as the more mundane, materialistic, and colder life of the north. But most of all he loved Rome's rich cultural history, the remnants of hundreds and thousands of years that the city simultaneously displays in an incomparable manner. From his many journeys to the Eternal City, Freud brought home a large collection of artworks from all epochs. On display in his practice and living quarters, first in Vienna and then in London, they had become a part of his everyday life. More than this, the overlaying, intermingling, and nestling of separate strata of history and culture that fascinated Freud in Rome became an organizing metaphor, if not model, of his psychoanalytical account of human memory and mind. Studying the mental life of his patients, he conceived of himself as an archeologist digging into deep and entombed areas of their past, discovering layers and nether regions that remerged in the form of memories and dreams.

Yet Freud did not only investigate the memories and dreams of his patients, but also used his own dream-memories, including some of his Rome memories. In his *Interpretation of Dreams* he describes how he once dreamt, reflecting a longing to visit Rome, that he was looking out of a railway carriage window at the river Tiber and the bridge Ponte Sant'Angelo: "[T]he train began to move off, and it occurred to me that I had not so much as set foot in the city" (Freud, 1900, p. 194). What the dreamer glimpsed through the carriage window was a classical Roman scene including the Dome of Saint Peter's and Castel Sant'Angelo. This was a beautiful vision indeed, so beautiful that it had been a favorite subject for many engravers and photographers of the day. Freud notices this in commenting on his memory-dream: "The view that I had seen in my dream was taken from a well-known engraving which I had caught sight of for a moment the day before in the sitting-room of one of my patients" (1900, p. 194).

I. FREUD'S SNAPSHOTS

Carefully examining the possible engravings and other images that might have triggered Freud's dream, Mary Bergstein (2010) found that there was most likely not just one but an array of pictures, especially for someone so captivated by all things Roman. The particular view of the river Tiber and the Ponte Sant'Angelo, for example, was taken by photographer Altobelli in 1868 and then widely reproduced as photogravure and albumen print. A number of subsequent photographers circulated variations of this image, which were often published in books about art history and travel, as well as in postcard and stereoscopic view cards; indeed, it also was a favorite among postcards sent back home by Viennese tourists. We can take this view as a case in point of how, in an age in which several new media of visual reproduction emerged, the meaning of the visual becomes more complex and ambiguous. In addition, it gains more explanatory weight. "The frequent replication and apparently seamless visual construction (carpentry) of photographic prints made their mental absorption faster and less conscious than that of a traditional work of art," writes Bergstein (2010, p. 11). While Freud, for one, conceived of his visual imagination in terms of traditional works of art like painting, drawing, and engraving, it was in fact strongly influenced by modern imagistic media such as photography that in his days had become ubiquitous, so much that it even affected ideas of mind and memory.

This becomes even more obvious in another detail of Freud's story about his Rome memory. Bergstein points out that the often-reproduced scene of the river Tiber could never have been visible in this composition from a train window, although Freud claimed to have observed it in exactly this way, presenting it as a memory within a compelling visual arrangement: "The view Freud glimpsed in the format of his dream was eminently photographic, framed and yet fleeting, a beautiful vision—a synecdoche for the whole concept of *Roma*—that slipped away with the departure of the train, leaving the dreamer both anxious and desiring" (Bergstein, 2010, pp. 12–13).

It has often been emphasized that Freud lived in the golden age of photography. Whether consciously or not, the photographic experience was one of the most distinct cultural experiences that left their mark on the expressive narrative imagery characteristic of Freud's psychological writings (Brockmeier, 1997). An essential part of the importance of photography for the cultural imaginary in the nineteenth and much of the twentieth century was its aura of authenticity. Photographs were typically viewed as documentary representations, capturing reality in a direct manner. "Photographs (including portraits and street scenes) were apprehended, like dream images, as an exquisite visual residue, as traces 'taken' from the continuum of live experience," as Bernstein (2010, p. 15) notes. She draws her argument on the widely accepted nature of photography in the West in this epoch as a testimony of "incontrovertible visual truth" against which fantasy and interpretation could be checked and measured, to the degree that "photographic images could be received as involuntary memory images, or memories" (Bergstein, 2010, p. 15). Memories, by the same token, were received as authentic visual imprints of past experiences, unmediated "snapshots" of the past. Not only this was the understanding of personal memories in Freud's psychoanalytical theory, it has also been the dominant understanding of memories in the memory sciences as well as in autobiographical literature and everyday discourse. Only very recently has this visual and archival view of personal or autobiographical memories been challenged.

Freud's dream-memory is particularly interesting in view of what I call the strong notion of the visual. This notion lays claim to a special explanatory power of the visual, indeed to its superior authority of authenticity and truth. It underlies many epistemological and cultural Western traditions, including the two just mentioned: the traditional psychological idea of autobiographical (or episodic) memories, of which Freudian psychoanalysis is one example, and the assumption of imagistic authenticity that has shaped the documentary understanding of photography and which I used as the backdrop to Freud's interpretation of his own Rome vision. The strong notion of the visual replies to the question of why a picture, as the proverb states, is worth a thousand words. The answer is, because a picture can present an immediate view of reality, unspoiled as it is from the vagaries and vagueness of language and its entanglements in interpretation. In a word, because an image is the truth, or at least it is closer to the truth than, say, a story.

The documentary understanding of pictures is part and parcel of photography as a modern cultural system to which Bergstein (2010) draws attention. I want, however, to take a look at something different, namely, the role of the strong notion of the visual in our cultural understanding of memories and remembering and, more in general, of understanding and knowing. In particular, I am interested in the reference to the visual that is inherent to countless ancient, premodern, and modern accounts of autobiographical memories—from everyday life to scientific and scholarly contexts. Often this reference comes with a shift in both the narrative and the conceptual structure of the account, a shift from reason to cause. Mostly this shift goes unnoticed; in many memory stories like Freud's there is a continuum from *giving a reason* that makes me believe or even be sure that this memory is a true and authentic past experience of mine to the conviction that that past experience is the *cause* of my memory. What is perceived here as causal builds on the supposedly imagistic nature of autobiographical and episodic remembering, the assumption that a personal memory is all the more authentic, reliable, and truthful the more it is visually present. Yes, I remember it very well because I have it clearly and evidently before my eyes—as if I would see it now! There is no doubt, *this* is the river Tiber with the Ponte Sant'Angelo that I once saw in Rome.

Is this just another case of a reason turning underhandedly into a cause, of something that I believe motivates or influences my thinking or acting and now spuriously appears as something from which my thinking or acting or remembering is a physical consequence (which would be the traditional definition of causation)? Are we faced then with a case of those "category mistakes" that are so common in everyday language use?

I think there is more to it than just a thinking (or speaking) mistake. Even if it is true that most things in the material world are the effects of causes that do not include human mental states, such a clear-cut distinction does not make much sense in the cultural worlds of human meaning making. Here causes and reasons are anything but clearly separated; certainly they are not in the myriad of stories we tell others and ourselves to make sense of ourselves and others and the rest of the world (Brockmeier, 2012). Slightly modifying an argument put forward by Donald Davidson (1963), one could say that many of the reasons given by people to explain their actions are in fact rationalizations. They rationalize an action as well as the intentions, considerations, and emotions connected and associated with it. That is, they aim to understand this action and the "rationale" behind it in light of socially plausible arguments and culturally acceptable storylines. And of course, narratives do this job very well, not least because they too can interpret the world in causal terms.

This is not to say there are no causes in the world; this would be to say there is no world. But the way we *explain* them is itself not a causal process but depends on our choice, a choice that includes a certain language, explanatory models and theories, and other cultural options and requirements that, in turn, then shape our explanation. So, if we want to, we can couch this explanation in causal terms; we even can do this in narrative form because narrative language offers, as already noted, probably the most sophisticated resources for both interpretive and explanatory reasoning. As Richard Rorty (1989, p. 6) puts the matter, the world does not speak—only we do, but "the world can, once we have programmed ourselves with a language, cause us to hold beliefs." Rorty agrees with Davidson that sheer causation is not under description, but explanation is. In other words, "when the die hits the blank something causal happens, but as many facts are brought into the world as there are languages for describing that causal transaction" (Rorty, 1991, p. 81).

It is in this hermeneutic sense that I understand Davidson's point that such interpretive rationalization is a species of ordinary causal explanation or, as I would call it, causal reasoning. Its framework, what Gadamer (1989) calls our horizon of understanding, is our cultural and narrative forms of life— which might include, as in Freud's case, things like the cultural system of photography—rather than any categorical (semantic or epistemological) logic. In the realm of human meaning making (which of course is comprised of remembering and forgetting) I find more appropriate the idea that there are as many causes as there are senses of because. This suggests an interpretive continuum overarching what was, in philosophical quarters before Gadamer and Davidson, understood as the polar opposite of cause and reason. It is hard to imagine a cultural system that can give shape to a more nuanced and fine-grained universe of senses of because than that articulated by the registers of narrative. It reaches from claims of strict causality and physical determination to vague and tentative interpretations of possible reasons one might or might not associate with an action or a thought or a memory.

II. VISUAL TRUTHS

I should make it clear that I do not consider in this short essay the basic assumption of cognitive and neuroscientific memory research that there are strictly causal brain mechanisms. These mechanisms are understood as materially carrying out the three core processes of memory, from the "encoding" of an experience or information to its "storing" and "recalling/retrieval." Instead, I focus on a different idea of "mnemonic causality"—or rationalization or narrative reasoning—one that draws on the strong notion of the visual.

Why has this notion become so influential in so many Western traditions, and why, in particular, has it had such a strong impact on our ideas of autobiographical memory and remembering? Let us recount for a moment what is at stake. Memories are notoriously unreliable and deceiving. Much memory talk, whether in everyday life, scientific memory research, or autobiographical literature, is about establishing particular memories as true and correct or as distorted and false. In fact, often when we deal with memories we are concerned with identifying whether a particular psychological or mental state is a memory at all, or rather a perception, an imagination, a dream, or a phenomenon that we have heard, read about, or seen on a photograph—like Freud. Recent neuroscientific studies have demonstrated that there is no neurobiological correlate that would allow me to determine if a certain scene on my mind is a memory, a present perception, or the imagination of a future or invented event. This has further supported the view that remembering is a constructive, imaginative, and creative process that is comprised of ongoing interpretative acts, rather than the retrieval of information preserved in a mental—or neuronal—storage. What complicates discerning the status of a mental phenomenon as a memory is that many times there is no intersubjective criterion that allows us to confirm through other persons who, perhaps, were present at an event that we might or might not remember. Moreover, memories can be contested; they can struggle for dominance in the face of alterative or competing memories from other people, for example, in arguments or in court. In all these cases, the strong notion of the visual backs up the claim to authenticity and truthfulness of a memory—oftentimes, as noted, even in terms of cause and effect. No doubt, this is a memory of the river Tiber because I clearly and evidently see it in my mind!

I want to foreground two further aspects of the cultural meaning system of the visual that help explain its far-reaching impact, which even affects our idea of "mnemonic causation." One is its capability to evoke immediacy across space and cultural difference, the other its capability to evoke the presence of phenomena over time and historical difference.

Space first. I have indicated that the strong notion of the visual is entwined with a "cultural system" of plausibility and reasoning, a concept that I use in the sense of Clifford Geertz's (1983) essay "Common sense as a cultural system." Geertz maintained that many anthropologists, in order to convince their audience of the accuracy and truthfulness of their descriptions of distant, often unknown, and never-before-seen cultural worlds, try to conjure up these worlds in their writings in the most suggestive and immediate fashion. Linguistically, they create a sense of "being there," of being a nonbiased and credible eyewitness at the scene of cultural action. The Oxford anthropologist E. E. Evans-Pritchard, instrumental in establishing the discipline of social anthropology, was a master of this trade. In examining Evans-Pritchard's style, Geertz (1988) emphasizes the "optical" and "graphic" quality of his writing, aiming at an intensely "visual representation of cultural phenomena" (p. 64). Geertz speaks of a "see-er's rhetoric" meant to present Evans-Pritchard's point of view in a quasi-documentary fashion by using specific narrative techniques that Geertz calls "ethnographical snapshots" and "anthropological transparencies" (pp. 64–67). In this way, the anthropological account assumes an exceptional imagistic quality, constituting the textual equivalent of a "magic lantern presentation" (p. 64). If we feel that we observe, indeed, take part in such an immediate manner in a ritual of witchcraft or magic among the Azande in Central Africa—the subject of Evans-Pritchard's first monograph—we cannot find the representation of the Azande (or Zande) tricksters' beliefs about causation anything but evident and reasonable. In Evans-Pritchard's studies, as some have argued, this sense of neutral "correctness" and the plausibility of the implied "sense of because" even extended to the tricksters' beliefs themselves. Viewed in the light of this magic lantern, they did not appear foreign anymore.

Why did Evans-Pritchard use this strategy of visual truth and plausibility? He wanted to demonstrate, Geertz suggests, that our established frameworks of social perception and reasoning—and here the idea of common sense as cultural system comes into play—are completely adequate and reasonable in order to understand even the oddest and most outlandish cultural phenomena. We can suspect that what Geertz identifies in this conclusion as a reason, Evans-Pritchard saw as a cause.

Turning to time, it is not difficult to refer to a great number of historical writings in which the same "see-er's rhetoric" is used to evoke a sense of immediacy and being there, regardless of how much historical time has passed. Viewed in a detailed close-up, the past ceases to be a foreign country. It hence might be more interesting in this context to consider how the strong notion of the visible affects a variation of historical time, namely, autobiographical time. The most developed genres of individuals' temporal self-localization (or self-historization) are autobiographical narratives: memoirs, autobiographies, childhood memories, and the like. Take childhood memories; there is, however, a fundamental aporia of autobiographical memory accounts that has been often discussed, especially by writers concerned with their early memories. It results from the fact that what we call childhood memories are experiences of the past that, in terms of the individual's life span, took place long ago. Yet if I speak about this memory experience in the present of an autobiographical narration, this unavoidably occurs in words from today, words that are given to that experience a long time after it originally took place. These are new words, foreign words, and they can be perceived as foiling the rememberer's intent to capture their memories as original and immediate as possible. This, the representation of one's own personal memories in their most authentic and truthful gestalt, is indeed what has propelled many modern autobiographers (e.g., Eakin, 1999), irrespective of what the contemporary study of remembering has revealed about the permanently changeable, reconstructive, and fluid nature of our memories.

Examining the childhood memories of the Italian writer Giuseppe Tomasi di Lampedusa (1896–1957), Alessandra Fasulo and I have pointed out some exemplary narrative and cognitive strategies used in autobiographical literature to face the aporia and find a path through what is perceived as the obstacles that language puts between us and our memories (Brockmeier & Fasulo, 2004). In his autobiographical writings *Ricordi d'infanzia* (childhood memories) that Lampedusa composed while working on his celebrated novel *The Leopard* (1960), he meditates extensively on this problem. His conclusion is that he has to give up trying to gain linguistic access to his early childhood memories. The words of a little boy are too "vague" and "imprecise" to genuinely capture his experiences. Even if one would be able to recall them, they would fail to represent the true richness of early memories. Instead, Lampedusa decides to focus on what he takes to be an incomparably more exact and reliable dimension of experience present and past: the space in which they occur, that is, their visual dimension. Focusing on the imagistic nature of early memories yields two advantages. It ensures a high degree of objectivity, because the adult narrator can, at least to a degree, verify the places in which the child experienced his world, and it offers a pre- or nonlinguistic access to the past. In this way, weakness turns into strength: "The mind [of the child] kept a highly vivid visual impression, because in those early days it was not yet bound to any words" (Tomasi di Lampedusa, 1993, p. 78; all translations by J. B.).

What, according to Lampedusa, is reconstructed in this manner is the perspective of the child who absorbs the events of his environment through his eyes and localizes himself through his sense of space, both being prelinguistic modalities. Consider the scene when Lampedusa's family—Sicilian aristocrats—learn about the assassination of the Italian King Umberto, on July 29, 1900. The three-and-a-half-year-old sits on the floor when his father bursts in to announce the news. "It was late morning, about 2 o'clock, I believe, and I see the strong light of the summer that came in from the window which was a French window, wide open, whereas the shutters where closed" (Lampedusa, 1993, p. 31) The writer goes on to say, "I don't remember the words nor their sense, I still 'see,' however, the effect they made: my mother dropped her silver hair brush with the long handle that she had in her hand, Teresa said, 'My God,' and the entire room was stunned ... I still 'see' the bands of light and shadow from the balcony" (Lampedusa, 1993, p. 31; quotation marks original).

Lampedusa's strategy of the glance completes various stylistic registers of spatial and perceptual organization (Brockmeier & Fasulo, 2004). The primary goal is to evoke a sense of visual immediacy, of being there. Of being where? In this case, it's a different, earlier time of one's life, one that, strictly speaking, is before language and any conscious autobiographical sense of time. Yet like many writers, Lampedusa widens the narrative spectrum of the glance to also embrace nonlinguistic—psychological and bodily—qualities such as tension, attention, and emotional arousal. What all these forms of remembering purport to skirt is the unreliable world of words, getting directly to the "real things" and, in this way, envisioning early experiences in precisely the way the little boy perceived them. The adult autobiographer, then, only gives a report of those states.

III. VIEWING, UNDERSTANDING, AND KNOWING

for the knowledge upon which we can establish a certain and indubitable judgment must be not only clear, but also distinct. I call that clear which is present and manifest to the mind giving attention to it, just as we are said clearly to see objects when, being present to the eye looking on. (Descartes, 1901/1644, I, p. 45)

It seems to be irrelevant on this account that the putatively nonlinguistic strategy of the glance is, of course, a linguistic arrangement. At stake is a text, an autobiographical story that taps into an established repertoire of narrative and stylistic techniques to conjure up "incontrovertible visual truths." This figure is, as we saw, a crucial element of the strong notion of the visual. Whether they are aware of it or not, Freud, Evans-Pritchard, and Lampedusa all draw on a close association among vision, photographic images, and involuntary memories. The underlying assumption is that all categories of imagery partake of the same sphere of authenticity and originality that, in turn, solidifies their particular claim to truth. Freud's mental snapshots through the window of a moving rail car, Evans-Pritchard's magic lantern, and Lampedusa's strategy of the glance are all attempts to rationalize an account in a way that Davidson calls ordinary causal explanation.

I noted that the explanatory reasoning that is afforded by the strong notion of the visual comprises a broad and nuanced spectrum of "senses of because" reaching from everyday life to academic discourse and literature. This enormous adaptability and malleability is one reason why, I believe, this notion has been so influential in a number of Western traditions. The Austrian psychoanalyst, the English anthropologist, and the Italian writer all used it with great ease and creatively adapted it to their reasoning. To conclude, let me mention another reason that refers to the broader historical backdrop of this notion. It results from the fact that the privileged claim of visuality is deeply rooted in our cultural life worlds, and first of all in our languages. It has often been pointed out that many words for knowing, thinking, and understanding in Indo-European languages stem from visual activities and imagistic experience, equally in new or old languages. Ancient Greek has played a particularly prominent role in this respect. Mediated through Latin, its visual and sight-related outlook upon the world shaped the philosophical, artistic, and spiritual vocabulary of knowing, experiencing, remembering, and imagining in the Western tradition from Antiquity to modern times (Konersmann, von der Lühe, & Wilson, 1995).

Of course, words are never only about words. Visuality was at the very heart of ancient Greek culture. Imagery, performance, and spectacle permeated all aspects of everyday life and thought. Literally and metaphorically, the visual sphere dominated not only arts and architecture, myth and ritual, but also courts and political events. Literature, theater, and philosophy hosted countless instances of viewing and optical experiences, continually engaging with sight-related language. As a consequence, the concern with seeing became more and more differentiated. Certain forms of seeing were associated with false perception, mere appearance, and deceptiveness. Still, seeing was the most secure means into knowledge, understanding, and wisdom, both on the sensuous level and on the intellectual and spiritual level of the soul whose forms of knowing were likewise conceived as forms of seeing.

At the same time, the interplay among viewing, understanding, knowing, and imagining was a central topic of theoretical reflection; it had a crucial place in Plato's and Aristotle's philosophizing. There is no doubt, in this cultural world the center of the mind was the mind's eye. After Aristotle had referred, in his *On Sense and the Sensible*, to a passage by the pre-Socratic philosopher Empedocles in which the eye was likened to a lantern, this passage became canonical in the entire tradition dealing with viewing and knowing. The passage said that in this lantern the primordially eternal fire is held, from where it reaches to the outside and reconnects with the daylight that moves in the opposite way. On this account, vision is a two-directional process in which the glance is linked both to the visible and to truth and timeless knowledge.

The Western philosophical tradition, it has been said, consists of a long series of footnotes to Plato. It certainly includes many footnotes to the strong notion of the visual that originated with the ancient Greek idea of a fusion of viewing, understanding, and knowing, an idea that, as I have suggested in this chapter, has affected even our modern understanding of remembering, authenticity, and causality.

REFERENCES

Bergstein, M. (2010). *Mirrors of memory: Freud, photography, and the history of art.* Ithaca, NY: Cornell University Press.

Brockmeier, J. (1997). Autobiography, narrative and the Freudian conception of life history. *Philosophy, Psychiatry, & Psychology, 4,* 175–200.

Brockmeier, J. (2012). Narrative scenarios: Toward a culturally thick notion of narrative. In *The Oxford handbook of culture and psychology* (pp. 439–467). Oxford & New York: Oxford University Press.

Brockmeier, J. (2015). *Beyond the archive: Memory, narrative, and the autobiographical Process*. Oxford & New York: Oxford University Press.

Brockmeier, J., & Fasulo, A. (2004). Spazio, tempo e ricordo. La spazializzazione della memoria nei ricordi d'infanzia di Tomasi di Lampedusa [Space, time, and remembering: The spatialization of memory in the childhood memories of Tomasi di Lampedusa]. *Rassegna di Psicologia* (Special Issue: Cultura e memoria autobiografica), *XXI*(1), 35–61.

Davidson, D. (1963). Action, reasons, and causes. *Journal of Philosophy*, 60(23), 685–700.

Descartes, R. (1901/1644). Principles of philosophy. In J. Veitch (Ed. & transl.), *The method, meditations and philosophy of Descartes*. Washington, DC & London: M. Walter Dunne Publisher.

Eakin, P. J. (1999). *How our lives become stories: Making selves*. Ithaca, NY: Cornell University Press.

Freud, S. (1900). The interpretation of dreams. In J. Strachey (ed.), *The standard edition of the complete psychological works of Sigmund Freud*, vols. 4 and 5 (pp. 1–626). London: Hogarth Press.

Gadamer, H. G. (1989). *Truth and method*, 2nd rev. ed. New York: Crossroad (original work 1960).

Geertz, C. (1983). Common sense as a cultural system. In G. Geertz (ed.), *Local knowledge: Further essays in interpretive anthropology* (pp. 73–93). New York: Basic Books.

Geertz, C. (1988). *Works and lives: The anthropologist as author*. Stanford, CA: Stanford University Press.

Konersmann, R., von der Lühe, A., & Wilson, W. (1995). Sehen [Viewing]. *Historisches Wörterbuch der Philosophie* [Historical dictionary of philosophical concepts], vol. 9 (pp. 121–161). Basel, Switzerland: Schwabe.

Rorty, R. (1989). *Contingency, irony, and solidarity*. Cambridge & New York: Cambridge University Press.

Rorty, R. (1991). *Objectivity, relativism, and truth, Vol. 1: Philosophical papers*. Cambridge & New York: Cambridge University Press.

Tomasi di Lampedusa, G. (1993). *I racconti*. Milano, Italy: Feltrinelli.

Part Four

. . . .

Causal Concepts and Medical Contexts

11

The Notion of Cause in Biomedicine

John Grimley Evans

A fundamental property of living organisms is adaptability; without the ability to recognize and to avoid or deal with noxious threats from the environment, an organism would not continue to live and, more important, reproduce. The nervous systems of the higher animals have therefore evolved in ways that subserve the dual functions of finding food and avoiding being food. Sense organs and their associated neural networks have adapted to recognize patterns in space and in time that support these two life priorities. In particular, perception of, and reaction to, temporal patterns depend on memory; the biological significance of memory lies not in recalling past times but in predicting what is likely to happen next.

The astonishing biological success of *Homo sapiens* is to a significant degree due to its ability to deduce how the world works and so change and manipulate it. Identification of causal relationships is an important element in this aim, and closely relevant to this is some capacity to assess probability. Behavior that embodies a response to probability is not specifically human and does not necessarily require consciousness. Neural networks typically become habituated to repeated stimuli unassociated with hazard or reward. Probability plays a part in Pavlovian conditioning; the extinction of inconsistently reinforced conditioning in rats takes more repetitions than that of the consistently reinforced. *H. sapiens* is not innately a good estimator of probability, as research into gambling reveals, but most individuals readily apprehend a polarity between a situation in which B always and only follows A and that in which A and B occur independently. Basic human reasoning is liable to infer causality in the first case, though not always correctly. If, within living memory, the winter solstice has always and only become apparent on the morning a virgin is sacrificed, farming folk will not want to risk stinting on virgins. In such situations, causation arises as an issue only if a plausible alternative hypothesis for the A-to-B sequence is generated. Empirical science depends on the formulation of such alternative hypotheses and a comparison of their predictive powers. Comparison is preferably made by experiment but otherwise by systematic observation of the consequences of natural variation (what happens, for example, to the winter solstice in a year when there are no virgins available?).

More often in the world of biomedicine—and in life generally—the relationship between A and B is modulated by other influences. Even if A is necessary for B to happen, B may not always follow A if other necessary conditions are wanting. B may happen for other reasons not involving A. Complete understanding requires elucidation of the mechanism of causation, but it is bad science to exclude causality on the ground that a mechanism cannot, at present, be identified. In the context of evolution by natural selection, it is also bad science to reject causality because the reason why it should have evolved, that A should cause B, cannot, at present, be identified. In the practical world it may be impossible or too expensive to establish a causative relationship by experiment; if a postulated cause calls for a decision, a choice may have to be made that is appropriate to risk and benefit, essentially the relative nett costs of Type 1 and Type 2 errors. (In this context Type 1 is concluding that a hypothesis is correct when it is not; Type 2 is concluding it to be wrong when it is right.)

I. THOUGHT AND WORDS

For more than two millennia, philosophers have been intermittently concerned with the notion of causation, its nature, its mechanisms, how it is apperceived, and how it can be identified. Specific concerns have included criteria such as contiguity, directionality, and simultaneity. Contiguity and simultaneity can now be subsumed and reconceptualized in the context of a view of causation as involving transmission of information and transformation of energy. There is also no modern revulsion from the notion of action at an apparent distance, and in the biological realm, a time delay between a cause and its significant effect is common. There have been concerns that chemical equations are on paper reversible and so cause and effect are in principle interchangeable. Current thinking seems to have assimilated the Second Law of Thermodynamics and the concept of entropy to the degree that we are happy in an empirical acceptance of directionality in time. However, as discussed later, even without any implied option of reversibility, directionality remains an issue in the perception, if not the nature, of causation in biomedicine.

As in all matters that have intrigued philosophers, especially those, like causation, that involve an element of reification, problems of language intrude. Russell (1913) pleaded for the word "cause" to be extruded from the philosophical vocabulary for being "so inextricably bound up with misleading associations." He pointed out that in the "gravitational astronomy" of his day, the word did not occur, and he seems to have envisaged the possibility of science as an all-embracing system of predictive equations. The biological world has a complexity that precludes such an ideal except possibly at a molecular level. Moreover, as a product of incomplete knowledge, and possibly because of the ultimate nature of things, predictive equations in biomedicine have to be created in probabilistic terms.

Scientists are semantically privileged in being at liberty to create and use words to suit the insulated needs of their fields of study. Definitions need to be precise, consistently used, and heuristic, but correspondence with the use of the same or similar words in other contexts is of lower priority. Physicists do not worry that "charm," "strange," or "spin" may to the common mind imply properties that quarks are not being claimed to possess. In its choice of terminology, biomedicine has a duty to be less rarified than physics because its scientific mission embodies an aim to improve the human condition, and ultimately this has to be done through human communication. Biomedical scientists therefore have to be aware of the range of ambiguities that their use of language can excite. "Cause" as a verb or noun is much used both in biomedicine and in "ordinary" language. There are some systematic differences: scientists are likely to speak of "a cause" and be misinterpreted as talking about "the cause." In the language of politics and the media, "cause" can also be deployed in implications of responsibility or culpability. A well-known example of the divergence of medical and legal thinking arose in the thalidomide case. The manufacturers sought to avoid blame for the increase in the numbers of babies born with limb deformities to mothers who had taken thalidomide in early pregnancy. The defense urged that the drug did not "cause" the deformities but facilitated the survival of deformed fetuses that would otherwise have spontaneously aborted. This ingenious casuistry conceded the issue of causation; the debate was over the mechanism and hence the culpability to be attached. Culpability is not a concern proper to science, but legal and moral implications of causation can ensnare an innocent medical commentator.

II. INFORMATION AND ENERGY

Some coinings in science have been less happy than others. The concept of "information," as created in cybernetics but now universal in science, is particularly provocative to nonscientists, especially to philosophers tilting at neuroscientific windmills. In the empirical world the transfer of information is an integral component in causation, and much of the study of mechanisms in disease involves identifying the transmitters and detectors of information and the code of their communication. Transfer or release of energy is required to generate, or predispose to, a physical effect. In the traditional model, a stationary billiard ball hit by a moving one moves off at a speed and in a direction determined by the transmission of energy and information contained in the vector of velocity and direction of the moving ball. The principle of the Conservation of Energy predicts that some energy will be dissipated in the audible click of the encounter and in heat generated by the impact and the friction with the tablecloth, while some remains in the continued modified motion of the impinging ball. This model is insufficient to specify the consequence of the impact.

The consequence of a billiard ball striking another will differ from that of a billiard ball striking an egg or a vial of nitroglycerine; the latter contribute their own information and energy in determining the cascade of consequences of the encounter. Cascade and fan-out, characteristic phenomena of complex systems, are common features of causal interactions in living organisms.

III. ETIOLOGY AND PATHOGENESIS

Biomedicine has its raison d'être in disease, and has traditionally divided the focus of its attention between etiology (causes) and pathogenesis (mechanisms). Both are subsumable under "cause," and conventionally were valued for distinguishing thought about "why" things happen from "how" they happen. Since the distinction was originally made, the "why" question in biomedicine has split into two. One relates, as originally, to direct causation, the other to the evolutionary background of both cause and mechanism. Lack of vitamin C is the cause of the identifiable metabolic mechanisms (including impaired synthesis of collagen) that produce scurvy, but why cannot *H. sapiens* produce its own vitamin C? Almost certainly its ancestors could.

Pathogenetic mechanisms relate directly to information and energy. In the biological world, information is contained in such forms as the shape of folded protein molecules or the presence of specific chemical groupings, and energy can be transmitted in charged particles or changes in molecular structure. In some biological instances, energy is called from latency in molecules by a change in the ionic environment and the "flipping" of one molecular configuration to one of lower energy. Energy is more remotely involved in such transactions in providing for the motion that brings about the juxtaposition of the interacting molecules. A common motif in living material is the separation by a membrane of chemicals that would interact if in contact. Neuronal activity involves transmutation of the information of a chemical stimulus into an electrical change allowing the passage of ions down a concentration gradient across the cell membrane. Energy is then needed to pump the ions back out of the cell to be stored in the reestablishment of the gradient. The electrical change is conducted along the neuronal fibers to be transmuted back into chemical information for transmission to another cell. Pores in cell membranes open when the complex molecules occluding them reconfigure through contact with a messenger molecule bearing a relevant identification "tag." Passage of a chemical through the pore, especially if against a concentration gradient, may require energy and linkage to a carrier molecule to provide the necessary configuration and polarity. "Flipping" of unstable configurations may also be produced by the passive juxtaposition of a "template." Such a process is thought to underlie the generation of nonfunctional or toxic proteins in a brain infected by prion molecules. This proposed mechanism for disease requires that the modified proteins do not exhibit the information that they are abnormal or are otherwise immune to the body's normal mechanisms for removal of "junk."

IV. A QUANTAL WORLD?

Empirical sciences define their own boundaries, which widen to maintain coherence as knowledge increases. Biomedicine's frontier with physics is open but filtered. As empirical scientists, workers in biomedicine can factor gravity into their equations, their thinking, and their daily lives without worrying about the Higgs boson. Until something unpredictable happens, they can treat the laws of nature as a sufficient explanation of why rather than merely how things happen in a particular way or sequence. Empirical science lives therefore mostly in a Newtonian world, and biomedicine in particular rarely has to venture below the molecular level. This will change if fundamental biological processes are discovered at the quantal level. Penrose (1989) has speculated that quantal processes may play a part in the mechanisms of the human brain that are important in the generation of human (self-)consciousness. If this proves to be correct, there will be profound consequences for the development of medical science and for philosophy.

V. TELEOLOGY

Darwin's recognition (it is high time for the word "theory" to be dropped in this context) that the history of life on earth has involved evolution by natural selection leaves no place in biological ontogeny for purpose or foreknowledge (i.e., forecoding) of consequence as a cause. Evolution has no aim or direction; it is opportunist and feeds on the random. Human immune genes have not developed in order to counter invading organisms; the genes arose by chance but their possessors survive and pass them on. The same, of course, has to be said for the genes that permit perception of causation.

The contribution of purpose and goal seeking to causation of animal behavior is less clear, and pre-Darwinian verbal habits commonly persist in common speech with misleadingly teleological implications. An insect does not hide to avoid being eaten, something of which it has had no experience; it hides because hiding behavior allowed its ancestors to live long enough to breed. Purposeful behavior requires some form of pre-coding of the target situation. Some complex serial patterns of behavior that seem to seek—that is, are terminated by the appearance of—a particular situation can in insects be a Markov chain of "hard-wired" segments. Much of the behavior of birds is similarly nonpurposive although some species are documented as showing goal seeking in devising and using tools to get at visible but inaccessible food. But here the target is not a retained pre-coding, it is visible. Operant conditioning whereby rats can learn to pull levers to gain food or other rewards can give a more suggestive appearance of memory-mediated goal-seeking behavior, but is explicable in other ways not involving pre-coding of outcomes. *H. sapiens* may have to a unique degree an ability, beyond the limitations of experience or mimicry, to use the observed or described knowledge of others as determinants of behavior in the form of pre-coded goals.

There is obvious survival value in recognition of danger or in perception of benefit from situations previously unencountered.

It is impossible to avoid the topic of (self-)consciousness in the context of human goal-seeking behavior. It would be perverse not to acknowledge awareness in the pre-coding of a desirable but currently absent state as an intermediary in the behavior that an individual undertakes to attain that state. The vexatious notion of "free will" lingers on with its theological encumbrances in discussion of the causes of human behavior. The biomedical hypothesis (not assertion) has to be that "will" as observed and experienced, and whether "free" or not, is the result of neural events and therefore not primary in any causal sequence. This hypothesis is compatible with scientific epistemology in that it is comprehensive, compatible, and the most parsimonious, and in being falsifiable but not yet falsified. It is parsimonious in avoiding any implication of a cause of human behavior that is ontologically distinct from physical processes. It is comprehensive in embracing what needs to be explained, and compatible in that it does not negate anything that is known. It would be falsified by consistent demonstration of relevant mentative activity occurring without physical substrate. Ultimately, however, the issue may be settled only by the human-made creation of a conscious entity.

We are nowhere near this. Current neuroscience is answering questions different from those being asked by philosophers. Scruton (2014) has forged a form of cognitive dualism on the basis of such reciprocal misunderstanding. But neuroscientists and introspectionists are not discussing different things; they are talking about different aspects of the function of a single thing, the human brain. We do not understand how neural activity produces the "self-ness" that we all (presumably) experience, and possibly it may prove ultimately to be beyond human apperception in being literally unimaginable. Both neuroscientists and philosophers are unhelpful in sometimes talking as if the problem were resolvable in the present state of knowledge. Our present understanding of the relevant neural processes is far more rudimentary than claimed by some enthusiasts. Analogy with current computers is of limited utility and may in time prove to have been a distraction. Neurons are not transistors and, at a level above that of the single cell, the digital/analog dichotomy is less clear-cut in the neural than in the electronic world. It is true that a neuron behaves in a digital fashion by firing or not firing, but the probability of its firing is graded by its various inputs, and the effect of its output is commonly merged into a collective of a variable number of other cells. The preemptive distinction between the "mind" of a human and the "model of a mind" in a machine is a scholastic quibble. The main concern for scientific propriety is not to put ghosts into our self-machines unless we have to.

At a more banausic level, there is some utility in the computer analogy of brain function for practical medicine. Cause and remedy for undesirable behavior or mood are sought in the hardware and the software of the brain, the traditional polarity drawn between, respectively, psychosis and neurosis. The brain is part of the complex machinery of the body and not a freestanding entity. Hardware malfunction may come about due to chemical effects originating elsewhere in the body as in the delirium produced by toxic material entering the blood from an infected wound. More subtly, a depressive state may result when the brain's perception of a social situation leads to hormonal changes that affect, among other bodily functions, brain activity. Even when some brain malfunctioning, in delirium and dementia for example, is due primarily to hardware problems, the behavior of an afflicted person is determined in part by the present environment being misinterpreted by the programming of memories of past experiences. A schizophrenic illness may involve secondary rationalization of primary delusions—software modifications in response to a hardware malfunction. Similar relationships can be perceived in the genesis of depressive illnesses. Drugs can be used to modify the working of the hardware by facilitating or inhibiting the activity of some classes of neurons relative to others. Software modification requires reprogramming in some form of learning. Rational therapy would seek both hardware and software intervention, and there is evidence that a combination of drugs with cognitive behavioral therapy can be more effective than drugs alone for the treatment of depression (Wiles et al., 2013). Drugs as hardware modifiers are liable to be overused as a "quick fix" thought more cost-effective than attempts at re-programming. Sadly, medication, especially sedative in nature, can also be chosen to reduce inconvenience to others rather than to ease the distress of the patient. Respecting the brain as a computer may lead to more compassionate care.

VI. DISEASE

The starting point for biomedicine was, and is, disease. The primary species of interest was *H. sapiens*, but concern spread early to its farmed and other associated animals, and to plants of value to nutrition or the environment. There is no universal definition of disease, and in the biosphere, one creature's disease may be another's lifestyle. In *H. sapiens* the concept of disease and its definition has changed with scientific discovery and under sociopolitical influences. In practical terms in the modern Western world, disease is anything considered undesirable and for which amelioration is thought to be possible and is seen as, or decreed to be, a medical responsibility. The implications of "responsibility" provide for some fluid, disputed, and politically sensitive boundaries with other professions and social agencies, particularly where undesirable behavior is a focus of concern. Psychopathy, homosexuality, attention-deficit disorder, and senile dementia are among the entities that in recent years have moved one way or the other across the border between "disease" and merely "variant." The distinctions can be more expedient than rational; in some countries it is better to be defined as mad rather than dissident or criminal, unless it leads to lobotomy.

There has been a historical progression in the theory of disease that has contributed to the present lack of a single unifying concept. The early centuries of biomedicine were occupied with what Lord Rutherford is reputed to have called "stamp collecting" as distinguished from the "real science" of physics. But all science has to begin with the accumulation of observations; only when a collection has been made can the scanning for resemblances and patterns lead to the inductive hypotheses that provide material for the real work of observational and experimental testing.

In the absence of effective therapy, an early concern of medicine was to predict the natural history of an illness. Apart from practicalities such as the making of wills and arrangements for family survivors, it was helpful to be able to recognize the first few cases of an epidemic. The earliest basis for labeling (biomedical stamp collecting) was the recognition of a syndrome, the running together of particular symptoms and signs, perhaps including environmental or lifestyle factors. Early terms tended to be descriptive—"blackwater fever" (fever with dark urine), "whooping cough" (cough with a characteristic sound), and diabetes mellitus (much sweet-tasting urine). Vanity and ambition of doctors as well as convenience later led to a historical phase of preference for eponyms such as "Parkinson's disease" or "Huntington's chorea."

With increasing use of autopsy and microscopic examination of tissues, biomedical science came to look more to pathological findings to create concepts and definitions of diseases. Thus, "apoplexy" became subdivided by autopsy findings into the leaking of brain arteries (cerebral hemorrhage) and obstruction of blood flow through brain arteries (cerebral thrombosis). Through the nineteenth century, bacteriology developed rapidly and with it the recognition that some diseases, particularly epidemic diseases, were caused by a "contagium vivum." For these diseases the responsible organism became the defining feature, the necessary cause. Early enthusiasm called for criteria to be agreed for proving that an organism found associated with an instance of disease was indeed the cause. Robert Koch (1884) proposed four such criteria, of which the first was that the suspect bacterium must be found in abundance in all organisms suffering from the disease, but should not be found in healthy organisms. This quickly lost its universality with the important discovery that some asymptomatic people were carriers of cholera or typhoid bacilli. Thus, it became accepted that in a disease defined by being the consequence of a necessary cause, that cause might not be a sufficient cause. By the end of the nineteenth century the general "seed and ground" model of disease became widely accepted in its recognition that whether the necessary seed of a disease produced its characteristic syndrome depended not just on the infecting organism but also on the susceptibility of the individual. From the later nineteenth century, attacks on the "ground" for disease were mounted through the various aspects of public health including sanitation, better housing, education, and vaccination. By the middle of the twentieth century the discovery of sulfonamides and antibiotics, coupled with programs for isolation and quarantine and means for controlling disease vectors such as mosquitoes, offered control of the "seeds"—the necessary causes of infectious diseases—by prevention and treatment. A classical evolutionary "arms race" has resulted as bacteria develop resistance to antibiotics, and viruses bypass acquired immunity by mutation or hide in animal reservoirs.

Medical science also concerned itself with diseases due to specific agents other than bacteria and viruses (and later rickettsia and prions). The responsibilities of empire led to the recognition and study of tropical parasitic diseases. Concern for the productivity of industry and its workforce identified dangerous chemicals such as beta-naphthylamine as a cause of bladder cancer in the rubber industry. Silicosis, asbestosis, and other industrial dust diseases were recognized and brought under control. Tobacco smoking was identified as a cause of lung disease in Germany in the 1930s—though the finding was lost sight of following the chaos of the 1939–1945 war (Proctor, 1999)—and urban air pollution was established as a cause of bronchitis in Britain in the 1950s.

In the later twentieth century, the emphasis of medical activity shifted toward the noninfectious and chronic illnesses and a new conceptual framework for causation of disease emerged. One driver of the conceptual shift was failure to identify single necessary agents in the etiology of diseases such as coronary heart disease and most cancers. There were also social, economic, and political pressures in the developed world calling for health care to be integrated into a broader conception of well-being. Public health became broadened in conception from its original focus on the control of epidemics, the productivity of workers, and the fitness of armies, to the well-being of the general population. Disease prevention became integrated into medical science and teaching. Broadened into the wider settings of disease control or management, prevention became generalized into primary, preventing the onset of the target disease; secondary, preventing the recurrence of the disease in an individual; and tertiary, dealing with the consequences of the disease. Medical concern also widened beyond the individual patient to include his or her family, and even society at large.

Most modern chronic disorders, although diagnosable by symptoms, signs, and investigations, are defined fundamentally in terms of linked pathology and syndrome. Coronary heart disease received much research attention in the second half of the twentieth century and has furnished something of a paradigm for chronic diseases of public health significance. One important finding was that several syndromes—angina pectoris, myocardial infarction, sudden death—were all associated with the same defining pathology, partial or total obstruction of one or more of the arteries supplying blood to the heart muscle. Many environmental, lifestyle, and biochemical factors were found to be associated with these various syndromes. The pathology, in fact, represents a final common pathway from a range of different and interacting antecedent conditions. Hence was born the multifactorial model of disease in which there is no single or necessary cause. Causes and mechanism in the traditional vocabulary lose conceptual utility in becoming subsumed into a nexus of facilitatory and inhibitory interactions. Mathematical modeling showed the limitations of early linear and additive ideas of causation in that the various factors generally interact with each other multiplicatively.

At each interaction in the causal nexus there will be "random effects" in the sense that although the interaction leads to the expected consequence on average, sometimes the unexpected occurs. There are problems in the use of the term "random" in this context. The use of the word ranges from the mathematical purity of an implication of spontaneous and unpredictable chance events to the idea that "random" refers merely to the operation of laws of which the observer is ignorant. "Random" effects can also occur from errors, some unavoidable in the methods used, in observation or measurement. Medical statisticians may be content to treat the contingency in causal chains as mathematical randomness, while medical scientists, in a perhaps atavistic aspiration to ultimate determinism, seek to identify the sources of variance in explicable and potentiality modifiable processes. Be that as it may, the modern disease model is fundamentally probabilistic, and this is likely to prove to match a broader biological reality rather than being a temporary approximation awaiting more and better data.

VII. EPIDEMIOLOGY OF MULTIFACTORIAL DISEASE

The identification of the multifactorial nature of disease is an achievement of the science of epidemiology. Here the underlying concept, appropriate to acute or chronic disease, is of the interaction between extrinsic factors (in environment and lifestyle) and intrinsic (genetic) factors in the potential sufferer. An organism's genotype (DNA) does not necessarily predict its form (phenotype); how genes manifest depends to a greater or lesser degree on the environment and lifestyle of the individual organisms carrying them. Most individuals of *H. sapiens* carry genes that can lead to the deposition of body fat, but people do not become obese as long as energy expenditure matches food intake. In recent decades, epigenetic control of gene expression has provided a newly studied dimension to biomedical causation. A gene may be present in a cell but is not necessarily active as it can be switched on or off by the presence of specific molecules, methyl radicals for example, attached to the DNA strand nearby. Switching may occur during embryonic development as stem cells differentiate into forms specific for particular tissues or organs. Switching will also occur in response to the varying metabolic needs of an organism during processes such as growth, healing, or reproduction.

It now seems that genetic switches can be set early in life that permanently affect the metabolic pattern of an individual organism. Some form of chemical message produced by an adverse factor in a pregnant woman's environment— poverty or undernutrition—for example, can affect the genetic repertoire of the fetus in ways that influence lifelong susceptibility to diseases such as coronary heart disease and diabetes (Barker, 1995). It is to be suspected that some at least of such switches gave survival value in the past history of *H. sapiens*. The ability to save excess calories in the form of body fat would be of value in populations exposed to recurrent famine, even though in modern societies the same ability predisposes to type 2 diabetes (Neel, 1962). The chemical messages that bridge the category gap between such states as poverty and DNA methylation are as yet obscure but not implausible. Some may be mediated by inadequacies in the placentas of deprived mothers, but other possibilities are more intriguing. Marmot (2004) has accumulated evidence that a state of social subordination in human individuals produces low-grade but persistent hormonal changes that are analogous to those occurring in dominance-submission relationships in baboons. Epigenetic configurations are inheritable and there are alarming politicoethical implications in transgenerational transmission of the consequences of social disadvantage.

These findings exemplify "causes" that may precede their significant effects by half a century or more. There are many other instances of temporal separation of cause and effect in biomedicine; the time between asbestos exposure and its consequent mesothelioma is commonly measurable in decades. Time may be necessary for the accumulation of a sufficient "dose" of a causative agent. Radiation and some toxic chemicals provide examples. The genesis of cancer is thought to be a multistage process requiring the accumulation of a series of possibly independent changes in an affected cell. Such mechanisms explain why most cancers increase in incidence with age. One has to live long enough to die from them.

VIII. CORRELATION AND CAUSE

Elucidation of the causative nexus underlying a multifactorial disease such as coronary heart disease usually begins with a correlation being found between a measurable element in lifestyle or environment and the disease of interest. Here, the ancient concern with directionality in causation reemerges but in modified form. Commoner than the simple question of whether environmental factor A precedes or succeeds disease B in a causal sequence is the possibility that A and B are not themselves in a direct causal relationship at all but are cognate phenomena, correlated because they share causes, possibly remote in time. As a further possibility, A and B may share noncausal relationships with so-called "confounding variables." Age and sex are the most notorious examples of confounding variables, and every analysis of possible etiology begins in statistically "partialing out" their contribution to the pattern of association. The long-observed higher rate of lung cancer in men was not due to hormones but to the fact that more men than women smoked. The place of age in medical thinking has always been ambiguous. Age is a number determined by a date on a birth certificate and cannot logically be a cause of anything except social discrimination. The fact that many diseases become more common with age merely indicates that there are time-dependent processes in the extrinsic or intrinsic factors that determine disease. Time-dependent processes might include accumulation of an environmental chemical toxin, cumulative risk of genetic mutation due to cell division errors, or cumulative radiation damage due to cosmic ray bombardment. Age-associated diseases are caused like any other diseases, but not by age.

Table 11.1 Bradford Hill's Criteria for Causality

Strength	Consistency	Specificity	Temporality
Biological gradient (dose-response relationship)	Plausibility		
Coherence	Analogy	Experiment	

Bradford Hill (1965) was one of the first to attempt defining criteria for deciding whether a correlation between an extrinsic factor and a disease was likely to causative rather than due to confounding. The distinction is important since experimental validation may be impossible and removing the factor might be expensive and, especially if commercial interests are affected, controversial. A version of Hill's criteria are listed in Table 11.1.

The *strength* of an association between a consequence and an antecedent is commonly represented in some form of risk ratio, essentially the probability of Y when preceded by X divided by the probability of Y in the absence of X. As indicated earlier, a frequent methodological problem is that of "extraneous variables" that are linked with both X and Y but are of no etiological relevance.

Bross (1966) explored the levels of ratios to be expected of an extraneous variable and found that its association with the variables of interest have to be very high if they are to match the risk ratios produced by truly causative relationships. However, very high-risk ratios, as found, for example for lung cancer and smoking, are rare and a risk ratio has to be judged in terms of both its statistical and public health significance. Thus, it might be prudent to implement a low-cost public health program for a common and serious disease at a lower risk ratio than shown by a less common and serious disease requiring an expensive program. As Bross also pointed out, the relevant language (that is to say the thinking) has to be stochastic (i.e., probabilistic) rather than causal.

Consistency of findings in multiple and independent observations is suggestive of a causative relationship and forms the rationale for the meta-analyses of enthusiasts of the so-called evidence-based medicine movement. Unfortunately many series of observations that are susceptible for meta-analysis, although independent, are similar in form and so at risk of similar forms of bias. Meta-analysis can therefore consolidate the evidence for fallacy and should not be allowed to displace other forms of critical analysis.

The criterion of *temporality* requires the putative cause to be demonstrably antecedent to the consequence. However, irrelevant factors can also precede.

The criterion of a *biological gradient* is often analogized to the concept of a dose-response relationship shown in a pharmacological experiment that higher doses of a drug produce commensurately greater effects. If demonstrable, it can provide quite strong supportive evidence for causation. A frequent problem lies in quantifying the actual dose levels of a possibly causative agent.

Individuals' reports of their consumption of cigarettes and alcohol are notoriously unreliable, and the exposure of individuals in a community or workplace to an environmental toxin may vary with lifestyle. Unrecognized interacting factors can also attenuate biological gradients; concurrent smoking may affect susceptibility to industrial dust disease.

The assessment of the *plausibility* of a hypothesized causative relationship requires judgment. Plausibility is high, for example, if a physiological mechanism for the relationship is known to exist. A relationship should not, however, be dismissed if no mechanism is known; one may be discovered later, especially if looked for. Plausibility can also be biological; it is plausible that abnormal behavior might result from adaptation to previous psychological trauma. Logic requires that the plausibility cited as supporting a causative hypothesis is not the same plausibility that led to the hypothesis being formulated in the first place.

Coherence with other forms of evidence, for example with experimental animal studies, can be supportive. It should not be regarded as crucial or it might weigh against new discoveries.

Analogy can rarely carry much weight evidentially but can contribute in directing search for etiological factors. Cough and wheeze experienced by workers on Mondays that persist through the week but then eases over Saturday and Sunday is clearly analogous to one of the industrial dust diseases such as bagassosis.

Experiment underpins the fundamental epistemology of empirical science. Experiments can be performed involving individual participants in groups or by repetitive intervention in a single individual in an "*n* of 1" design (Price & Grimley Evans, 2002). Rarely can an experiment be carried out with adequate control groups at a population level. Powerful evidence can be obtained by an intervention that affects some members of the population more than others. Following the Royal College of Physicians' (1962) report on smoking and lung cancer, a higher proportion of doctors gave up smoking than did other British men and showed a correspondingly more rapid reduction in subsequent lung cancer rates.

IX. THE END OF CAUSATION IN MEDICINE?

As noted above, Bross (1966) expressed explicitly a growing awareness of the diminished utility of the concept of "cause" in the evaluation of multifactorial disease. He made a plea for abandoning "causal" in favor of "stochastic" language for dealing with the emerging science of chronic disease. What is relevant is the degree of risk associated with a factor not whether the risk if conveyed by direct cause or by a facilitatory effect on some other causal sequences. The relevant epidemiological measure of such a possible composite influence is the "population attributable risk," an estimate of the proportion by which the incidence of a disease might fall if the factor were removed. The measure applies to the population not necessarily to an individual; some nonsmokers get lung cancer.

Bioscience is empirical, and whatever the statistics, the ultimate criterion has to lie in experiment, or where that is impossible, in a critical evaluation of spontaneous or induced change in the factor of interest. The fall in lung cancer deaths in male doctors following the publication of the famous report of the Royal College of Physicians (1962) dealt with the notion raised by tobacco companies that lung cancer is not due to smoking but due to genetic factors that also predispose to smoking. There probably are both genetic and experiential factors that predispose to smoking and it is now generally accepted in epidemiology that attributable risk embraces contributory and interacting influences. But it does imply that reducing the risk variable would reduce the target disease. The problem, as already noted, is that a randomized controlled trial may be impossible and policy-makers have to act on evidence that is scientifically incomplete. When social policy is affected, other things may be happening at the same time so that the evidence may be doomed to be incomplete forever. This needs to be faced; it may be true, as the tobacco industry claims, that "mere statistics" (observational statistics that is) "cannot prove a causal relationship." But empirical science never "proves" anything. It generates a hypothesis and the burden of "proof" is to show it false. All that can be done is to discourage tobacco smoking and watch the incidence of lung cancer fall. The relationships between the various chemical components of tobacco smoke and cellular changes predisposing to malignant change are possible mechanisms to be explored in the laboratory. The question of whether smoking "causes" lung cancer or merely facilitates the causative action of other factors becomes otiose or, in the mouths of lawyers and tobacco companies, an obstruction to necessary action.

As Russell (1913) noted, careless talk of "cause" can be "inextricably bound up with misleading associations." He was right for medicine as well as philosophy. Unfortunately the less tendentious "is associated with an increase in the probability of" is somewhat cumbersome.

REFERENCES

Barker, D. J. P. (1995). Fetal origins of coronary heart disease. *British Medical Journal 311*, 171–174.

Bross, I. D. J. (1966). Spurious effects from an extraneous variable. *Journal of Chronic Diseases 19*, 637–647.

Doll, R., & Hill, A. B. (November 1956). Lung cancer and other causes of death in relation to smoking; a second report on the mortality of British doctors. *British Medical Journal 2*, 1071–1081.

Greenland, S., & Robins, J. M. (1988). Conceptual problems in the definition and interpretation of attributable fractions. *American Journal of Epidemiology 128*, 1185–1197.

Hill, Austin Bradford. (1965). The environment and disease: Association or causation? *Proceedings of the Royal Society of Medicine 58*, 295–300.

Koch, R. (1884). Die Aetiologie der Tuberkulose. *Mittheilungen aus dem kaiserlichen Gesundheitsamte 2*, 1–88.

Marmot, M. G. (2004). *The status syndrome: How social standing affects our health and longevity*. London. Bloomsbury Publishing Plc.

Neel, J. V. (1962). Diabetes mellitus a "thrifty" genotype rendered detrimental by "progress." *American Journal of Human Genetics 14*, 353–362.

Penrose, R. (1989) *The Emperor's new mind*. Oxford: Oxford University Press.

Price, J. D., & Grimley Evans, J. (2002). N-of-1 randomized controlled trials ('N-of-1'): Singularly useful in geriatric medicine. *Age and Ageing 31*, 227–232.

Proctor, R. N. (Date). *The Nazi war on cancer*. Princeton: Princeton University Press.

Royal College of Physicians. (1962). *Smoking and health*. London: Royal College of Physicians.

Russell, B. (1913). On the notion of cause. *Proceedings of the Aristoteleian Society 13* (new series), 1–26.

Scruton, R. (2014). *The soul of the world*. Princeton: Princeton University Press.

Wiles, N., Thomas, L., Abel, A., et al. (2013). Cognitive behavioural therapy as an adjunct to pharmacotherapy for primary care based patients with treatment resistant depression: results of the CoBalT randomised controlled trial. *Lancet 381*, 375–384.

EDITORS' COMMENTARY

The most fundamental question in the philosophy of causality is simply this: under what circumstances, and with respect to what body of knowledge, can we go on from observing a correlation between prior events, perhaps as states of a presumed causal mechanism, and a viable claim to have proven a causal relation between prior conditions and subsequent effects? Biomedical studies are forever running up against this problem, as indeed are most causal contexts. Unknown to philosophers, it seems—but prescient—are the conditions proposed by Bradford Hill and quoted by Grimley Evans. The list includes the strength or efficacy of a condition; the consistency of its effect; its temporal relation to the presumed effect, recent or distant; and the medical notion of "biological gradient," which reflects the relation of response to the dose of some treatment. Also, the plausibility of the connection being causal, and, as we emphasized in the opening chapters, this involves beliefs about possible causal mechanisms, coherence of the claim with all else known in the situation, and the existence of analogue cases (e.g., double-blind organization).

Historically, probably, the next most important issue has been the nature of the temporal relation between cause and effect, be it event concomitance or the agentive exercise of powers. When we declare a cause is always temporally prior to its effect, are we reporting a matter of fact that might have been otherwise or a feature of the concepts of cause and effect? If a certain event or action came after an event, then it was an effect and the prior event was its presumed cause. The information/energy transition as features of a linked sequence of events is a good fit with causal relations as picked out by physicists, chemists, and biologists, as well as by historians and detectives.

Grimley Evans points out that the majority of research projects in biomedicine reveal that there are many *factors*, some perhaps unknown at the time of research, that have to be taken into account in descrying the conditions that bring about a medical phenomenon. In this context, "factor" seems to be just the right word. It follows that any selection among such factors, made for whatever reason, from moral to economic, will result in a probabilistic estimation of the likelihood of a certain outcome. Researchers presume the presence of unknown factors because the known factors leave at least something unexplained in the origins of a condition.

In the transition from medical science to social policy apropos of some medical phenomenon, usually thought to be undesirable, the key concept is "risk." The operating assumption is then: the lesser the risk, the less the medical condition is likely to appear. In the well-worn case of smoking, it seems that there are probably both genetic factors and influences from life experiences, parental models, peer pressure, and advertising. So there are many factors that predispose someone to take up smoking. As Grimley Evans puts it, "attributable risk embraces contributory and interacting influences." The classical concept of causality, be it Humean exceptionless concomitance or the exercise of agentive powers, is deterministic. That is, if the necessary conditions are achieved, the effect must occur. But medical science can reach only as far as predispositions, which suggests that the completion of the necessary conditions must involve, perhaps, idiosyncratic features of the life and character of each individual. This level of granularity can obscure the relationships between causes and effects. If a condition is relevant, we must have learned of its efficacy in parallel cases, and this thought raises tricky questions about similarities and differences and degrees of intensity.

Another long-running issue in philosophical writings of causality has been the question of the priority of events as causal triggers, circumambient conditions as necessary to the efficacy of a trigger, and causal mechanisms as the underlying essence of the causal relation in determining the meaning of "c causes e." Grimley Evans shows how biomedical research is set in a frame in which both causal triggers in relevant circumstances and causal mechanisms have an essential part, such that none of these can be picked out as *the* cause. Illustrated with several telling examples, Grimley Evans links the distinction between the etiology of a disease from pathogenesis—the former being a trigger event with its necessary background conditions and the latter the mechanism that is activated by the trigger event in the given circumstances.

Grimley Evans's analysis shows that at the point at which biomedicine, ethics, and social policy converge and differentiate again, the whole gamut of causal concepts laid out in the initial chapters are at work. None could be eliminated from the story without the practice of biomedicine and linked social policy simply falling apart for lack of a coherent set of background assumptions.

12

Causes and Consequences: Pain Research and the Placebo Effect

John C. Lefebvre and James T. Bednar

I. INTRODUCTION

At first glance, most people would believe that the causes of pain are very straightforward. When individuals sustain an injury, such as a cut or a burn to the skin, the injury is immediately followed by the perception of pain. Thus, the cause (injury and/or tissue damage) and the consequence (pain) seem to be clearly related. In fact, the modern scientific definition of pain alludes to the inherent relationship between injury and the experience of pain. According to the International Association for the Study of Pain (IASP), pain can be defined as "[a]n unpleasant sensory and emotional experience that is associated with either tissue damage or is described in terms of tissue damage" (IASP, 2011; Loeser & Treede, 2008; Merskey & Bogduk, 1994). Furthermore, it is often assumed that the degree of pain experienced is directly proportional to the amount of tissue damage experienced (Melzack, Wall, & Ty, 1982). It is also considered part of a group of sensations that also include itch and tickle (Aydede, 2013).

In the commonsense view, pain is the product of a sensory process as is the perception of the color of an object or the pitch of a sound. Using this analogy, pain cannot be easily separated from the causal stimulus in the environment. People rarely identify the experience of pain without referring to the location (low-back pain) or the perceived cause of the pain (sunburn). In this way pain is seen as an object to be perceived in the environment. One problem with this commonsense approach is that pain is also completely subjective and thus incorrigible (Aydede, 2013). There is no objective object that others might be able to perceive independent of the individual experiencing pain. The definition of pain proposed by the IASP (2011) carefully avoids linking the source or the cause of the pain to a specific stimulus. Thus, it is conceptualized as an experience in itself and not secondary to other objects. In fact, research and experience have shown that there is a tension between the perceived cause and the subjective experience of pain. For example, there are pain conditions that do not have a clear stimulus or event (e.g., phantom limb pain) and there are situations where pain is not experienced despite significant tissue damage (e.g., stress induced analgesia in battle). Thus, while pain and a particular stimulus would appear to be related, this conception reflects a traditional view of pain that is not completely accurate.

For centuries, the association of injury and pain has dominated our conceptualization of causality in pain research and theory. In 1664, René Descartes proposed that pain was a means of alerting the body of potential danger (Melzack & Wall, 1988). In the model, Descartes proposed that a thin filament extended from the periphery to the brain. Agitation of the filament due to close proximity to a noxious stimulus elicited movement in the filament to alert the individual to danger. The analogy that is often used is of a rope that pulls on the bell in the steeple of a church. Similar to the modern concept of the reflex, the individual would withdraw to avoid additional damage to the body. In this view, pain serves as an alarm system; pain alerts the individual to actual or potential tissue damage (Melzack & Wall, 1988).

Sensory research on receptors in the skin led to the development of specificity theories (Skevington, 1995). In this view, a number of receptors were discovered under the skin and were assumed to represent different sensory experiences. Among these receptors (also known as nociceptors), the free nerve endings were considered the most likely candidate to be responsible for pain sensation and transmission. These specific pain receptors would transmit on specific pain tracts in the spinal column to specific areas of the brain responsible for pain. The Cartesian/Specificity theories have a great deal of intuitive appeal in terms of causality. The theories are intuitively appealing because they offer a mechanism that is unidirectional in terms of causality; pain signals travel in only one direction from the periphery to the central nervous system (CNS). The theories also keep the cause and the consequence as distinct particulars and not as a complex interplay among factors. You have a specific cause (tissue damage) and a specific consequence (pain). They also suggest that pain will be at a constant intensity as long as the injury is not healed and the receptors remain active. As long as the receptors remain active or the specific cause is active, the specific consequence will remain. Thus, these models would also suggest that the cause of analgesia is simply the removal of the cause of pain.

Although the Cartesian/Specificity theories may provide a simple and intuitive causal story, they are insufficient in terms of explaining a number of painful experiences. For example, chronic pain does not seem to follow from what was described by these theories. While the argument could be made that pain resulting from tissue damage may have been present at first injury, the prolonged experience of pain after recovery seems to contradict the pain as a simple alarm paradigm.

In the 1960s a new theory was proposed that placed a greater emphasis on the interaction between the CNS and the sensory system. The Gate Control

Theory of pain proposed that the brain was not simply a passive receiver of pain signals. Rather, mechanisms within the CNS were actively modifying the pain signal as it moved through the sensory system. With the addition of central control, psychological factors such as mood, beliefs, expectations, memory, behavior, and attention could influence the nature of the pain experience. The Gate Control Theory makes determining causality a bit more complicated because it allows for pain to be modified, or even blocked, over the course of time. Thus, pain may not directly reflect the degree of tissue damage (Beecher, 1946; Turk & Okifuji, 1999), or may be present without clear pathology as in individuals with phantom limb pain (Melzack & Loeser, 1978; Nikolajsen & Jensen, 2001), or even low-back pain (Loeser, 1980; Waddell, 1996). Pain also fluctuates naturally. Some persistent conditions may not be painful all the time. Thus, a range of situations may increase or decrease the intensity and functional interference of pain.

The move away from Cartesian/Specificity theories toward Gate Control Theory highlights five shifts in the way cause and consequence have been conceptualized in pain research.

- *The causal relation between pain and injury/tissue damage:* Whereas the Cartesian/Specificity theories conceive of pain as an effect that arises only from injury/tissue damage, Gate Control Theory does not: injury/tissue damage is neither causally sufficient nor causally necessary for pain.
- *The causal direction between the sensory system and the central nervous system in pain perception:* In the Cartesian view, the interaction between these systems in pain perception runs only in one direction: from the sensory system to the CNS, ultimately to a specific part of the brain, where the mind perceives/experiences the signal as pain. In the Gate Control Theory, signals from the CNS interact with signals from the sensory system; pain perception depends on the interaction of these signals in both a top-down (CNS to periphery) and bottom-up (periphery to CNS) fashion.

Among these, the latter deals with causal directions between two bodily systems; we should also note two further shifts in regard to the nature and existence of causation with respect to the mind and the body.

- *The classification of pain with respect to mind-body causation:* A person, in Descartes's view, is a composite of a mind and a body causally interacting with each other. In this view, causal interactions between mind and body can be classified according to whether (1) the mind causes a change in the body or (2) the body causes a change in the mind. Intentional action is Descartes's paradigm case of the mind causing changes in the body: a person's mind decides to raise her or his arm and her or his arm rises. Pain, by contrast, is Descartes's paradigm case of the body causing changes in the mind: a person's arm is injured and his or her mind experiences pain. The Gate Control Theory would reject classifying pain strictly as falling under (2)—and, for that matter, a contemporary Cartesian dualist would do well to do the same. In the Gate Control Theory, psychological factors such as mood, beliefs, expectations, memory, behavior, goals, and attention influence the nature of the pain experience. Indeed, the phenomenon of placebo analgesia suggests quite strongly that the mind is not merely a passive receiver of sensory input from the periphery but an active modifier of the experience of pain.

Implicit in Descartes's classificatory scheme is substance dualism where the mind and the body are distinct causal agents. This brings us to the fourth shift:

• *Mental causation with respect to the immateriality of the mind:* In Descartes's view, the mind and body are metaphysically distinct: the former being immaterial substance, the latter being material substance. As to how immaterial and material substance can interact causally, Descartes ultimately responds: "It is one of those self-evident things which we only make more obscure when we try to explain it" (Cottingham, Stoothoff, Murdoch, & Kenney, 1991, p. 358). The rejection of immaterial substance is nearly universal in contemporary science and philosophy. Nevertheless, the convergence in the rejection of Cartesian dualism has not lead to convergence upon a successor view. In fact, there seem to be two focal points. On the one hand, there are theories that identify the mind with the brain—mental states/properties/events are brain states/properties/events. In this view, mental causation is not problematic—at least, it is no more problematic than physical causation. However, some materialists go further: if the mental is just the physical, we can and should eliminate talk of the mental from scientific theorizing. This view is called eliminative materialism. On the other hand, there are theories that reject substance dualism and accept property dualism: while there are only material substances upon which all properties depend, mental properties are distinct from physical properties. While such theories block the eliminativist move, they seem to render mental states causally inert.

In light of the fourth shift, one might wonder where this leaves the claims in the third shift regarding the role of psychological factors in pain experience.

This chapter provides a survey of some of the conceptual and methodological ways that people have approached the relationship between cause and consequence in pain research. In order to better understand the cause-and-consequence relationship, special attention will be focused on research and theory on the placebo effect. The phenomenon of placebo analgesia makes this question particularly acute. In their review of placebo analgesia research,

Price, Finniss, and Benedetti (2008) identify, among issues for future discussion and research, the following: "Powerful placebo effects reflect mind-brain-body relationships, and there is a need to philosophically resolve explanations of these relationships without resorting to eliminative materialism or forms of dualism that completely divide the mind from the body" (p. 586). The chapter concludes by revisiting the notion of eliminative materialism, which we contend inevitably raises broad issues regarding the relationship between causation and explanation in pain research.

II. CAUSALITY IN PAIN RESEARCH

The origins of causality in pain research are no different than those found in other areas of science that have a strong relationship biological inquiry (Okasha, 2012). Given the nature of change in biological systems, as well as the heterogeneity of the samples used, there has been more of an emphasis on defining the degree of certainty around a causal relationship. Ronald Fisher argued that causal inferences in these types of studies would be possible only if appropriate controls were implemented (Okasha, 2012). This required the use of randomization in order to distribute individual differences between experimental groups. Thus, in order to show that an experimental manipulation had an effect, there had to be a consistent change in one group compared to another group that was greater than what would be expected with natural variation within the samples. In a randomized study, the assumption is that causality could be assigned to the experimental manipulation if the natural variation within the groups was thought to be equal.

The emphasis on randomization that Fisher advocated has become the metric by which all other methodologies are compared (Okasha, 2012). While this may be the sought-after approach, it leads to problems in the study of causation in pain research. Random assignment is possible if the pain stimulus is an acute experimental pain (e.g., electric shock, thermal pain, cold pressor) presented to a healthy participant. However, when studying chronic or persistent pain, randomization is not possible given the experience of pain predates the study. Thus, research often quickly highlights the inherent differences between acute and chronic pain studies given that prior experience may influence the results of the study. Furthermore, the bulk of the studies are not designed to elicit pain but to assess the degree to which specific factors influence pain intensity and unpleasantness. Thus, these studies are more interested in determining what causes variations in pain and not what causes pain initially.

III. PLACEBO ANALGESIC EFFECT

One of the more interesting approaches to the study of cause and consequence in pain research can be found in the work on placebo analgesia. Because of the limitations placed on assessing causality in pain, one interesting approach is to assess how placebos can be used to modify the experience of pain, producing a degree of analgesia, often using methodologies that isolate the role of psychological and other factors.

Interest in placebo analgesia has grown tremendously over the past 40 years (Miller & Kaptchuk, 2008). This interest is due to a number of factors including the desire either to control placebo effects in clinical trials or to capitalize on the therapeutic effects of placebo analgesia. Placebo analgesia has often been maligned because it suggests that the reduction in pain that often accompanies the placebo was caused by psychological rather than "actual" therapeutic effects (Wall, 1999). This suggests either that the analgesic effect is not real in that people reported incorrect values and simply wanted to give the impression of improvement or that the original level of pain in some way was not based on actual pathology but was psychological and thus immutable in terms of treatment.

The term "placebo" has been defined as "to please" and has traditionally been associated with a negative connotation (Fields, 2004; Finniss, 2013). In terms of medical practice, in 1772 William Cullen presented a series of examples where a physician used placebos in order "to please" patients with incurable diseases because of the expectation on the patient's part to receive treatment. Later, the term "placebo" became more associated with the situation where a medicine was given in order to please rather than to treat the patient (Finniss, 2013). Especially in reference to a pharmacological intervention, a placebo was defined as a "sugar pill," something that is inert and should not provide any therapeutic effect. The placebo effect would thus be any changes in the condition that were brought about by the administration of the placebo. Despite the possible beneficial effects of a placebo, in many respects, there has been a negative connotation associated with placebo (Fields, 2004; Wall, 1999). The suggestion is that using a treatment that should not provide any relief from symptoms is a fraud. Any relief obtained from this approach must be due to the imagination of the patient subsequent to the deceit on the part of the practitioner (Finniss, 2013). Thus, you have the tension between the desire for the patient to find relief juxtaposed over the skepticism of the practitioner over what is actually providing the relief (Kaptchuk, Kerr, & Zanger, 2009).

The placebo effect has a long history in the treatment of pain. The placebo analgesic effect has been defined as the mean reduction in pain that results from the administration of a placebo (Price, 1999). This can be measured in a repeated measures approach where pain is assessed prior to and after the administration of a placebo and the associated reduction is defined as the placebo effect (Price, 1999), or by comparing between two groups where one serves as a control and the other receives the placebo (Fields, 2004).

Starting with Fisher's view of causation, the "gold standard" for research is the randomized clinical trial. The goal in this methodology is to show that an active agent (usually a medication or other form of treatment) provides a degree of pain relief after all other factors are controlled. The assumption that the active agent will be effective in producing analgesia can be derived from clinical or experimental observations, or through theoretical insight. In order to prove that any analgesia that is produced is caused by the active agent, it is subjected to a randomized clinical trial. In this methodology, a participant is randomly assigned to one of at least two conditions. In the first condition, he/she is administered the active agent whether it is pharmaceutical or psychological. In the placebo-control condition, they are provided with another agent that should mimic the active agent in every way, except that it does not contain what is believed to be the active agent. Both the participant and the person providing the treatment should be blind to the condition. Thus, neither should be aware as to whether the participant is receiving the active agent or placebo control. Additional controls may also be included such as a "treatment as usual" condition in order to assess natural fluctuations in pain. Also, some behavioral treatments may want to demonstrate that they are equal to or better than an existing treatment. In the end, the goal is to demonstrate that the active agent consistently shows a greater analgesic effect than the control groups including the placebo control. The assumption is that any effect on pain above and beyond what is found in the placebo control is due to the efficacy of the active agent alone. Usually, if there is no differential effect between the treatment and placebo conditions, the trial is thought to be a failure and the treatment effects are thought to be imaginary.

While this seems straightforward, there are problems that arise in this design. First, the ideal situation would be that both the participant and the person delivering the treatment would be blind to the condition. This is possible in pharmaceutical research where the pill containing the active ingredient and the one without the active ingredient are similar and it would be difficult to differentiate the two. However, in some situations, it would be impossible to mask the condition from the person providing the active or placebo treatments. For example, in psychological treatments for pain, the active treatment may be one form of therapy and the control may be another form of therapy that is not believed to have an effect or as strong an effect on pain. Also, the expectations of providing the active agent may lead to subtle cues and behaviors on the part of the clinician leading to a demonstrable placebo effect (Gracely, Dubner, Deeter, & Wolskee, 1985).

Not all people respond equally to the placebo effect. Henry Beecher (1955) was one of the first to try and better understand the role of the placebo effect in producing pain relief and in the treatment of other illnesses. As with others, Beecher believed that the placebo effect was a nuisance that was interfering with effective treatment or hampering research. He noted that the placebo was hard to identify because it mirrored in many ways what would be expected of the actual treatment, even the toxic side effects of the medications. Not only was it mimicking the beneficial effects of the treatment, but it was also causing the same unwanted side effects. In his review of 15 studies, the results suggested that taken together, approximately 35 percent of the samples in the studies reviewed showed consistent therapeutic effect from a placebo.

Beecher was quick to label those who received relief from the placebo as reactors and those who did not as nonreactors. This suggested that some people were more likely to produce a placebo response and this needed to be minimized in research protocols. In more recent studies trying to quantify the percentage of participants who show a placebo response, the result varies between approximately 27 percent and 56 percent when compared to nontreatment control groups (Price et al., 2008).

Role of Learning and Expectancies in Placebo Analgesic Effect

Research on the placebo effect has gradually shifted over time. As we have demonstrated above, the original view of the placebo was of a nuisance variable that needed to be controlled in order to better understand the true cause of pain relief. However, over the past 20 years, the emphasis in research has started to assess the degree to which key variables are important in creating treatment effects for both the placebo and the "true" treatment.

The emphasis in all of the research is on the effects of expectations of relief. There are several different ways to create these expectations, which include learning, social observation, and the environmental context (Price et al., 2008). In terms of learning, some of the earliest work was on the classical conditioning of the placebo response in humans and animals (Wickramasekera, 1980). Analgesia can be considered an unconditioned response (UCR) to the effects of an analgesic treatment that would serve as an unconditioned stimulus (UCS). Thus, over repeated presentations, other stimuli that would normally not elicit a response (neutral stimulus) will come to signal the delivery of the UCS and come to be associated with pain relief. These neutral stimuli, such as the pill itself, the location of the treatment, the physician, can all signal and thus elicit a conditioned response (CR) of pain relief that is essentially identical to the actual pain relief (Price, 1999). In other words, people have suggested that the neutral elements associated with pain relief are responsible for people expecting that the treatment will be effective and thus leads to the placebo responses.

For example, in a classic study by Voudouris, Peck, and Coleman (1990), the authors showed that there is the possibility of simulating an analgesic effect. In the study, 40 participants were randomly assigned to one of two experimental conditions. All of the participants attended an initial session where half of them were informed that they were to receive a powerful analgesic cream that will lead to significant pain relief. The other half of the participants was informed that the cream was a neutral cream with no special analgesic properties. In reality, the cream was a simple pink-colored cold cream that included some rubbing cream to give it a distinct medicinal smell. All participants were then presented with a series of painful electrical stimuli. During the conditioning phase of the study, half of the participants in the placebo and the neutral condition covertly received electrical stimuli that were reduced by 50 percent after the application of the cream. Thus, to the participant, the application of the cream was effective in decreasing the level of pain from a baseline assessment. In the final session, all participants were asked to rate the degree of pain they experienced with and then without the cream. The results showed that those who associated the cream with pain relief reported a decrease in pain after conditioning. These results suggest that once a treatment has been associated with pain relief, the neutral properties of the treatment (e.g., the location, the color, the smell) will take on the properties of the treatment and produce the analgesia.

As mentioned above, the consistent presentation of a neutral stimulus with a UCS will lead to the association of the neutral stimulus as a signal for the UCS. In other words, the neutral stimulus may lead to an expectancy of the presentation of the UCS. Thus, another theory that has emerged from the classical conditioning literature is the expectancy theory. In their study, Montgomery and Kirsch (1997) wanted to assess the degree to which the placebo effect detected by Voudouris and colleagues (1990) would disappear after the person was told about the deception. If the association was a learned association it should not be affected by changing the expectancies of the individual. The study included 48 participants who were provided with a brownish medicinal smelling cream that the research team introduced as an experimental topical analgesic. During a pretest, each participant provided a baseline assessment of pain with and without the application of the cream. Participants were assigned to one of four conditions. In the uninformed condition, the participants experienced the same type of conditioning as in the study by Voudouris and colleagues (1990) where the intensity of the stimulus was covertly decreased by 50 percent. In the informed condition, the participants were informed that the intensity of the pain stimulus would be decreased by 50 percent in order to test the efficacy of the cream at lower levels. For the extinction condition, there was no change in stimulus intensity. Finally, in the no-treatment condition, the participants were not exposed to any of the conditioning trials. At posttest, all participants were again presented with a series of pain stimuli with and without the cream and asked to rate the experience of pain. The findings of the study showed that the results shown by Voudouris and colleagues (1990) were due to expectancy effects. The uninformed condition consistently showed the greatest placebo effect when comparing their pre- and posttest pain ratings. Those in the informed condition received the same degree of stimulus reduction, but did not attribute it to the analgesic effects of the cream and thus showed no placebo effect.

Finally, a placebo response can also be obtained via observational learning. All of the research covered so far suggests that direct experience with the placebo analgesia is necessary. However, in a study by Colloca and Benedetti (2009) the authors demonstrated that observational social learning can also lead to a placebo effect. In the social learning condition the participants observed another individual receive supposed relief from an acute electrical pain stimulus. However, this individual was a confederate who was trained to mimic the analgesic response. The confederate always rated the stimulus paired with a green light as being less intense compared to one paired with a red light. In the conditioning group, the participants received an experience similar to the Voudouris and colleagues (1990) study where they expected the pain to remain stable but was surreptitiously decreased to mimic analgesia. As with the social learning condition, those stimuli paired with a green light were less intense compared to those paired with the red light. Finally, in the verbal suggestion condition the participants were informed that a green light would precede a stimulus of reduced intensity. The results of the study found that those individuals in the observational learning condition rated the stimuli presented with the green light as being less painful compared to those paired with the red light. Those in the conditioning group also showed a placebo effect related to the presentation of stimuli associated with the green light. Finally, no effect was found for those in the verbal suggestion condition. Further analyses showed that there was no significant difference in the degree of placebo analgesia between those participants in the observational and conditioning groups. Both of these groups showed a greater placebo effect compared to those in the verbal suggestion condition. These results suggest that belief and expectancy are not enough, observation or direct experience is necessary.

Role of Context in Placebo Analgesic Effect

Recently, Miller and Kaptchuk (2008) have suggested that a better understanding of the placebo response would be achieved if it was redefined as "contextual healing." In this view, healing whether through the direct effect of the treatment and/or the environment of the clinical setting, the expectations of relief, or previous treatment experiences would all contribute to the treatment effect. Thus, treatment would be as much about the ritual of treatment as with the actual treatment.

In order to separate the effect of the treatment from the rituals associated with treatment, a number of studies have attempted to assess the degree to which a treatment is effective when delivered without the patients' knowledge. One of the first studies to use this open-hidden paradigm was conducted by Levine and Gordon (1984). In the study, 96 individuals who had undergone third molar extraction were randomly assigned to receive either naloxone (an opiate antagonist that increases pain), naloxone vehicle (neutral substance), or morphine (opiate analgesic that decreases pain). All of these substances were to be delivered through an intravenous system. Each group received their assigned substance in a double-blind design. In one group, they received the medication via an open infusion where someone next to their bedside was overtly administered the substance. In another condition, the participants received the substance in a hidden fashion via someone in another room. Finally, the remainder of the sample received the substance via a preprogrammed infusion pump. The effect of each substance was determined by the change in pain level 50 minutes following administration. The results suggested pain levels in those receiving the naloxone vehicle in the open administration showed as much of a decrease in pain as those receiving 8 mg of morphine through the infusion pump. The results also found that those who were given the vehicle using the hidden approach showed some degree of placebo effect, suggesting that even very subtle cues that they were receiving a substance were enough to produce a placebo response. Thus, the results of the study suggest that the method of administration is incredibly important in determining the efficacy of a treatment. Those who received the vehicle in an open method where they knew they could be receiving a pain medication showed a stronger placebo effect compared to those who received the vehicle through an infusion pump.

These results were replicated and expanded in a study by Amanzio, Pollo, Maggi, and Benedetti (2001). The study used a sample of 278 patients who had undergone thoracic surgery for a variety of conditions. In the open condition, a physician administered a bolus of a substance in plain view of the patients. The patients were told that the medication was a strong painkiller. The patients were actually treated with one of four different analgesics depending on the severity of the surgery (buprenorphine, tramadol, ketorolac, metamizol). In the hidden condition, similar to Levine and Gordon (1984), the medication was delivered via a preprogrammed infusion pump. Thus, in this condition the patients had no idea they were receiving any analgesic medication. The results showed that the reduction in pain was significantly greater for those in the open condition compared to those in the hidden condition regardless of the type of medication. The results also showed that the analgesic effects started sooner after injection in the open condition compared to the hidden condition.

Amanzio and colleagues (2001) also conducted a study using a separate sample to assess the degree to which the analgesic effects of the placebo response could be reversed using naloxone. In the experimental pain study, a sample of 86 healthy volunteers was exposed to ischemic arm pain. In this procedure, a blood-pressure cuff is placed around the upper arm and inflated to a pressure that would lead to blood not being able to flow adequately to the forearm. As the individual squeezes and releases an exercise device, they begin to experience an increasing degree of pain. They are then instructed to stop the exercise when the pain becomes intolerable. The squeezes are timed and coordinated. The amount of time it takes from the first squeeze to reach this level of pain is the dependent variable. All participants had a needle inserted into their forearm through which medications could be administered. In the no-treatment condition, the participants were not provided with any substances and served as the natural pain history condition. As with the clinical pain study presented above, in the open condition the participants witnessed the researcher deliver a substance in clear view and were told that they were receiving a powerful pain killer that would increase pain tolerance (increasing the amount of time until intolerable pain). In the hidden conditions, the substances were delivered through a preprogrammed infusion pump. In the hidden naloxone condition, the participants were given naloxone through an infusion pump. In the hidden ketorolac (a non-opiate analgesic) and naloxone condition, the participants received a bolus of ketorolac followed by naloxone. Given that ketorolac is not opiate mediated, the naloxone should have no effect on the medication. In the hidden ketorolac condition, the participants were given a bolus of ketorolac. This group should show an analgesic effect with the least placebo effect. Finally, two groups were those that received the open administration of ketorolac and those who had the open administration of the ketorolac and naloxone combination. The results mirrored those found in the clinical pain study. Namely, those who were in the condition to receive the open administration of ketorolac showed a greater decrease in pain compared to those who received the hidden administration of the medication. The results also showed that there was no difference in pain tolerance between the open and hidden conditions where ketorolac and naloxone were delivered. Thus, adding naloxone blocks the placebo effect but does not reduce the effect of ketorolac. Thus, the increased treatment efficacy of open ketorolac was mediated through the opioid-based placebo effect.

In summary, the results of the studies presented in this section demonstrate that learning and expectations of relief are powerful enough to produce analgesia even in the absence of an active treatment. While others would believe this to be a nuisance, it suggests that the brain is not a passive recipient of pain signals, nor is the active agent in treatment solely responsible for any analgesic effect. Given this information, logically if we could determine what parts of the CNS are active when pain is present and demonstrate changes in these areas after treatment or placebo, we could discover the ultimate cause of pain.

IV. BIOLOGICAL BASES FOR PAIN AND THE PLACEBO ANALGESIC EFFECT

Beginning with Descartes, the assumption has always been that the ultimate cause of the experience of pain would be activation of specific areas of the human brain. The assumption is that nociceptive signals sent to the brain would be ultimately interpreted as pain. Thus, it would be assumed that an area of the brain would be found that would be responsible for collecting and analyzing all of the nociceptive signals originating from the periphery that would ultimately cause pain.

However, the role of the CNS and of the cortex in the processing of pain was not clear at the start of the past century. Clinical observations of individual with significant lesions of the cortex did not seem to diminish the experience of pain (Bushnell et al., 1999; Head & Holmes, 1911). In addition, Wilder Penfield in his seminal work on mapping the cortex in conscious humans noted that pain experiences were very limited. Direct stimulation of the somatosensory cortex produced a tingling sensation that some reported as unpleasant but not necessarily painful (Mazzola, Isnard, Peyron, & Mauguière, 2011; Penfield & Boldrey, 1937). Thus, when providing direct electrical stimulation to the cortex, Penfield was unable to produce the experience of pain. Based on his clinical observations, he suggested that the brain was not actually involved in the experience of pain (Penfield & Boldrey, 1937).

The causal assumptions that underlie the clinical works of Head and Penfield is that pain originates in the brain and that stimulation of the "pain center" would lead to the experience of pain. This makes sense given that stimulation of the somatosensory cortex (S1) leads to the experience of tingling and other sensory experiences. However, these results also suggest that pain may be more complex in terms of its origins. There was no way to record activity in the cortex at the time of these studies. With the development of modern imaging technology, the ability to directly observe activity in the cortex and in subcortical areas has become a reality. The results of these studies have also brought about a change in the models that are used in explaining the experience of pain. Because of the complexity of the pain experience, the assumptions have always been that the experience of pain would require the involvement of several systems within the CNS and not a single location advocated by Descartes (Craggs, Price, & Robinson, 2014). Rather, the interplay among these different locations would be responsible for the different aspects of the experience of pain. Melzack, in trying to conceptualize the experience of phantom limbs and phantom limb pain, suggested that complex perceptions were not the product of a single location in the cortex, but of a complex interplay between different regions (Melzack, 1988). This concept of the pain neuromatrix was later extrapolated to the experience of pain (Melzack, 1990). More recently, this concept of the neuromatrix has been reformulated to become the pain matrix (Legrain, Iannetti, Plaghki, & Mouraux, 2011) and later the pain signature (Tracey & Mantyh, 2007).

The basis for the development of the pain matrix is based on the research on using neuroimaging technology. Apkarian, Bushnell, Treede, and Zubieta (2005) completed a meta-analysis of the role of different cortical and subcortical regions that are believed to be involved in the experience of pain. These would be the most likely candidates for the pain matrix. The results of their analyses suggested that main components of the pain matrix would be the primary and secondary somatosensory cortices (S1, S2), which the authors conclude are regions responsible for the sensory and discriminative features of pain (pain intensity and location). The insular cortex and the anterior cingulate cortex were also found to be activated during painful experiences. These areas are part of the limbic system and are believed to be responsible for the affective component of pain (pain unpleasantness). Finally, the prefrontal cortical areas and the parietal association areas are associated with cognitive variables such as memory and stimulus evaluation and are believed to be responsible for the evaluative aspects of the pain experience (evaluative component of pain). Subcortical areas that were identified by the meta-analysis included the thalamus, the basal ganglia, and the cerebellum (Apkarian et al., 2005). The majority of the studies assessed the activation of the brain in normal, pain-free individuals who experienced acute levels of pain. Research on the areas that are activated under chronic pain conditions suggest that very similar areas are activated. However, the pattern and the temporal nature of the activation are different. For example, when patients with chronic pain are given acute pain stimulation, there is a decreased level of activation compared to the same areas in pain-free individuals (Apkarian et al., 2005). Others have found that people with chronic pain also show a change in the location of activation compared to acute pain, with chronic pain associated with more activation in the rostral area of the cingulate cortex, suggesting a change in the affective response to pain (Schweinhardt et al., 2006; Tracey & Mantyh, 2007).

In terms of the placebo effect, the results of a number of studies show that context and expectations have a definitive pattern of activation. In general, studies have shown that placebo analgesia is associated with decreases in activity in the anterior cingulate cortex, the insular cortex, and the thalamus (Wiech, Ploner, & Tracey, 2008). Anticipation of a painful stimulus has been shown to increase activity in S1, the anterior cingulate cortex, the periaqueductal gray matter, the insular cortex, the prefrontal cortex, and the cerebellum (Apkarian et al., 2005). Stronger activation of the prefrontal cortex was also found to be correlated with greater placebo response (Tracey & Mantyh, 2007). In a study by Craggs et al. (2014), a sample of people with irritable bowel syndrome were given a standard placebo and an enhanced placebo condition. Compared to the standard placebo condition, the enhanced placebo condition showed increased activation in those areas of the brain involved in top-down modulation of pain. The areas of greatest interest in this study were those involved in memory (hippocampus, parahippocampal gyrus, temporal lobes), semantic processing (angular gyrus and Brodmann area 39), and affective processing (rostral anterior cingulate gyrus, ventral striatum). Thus, as with other studies, it appears that the same areas that are involved in the processing of pain are less active during placebo. Enhancing the placebo effect only increases the activation of these areas. Furthermore, the activation of the placebo effect appears to be reliant on areas of the cortex that are involved in memory and the affective processing of pain.

In terms of the causal link to pain, these studies set up an interesting question. On the one hand, the clinical observations of Penfield and others suggest that direct stimulation of the cortex does not appear to be related to the experience of pain without sensory input. The results of the neural imaging studies suggest that the experience of pain and placebo are related to widespread activation in cortical and subcortical regions. Perhaps, Penfield was simply not applying direct stimulation to the appropriate areas. For example, it would be very difficult to apply direct stimulation to subcortical regions in humans. In a study by Mazzola and colleagues (2011), the authors wanted to apply direct stimulation to the areas identified as belonging to the pain matrix. The study included 4,160 cortical stimulations from 164 epileptic patients. All patients had received electrode placement for diagnostic purposes.

The results of the study found that only a small percentage of the stimulations produced any painful sensations (1.4%). When analyzed, the results showed that pain was only reliably elicited when the medial part of the secondary somatosensory and the insular cortex were stimulated. These were areas that were not accessible to Penfield and his colleagues during surface stimulation. As with the studies of Penfield, stimulation of the primary somatosensory cortex was found to produce nonpainful paraesthesiae. Furthermore, the majority of the areas that have been identified as part of the pain matrix did not produce pain sensations when stimulated.

Others have proposed that perhaps the data on the pain matrix are not actually picking up on a pain system, but actually reflect a much broader system of detecting salience. Legrain and colleagues (2011) proposed that the activation in the pain matrix described above could also be interpreted as a salience detection system that lends itself across sensory systems. However, given the fact that most research covered in this chapter is on pain, the emphasis has been placed on the pain matrix interpretation. Legrain and colleagues (2011) proposed that the data suggest that the brain mechanisms thought to interpret sensory data and cause the experience of pain could actually be more involved in detecting the emergence and changes in pain intensity and location. Thus, the pain matrix described by others would represent a system within the brain that detects changes in sensory signals and direct attention and other resources to process the change. The results suggest that context and other factors thought to be important in the placebo effect would also be important in the determination of salience. This mechanism would also suggest that factors that influence attentional processes, such as hypervigilance and distraction, would also play an important role in the salience detection system. Thus, in their view, this system can also be applied to a threat detection system; pain, because of its nature, would be a focus of this system.

In summary, the goal of identifying what parts of the brain are consistently active during the experience of pain and pain relief has identified a number of areas that have been labeled as the "pain matrix." While these areas may be consistently associated with pain, there is some variability in the patterns of activation leading to a further discussion of "pain signatures." Despite this getting us potentially closer to discovering the ultimate cause of pain and pain relief, others have suggested that this may be more complicated. For example, some research suggests that direct stimulation of these areas does not produce the same sensory effects that are found in other sensory systems. Others suggest that these areas may be more likely associated with threat detection across all modalities and not just pain.

V. CONCLUSION

Common sense would suggest that pain is the consequence of an event that occurs in the environment leading to damage or potential damage to the body. The event in question triggers a series of events in the peripheral nervous system that lead to changes in the CNS, where pain is believed to serve a protective function. As with Descartes, this commonsense view suggests that pain is the product of the interplay between different neural circuits that ultimately produce the experience of pain. Thus, pain is seen as yet another sensory experience that has its own receptors, pain transmission system, and areas responsible for the processing of the sensory system. Therefore, in this reductionistic view, pain is simply the consequence of these changes within the CNS. It also suggests that with the proper imaging technologies, once the pattern is detected in the CNS, we will be able to objectively study the pain experience.

However, as has been described in this chapter, pain is more than the sum of these neural activities. Mental states/properties/events seem to be ineliminable aspects of pain and placebo analgesia. Placebo analgesia can be produced through stimulus-response conditioning that brings about beliefs and expectancies of analgesia. Other studies have suggested that observational learning and context are also causally relevant to placebo analgesia. Furthermore, open-hidden studies reveal that, even when people are in fact receiving an analgesic treatment, their beliefs about whether they are receiving the treatment significantly impact the overall analgesic effect of the treatment. Thus, the treatment context and the rituals that others dismiss as artifacts in the cause-consequence relationship are incredibly important in determining efficacy. Placebo analgesia, moreover, is increasingly being shown to have a neurophysiological components. The fact that naloxone blocks placebo analgesia just as it blocks the analgesic effect of morphine suggests that the aforementioned psychological and social factors influence the body's endogenous opioid system in producing analgesia. Neuroimaging studies are increasingly revealing that placebo analgesia and other forms of analgesia recruit similar regions of the brain. This suggests that placebo and active agents are in effect no different when it comes to producing pain relief. This nuisance as others have thought is actually using the same circuits in the production of pain and in the relief of pain.

All of these results argue against forms of property dualism according to which mental properties casually depend on physical properties but do not causally influence physical properties—also known as epiphenomenalism. These considerations also argue against eliminative materialism as a theory of mind-brain-body. Fortunately, a materialist need not be an eliminative materialist. In fact, there is a great deal of ambiguity in regard to what the latter view is. By way of conclusion, then, we wish to highlight a few issues regarding eliminative materialism.

- *Elimination versus reduction:* In its inception, eliminative materialism has vacillated between two different notions: (1) mental states do not exist and should accordingly be eliminated from scientific theorizing and (2) mental states exist but are reducible to brain states (Ramsey, 2013). Here we wish to point out that a materialist is perfectly happy with (2), but this does not mean mental talk should be eliminated from scientific explanation any more than talk of water (now reduced to H_2O)

should be eliminated. Some concepts may need to be abandoned, just as talk of demons has been abandoned. Others, however, will be reinterpreted in light of current theory. Recent pain research seems to follow more along the lines of (2) than of (1).

- *Empirical versus regulatory claim:* Taking eliminativism proper to claim (1), there is a further question as to the status of the claim. We cannot cover here the arguments for the claim, but we wish to note that it is proposed as an empirical claim but often serves as a regulatory one. In other words, science should proceed on the assumption of (1). Strong assumptions do have their methodological merits: they tend to be easier to disconfirm. Thus, there might be a reason to proceed along the lines of (1). But this reason is undercut if no results, in the name of methodological presumption, can count against it. Relatedly, eliminative materialism seems like a promissory note: someday neuroscience will be so well developed that (1) will be vindicated (Ramsey, 2013). Many have claimed that there is not much to be gained debating (1) before neuroscience is thusly developed.

In the end, we must go back to the statement that was made by Price and colleagues (2008) that suggests that the experience of pain and the placebo analgesic effect warrant a new discussion about the theory of mind that does not rely on eliminative materialism. Although pain will ultimately be explained by looking at activation patterns within the CNS, there is no guarantee that this is the actual cause of the pain and analgesia.

REFERENCES

Amanzio, M., Pollo, A., Maggi, G., & Benedetti, F. (2001). Response variability to analgesics: A role for non-specific activation of endogenous opioids. *Pain, 90* (3), 205–215.

Apkarian, A. V., Bushnell, M. C., Treede, R. D., & Zubieta, J. K. (2005). Human brain mechanisms of pain perception and regulation in health and disease. *European Journal of Pain, 9* (4), 463–463.

Aydede, M. (2013). Pain. In Edward N. Zalta (ed.), *The Stanford Encyclopedia of Philosophy*. Retrieved from http://plato.stanford.edu/archives/spr2013/entries/pain/

Beecher, H. K. (1946). Pain in men wounded in battle. *Annals of surgery, 123* (1), 96.

Beecher, H. K. (1955). The powerful placebo. *Journal of the American Medical Association, 159* (17), 1602–1606.

Bushnell, M. C., Duncan, G. H., Hofbauer, R. K., Ha, B., Chen, J. I., & Carrier, B. (1999). Pain perception: Is there a role for primary somatosensory cortex? *Proceedings of the National Academy of Sciences, 96* (14), 7705–7709.

Colloca, L., & Benedetti, F. (2009). Placebo analgesia induced by social observational learning. *Pain, 144* (1), 28–34.

Cottingham, J., Stoothoff, R., Murdoch, D., & Kenny, A. J. P. (1991). *The Philosophical Writings of Descartes: Vol. 3, The Correspondence.* Cambridge, UK: Cambridge University Press.

Craggs, J. G., Price, D. D., & Robinson, M. E. (2014). Enhancing the placebo response: Functional magnetic resonance imaging evidence of memory and semantic processing in placebo analgesia. *The Journal of Pain, 15* (4), 435–446.

Fields, H. L. (2004). Placebo Analgesia. In R. H. Dworkin & W. S. Breitbart (eds.), *Psychological Aspects of Pain: A Handbook for Health Care Providers* (pp. 623–641). Seattle, WA: IASP Press.

Finniss, D. G. (2013). Historical aspects of placebo analgesia. In L. Colloca, M. A. Flaten, & K. Meissner (eds.), *Placebo and Pain: From Bench to Bedside* (pp. 1–8). London: Elsevier.

Gracely, R., Dubner, R., Deeter, W., & Wolskee, P. (1985). Clinician's expectations influence placebo analgesia. *The Lancet, 325* (8419), 43.

Head, H., & Holmes, G. (1911). Sensory disturbances from cerebral lesions. *Brain, 34,* 102–254.

International Association for the Study of Pain, IASP Taxonomy Working Group. (2011). *Descriptions of Chronic Pain Syndromes and Definitions of Pain Terms: Classification of Chronic Pain,* 2nd edition. Retrieved from http://www.iasp-pain.org

Kaptchuk, T. J., Kerr, C. E., & Zanger, A. (2009). Placebo controls, exorcisms and the devil. *Lancet, 374* (9697), 1234.

Legrain, V., Iannetti, G. D., Plaghki, L., & Mouraux, A. (2011). The pain matrix reloaded: A salience detection system for the body. *Progress in neurobiology, 93* (1), 111–124.

Levine, J. D., & Gordon, N. C. (1984). Influence of the method of drug administration on analgesic response. *Nature, 312* (5996), 755–756.

Loeser, J. D. (1980). Low back pain. In J. J. Bonica (Ed.), *Pain.* New York: Raven.

Loeser, J. D., & Treede, R. D. (2008). The Kyoto protocol of IASP basic pain terminology. *Pain, 137* (3), 473–477.

Mazzola, L., Isnard, J., Peyron, R., & Mauguière, F. (2011). Stimulation of the human cortex and the experience of pain: Wilder Penfield's observations revisited. *Brain, 135,* 631–640.

Melzack, R. (1988). Labat lecture. Phantom limbs. *Regional anesthesia, 14* (5), 208–211.

Melzack, R. (1990). Phantom limbs and the concept of a neuromatrix. *Trends in neurosciences, 13* (3), 88–92.

Melzack, R., & Loeser, J. D. (1978). Phantom body pain in paraplegics: Evidence for a central "pattern generating mechanism" for pain. *Pain, 4,* 195–210.

Melzack, R., & Wall, P. D. (1988). *The Challenge of Pain, revised edition.* London, England: Penguin Group.

Melzack, R., Wall, P. D., & Ty, T. C. (1982). Acute pain in an emergency clinic: Latency of onset and descriptor patterns related to different injuries. *Pain, 14* (1), 33–43.

Merskey, H., & Bogduk, N. (1994). *Classification of Chronic Pain*, IASP Task Force on Taxonomy. Seattle, WA: International Association for the Study of Pain Press.

Miller, F. G., & Kaptchuk, T. J. (2008). The power of context: Reconceptualizing the placebo effect. *Journal of the Royal Society of Medicine, 101* (5), 222–225.

Montgomery, G. H., & Kirsch, I. (1997). Classical conditioning and the placebo effect. *Pain, 72* (1), 107–113.

Nikolajsen, L., & Jensen, T. S. (2001). Phantom limb pain. *British Journal of Anaesthesia, 87* (1), 107–116.

Okasha, S. (2012). Causation in biology. In H. Beebee, C. Hitchcock, & P. Menzies (eds.), *The Oxford Handbook of Causation* (pp. 707–725). Oxford, UK: Oxford University Press.

Penfield, W., & Boldrey, E. (1937). Somatic motor and sensory representation in the cerebral cortex of man as studied by electrical stimulation. *Brain, 60*, 389–443.

Price, D. D. (1999). Placebo analgesia. In D. D. Price (ed.), *Psychological Mechanisms of Pain and Analgesia* (pp. 155–181). Seattle, WA: IASP Press.

Price, D. D., Finniss, D. G., & Benedetti, F. (2008). A comprehensive review of the placebo effect: Recent advances and current thought. *Annual Review of Psychology, 59*, 565–590.

Ramsey, W. (2008). Eliminative materialism. In Edward N. Zalta (ed.), *The Stanford Encyclopedia of Philosophy*. Retrieved from: http://plato.stanford.edu/archives/sum2013/entries/materialism-eliminative/

Schweinhardt, P., Glynn, C., Brooks, J., McQuay, H., Jack, T., Chessell, I., Bountra, C., & Tracey, I. (2006). An fMRI study of cerebral processing of brush-evoked allodynia in neuropathic pain patients. *Neuroimage, 32* (1), 256–265.

Skevington, S. M. (1995). *Psychology of Pain*. West Sussex, England: John Wiley & Sons.

Tracey, I., & Mantyh, P. W. (2007). The cerebral signature for pain perception and its modulation. *Neuron, 55* (3), 377–391.

Turk, D. C., & Okifuji, A. (1999). Assessment of patients' reporting of pain: An integrated perspective. *The Lancet, 353* (9166), 1784–1788.

Voudouris, N. J., Peck, C. L., & Coleman, G. (1990). The role of conditioning and verbal expectancy in the placebo response. *Pain, 43* (1), 121–128.

Waddell, G. (1996). Low back pain: A twentieth century health care enigma. *Spine, 21* (24), 2820–2825.

Wall, P. D. (1999). The placebo and the placebo response. In P. D. Wall & R. Melzack (eds.), *The Textbook of Pain, 4th edition* (pp. 1419–1430). Edinburgh: Churchill Livingstone.

Wickramasekera, I. (1980). A conditioned response model of the placebo effect. *Biofeedback and Self-Regulation, 5* (1), 5–18.

Wiech, K., Ploner, M., & Tracey, I. (2008). Neurocognitive aspects of pain perception. *Trends in Cognitive Sciences, 12* (8), 306–313.

EDITORS' COMMENTARY

The search for the causes of pain has undergone a fascinating evolution, as discussed in this insightful chapter by Lefebvre and Bednar. The point of departure for this story is the assumption that pain is caused by tissue damage, which seems like a straightforward account that would be valid for all humans across cultures. Here, we seem to be faced with simple efficient causation. Of course, there are many complicated aspects to the human experience of pain, and so we quickly learn that we also need to consider other types of causation, particularly final cause to do with meaning and how stimuli are perceived and interpreted.

One of us worked at McGill University at the same time that one of the authors (John Lefebvre) was a student there, which happened to also coincide with the tenure of Ronald Melzack, who co-developed the wall theory of pain during his decades of research at McGill. Melzack approached pain from a psychological perspective. For him, psychological interpretations intervene between the physical changes (tissue damage) and the actual feeling of pain. The incorporation of psychological factors necessarily leads to a far more complicated kind of causation to be considered. Now, what happens in the brain —cognition—can take central place.

We have entered an era of neuroscience research when every study has to have an fMRI image to tell us what the brain is doing when a person feels jealous or expresses racial bias, or feels pain, or does anything else. This is akin to the heyday of behaviorism when the new technologies and language of behaviorist researchers took over all of psychology. Inevitably, there are now hundreds of neuroimaging studies that attempt to identify the "pain centers" in the brain. The assumption is that such centers "control" pain experiences. By manipulating these "pain centers," it is assumed we will be able to causally impact the experience of pain. Of course, research using fMRI is fast being overtaken by studies using other technologies to study pain, such as optogenetics (Iyer et al., 2014). But irrespective of the particular technology being used, the challenge raised by the Gate Control Theory of pain remains: what are the processes resulting in the wall being or not being raised? To address this question, it may be necessary to incorporate both causal and normative accounts of behavior (Moghaddam, 2005).

REFERENCES

Iyer, S. M., Montgomery, K. L., Towne, C., Lee, C. T., Ramkrishnan, C., Deisseroth, K., & Delp, S. L. (2014). Virally mediated optogenetic excitation and inhibition of pain in freely moving nontransgenic mice. *Nature Biotechnology, 32*, 274–278.

Moghaddam, F. M. (2005). *Great Ideas in Psychology: A Cultural and Historical Introduction*. Oxford: Oneworld.

13

Questioning Causation in Mental Health

Paul Steinberg

The mental health field, indeed the field of psychiatry, has had more than its share of bizarre theories of causation. Perhaps the most striking of all the illogical psychiatric notions has been the theory of the schizophrenogenic mother causing schizophrenia. Coined by Frieda Fromm-Reichmann and promoted by Silvano Arieti, two well-respected postwar psychiatrists, this theory postulated that a nurturing figure in a child's life might continuously create double binds and Catch-22's and that these interactions would ultimately lead to auditory hallucinations—the hearing of voices that were not present in reality—and to horrific paranoid delusions including the typical belief in schizophrenia that something or someone, often in outer space, is controlling one's thoughts and feelings and actions.

No doubt a parent-child interaction that is filled with double binds can cause confusion and a bit of neuroticism, especially if the child is unable to escape from these interactions. But it is more than a considerable stretch to think that a mother or any parenting figure could somehow produce the profound symptoms associated with schizophrenia.

Competing for bizarreness in causation in the early twentieth century is the notion of the "refrigerator mom" causing autism. According to this theory, a cold and unengaged mother can create in her child an inability to understand language, a severe deficiency in what we call "receptive language"—a more-than-profound disability that makes it impossible for the child to use language to make sense of the world and to communicate with others and for others to communicate with him. Quite a stretch, again, in looking at causation.

As we can see, these theories took nature versus nurture, genetics versus the environment, and ran totally with nurture. And not just nurture: the theories assumed that the nurturer herself, the mother in virtually all cases, was the culprit, the cause of dreadful and disturbing symptoms and conditions. To put it mildly, mothers took it in the ear: not only were they facing the task of dealing with a young child with autism or a teenager with schizophrenia—each being terribly disabling conditions—but they also were considered the source and the cause of these illnesses. The ultimate in blaming the victim, the ultimate in guilt induction.

In the early 1900s Sigmund Freud noted that in the future we would find biochemical and physiological causes for these kinds of mental illnesses. But in the late nineteenth century and the early- to mid-twentieth century, our knowledge of the genetics and the biochemistry of the brain was quite primitive.

The thick skull surrounding the human brain has not helped matters. Even when Ivan Pavlov was able to look at the biochemistry of the stomach and gastrointestinal tract in the late nineteenth century—looking at the stomach's response to powdered meat or the anticipation of powdered meat in hungry dogs—the brain was still off-limits. Short of drilling holes in the skull, there was no way to look at the chemistry and physiology. So, the environment, the so-called "nurturing environment" (more accurately, the unnurturing environment) and the specific nurturer were the only causal factors that could be examined in explaining the human condition and the many various mental illnesses.

This inability to look at biochemical and physiological causes for major psychiatric disorders had a pronounced effect on treatment. Indeed the only treatments available were environmental ones—specifically talk therapy, or psychotherapy and psychoanalysis. The notion was that we could find a better nurturer, a better mothering figure to resolve the symptoms and the condition—a nurturer that could be infinitely more helpful and nurturing than the schizophrenogenic mother or the disengaged refrigerator mom. Although still quite helpful for anxiety and depression, talk therapy was used for conditions like schizophrenia and autism and mania—conditions that in their acute phases were and are unresponsive to talking and reasoning.

In the past 30–40 years, the pendulum has swung in the opposite direction. Now in the mental health field, the focus is almost exclusively on the biochemistry and physiology of the human brain, on the genetic elements involved in causality. Based on the fact that certain medications can be effective in treating conditions like schizophrenia and manic-depressive illness (bipolar illness), we have developed theories that associate these conditions with a particular biochemical substance or neurotransmitter, be it serotonin or norepinephrine or dopamine.

But, given the history of psychiatry, these hypotheses—for example, the serotonin hypothesis for depression—need to be taken with a considerable grain of salt and doubt. The biochemistry still eludes us. Yes, serotonin may have a considerable effect on mood and stress levels, but we are still unaware of the downstream effects of neurotransmitters like serotonin. Perhaps another neurochemical may have a more significant effect downstream than serotonin has. Again, that thick skull still makes it quite difficult to figure out the ways that the neurotransmitters interact and influence each other.

Even now in the twenty-first century, our ability to look at the human brain is limited. Imaging studies—with all their presumed promise—have so far turned out to be disappointing in looking at physiological changes in the brain and in looking at functionality. Computerized tomography (CT) scans and magnetic resonance imaging (MRI) can be extraordinarily helpful in looking at the anatomy of the brain—in looking for anomalies in the structure of the brain, in looking for tumors and swellings and edema and vascular changes. But these imaging techniques are relatively useless in our understanding of the physiology of the human brain.

Positron emission tomography (PET) scans can examine physiology through the use of glucose (a sugar) in parts of the brain as we do certain tasks. But, again, the capabilities are limited. Over the past century we have also been able to look at the postmortem brain, the brain in formaldehyde—and in the process discover the pathways going from the cerebral cortex to the midbrain, on to the brainstem and to the spinal cord.

Nevertheless, the functionality eludes us. How do the various areas of the brain interact and intertwine? For example, how does the amygdala in the temporal lobes interact with the prefrontal cortex? The amygdala is the seat of the sympathetic nervous system and the source of our instinctuality and our rapid response to stressors, and the prefrontal cortex is the most recently evolved and most sophisticated part of the brain, the area that allows us to think slowly and deliberately. We know that the pathways between these two parts of the brain are crucial in health and disease, but our understanding is still minimal.

How do the neurochemicals and neurohormones and various peptides interact in real time? And, again, how do these interactions produce a relatively healthy brain versus an unhealthy brain?

Even in the twenty-first century, we are left with speculations, theories, assumptions, hypotheses, conjectures, inferences, and suppositions. We are left with questions of correlation versus causation. Just because Prozac (fluoxetine, as the generic) is correlated with increases in serotonin levels in the synapses between brain cells does not mean that serotonin is the only crucial neurotransmitter in explaining mood disturbances, energy disturbances, and levels of stress and anxiety.

Ultimately in the process of attempting to understand neurochemistry and brain physiology, we have created what some have called a "mindless" understanding of the human brain, a mindless psychiatry. We have taken the most remarkable organ ever evolved on this planet and reduced it to relatively simplistic and reductionist biochemical causes and effects. The mind is nowhere to be seen.

Yet, despite our limitations, despite our potential mindlessness in understanding mental health, despite our uncertainties amid speculations, and despite our difficulties in distinguishing correlations from causations, let's take a look at aspects of mental health and mental illness—and figure out causation as best we can using our current technology and proficiencies.

* * * * * * * * * * * * * * * *

The most helpful paradigm in understanding health and disease and human behavior is what Matt Ridley, former science editor of the *Economist*, has called "nature via nurture." It all starts with the gene, with genetics—and then the environment supports and promotes that genetic element. Then a cascading effect—a virtuous spiral or a vicious spiral, depending on one's point of view—may ensue.

Let's start with schizophrenia, now that we know that nurture and the environment and the actual nurturer are not the causes of this debilitating illness. But that fact may be all that we know. We still do not have a clear-cut sense of what causes this illness. Seemingly healthy teenagers or young adults can develop a loss of touch with reality, can develop a set of paranoid delusions, a notion that something or someone is controlling one's thoughts and actions, a set of disturbing and unsettling and distracting auditory hallucinations—not just voices inside one's head but also static-like sounds and distortions.

It may start with a genetic predisposition. Several genes have so far been implicated, but not one of those genes has stood out. This has led to speculation, perhaps spurious, that schizophrenia is a bunch of different illnesses all leading to a final common pathway, all leading to a similar set of symptoms.

But here is one hypothesis that is gaining traction: a certain gene puts the body and brain in a position of being more sensitive to a specific virus in utero or in infancy—possibly the influenza virus. In fact, when the human population has faced influenza epidemics in the past, a peculiar phenomenon has come into play 15–20 years later: a virtual epidemic of schizophrenia has appeared in that 15–20-year time frame.

Some researchers have speculated that, when the human organism is challenged by the influenza virus, antibodies are formed to attack the virus, to kill the virus, and to remove the virus. In certain vulnerable people who have a specific genetic makeup, these antibodies attack not just the virus but also the cells of the brain's prefrontal cortex—with the cells of the prefrontal cortex somehow resembling the protein and peptide structure of the influenza virus in genetically vulnerable individuals. The prefrontal cortex, this highly sophisticated part of the brain, is not particularly important in early childhood, but becomes crucial in adolescence and young adulthood as we face more intricate and complex demands of relationships and career. With the prefrontal cortex losing its cells, other parts of the brain overcompensate and overdevelop. Indeed the temporal lobes may become overstimulated and thus produce altered perceptions and unreal auditory phenomena. This illness and these symptoms, however, may not rear their head until one is in his or her teenage years or early twenties.

An analogous process may occur in juvenile diabetes, otherwise known as Type I diabetes mellitus—to be distinguished from adult-onset or Type II diabetes (often associated with obesity). In juvenile diabetes, certain genetically vulnerable children or teenagers may be exposed to the Coxsackie virus, one of a number of viruses that causes the common cold. Antibodies attack the virus, but also attack the islet cells of the pancreas, the cells that produce insulin.

The youngster, with diminishing amounts of insulin, is unable to manage glucose, to push glucose into muscle tissue. Muscle wasting and off-the-charts sugar levels in the blood can ensue unless one is able to get access to exogenous, or outside, insulin.

So, in essence, in both conditions—with schizophrenia and with juvenile diabetes—two elements are required in this hypothesis: first, a specific genetic loading is essential, a genetic vulnerability in which the influenza virus proteins are similar in certain individuals to the proteins and structure of the cells of the prefrontal cortex, in order to produce schizophrenia. And likewise the Coxsackie virus proteins must mimic the pancreatic islet cells to produce juvenile diabetes. But a second element is crucial: if a genetically vulnerable fetus or infant never gets exposed to the influenza virus, he or she never develops schizophrenia. Likewise, a genetically vulnerable child who never gets exposed to the Coxsackie virus cannot develop Type I diabetes.

Thus, a very different kind of nature via nurture than we usually expect: genes are critical, and the environmental factors that bring forth the disease are not our fellow human beings, our nurturers, our mothers, but instead a simple virus.

No one as yet has been able to prove this hypothesis for explaining schizophrenia. The evidence is indirect, based on epidemiology and maternal/pregnancy histories. Toxins and poisons may also be factors in producing this illness.

Again, the question is causation versus correlation. An influenza epidemic is correlated with a significant increase in schizophrenia numbers 15–20 years later. A true causation?

* * * * * * * * * * * * * * * * *

Let's take a look at a more common human condition, that of depression and anxiety. As much as 20–30 percent of the human population experiences depression or anxiety, to a point of its affecting their ability to function, over the course of a lifetime.

Some depressive diatheses may be almost purely genetic—the equivalent of manic-depressive (bipolar) illness but without mania, just as there can be manic-depressive illness with only episodes of mania without any depressive episodes. This kind of presentation of depression may reflect only a small percentage of cases of depression, but this depression can feel pervasive and intractable.

Here is how the former U.S. poet-laureate Jane Kenyon once described it:

When I was born, you (melancholy) waited behind a pile of linen in the
     nursery,
And . . . you lay down on top of me, pressing the bile of desolation into
     every pore.

Most of us are remarkably resilient psychologically and emotionally into our mid- to late adolescence, and once we reach 17–18 years of age, we become more vulnerable. But children with the emotional fragility that Jane Kenyon describes are extremely vulnerable from a very early age—thus reflecting a considerable genetic component, no matter what the effects of the environment might be. From the start of life, one can feel that "[a] piece of burned meat wears my clothes, speaks in my voice, dispatches obligations haltingly, or not at all. It is tired of trying to be stouthearted, tired beyond measure" (Kenyon).

Yet the more garden-variety depression does reflect more of a nature-via-nurture paradigm. The environment, a series of stresses and losses and traumas and abuses, can have a profound effect on our neurochemistry, especially if we have a certain genetic predisposition, a certain set of personality traits that can make us more vulnerable to anxiety and depression.

These personality traits can be described succinctly in the word "temperament." Temperament may not explain causation of depression in a complete and comprehensive way, but it does explain a genetic vulnerability, a part of our hardwiring that makes us more reactive to the environment.

Data on temperament come from studies on human infants by Jerome Kagan in Boston and corroborating studies on primates in the Laboratory of Comparative Ethology at the National Institute of Child Health and Human Development (NICHD) by Stephen Suomi in Poolesville, Maryland.

In a simple but elegant study, Kagan exposed infants to a series of noxious stimuli: a tape-recording of a screaming and yelling mother's voice, clowns, and popping balloons. The exposures occurred at 4 months of age, 9 months, 13 months, and 22 months—a time frame in early childhood that would minimize the effects of the environment while maximizing the presumed effects of hardwiring and genetics.

The findings were striking, as well as consistent throughout the four time intervals: approximately 20 percent of the infants (generally between 15 and 25%) unvaryingly were more reactive to these noxious stimuli than the other 80 percent. In response to each of the stimuli—popping balloons, clowns, and a screaming mother's voice—the 20 percent started bawling almost immediately. For approximately 70 percent of the children, their lips would pucker, their mouths would turn downward, and they appeared to be on the verge of tears before pulling themselves together. And, remarkably, 10 percent of the boys and 6 percent of the girls consistently started smiling and laughing in response to each of these three noxious stimuli. Nothing short of physical pain—certainly not any startling noise or clownish figures—could cause much of a negative reaction in these seemingly invulnerable kids.

Suomi's findings with rhesus monkeys were similar. When he discovered that approximately 20 percent of the monkeys were more sensitive and more emotionally reactive—wherever they had come from—he initially assumed that he had gotten a bad shipment of monkeys. Shouldn't a larger percentage of monkeys be tougher, less emotionally fragile, more insensitive, and less reactive in order to maximize the survival of the species? Yet even the monkeys he studied in the wild off the coast of Puerto Rico had the same balance of emotionally reactive and sensitive versus more laid-back and less reactive. As much as 20–25 percent of the monkeys in the wild were sensitive and reactive.

So, what is going on here, he wondered. It turns out that the sensitive and reactive monkeys, both male and female, become better parents, become actual leaders in the monkey community when they have had good, nonpunitive parenting. They are able to be more caring and more nurturing, more supportive of their fellow monkeys. But with punitive parenting they are also more vulnerable to stress and depression and apparent neuroticism.

For the more laid-back and less-reactive monkeys, the parenting they received mattered much less. They found ways to escape or fight back against punitive parenting, to blow off inappropriate and unnecessary parental responses. Good, nonpunitive parenting was fine for them as well, but they could care less. They were able to "do their thing" no matter what the environment imposed.

Suomi describes a group of female monkeys in each generation that became "super-moms." They were the sensitive and reactive females who were fortunate enough to have had nonpunitive and nurturing and caring parenting. Their sensitivity put them in good stead, able to respond in a delicate and perceptive and attentive way to the younger generation.

So, from an evolutionary standpoint, it makes sense for a sizeable minority of primates, including humans, to have this sensitivity and reactivity. It makes for better parenting, and at the same time, however, it makes for a greater vulnerability to stress and anxiety and depression. Caring has its costs.

But what is temperament? How do we define the hardwiring of the brain that leads to certain clear-cut personality traits? Reactivity and sensitivity and an inability to care less—traits that can be definitively seen in four-month-old human infants—are a significant aspect of human hardwiring and of temperament. Yet we are beginning to see other elements that can be delineated in our neurophysiology.

Brain-derived neurotrophic factor (BDNF) is one of those genetic elements. The valine form of BDNF is associated with an enhanced memory for emotionally laden events. In contrast, the methionine form of BDNF—with a simple change in one amino acid—is associated with a diminished memory for emotionally laden events. Those with the methionine BDNF are able to let things go, to not be as bothered by events of the past.

Not surprisingly, those of us with methionine BDNF are much less prone to anxiety and depression. We are preoccupied less with the past; we may be more engaged with the here-and-now and less focused on mistakes and regrets from minutes and days and years ago. We are more readily able to get into what is often called "flow states."

And yet, those of us who do not remember and learn from the past are condemned and doomed to repeat it. Memory and history are valuable, not to be thrown off lightly. But this capacity for memory may not benefit our mental health.

This polymorphism of genes—this variation in genes—is inordinately valuable for any species. Some members of the species can survive best under certain environmental circumstances, and in other environments, members of the species with a different genetic loading can survive and thrive.

Fortunately genes can be turned on and off during the life cycle. A dance is constantly being played out between our genes and the environment. And we are capable of learning and growing, of developing a repertoire for dealing with life. Accordingly, we can learn to care less and to be less reactive, we can learn to let go of events from the past, to forgive and forget. We may need help in doing so, we may need valued role models who can show us the way, we may even benefit from talk therapy, or psychotherapy, which as we will see later is a form of unlearning and relearning, all mediated by changes in the chemical makeup of our synapses.

How does our early childhood affect our ability to handle stress and trauma? Clues are available from the work of Moshe Szyf and his colleagues at McGill University. Looking at rat pups, Szyf noticed a considerable difference between pups whose mothers spent a great deal of time licking and grooming them versus pups whose mothers were neglectful. The offspring that had been licked and groomed grew up to be less fearful and better-adjusted adults. Then as adults they were able to provide the same level of care for their own offspring, the next generation and beyond.

Szyf and colleagues then looked at the brains, specifically the hippocampus, the area of the brain most involved in responding to stress, of the two types of rats. The better-adjusted rats had, in their hippocampuses, a more active form of the gene that encodes a molecule called glucocorticoid-receptor protein. Glucocorticoid is a neurohormone produced in response to stress. This neurohormone is essential for our ability to respond effectively to stress and struggles, but too much of it can create a sensation of being overwhelmed. A feedback loop exists that allows our brains to turn off the glucocorticoid production when we hit a crisis.

Rat pups that have had minimal maternal care have a weaker feedback system. They are less able to turn off glucocorticoid production, and they are more anxious and fearful and show an intensified response to stress. All of this is mediated, it appears, by either methylation or acetylation of the glucocorticoid-receptor gene. In a process we call "epigenetic," the rat pups with limited maternal care had more methyl groups added to the gene, whereas well-groomed and well-licked pups had more acetyl groups added to the gene. The acetyl groups made gene expression easier and allowed the pups to turn off excessive production of glucocorticoids when necessary. In essence, they were better able to nurture and support and soothe themselves, to lick and groom themselves metaphorically in the face of stresses and struggles. A simple difference: an acetyl group with an extra carbon and an added oxygen ($COCH_3$) compared to a methyl group with one less carbon and no oxygen as part of it (CH_3). And yet a remarkable change in rat pup behavior and response to stress.

Can causation—or even correlation—be that simple in understanding mental health and illness and response to stress? We are still figuring this out.

But wait. New biochemical and physiological aspects of mental health are coming into play and being recognized—aspects that focus on what goes right in the human brain, not just what goes wrong. Some people have a heightened capacity to remodel the brain in response to stresses and traumas, essentially to make lemonade out of lemons. This neural remodeling allows a person to develop a greater resilience and a greater flexibility in response to the slings and arrows of life.

Fibroblast growth factor (FGF) may be an essential element in this neural remodeling. In rat studies, rats that are inhibited, indeed rats that appear vulnerable, have a lower level of FGF. They are less able—and slower—to recover from stresses and traumas.

But here's the rub, as we look at causation: is a low level of FGF a trigger for a more profound depression—with this low level interfering with potential neural remodeling—or is it a consequence of a profound depression? We still do not know which comes first—the old chicken-and-egg question.

In studying mental health and disease, we also can look at the phenomenon of telomeres. Telomeres are a region of repetitive nucleotide sequences at the end of chromosomes, and they serve to protect the chromosome and its genes from deterioration and from fusion with neighboring chromosomes, specifically during chromosome replication. As we age, telomeres begin to shorten. Our genes and chromosomes become more fragile and vulnerable.

Evidence is evolving, however, that certain activities and responses can minimize the shortening of the telomeres and lead to a longer and healthier life span. It appears that three elements are protective of telomeres, of chromosomes, of our longevity and health: exercise makes a difference, as does good sound sleep, as well as omega-3's in the diet. Again, though, causation versus correlation.

In contrast, certain personality traits and experiences and mental health factors can shorten telomeres. Pessimism and cynicism and hostility can exacerbate the shortening of telomeres. Likewise intrauterine exposure to stress as well as traumas and abuses in early childhood appear to intensify the shortening of telomeres. And low educational exposure makes one vulnerable to this shortening of telomeres. Yes, the slings and arrows, the outrageous fortunes of life, have a way of limiting our health, our longevity, and our emotional well-being. All of it is intertwined. There is no mind-body dichotomy.

* * * * * * * * * * * * * * * * * *

Alcohol, or drinking, problems offer an alluring opportunity to see nature via nurture at work. For centuries having been seen as a reflection of moral turpitude, drinking problems have in the past 80 years come be seen as a medical problem, as a disease, not unlike diabetes or heart disease. For better or worse, drinking problems have been taken out of the moral realm and moved into the medical and psychiatric realm—a major change in our thinking about causation. As the saying goes, if it quacks like a duck and walks like a duck, then it is a duck. And if a particular phenomenon acts like a disease, then it must be a disease.

So, what have we come to understand about alcoholism in the past few decades? Clearly genetics plays a crucial role, and the environment can readily reinforce the effects of genetics.

We can start with an old Japanese proverb: first the man takes a drink, then the drink takes a drink, then the drink takes the man. If any of us drink long enough and hard enough, we will eventually reach a point at which we will have lost control over our drinking. But how do we determine whether someone has reached the third phase of the above-noted Japanese proverb? When do we know that someone has lost control over his or her drinking?

A strong case can be made that someone who has one or two drinks regularly, even on a daily basis, does not have a genuine drinking problem. In fact, some research shows that regular controlled drinking is healthier for the body and mind than complete teetotaling. Yet someone who drinks only a few times a year, but each time he drinks to get drunk, may indeed have a drinking problem. Generally a person who has lost control over his or her drinking will acknowledge, "If I have one drink, I'll then have two; and before I know it, I'll be up to six, eight, ten or more."

No blood tests or imaging studies can determine if someone has a drinking problem. Indeed there is only one true test for a loss of control over drinking, a test developed by Rachel Fox, essentially a 40-day trial of controlled drinking. In this trial, the person with a possible drinking problem is paradoxically asked to drink whenever and wherever he or she wants during a specified 40-day period—but no more than two drinks (two glasses of wine or two beers or two shots, or any combination of these drinks) per any 24-hour period. Being sober and abstinent for 40 days proves nothing. Can they consistently have one or two drinks in a 24-hour time period and be able to stop? Do they have control?

Most people with drinking problems around the world turn out to have a genetic predisposition. They have what we have come to call a "low reactivity" to alcohol, a very high alcohol tolerance that they may have been born with. Marc Schuckit at the University of California at San Diego has taken 16-year-olds who have not been exposed to much previous alcohol and measured their reactivity to large boluses of alcohol. Could they walk a straight line? Did they slur their speech? Did their blood cortisol levels increase significantly in response to the challenge of large amounts of alcohol? As Schuckit has pointed out, the genetics would have been more obvious if he could have done his study with five-year-olds, but he, of course, could not get such a study approved by the university ethics committee.

Approximately 20 percent of the teenagers had low reactivity to alcohol: they could walk a straight line, they did not slur their speech, and their cortisol levels barely budged in response to large amounts of alcohol. Within the next 5 and 10 and 15 years, these were the then-young adults who ultimately and almost invariably developed drinking problems. They much more readily reached the third phase of the Japanese proverb; they were able to drink with impunity, without any adverse effects.

What role does nurture play? George Vaillant, a psychiatrist and alcohol researcher in Boston, has looked at first-generation Italian-American families and compared them to first-generation Irish families—with the realization that, within two to three generations of living in the United States, all bets are off with assimilation having taken hold. Vaillant removed families from the study if the families were studded with alcoholism, the families appearing to have a clear-cut genetic component to alcoholism.

The study—perhaps not replicable now with Southern European drinking patterns having come recently to resemble longstanding Northern European drinking patterns—was done in the early 1980s. It showed that the prevalence of drinking problems in first-generation Italian families was much lower than in the Irish families. And how the children in each group were taught to drink was 180 degrees opposite: in the Italian families, the kids were taught to drink from a very early age, but abuse of alcohol was not to be tolerated. In contrast, in the Irish families, children were not allowed to go near alcohol, but when they reached a certain age, they were expected to "tie one on," to prove how macho and adult they were by drinking as much as possible.

The evidence supports the notion that *if* you have low reactivity to alcohol and *if* you grow up in a culture with no exposure to alcohol until you are expected (in your late teens or early twenties) to drink everyone else under the table, you will be in real trouble with alcohol. The third phase of the Japanese proverb beckons. The drink is consuming you, not vice versa. Again, a long way from moral and spiritual depravity as a cause for drinking problems. Does this new nature-via-nurture causation ring true? It certainly fits together with a perspective from Alcoholics Anonymous: "I am not responsible for my illness, but I am responsible for getting help for my illness!"

In thinking about causation with alcoholism, as well as with other mental health conditions including schizophrenia and depression, we often do not look for deeper "why's," deeper aspects of causation. For example, with drinking problems, we might wonder why some human beings have developed a capacity to metabolize alcohol quite effectively, why they have developed this high tolerance for and low reactivity to alcohol. What evolutionary pressures caused this heightened capacity to drink alcohol with impunity, and thus be more vulnerable to developing drinking problems?

In contrast, many Asians cannot tolerate much alcohol. They are missing an enzyme, alcohol dehydrogenase, that helps in the metabolizing of alcohol. Alcohol indeed gets metabolized into toxic aldehydes including formaldehyde, and many Asians experience considerable flushing, an uncomfortable "Asian glow," after just one or two drinks. This flushing and this high reactivity to alcohol provide a protection against excessive drinking. But, again, why?

Why have some people evolved to have a high reactivity to alcohol and others a quite low reactivity?

Similar questions come up with culture. Why have some cultures cultivated heavy drinking, have promoted it and supported it? The Irish mode of how we teach our children and teenagers to drink has become a way of operating here in the United States. Kids are not allowed by law to be taught how to drink in a controlled and responsible way, until the age of 21. And at 21 the message is to get wasted, to prove you can handle large amounts of alcohol. Colleges have come to realize that one's 21st birthday is potentially the most dangerous day of a student's life.

Yet other cultures—until recently the Southern European and Mediterranean cultures—have created approaches that support controlled drinking and flog out-of-control drinking. Still other cultures—Moslem societies and even here in the United States in the 1920s with Prohibition—outlaw drinking entirely. And why? Why do different societies and tribes develop completely different approaches to dealing with a ubiquitous substance like alcohol?

Interestingly, drug problems—including marijuana and cocaine and opiates—have a different set of causations, we believe, than alcohol problems. Temperament may play a role: some people are much more willing to take risks, to flaunt the law, to ignore warnings about the impact and addictiveness of certain drugs. The Japanese proverb still applies: for example, first the man snorts cocaine, and in short order, given how addictive cocaine can be, cocaine snorts the man.

* * * * * * * * * * * * * * * * *

So far, our look at causation in recent years has focused on genetics and physiology and biochemistry—a mindless psychiatry, a look at mental health without looking at the mind. Learning and conditioning, however, play a crucial role in mental health and in mental unease and mental disease.

Eric Kandel, the 2001 Nobel Prize winner in Medicine and Physiology, has helped to bring the mind and its learning and unlearning and conditioning into clearer focus. A neurophysiologist and psychiatrist and psychoanalyst by training, Kandel wrote a seminal paper in the late 1970s called "Psychotherapy and the Single Synapse." Too often the mental health field examines and treats brain conditions in a global way, with medications that work throughout the brain, with physical treatments like electro-convulsive treatment that likewise work throughout the brain. But what happens at the single synapse level?

Kandel studied snails that have limited neural or brain tissue, that also have such large neural cells that they can be seen virtually with the naked eye, without a microscope. Baby snails, when exposed to a predator, figure out how to escape, and their neural synapses after exposure to the predator are markedly different than before the exposure. Learning happens, and it is mediated by biochemical changes at the synaptic level—in the chemical makeup of the area between neural cells. When later exposed to an animal that looks like a predator, but is actually a friendly animal, the snails continue to "run," to escape. As Kandel points out, if the young snails are going to be spending a good deal of time around the faux predator, these snails will have to go through a relearning process, a further change in their synaptic makeup. It will be crucial for them to make distinctions between the genuine predator and the faux one—to note the differences between the two and not just see the similarities.

Kandel's essential point is that talk therapy, or psychotherapy, is a pivotal way for people to learn and unlearn and relearn, to figure out how to deal with the everyday traumas of everyday life, to change the biochemistry of the brain one synapse at a time. Traumas are ubiquitous—not just in war zones or in abusive households or in dangerous neighborhoods, although those settings produce more profound traumas. When we are menacingly cut off on the highway, we experience a trauma, and we then may change our driving habits to avoid that lane or that highway for the next several days. At the single synapse level, our brain chemistry has changed; we have learned for better or worse to avoid that situation. But if we need to continue to use that lane or highway in the future, we may need to unlearn and relearn—to make distinctions between the situation yesterday and the situation today: the menacing driver is nowhere to be seen, the weather and traffic patterns are different today than yesterday.

We are still in the primitive stages in understanding the communication between brain cells, in even understanding the various neurochemicals involved in learning and unlearning. Psychiatric researchers have focused on certain neurotransmitters like serotonin and dopamine and norepinephrine. But other more newly discovered neurochemicals like the endocannabinoids—our own internal cannabinoids that have the same effect as cannabis in marijuana—may be just as critical in determining how we cope with life and its traumas. Indeed the endocannabinoids may be the crucial chemical that allows us to care less, to be less reactive to negative experiences.

But who knows? We are still figuring out causation versus correlation. Exercise is known to increase the release of endocannabinoids, to create what runners call "the second second-wind"—an ability to care less, to blow off problems from a few hours earlier, to not sweat the small stuff, and to see everything as small stuff. Are the endocannabinoids the cause of this change, or are they simply correlated with this change? Or are there other hitherto unknown neurotransmitters that are even more crucial?

Only one thing is certain: we know a heck of a lot more than we did a century ago. Yet the brain remains one of our still-enduring mysteries. We continue to figure out causative factors and to separate them from correlative factors. Even with autism we have moved well beyond the refrigerator mom hypothesis. Indeed, autism appears to be correlated with a continuing development of new pathways and neural connections and neural wirings in a young child's brain—but without the pruning and culling of these neural connections, a pruning that is essential for normal brain functioning. The young child is left with "noise," with blather and babble, with an inability to distinguish one sound from another. No wonder then that everything seems normal in the first year, and then everything goes to hell in brain function subsequently. But there is no evidence whatsoever that mothers and other nurturing figures have caused this brain disease; nor is there evidence that vaccinations and immunizations—a theory proposed in the past decade—would cause autism.

The vaccination hypothesis is a fine example of correlation rather than causation. Vaccinations were connected temporally with the development of autism: a seemingly normal child would get his or her early childhood vaccinations and within days or weeks would suddenly lose the capacity to understand language. Too easy to make causative assumptions based on these temporal connections.

A cautionary tale: We still have a long way to go in distinguishing causations from correlations. Our knowledge, as profound as it is, still has significant limitations. For many of us, though, the only thing that may rival the human brain for endless mystery and endless fascination may indeed be astrophysics and the universe itself.

EDITORS' COMMENTARY

In his discussion of a genre of explanations of the causes of certain psychopathologies, Paul Steinberg highlights the claims by some psychiatrists to have found the causes of these conditions in alleged relations between mothers and children. His analysis in the example that initiates his exploration of the causal concepts in use in mental health contexts makes use of agency concepts rather than either regular antecedent conditions or mechanisms. Mothers are the agents that bring about certain psychopathologies in the children. Steinberg notices that, in many ways, these alleged agents are singled out so that someone can be blamed for bringing about a deviant development process. However, a closer examination of his analysis reveals that it makes use of a more subtle pattern of causal concepts: *chains* of causal agents. There has been much discussion of chains of causally relevant events, but not much of a pattern of causality that depends on chains of agents.

The refrigerator mother is an agent in acting in a certain way, and her actions are the agents that distort the normal development of the child who develops a psychopathology. Mothers who present their children with double-bind situations cause those children to become schizophrenic. So it is what the mother does that is the distorting agent.

Stepping away from this type of theory, Steinberg points out that the popular alternative was to find the causes of mental abnormalities in biochemical phenomena. Sometimes these causes were remote from the site if the disturbance in genetic abnormalities and sometimes, for example, in the case of neurotransmitters is functional at certain specific sites in the actual nervous system of the person. By employing chemical action on these chemicals, their distressing effects could be mitigated. However, this was rarely successful on its own.

Scanning has made possible closer examination of a person's brain as an active organ, but, as Steinberg remarks, not only are we far from understanding how the various processes and substances interact but we have also been led into the trap of the "mindless" person. So far, correlations have fallen short of causes.

Taking the specific case of schizophrenia, Steinberg shows how the limitations in linking seemingly salient groups of genes as the distal factor in schizophrenia leave the question of the onset of the symptoms in any particular person—the site of proximal causes—unanswered. There has been the suggestion that an internal sequence of agents is redirected by an external event, such as an attack of influenza. If we turn to the balance between nature and nurture, in this context, Steinberg cites two important studies that tend to open up what seemed a simple relationship between nature and nurture. When subjected to noxious stimuli, some infants are upset but others are indifferent—reminding one of Bowlby's discovery of different types of responses to separation from the mother. The other study reveals that "problem drinkers" do have a distinctive genetic makeup that may predispose them to drinking too much alcohol for their general health. From the point of view of the extraction of causal concepts, we gain a picture of how genetic background conditions and the differential effect of similar triggers establish habitual behavior. Here we might even see a form of Aristotle's material and efficient *aitia* at work.

Turning the tables once again, Steinberg points out that the conditions of life that many people encounter and, for some, engender depression, do have an effect on the biochemistry of the person thus afflicted. Despite the popularity of turning increasingly to genetics and biochemistry for causal hypotheses, chains of agents or chains of events, the reality of the onset of depression opens up cultural and historical conditions as effective and, perhaps, candidates for causes.

Steinberg looks at other cases in which causal concepts seem to be at work: the learning and relearning that comes about after a trauma transforms (causes?) a change in our life patterns, and even in those of snails, but, as he points out, the search for a causal mechanism or for an authenticated causal agent actively producing change leaves us still with the distinction between correlation and causation unresolved in many cases.

14

Understanding the Person with Alzheimer's Disease from a Causes-and-Consequences Perspective

Kate de Medeiros and Steven R. Sabat

According to the *Diagnostic and Statistical Manual of Mental Disorders, 5th ed.* (*DSM-V*; 2013), Alzheimer's disease (AD) is a neurocognitive disorder causing a decline from previous levels in one or more of the following: learning, memory, language, perceptual-motor skills, executive function, social cognition, attention. At present, more than 5 million people in the United States have been diagnosed, and as the number of people who reach old age increases, the numbers worldwide continue to grow at an alarming rate (Thies & Bleiler, 2013). AD is debilitating emotionally and financially to those diagnosed and to their caregivers. In the absence of a cure or preventive measures, it is of paramount importance to help individuals and families cope with the effects of the illness as best as possible. How we cope, however, will depend on understanding the person diagnosed and his or her actions. That is, how we understand what causes the person's actions will affect how we treat the person, and how we treat the person will have still further effects on the person diagnosed and his or her loved ones.

During most of the twentieth century, a biomedical approach to understanding people with AD was dominant. From this point of view, AD is a biological disorder and alterations in the diagnosed person's actions were understood as being caused by pathological processes in the brain, especially amyloid plaques, neurofibrillary tangles, decreases in the levels of neurotransmitters, and losses of brain cells in many areas, including the hippocampus. In the last 25 years, other approaches have focused on more than the biophysiology of the person diagnosed. These new approaches include the *bio-psycho-social* approach (Bender & Cheston, 1997; Cotrell & Schulz, 1993; Downs, 1997, 2000; Downs & Bowers, 2008; Kitwood, 1990, 1993, 1997; Sabat, 2001) and the *situated embodied agent (SEA)* view (Hughes, 2001; Kontos, 2004, 2005). The former includes biological aspects, but focuses also on the subjective experience of the person diagnosed (psychological part) and the social world's effects on the person. The SEA view, recognizes the person diagnosed as (a) being embodied and able to express himself or herself in pre-reflective actions; (b) being situated in a social, cultural, spiritual, value-laden environment that is personal and extra-personal; and (c) having intentions that he or she chooses to act upon (agentic).

In summary, these newer approaches emphasize the idea that the actions of the person diagnosed can be due to:

- Brain damage
- The person's reactions to the effects of brain damage
- How others treat him or her
- The social, value-laden situation in which the person lives and has lived

In this chapter, we shall explore (1) how these different approaches can lead to very different interpretations of the same actions on the part of the person diagnosed (causes of actions) and (2) how these different interpretations lead to different ways of treating the person (the consequences).

I. THE FUNDAMENTAL ATTRIBUTION ERROR

One interpretive dynamic that affects how we understand and treat people with AD is what psychologists have called the "fundamental attribution error" (Jones & Nisbett, 1972). When applied to people with AD, it indicates that others view alterations in the person's actions as due to the person's "disposition" or nature (in this case the disease), rather than to the situational circumstances surrounding the person. So, the person is acting in this or that way because it is symptomatic of AD rather than due to external situations. This interpretation is quite common in Western culture. Thus, the treatment that follows will be medical/pharmaceutical rather than social or psychological.

Particular alterations in the actions of the person with AD truly are due to the effects of brain injury. For example, when a person repeatedly asks the same question even though it has been answered each time, the person is showing the effects of damage to what is called the "explicit memory system," of which the hippocampus is an important part (Sabat, 2006). In addition, there are depletions in the person's neurotransmitters, especially acetylcholine, making the transmission of neural impulses among the brain's neurons much less efficient than before. Given these causes, the treatments so far have been medications, such as Aricept (i.e., donepezil), that allow acetylcholine to remain in the synapses longer than it otherwise would, and some efficacious effects have been found. Thus, we have a biomedical cause and a biomedical treatment as a consequence. This is all well and good as far as it goes. Problems can arise, however, when we explore other aspects of the person's actions and examine the causal interpretations that are offered.

II. UNDERSTANDING "BEHAVIORAL PROBLEMS" THROUGH A BIOMEDICAL LENS

As mentioned earlier, biological approaches to understanding dementia focus on relating outcomes, such as behaviors (e.g., aggression) or actions (e.g., wandering), to physical changes in the brain rather than social or environmental circumstances. "Behaviors that challenge" (Keady & Jones, 2010), labeled as neuropsychiatric symptoms (NPS), are "signs and symptoms of disturbed perception, thought, mood, or behavior" (Livingston et al., 2005, p. 1996), and include delusions, aggressive behavior, hallucinations, agitation, depression, apathy, sleep impairment, wandering, repetitive vocalizations (e.g., repeatedly yelling for help), and others (Sink, Holden, & Yaffe, 2005). In AD specifically, apathy, agitation, depression, anxiety, and irritability are common; delusions and hallucinations are less common (McKeith & Cummings, 2005).

NPS are important to consider in the context of action and causal interpretations for several reasons. First, researchers have estimated that NPS occur in 50–98 percent of people with dementia, with prevalence varying by dementia type (e.g., AD) and stage (e.g., mild, moderate, severe) (Sink et al., 2005). Second, the real consequences for people who exhibit what are labeled as NPS include medication, hospitalization, and relocation from home to a formal care facility. In fact, the presence of NPS is cited as the primary reason for persons entering formal institutional care (Keady & Jones, 2010; Sink et al., 2005). Finally, NPS have been associated with stress experienced by caregivers, which in turn can lead to higher rates of depression and poorer health (Zarit, Stephens, Townsend, & Greene, 1998).

The question we raise herein is not whether NPS exist; behavioral disturbances are well documented. Instead, we seek to raise awareness regarding how behaviors and actions are interpreted (or misinterpreted at times), leading to fundamental attribution errors. For example, a person in a formal dementia care residence may be confused about where he or she is and consequently shows signs of irritability. Although the irritability itself is not directly linked to a medical cause, there is a medical cause for the confusion itself: the person experiences difficulty recalling information related to his or her location and the reason for being there. In practice then, even well-intentioned ways of examining causes of a certain behavior will likely end up with an explanation (e.g., brain changes lead to irritability) based on the disease itself rather than on something social or environmental (e.g., annoying music is playing loudly, causing a person to become irritable). We note that many formal dementia training programs stress the importance of "decoding" a person's behavior or trying to understand why a particular behavior is occurring by finding clues for the reasons behind the behavior, identifying possible motives, and developing, applying, and evaluating appropriate interventions (Keady & Jones, 2010). In our example, if the care providers viewed the "irritable" person as someone who may be frightened or confused about location, they might develop an appropriate social intervention (e.g., having a conversation with the person to offer explanations) rather than a medical one.

The following sections provide examples of such errors for two groups of people with AD specifically: those participating in adult day care center programs and those living in a secured dementia care residence.

III. ADULT DAY CARE CENTERS

Adult day care centers in the United States house programs for people with physical or cognitive challenges. In 2012, there were approximately 4,800 such centers in the United States (Harris-Kojetin, Sengupta, Park-Lee, & Valverde, 2013). Based on their legal capacities, day centers could potentially serve over 275,000 people daily, although data on actual usage are not available (Harris-Kojetin et al., 2013). Services provided at adult day centers generally include medical care, medication administration, physical therapy, and the opportunity to socialize with others (Siebanaler, O'Keeffe, O'Keefe, Brown, & Koetze, 2005). A licensed nurse specialist is usually required to supervise other care workers.

People attending adult day centers typically decide how often to attend, up to five days per week. Two important advantages of adult day care are (1) caregivers are given a regular respite from their caregiving responsibilities to pursue other activities or to go to work and (2) persons attending such centers are able to avoid social isolation in many cases, while being able to return to their homes each evening, thereby delaying or eliminating the need for formal dementia care residential settings such as assisted living or nursing homes. Caregivers who use adult day care services report experiencing less stress than do those providing all care within the home. There are virtually no data, however, on how people with dementia themselves view the experience of adult day care.

Although many people use adult day care services for social opportunities, the centers themselves are framed predominantly as providing medical services. For example, one adult day service advertisement includes the following description: "It is our primary focus to ensure that your loved one achieves an overall improvement in their quality of life through the effective management of chronic conditions, cognitive and physical stimulation, and medical management in a cost-effective environment" (Active Day, 2014). Consequently, this medical framing of the day care's purpose poses a risk that staff and/or family members may interpret the actions of people in adult day centers through a medical lens rather than through a more comprehensive bio-psycho-social model.

IV. CASE EXAMPLES: DELUSIONS AND IRRATIONAL HOSTILITY

As mentioned, some people with AD attend day centers during the week for social engagement and to give their carers respite or because their primary carers work. In one such situation, the spousal carer informed the second author that his wife, Mrs. D, who had been diagnosed four years earlier, (1) had developed a delusion about having a job and (2) she had become "irrationally hostile" toward him after he brought her home from the day center. Irrational hostility is said to be symptomatic of AD, even in the early stages, while delusional thinking is often more common in later stages of the disease. Especially in the case of the latter, pharmaceuticals are generally prescribed. Further investigation into these situations revealed a story that went beyond the biological level.

Regarding the report that Mrs. D was delusional about having a job, it turned out that at the day center, she had constructed a social persona describable as "the life of the party." She grew up in a show business family and at the day center told jokes and sang old songs that the other participants enjoyed greatly. The staff recognized her open, warm, gregarious nature and made her a liaison, of sorts, to help integrate new participants into the day center community. She found great purpose and meaning in this role and would hurry her husband in the mornings to take her to the day center because she did not want to be "late for work." Mr. D assumed that his wife had a delusion about being a paid employee (having a job) and that this delusion was symptomatic of AD. When asked about her "job," she was quite clear in explaining that she "worked to cheer people up" at the day center, because "many of them are depressed." Thus, she did not at all believe that she was a paid employee anywhere and had no delusion at all. She was using the word "work" to describe the meaningful things she was doing with and for people at the day center. In this example, the husband interpreted his wife's actions through a medical lens, attributing AD as the cause of her "delusions."

In the case of Mrs. D exhibiting "irrational hostility," the social situation that preceded her acting in a cold, angry manner toward her husband was as follows: When he arrived at the day center to pick up his wife, Mrs. D was standing in the hallway, engaged in conversation with staff members and the second author. As she was talking, Mr. D began tucking Mrs. D's turtle neck top into her slacks, as if she looked disheveled, which she did not. Her facial expression signaled embarrassment, humiliation, and anger, but Mr. D did not see this, as he was occupied with "fixing" his wife's attire. In subsequent days, Mr. D reported that "the AD is getting worse—she was irrationally hostile with me after I brought her home from the day center." Mr. D did not understand that his wife's anger was due to his having humiliated her, and so, lacking any explanation for her anger, he attributed it to AD, thereby committing the fundamental attribution error. When informed about the social context and what his actions toward his wife meant to her, he was terribly sorry for not having realized the effect of what he was doing. Consider, though, what could have happened had Mr. D informed the physician treating his wife that Mrs. D was "irrationally hostile": without any socially contextual information, the physician would have contextualized Mrs. D's actions as a biomedical outcome of AD, as "irrational hostility," perhaps requiring medication. If, on the other hand, we adopt a bio-psycho-social view, or an SEA view, then Mrs. D was not "irrationally hostile" at all. Rather, she was "right-eously indignant" about having been humiliated in public.

Aimless Wandering

Another common problem observed in people with dementia is "aimless wandering," which can involve anything from pacing back and forth to walking for stretches of time. It is important to note that there are very few medical parameters defining what constitutes "wandering." In most cases, it is the perception of the caregiver (formal or informal) that determines this label. For example, a person who appears to the caregiver to be walking without a clear end goal in mind (e.g., traveling from one's room to the kitchen for a meal) runs the risk of being labeled as "wandering."

The example of Mrs. R. is illustrative. Mrs. R was diagnosed with AD four years earlier and attended an adult day center four to five days per week. She would often be seen walking up and down the long hallway that led to the various rooms. People who knew her only as someone diagnosed with AD referred to this as "aimless wandering" because she was seemingly unable to reply to questions such as "Where are you going?" Perhaps she could be described also as "agitated."

Unlike Mrs. D, Mrs. R had severe problems recalling the words she wanted to use when speaking. At the same time, though, she was extremely helpful while at the day center, setting tables for lunch meals, noticing that people in wheelchairs or using walkers needed help in opening doors, and opening the doors for them. That is to say, her understanding of others' needs was clear and her ability to focus her attention on moment-by-moment situations was still quite intact as was her ability to execute proper plans of action.

Among the customary activities at the center were small group discussions led by staff. During this activity, Mrs. R absented herself and walked in the hallways. Without knowledge of the larger social context, Mrs. R could, indeed, be described as wandering aimlessly, which would be considered a pathological action caused by AD. With knowledge of the social context, however, her action could be described more aptly as taking a walk in the hall so as to avoid the humiliation and embarrassment that she would feel when her turn to talk would arrive and she would be unable to speak fluently and coherently. That is, her acting in this manner exemplifies "semiotic behavior"—behavior that is driven by the meaning of a situation and, therefore, hardly "aimless" at all.

V. AD IN THE CONTEXT OF LONG-TERM CARE

Some people with AD, for one or another reason although often because of NPS, cannot be cared for properly at home, and therefore become residents in specialized dementia care units. Two types of specialized dementia care units exist in the United States: (1) assisted living and (2) nursing home-level care.

These differ in the method of payment (private pay vs. government subsidized), government oversight (each type is subject to different state and federal regulations), and the level of care provided. Both types of care are important to consider in relation to people with AD because (1) many people with AD eventually are admitted to a specialized care unit, (2) the use of standardized tools to monitor behaviors reinforces the notion of a medical reason behind a particular action, and (3) the physical and social environments of long-term care (LTC) settings create a structure where it is difficult for the person with AD to escape the fundamental attribution error by staff, clinicians, and family.

Standardized assessment methods in LTC provide clinicians, staff, and government oversight agencies a means of looking at potential changes in various physical, cognitive, and behavioral aspects of persons over time. Common methods meant to inform staff within a care unit include the Psychogeriatric Dependence Rating Scale (PGDRS) (Wilkinson, 1980), whereby nursing staff rate the frequency of 16 types of behaviors for the prior five shifts. Behaviors include wandering, demanding interaction (described as "Does the patient demand conversation or other social interaction from the nursing staff by making a positive approach?), passive physical aggression ("Does the patient refuse to obey demands or follow instructions?"), and others. Note that the noun "patient" is used rather than resident, thus reinforcing a medical context. Monitoring people in this way allows staff to address any behaviors that may have changed or worsened through changes in medication or psychosocial interventions.

On a larger scale, the Long-Term Care Minimum Data Set (MDS) is an instrument that all Medicare- or Medicaid-certified nursing homes are required to complete for each resident. In addition to questions regarding medical conditions, level of care needed, and recent adverse events (e.g., falls), there are questions requiring staff to assess a variety of domains, including the resident's mood (e.g., "short temper," energy, self-depreciation), wandering (to include presence and frequency), and others (Centers for Medicare & Medicaid Services [CMS], 2012). The purpose of gathering such information is to collect data as well as enable the government to monitor the appropriateness of care provided, such as whether medications are being properly used.

Although the PGDRS or MDS may provide a record to evaluate a person's decline or progress over time, such tools also reinforce the connection between "disease" and "behavior" for staff. Walking becomes wandering; wandering, listed on the PGDRS and the MDS, then becomes a consequence of dementia. In addition, a resident's failure to comply with a caregiver's request, such as getting out of bed, can be labeled as "manipulative" or "combative to care" rather than the resident's desire to sleep longer. Interestingly, as is illustrated in the example of Mrs. T below, manipulation of residents by staff is not considered to be problematic.

VI. CASE EXAMPLES: DELUSIONS AND IRRATIONAL HOSTILITY

Although labeling of various behaviors may occur differently in LTC than in adult day care or home settings, such labels are present nonetheless. Consider the case of Mrs. T, a widow residing in specialized and secured assisted living facility for people with dementia. Staff reported that every morning, Mrs. T. put all her belongings in a suitcase and waited for her son to pick her up. As the hours passed, Mrs. T. became increasingly upset as she waited, sometimes refusing to go to the dining room fearing that her son would arrive and be unable to locate her. Staff described this behavior as "delusional"; Mrs. T's son rarely visited and had not notified the facility that he would be coming. They further described her behavior as "irrationally hostile," especially when she declined to join activities or unpack her belongings.

Staff often shook their heads and made comments about Mrs. T. "not knowing any better" because of her dementia or even "fixating" on her son because of her disease. As it turned out, the origin of Mrs. T's belief that her son was coming that day was directly rooted in the staff's actions. Every morning, to get her out of bed and dressed, the morning care staff (unbeknownst to the rest of the staff) would tell Mrs. T that she needed to get up and get ready because her son was coming to take her home, something that simply was not true. This, as it happens, is a form of malignant social psychology that Kitwood (1997) called "treachery," wherein people deemed healthy use forms of deception to manipulate a person with dementia in order to secure their compliance. Under the belief that her son was coming to take her home, Mrs. T. then packed her belongings and waited. Her hostility toward staff was directly due to her having been told that her son was coming, on the one hand, and being asked to go elsewhere in the facility, on the other, and hardly due to any biomedical condition. Her actions had deep personal and logical meaning given what she was told by staff in order to manipulate her in the first place.

Another example of hostile behavior is revealed in Mr. A., who also lived in a specialized dementia care assisted living residence. In this setting, staff created and used a "daily life plan," which was meant to provide information for other staff on how best to deliver care to the resident, personal data, favorite activities, and any notes on how to manage challenges or problems with the resident. The following is an excerpt from Mr. A's daily life plan:

> Strategies to help him get out of bed: Turn on alarm. Strip bed when he gets up to use the bathroom. Will get dressed if clothes are set out. Must shower first thing. Won't refuse if he's sleepy. Particular about washing, rinsing and drying. Does each step three times. If he is rushed, he gets agitated and refuses care. Likes very warm shower.

On the second page, under the heading of "sleep habits," the following was written: "Early riser, late to bed."

There is much worth noting here. First, there seems to be a disconnect between the belief that Mr. A prefers to wake up early and the practice of tricking him into staying awake by removing his bedding when he is using the restroom. Perhaps because Mr. A. likes to stay up late, he may also like to sleep later than the staff would prefer. His preference of sleeping late became a problem that staff devised a means to fix, by turning on his alarm clock. Another important aspect is the use of the word "agitated," which is a common NPS associated with AD. "Agitated," as opposed to "annoyed" or "upset," frames Mr. A's reaction as an NPS rather than a desire to adhere to a preferred morning ritual. Mr. A. may have used the bathing routine of washing, rinsing, and drying three times for most of his life. Becoming upset by being rushed through a morning routine, or being forced to carry out the routine at a time that is not of one's own choosing, is a logical reaction that most people deemed healthy would have. Yet, the fundamental attribution error is committed by placing these actions in the context of the disease, not the circumstances.

Aimless Wandering

As mentioned earlier, determining what constitutes "aimless wandering" is often left to the observer. Many dementia LTC facilities contain what is called a "wandering loop," which is usually a hallway that circles the perimeter of the secured part of the building, providing residents with a place to walk because they otherwise have little opportunity for exercise or privacy. The fact that such a hallway is called a wandering loop immediately pathologizes any walking done by a resident in this hallway. Mr. H., a resident in the nursing home section of a specialized dementia care facility, was described by staff as spending his days wandering aimlessly through the hallways, as otherwise unresponsive, subject to anger, and lacking social cognition. On one occasion, the first author joined Mr. H. on his walk. After introducing herself to Mr. H., he immediately asked her if she knew how to open the doors. Thus, he recognized that she was not a resident and therefore might not have such knowledge. He invited her to accompany him. As they walked, he would motion for her to stop prior to examining intersections of hallways. He then carefully proceeded forward, looking both ways for staff members and, if "the coast was clear," motioned for her to advance. If staff were present, he would stop and simply look around, perhaps to avoid arousing their suspicions. His purpose for walking, as it turned out, was to find a way out of the unit. The walk continued in this manner until they finally reached the main door. When the first author was unable to open the lock, Mr. H. shook his head and suggested they try another door.

The point of this example is that, as in the case of Mrs. T above, Mr. H. was clearly walking with a purpose, namely, to leave. He seemed to have a deep mistrust for others at the nursing home and saw, in his new walking partner, a possible ally. That his intact social cognition and clear motives were dismissed by staff members so readily discounted Mr. H's experience of being held against his will in a strange place, surrounded by strange, even threatening, people, and prevented staff from understanding and sympathizing with his point of view. Indeed, the staff clearly made the fundamental attribution error by failing to appreciate what the situation meant to Mr. H as a person.

VII. SOCIAL CONSEQUENCES OF THE FUNDAMENTAL ATTRIBUTION ERROR

In previous sections we described some of the physical consequences (e.g., medication) of interpreting as pathological the actions of people with dementia. Terms such as "wandering" reflect the assumption that the person with dementia cannot make a purposeful choice (e.g., to walk for exercise). In this section, we address some of the social consequences (e.g., loneliness, isolation) of overlooking or devaluing the personhood of someone with AD. In other words, viewing the person with AD through a lens that focuses on and emphasizes pathology will affect the quality of opportunities that the person has to interact with others socially.

Here, we focus briefly on the topic of friendships. Rarely have researchers examined how new friendships unfold between people with dementia in LTC settings (de Medeiros, Saunders, Doyle, & Mosby, 2012). Although such settings provide structured social activities for people with AD, staff at many LTC settings assume that someone deemed healthy is needed for a successful social encounter to occur. In other words, people with AD are often viewed as incapable of initiating meaningful social encounters themselves outside of guided activities.

In LTC settings in general, residents' ability to socialize is determined by several factors beyond their control such as physical layout of building, other residents' willingness to socialize, and presence of staff in public spaces, among others. In a specialized dementia care environment, these barriers become more pronounced given the restricted space and limited number (10–20) of other residents. For example, placement of furniture may make it difficult for a resident to move from one side of the dining room to another, thereby limiting the number of people with whom one could talk. Staff themselves limit social engagement among residents by interrupting their conversations, guiding residents to specific seats based on their opinions of who among the other residents would make an acceptable social partner for that person, or playing music at too high a volume for people to talk above (de Medeiros et al., 2012).

The following conversation occurred in the dining room of a specialized unit for people with mid-stage dementia. The dining room featured a "men's table," where the same four men were guided by staff to sit for meals each day since staff believed they preferred to sit together because they shared many interests in common. On this particular day, Mr. J. was being guided to the men's table by Sally, a staff member.

Sally: How are you doing, folks?
Mr. J: How are you doing?

Sally: Good. Is everything OK?

Mr. J.:   Everything is fine. [speaking to one of the men at the table] Mr. S. How are you? How are you, boss?

Mr. S: I am fine. Yourself?

Mr. J: I am alive. [The people at the table laugh.]

Sally: Look, it's a Valentine's Day Card.

Mr. J: Yeah, don't tell me.

Sally: It's very cute.

The conversation between Sally and the tablemates continued for a bit, ending when Sally offers to "do some visiting" with a third person at the table, Mr. B. Although well intentioned, Sally took responsibility to manage the conversation between the men. She interrupted Mr. J's dialogue by introducing a topic that was not of interest to him. She did not provide the men any privacy for any conversations they may have wanted to have on their own. She also took it upon herself to "visit" with Mr. B. Overall, the reason for placing the men together at this table is thus negated by Sally's presence and oversight. There was no way of knowing what sorts of relationships could have developed or what conversations could have been shared among these men, because they were never given the opportunity to interact with each other.

VIII. CONCLUSION

The consequences of using the diagnosis of AD as a biomedical "explanation" of what people do are clear:

1. Biomedical remedies are sought.
2. The subjective experience of the person diagnosed is not given serious, thoughtful attention.
3. Dysfunctional social treatment of the person continues.
4. Reactions to socially dysfunctional treatment are seen as symptomatic of illness rather than logical reactions to treatment that Kitwood (1997) called "malignant social psychology" and people with AD continue to be misunderstood.
5. Actions such as Mrs. R's and Mrs. T's are seen as being pathological results of disease rather than logical examples of self-protection and self-respect, and Mrs. R and T are not seen as persons who understand the meaning of situations and act as would most persons deemed healthy.
6. Caregivers feel helpless in the face of the disease and see their loved ones primarily in terms of defects.

The consequences of using the larger social context as influencing the actions of people diagnosed with AD are likewise clear:

1. The subjective experience of the person is respected, is understood, and can gain sympathy of others.
2. Socially dysfunctional treatment is recognized as such and ceases.
3. People with AD are recognized as able to understand social situations and to respond to those situations as they did in healthier days.
4. People with AD are treated as people rather than as patients or as instantiations of disease entities.
5. Caregivers are able to appreciate their loved ones' remaining strengths and respond accordingly, thereby not exacerbating the effects of AD.
6. Medication is not used unnecessarily; extant excess disability ceases.

Finally, considering how the fundamental attribution error functions in dementia care raises two important questions regarding the personhood of those diagnosed:

1. Does the hegemony of the medical model prevent Mr. R from receiving the very information he needs to help his wife avoid feeling depersonalized and then ignored and then depressed? Might there be some improvement in her condition if she weren't unwittingly treated as a nonperson?
2. What type of authority is privileged in the context of care—medical or person focused? The language of medical authority (e.g., labels such as agitation and wandering), even when coming from a layperson (e.g., Mrs. R's husband), often takes precedence in nonmedical decisions about care. In both cases, the complexities of the person are replaced by the "simplicity" of a medicalized answer and the effects of this are precisely what we hope to bring into question, for providing humane care would seem to require attention to and support of the complexities of the person.

REFERENCES

Active Day Senior Care. (2014). Welcome to the Active Day and Senior Care Centers of America. Located at: www.seniorcarectrs.com. Accessed on August 12, 2014.

Bender, M. P., & Cheston, R. (1997). Inhabitants of a lost kingdom: A model of the subjective experiences of dementia. *Ageing and Society, 17,* 513–532.

Centers for Medicare & Medicaid Services. (2012). Long Term Care Minimum Data Set (MDS). Located at: http://www.cms.gov/Research-Statistics-Data-and-Systems/Files-for-Order/IdentifiableDataFiles/LongTermCareMinimumDataSetMDS.html. Accessed on July 29, 2014.

Cotrell, V., & Schulz, R. (1993). The perspective of the patient with Alzheimer's disease: A neglected dimension of dementia research. *The Gerontologist, 33,* 205–211.

de Medeiros, K., Saunders, P., Doyle, P., & Mosby, A. (2012). Friendships among people with dementia in long-term care. *Dementia, 11*, 363–381.

Diagnostic and Statistical Manual of Mental Disorders, 5th Edition. (2013). Washington, DC: American Psychiatric Association.

Downs, M. (1997). The emergence of the person in dementia research. *Ageing and Society, 17*, 597–607.

Downs, M. (2000). Dementia in a socio-cultural context: An idea whose time has come. *Ageing and Society, 20*, 369–375.

Downs, M., & Bowers, B. (Eds.). (2008). *Excellence in dementia care: Research into practice.* New York: Open University Press/McGraw Hill.

Harris-Kojetin, L., Sengupta, M., Park-Lee, E., & Valverde, R. (2013). *Long-term care service in the United States: 2013 overview.* Hyattsville, MD: National Center for Health Statistics. Access online at: www.cdc.gov/nchs/data/nsltcp/long_term_care_services_2013.pdf.

Hughes, J. C. (2001). Views of the person with dementia. *Journal of Medical Ethics, 27*, 86–91.

Jones, E. E., & Nisbett, R. E. (1972). The actor and the observer: Divergent of the cause of behaviour. In E. E. Jones, D. E. Karouse, H. H. Kelley, R. E. Nisbett, S. Valins, & B Weiner (eds.), *Attribution perceiving the causes of behaviour*, pp. 79–94. Morristown, NJ: General Learning Press.

Keady, J., & Jones, L. (2010). Investigating the causes of behaviors that challenge in people with dementia. *Nursing Older People, 22*(9), 25–29.

Kitwood, T. (1990). The dialectics of dementia: With particular reference to Alzheimer's disease. *Ageing and Society, 10*(2), 177–196.

Kitwood, T. (1993). Towards a theory of dementia care: The interpersonal process. *Ageing and Society, 13*, 51–67.

Kitwood, T. (1997). *Dementia reconsidered: The person comes first.* Buckingham: Open University Press.

Kontos, P. (2004). Ethnographic reflections on selfhood, embodiment, and Alzheimer's disease. *Ageing and Society, 24*(6), 829–849.

Kontos, P. (2005). Embodied selfhood in Alzheimer's disease: Rethinking person-centred care. *Dementia: The International Journal of Social Research and Practice, 4*(4), 553–570.

Livingston, G., Johnston, K., Katona, C., Paton, J., Lyketsos, C. G., & Old Age Task Force of the World Federation of Biological Psychiatry. (2005). Systematic review of psychological approaches to the management of neuropsychiatric symptoms of dementia. *American Journal of Psychiatry, 162*(11), 1996–2021.

McKeith, I., & Cummings, J. (2005). Behavioural changes and psychological symptoms in dementia disorders. *The Lancet Neurology, 4*(11), 735–742.

Sabat, S. R. (2001). *The experience of Alzheimer's disease: Life through a tangled veil.* Oxford: Blackwell Publishers.

Sabat, S. R. (2006). Implicit memory and people with Alzheimer's disease: Implications for caregiving. *American Journal of Alzheimer's Disease and Other Dementias, 21*(1), 11–14.

Siebanaler, K., O'Keeffe, J., O'Keefe, C., Brown, D., & Koetze, B. (2005). *Regulatory review of adult day services: Final Report.* Washington, DC: Department of Health and Human Services. Accessed online at: aspe.hhs.gov/daltcp/reports/adultday1.pdf.

Sink, K. M., Holden, K. F., & Yaffe, K. (2005). Pharmacological treatment of neuropsychiatric symptoms of dementia: a review of the evidence. *JAMA, 293*(5), 596–608.

Thies, W., & Bleiler, L. (2013). 2013 Alzheimer's disease facts and figures. *Alzheimer's & Dementia: The Journal of the Alzheimer's Association, 9*(2), 208–245.

Wilkinson, I. M. (1980). Psychogeriatric dependency rating scale: A method of assessment used by nurses. *British Journal of Psychiatry, 137,* 558–565.

Zarit, S. H., Stephens, M. A. P., Townsend, A., & Greene, R. (1998). Stress reduction for family caregivers: Effects of adult day care use. *The Journals of Gerontology Series B: Psychological Sciences and Social Sciences, 53*(5), S267–S277.

EDITORS' COMMENTARY

Contemporary thinking has much expanded the range of conditions that are implicated in the explanation of the behavioral and cognitive deficits that make up the syndrome of Alzheimer's disease. These can be due to: brain damage; the person's reactions to the effects of brain damage; how others treat him or her; the social, value-laden situation in which the person lives and has lived. Sebat and de Madeiros describe how these different approaches can lead to very different interpretations of seemingly the same actions on the part of the person diagnosed, each of which paints a different picture of what is responsible for those actions. That is, in a general way, different interpretations arise as to their causes and how these different interpretations lead to different ways of treating the person in terms of different views as to what is responsible for what a person can and cannot do. These may include biological changes in the person's brain, but also—and this is the consequence of new thinking in this field—many other features of a human situation, including the ways other people behave and the social and historical situation that a person is embedded in.

What kinds of causes are implicit in this account? We can start by noting the way the general pattern of standing conditions and momentary triggers shapes much of the discussion. Each opens a causal question: what brought this kind of condition about, and what agent is responsible for the advent of the relevant trigger? It also raises the question of why some events are triggers for the display of Alzheimer-type behavior and some are not.

However, in the analysis of the overall pattern of causal concepts, the role of time was fundamental—and that was presented as rooted in the flux of change. In the case of the "causes of Alzheimer's disease," Sabat and de Medeiros's presentation draws attention to changes that are intrinsic to the person, neurological and psychological, and to changes that are extrinsic to the person. Extrinsic changes include ways in which the social and moral contexts emerge around a person once that person has been so diagnosed. Diagnosis itself becomes a causal factor in the sense of a potent agent acting on the individual and creating an environment that further extends the aura of the original changes. A simple example is the change in a person's life that comes about when the diagnosis of Alzheimer's leads to the withdrawal of the license to drive a car. In diseases such as viral infections, and conditions such as broken bones, the diagnosis exists independently of the disease. In the case of Alzheimer's, it becomes an intrinsic part of the condition. Thus, we encounter a kind of cyclical causality, which we find in the self-fulfilling prophecy as the act of professing becomes a causal factor in the genesis of the consequential state of affairs. We could envisage two patterns of this general sort—one might lead to a static repetition of syndrome and diagnosis, in which each perfectly replicates the other. But we also seem to have cases in which the product of the action that is triggered by the reaction of the first act is slightly different—this engenders a slightly different diagnosis, and so we have a progressive development. In one case, cited by Sabat and de Medeiros, the reciprocal causal reflection leads to progressive worsening of the condition and, in another, to its betterment. There is also the type of case cited by Sabat and de Medeiros, in which the stress induced in a caregiver begins to have an effect on the person being cared for that exacerbates the stress suffered by the caregiver. Which of the patterns of causality brought out by the philosophical survey of causal concepts seems to be appropriate in these cases? The simplest and perhaps most superficial analysis exemplifies the "this rather than that" pattern—the diagnosis makes more probable that the condition will worsen, which will affect subsequent diagnoses. Then we have a platform for looking for the mechanisms which sustain these processes—and they appear to be familiar patterns of reasoning. Does holding a certain premise cause the thinker to draw a certain conclusion? At least we can say this: if the reasoner does hold a premise that does entail a certain conclusion with relevant ancillary matter, and that would be a piece of valid reasoning by the logic of our culture, then we might want to extend the scope of causal concepts to cases like this on the grounds that holding this premise, rather than some other, makes it more likely that the reasoner will draw that conclusion.

The second fundamental point, apropos of the use of causal concepts, emerges in considerations of care. It is not only bound up with a certain biomedical slant toward AD but is embedded in the very words used to describe what the sufferer's behaviors mean. Essentially, the sufferer is stripped of personal agency. In case after case, Sabat and de Medeiros demonstrate the malign effects of this practice, intended for the next of reasons. It occurs most strikingly in the language used to describe what AD sufferers do. For example, "aimless wandering" is used in place of "going for a stroll." The former is non-agentive while the latter is agentive. Instead of "annoyed" or "resentful," the

AD sufferer is described as "agitated." Again, the use of this word moves the causality of the conduct of the patient from the agentive to the passive domain, thus deleting personhood and the personal agency that goes with responsibility and control and meaningfulness. To be agitated is to be the victim of a neurological or biochemical process. As such, it is shorn of any meaning it might have in the concrete context of actual situation and, perhaps, its history.

Part Five

. . . .

Causal Concepts and Collective Behavior

15

Causality and Protracted Violent Conflicts: The Case of Internally Displaced Persons

Daniel Rothbart and Sudha G. Rajput

Why do certain identity groups—ethnic, religious, nationalist—resort to violence as a means for settling their grievances against an adversary? The answer to this question represents a primary goal of conflict analysts. With their attempts to find the "why" of protracted violent conflict among identity groups, such analysts routinely resort to various notions of causality. In their studies of specific conflicts, researchers invoke ideas about causal processes, mechanisms, factors, or systems that are responsible for producing such violence. Such notions are inextricably linked to attempts to explain why such conflicts occur, how they evolve, and what the opportunities for their possible resolution are. The dynamics of relations among those engaged, or engulfed, in violence rest on different kinds of causal processes. Attempts to reduce such processes to a single form, such as human-oriented causality, are bound to fail.

One way to illustrate this centrality of causal notions in the analysis of protracted violent conflicts is to identify the working assumptions of a vast majority of conflict research. We identify three such assumptions. First, protracted violence conflicts are complex, involving a wide range of stakeholders spanning various sectors of society. Within the internal dynamics among such stakeholders are causal processes of various kinds, such as those processes in which some stakeholders seek influence, control, or possibly to dominate others. For example, in the prelude to many conflicts, political leaders resort to various forms of manipulations to persuade a reluctant civilian population to support, and possibly sacrifice themselves for, the "just cause" of war, which illustrates such processes.

A second working assumption is that protracted violent conflicts are deeply rooted in social and political systems that create the preconditions for rebellion. In such cases, certain marginalized segments of the general population believe that their suffering finds its source in the domination of those who control their reins of power in various sectors of society. This notion of deep-rooted systems is fundamentally causal.

Third, the impact of such conflicts extends far beyond the battlefield to those who are not directly involved in the violence.[1] For many survivors, the sense of devastation they experience can turn to hatred, hostility, and enmity that, in turn, can serve as a prelude to subsequent violence.

In this chapter, we examine one sort of causal process that is ubiquitous among conflict protagonists. This is a process in which a certain segment of the population, such as a minority population who feels marginalized from the national centers of power, prestige, and promise, resorts to violence out of frustration and as a reaction to their plight. In Section 1 we focus in particular on a primary aspect of such a reaction—the moral emotions of the conflict protagonists. Then, in Section 2, we extend the study of moral emotions to those who are neither conflict protagonists nor militants. We examine the plight of those civilian noncombatants whose lives are negatively impacted, through various causal processes, by the violence. We give special attention to those civilians who are forcibly exiled from their homes to seek safe haven in an in-country community. Many of these internally displaced persons (IDPs) experience a deep sense of social-psychological devastation that is charged with shame, humiliation, and guilt. We present findings of a case study of a group of IDPs from Kashmir, whose exile from their homeland brought on trauma that is awash in moral emotion. We argue that such trauma constitutes an affliction to the moral life of IDPs, that is, a rupture to their sense of self in relation to others that is steeped in moralistic sentiments, thoughts, and judgments. This is a trauma that deeply impacts the moral plane of their lives.[2]

I. RELATIVE DEPRIVATION

According to one widely cited conflict theory, some violent conflicts are fueled by a group's frustration reactions to their sense of relative deprivation. In such cases, a group believes that their rights are denied, their expectations from society are unmet, and their elemental needs are unfulfilled. As Ted Gurr argues, relative deprivation occurs when the group's value expectations are unfulfilled and will remain so given the limited capacities from their placement in society (Gurr, 1968, 1970, ch. 2). In such cases the deprived group experiences a psychological tension, or internal struggle, between what they regard as their expected rights that society should recognize and the limited opportunities for actually having their expectations realized.

---

[1] By any reasonable measure, civilian noncombatants suffer more than combatants in protracted violent conflicts. Violence against civilians, either intentionally targeted or unintentionally engulfed in the hostilities, is deeply embedded in the character of such conflicts, as one author has argued elsewhere (Rothbart & Korostelina, 2011, ch. 1).

[2] We are invoking Erving Goffman's notion of a moral career, which he develops regarding the moral career of mental patients (Goffman, 1968, ch. 2).

The frustration-reaction system is conceived as a social-psychological response—a causal mechanism—to the realization of one's deprivation. The result of such tensions are contradictory emotions of hope and despair—hope that they should be afforded certain rights, opportunities, and privileges associated with membership in society and despair over the realization that their value expectations are not met. In such cases, the group feels socially handicapped by their degraded social placement, status, or station. Frustrations foster anger, bitterness, humiliation, hatred, or possibly demonization of the dangerous other. For many identity groups, certain traumatic episodes foster a sense of collective suffering, survival, heroism, endurance, strength, and possibly well-being (Volkan, 1997, ch. 5).

Such frustration reactions are charged with moral emotions. A moral emotion should not be understood as a momentary feeling, a pain from a pinprick. It is rather a dynamic process, that is, a social-psychological force with intensity and direction.[3] Negative moral emotions are experienced as a tension, an imbalance, or a disturbance in one's relations with others. For example, with humiliation, one takes on a sense of being disgraced in the eyes of others. The humiliated person ponders, or broods, over his or her diminished moral worth or social status in a social space. In some cases, the humiliated person experiences an acute form of disorientation, which people often express in terms of not knowing what they are, but which can also be seen as a radical uncertainty of where they stand, as if losing one's bearings for navigating through treacherous waters (Taylor, 1989, p. 28). Such emotions can be understood as a lingering condition of one's life, experienced as a state of being ill-at-ease in relations with others.

To develop this theme further, we offer the following defining elements of any moral emotion: (1) biophysical response to an encounter, interaction, or experience; (2) normative assessment of an encounter, interaction, or experience; (3) a capacity to spread from one person to others; and (4) a positioning system underpinning such practices.

The biophysicality of any emotion reflects a psychic tension, disturbance, agitation, rupture, disintegration, or possibly disorientation of the individual in relation to a social order.

In such cases the body undergoes psychochemical changes—secretion of adrenalin, increased heartbeat, changing respiration, and perceptual intensity. Blood flow to the muscles intensifies the capacity for running away, and a surge of cortisol from the adrenal glands pumps glucose to the bloodstream, providing extra energy. Through such mechanisms, the fear is thoroughly embodied. And in the conventional (neuropsychological) interpretation, the triggering events are causes of the embodied responses.

---

[3]We invoke Kurt Lewin's field theory of psychology for an understanding of a moral emotion (Lewin, 1951, ch. 5).

Moral Emotions Are Not Explained by Biophysical Conditions Alone

Going beyond momentary changes in the body, moral emotions linger, persist, and may come and go over time. Such emotions are not instantaneous feelings. They remain with the person. For example, an emotion of compassion typically stays with the person, characterizing his or her state of responsiveness to experiences, encounters, and episodes over time. One cannot experience such emotions without some sense of moral judgment about what is morally good or bad, right or wrong, or virtuous or vicious (Williams, 1985, p. 129).

Moral emotions are normative responses to life's encounters, interlinked with assessments of events, experiences, and encounters. Such emotions are not removed from the weave of life. They invoke memories of the past, responses to the present, and aspirations for the future (Coulter, 1986, p. 120). For example, humiliation is experienced as a disgrace that tacitly invokes social mores and notions of intrinsic values and disvalues in life. In like measure, shame is neither momentary nor cut off from the life's experiences. To be humiliated implies an understanding and judgment about events in the world and a way of being that occurs both in the head and in meaningful social events or encounters with others. The "substance" of such emotions is deeply socialized. As Martha Nussbaum has shown, emotions are inseparable from the landscape of our mental and social lives, thoroughly suffused with intelligence and discernment (Nussbaum, 2011, p. 1). Emotions are experiential responses from which we register the damages we have suffered, might suffer, or luckily avoided (Nussbaum, 2011, p. 6).

> A moral emotion can spread, like a contagion, in ways that overwhelm those afflicted with the emotion and impact others who are affected by the display of emotion. (Hatfield, Cacioppo, & Rapson 1994, "Introduction")

One can "catch" the emotions of joy, love, anger, fear, and sadness of those around them. In tightly knit groups, the display of prosocial emotions has the effect of bringing individuals closer together, as with expressions of displays of affection, forgiveness, kindness, warmth, or love. Of course, the display of negative emotions, such as anger, has a divisive impact on social relations. In conflict settings, stories about the dangerous Other are filled with emotional impact, raising individuals to a fever pitch of terror that often precedes the collective campaign of militant retaliation against an enemy.

The social force of a moral emotion is typically conveyed through storytelling practices, public speech, and collective action. Such force can persuade, extol, overwhelm, transform, compel, and possibly deceive. In the prelude to conflicts, particular attention is given to riveting episodes of suffering, abuse, devastation, humiliation, or, in some cases, extermination. The stories about the enemy's criminality, depravity, and malice impact notions of identity and difference, accentuating normative notions. There is a sense of urgency to redress the injustice, to take corrective action, and to demand a "just" response.

> Such stories invoke and then contribute to a system of positioning, in terms of which the storytellers are tacitly situating the actors within the stories in relation to the socially sanctioned moral rights and obligations and positive and negative character traits. (Harré & Moghaddam, 2003, ch. 1; Harré & van Langenhove, 1999, ch. 1)

A position represents a stance one takes, or is given, through storytelling, that is, one's discursive "placement" based on the local moral order. As the violence between conflict protagonists intensifies, the stories about the enemy's criminality filter down to notions about essential and eternal differences. "They" are inherently bad, vicious, or unjust. "We" are morally pure and endowed with virtues that inhere in a birthright connected to a sacred homeland, the legacy of a country's monarchy, or a social order made sacred by an approving God (Rothbart & Korostelina, 2011, ch. 8). The "reality" of such differences can be cast as a group's collective axiology, implying a sense of essential difference in terms of moral constructs. Birth in a sacred homeland secures one's virtues, whereas birth in the enemy realm confers certain vices that are linked to the profane foreign territory.

Of course, the lives of many participants in violent conflicts are filled with moral emotions. One such group includes those noncombatants who are engulfed in the brutality and suffer from its effects. We turn to the case of IDPs who were exiled from their homes in Kashmir in 1989.

II. IDPS: A GLOBAL CRISIS

A violent conflict between Muslims living in Kashmir and the Indian authorities governing this region erupted in 1989. In that year, the Kashmir Valley was home to a Muslim majority and a Pandit minority, the latter representing approximately five percent of the population. According to Indian authorities, Islamic extremists, seeking independence from India, waged a guerilla-style war against the legitimate government administration. The protesting Muslims sought self-determination and resorted to violent clashes against the Indian military. Massive protests by Muslims took hold of the valley, leading to violent confrontations with the Indian army. The separatist movement, known as the Jammu Kashmir Liberation Front, claimed a "secular" agenda of liberation from the Indian rule. Yet, the ideological motivation of the Islamic extremists included a campaign to drive non-Muslim "infidels" out of the state and establish the Order of the Prophet (Gill, 2003, pp. 1–2). According to a former director of the Indian police, "since late 1989, Jammu and Kashmir has been in the grip of a vicious movement of Islamist extremist terrorism" (Gill, 2003, pp. 1–2). The militants targeted anyone who openly expressed pro-India policies. Kashmiri Pandits, the Hindu minority of the valley, were "specifically targeted as they were perceived to be symbolizing Indian presence in the Valley, as they professed a different faith" (Rai, 2011).

Many Hindus were targeted, threatened, abducted, or killed, resulting in panic among the minority Hindu community of the Kashmiri Pandits. The primary motivation for leaving Kashmir was fear of the violence in the valley. Before their exile, accounts circulated about villages being looted, girls raped, and innocent civilians killed. One IDP, a shopkeeper in the Kashmiri "migrant market," reports that he "saw many deaths." Another IDP said that he was "still in shock" from witnessing sexual violence against girls. He said, "From 1986, things began changing in Valley, more Islamitization, temples began to be destroyed, curfews became routine. Over there is danger, threat and no freedom. 84% of the houses have been burned."

For the Pandits living in the Kashmir Valley, 1989 was a year when "the guns were never silenced," turning certain regions, such as Srinagar, into war zones (Rahul Pandita, November 2013, personal communication). After 1989, large numbers of Kashmiri Pandits, seeking to escape the targeted killings, found refuge in regions throughout India, with large numbers settling in Jammu and Delhi (Sekhawat, 2009). The total number of Kashmiris forced from their homes was approximately 250,000. They included school teachers, professors, doctors, singers, farmers, and businesspeople; males and females; and young and old, between the ages of 3 months and 70 years (Rajput, 2012). Some were ready for retirement, while others were yet to enter school. They owned land, orchards, and farm animals. Evicted from their ancestral homes 26 years ago, these displaced persons, plus a full generation of descendants, continue to live as "Kashmiri Migrants," which was a term of derision given by local community members.

The phenomenon of IDPs is widely recognized as a global crisis, with more than 28 million displaced worldwide in 2013 (UNHCR, 2013). IDPs are people who are forcibly exiled from their home but who remain displaced within their own national borders. The United Nations has recognized three primary contexts for causing such displacement: natural disasters, infrastructure development projects, and violent conflict. Particularly troubling are cases in which violent conflicts cause displacement of large portions of the population. The duration of their exile is not short; the United Nations has recognized 33 refugee/IDP situations that are protracted, involving at least 25,000 people exiled for more than five years. Many of these situations extend for decades, with little hope for their return to their ancestral homeland.

Many IDPs are subjected to suffering and hardships of various sorts from the initial phases of their exile. Going beyond deprivations of their element needs, their trauma is emotionally charged, affecting their sense of self in relation to others, such as community members, government officials, and other IDPs. In this section, we report on the findings of a study by Rajput (2012), which was conducted as part of a doctoral dissertation for the School for Conflict Analysis and Resolution at George Mason University.

For this study, 94 interviews were conducted in Delhi, Jammu, and Srinagar. Interviewees came from 14 IDP camps, so-called migrant markets, Delhi- and Kashmir-based ministries, and NGOs. The research also includes interviews with representatives of media, academia, charitable organizations, and the host communities (Rajput, 2012). State policies were investigated through semi-structured face-to-face interviews with key stakeholders of this displacement, such as top-level policy-makers, policy implementers, and IDP camp administrators. Oral histories, constructed by living with the families in "Migrant Township" quarters, represent the voice of the participants. Subject-matter experts who were interviewed were those with a direct role in policy-making, such as officials from the Ministry of Home Affairs, the Kashmir State House, and the National Minority Commission. The selection criteria included only those who were displaced due to the 1989 militancy. The participants interviewed from the local communities represent a spectrum of ethnicities, such as Dogra, Hindu, Muslim, and Punjabi. The IDP families interviewed represent a range of economic and social diversity, before and after displacement.

A majority of IDPs interviewed experienced trauma that finds its source beyond their desperate search for essential food, water, and shelter. Following their displacement, the IDPs entered a world of radical uncertainty about their capacity to survive the ordeal. In the initial period of displacement, they were vulnerable to a wide range of dangers, both known and unknown, and were consumed by their search for a safe haven for themselves and their loved ones. A sense of impending doom washed over some IDPs, as they experienced a sense of despair about the future for themselves and their loved ones. If fortunate enough to survive their ordeal of exile, the IDPs were then barraged with unfamiliar rules, norms, and regulations in their new residence, many of which were opaque to them. Strange sorts of interactions occurred. New challenges in their relations with local community members, government officials, and other IDPs created a deep sense of alienation that goes to the heart of who they are as Kashmiris. They experienced a rupture, as if a kind of normative injury, to their sense of self in relation to others. The dignity that they may have felt before displacement is replaced by the humiliation of being cast as migrants, as temporary people who are dislocated from their "natural" homes and are disturbing the "natural" social order. With the identity-marker of migrancy comes the stigma from local community members of "polluting the local values" with "strange ways" that are alien to the local community.

As migrants, the IDPs are seen by the local community members as broken, damaged, or unnaturally separated from the proper place, as if washed away in human floodtides (Malkki, 1995). A migrant is viewed as suffering from a troubled past—displaced from one's ancestral home—and bound for a precarious future. As such, migrants are vulnerable to a wide range of forces beyond their control, both natural and "human-made." In being displaced, they are often viewed by local community members with disgust from what happened to them and for lacking ancestral roots in the community. They have been, and continue to be, buffeted about by others.

Their migrancy stories are now part of the IDPs collective lore. Such stories capture their extraordinary experiences that break with their sense of morality, as if creating a warping effect on time itself. "It is an injustice to call us migrants," laments this IDP, a shopkeeper in Delhi's "migrant market," as the locals call it. Another IDP expressed a mild threat in claiming that the IDPs may have reached their limit in holding back their anger and retaining peaceful relations with others; retaliation in response to such indignities would be understandable.

With this stigmatization, many IDPs feel a sense of loss of pride compared to what they may have enjoyed in the valley. Memories haunt them with comforting recollections—or exaggerations—of a former life with images of comfort, safety, and well-being. Exile represents a departure from normality. Memories of life in the valley are charged with yearnings, hopes, and dreams for a kind of salvation from their current plights. Such emotions foster a collective humiliation about their state of being in this world of migrants, fueled by a sense of impotence from the conditions associated with displacement. The lure of the past is motivated in part by attempts to escape psychologically from their current struggles. Such humiliations carry with them a strong sense of resentment for losing control of their own destiny. Their lives rest in large measure on the good graces of others. Subjected to threats of various kinds, their survival rests on what militants in the valley do or do not do to them, how local community members will treat them, and what policies and services government agencies will provide for them, without regard for their participation.

These IDPs are pained by the piercing gaze of others—degradations that in turn impact their sense of self in relation to others. The loss of pride they experience negatively impacts their sense of self, representing a major transformation of self-image in relation to their life in the valley. Their diminished self-worth is conveyed in the stories about degrading encounters with others, such as the community members, government officials, and other IDPs. Many of these stories take the following narrative form: "I see how you are evaluating me through your lens, how you are imposing a degrading social status that is beneath your own, seeking to put me in my place according to your norms for proper behavior, thoughts, and feelings." For some IDPs, the response to this sense of stigmatization is a negative projection of the Other as dangerous, alien, or corrupt, as illustrated in the testimony that the government officials are corrupt, self-serving, and negligent.

The following four themes emerged from this research: (1) adjusting to a new community, (2) relations with local community members, (3) a sense of the future, and (4) assessment of government services.

Adjusting to a New Community

The IDPs' material losses from their exile were extensive. Some displaced persons "left with nothing," as one IDP recalled. The despair they felt from such losses impacted their reactions to their new life in the camps. Some expressed their remorse about living in temporary housing or having shops that are not permanent. One IDP, a grandfather in Delhi's Dwarka camp, spoke of the degrading living conditions, such as the fact that "fifteen of us lived in one room like animals." Another IDP laments, "It is a demotion to be a migrant here on our soil, migrants in or own country." Such a status constitutes a major loss of honor. Another IDP, who is a social activist in Delhi's mainstream community, expressed a sense of humiliation in being forced into exile and then losing the right to die in one's ancestral homeland. One IDP, a grandfather in the Jammu camp, declared:

> My life was halved when we were evicted. Coming here, we felt lost; as we are one among many Pandit families. In the valley we were unique and recognized. Here there are 2,500 families in the camp; my Kashmiri Pandit identity is now replaced by a plastic identity card. They know me as a resident of flat #X. I am nothing. My blessing is that I was able to educate my children while living in the camp. I will go back to the valley only if circumstances are right.

This sense of lost uniqueness intensifies the suffering associated with their migrant identity.

A primary source of distress for many IDPs comes from their sense of failed responsibility to their children. Various reasons for such distress were given: the lack of adequate education for their children, the inability to teach them the Kashmiri language, the sadness over a child's maladjustment in the local community, and the fact that the children are not able to see the region in Kashmir where their family lived. For a father, the inability to teach his children the Kashmiri language represented a major challenge.

Another IDP, a mother with a teenage son, expressed despair over the education of her son and the lack of jobs available for her:

> My life was interrupted [from the exile]; when it was time for my son to study, we had to leave. I had never left Kashmir before. We were threatened. It is not the same here, but misery brings us together. We only interact with our own community here. In the valley, I had my own shop; here I am useless. Job policy came too late, when they offered jobs, my son was over-age. I am ashamed of this housing. Some NGOs came forward, but we were neglected; the government never asked how we live. We complained, and as a result, some have now gotten a two-room flat. I don't want to go back as there won't be any jobs.

Another IDP parent, a resident of the Rohini camp, expressed deep regret that his children are not able to see the region in Kashmir where their family lived:

> I went from camp to camp and finally got a government job. We were educated—that helped. It was hard to adjust to the heat. Here we live in our own community. I am OK, but my kids have changed, they do not understand where I am from. I have no identity here.

While expressing a sense of courage and reliance at finding a government position, the parent is saddened at feeling misunderstood by, and alienated from, the kids.

Many IDPs were grief stricken from being severed from one's family roots. Their grief rests on two kinds of value commitments—first, the value of the person who has left or died, and second, the value of the relationship between the griever and the person lost. This illustrates a critical element of grief generally. To grieve represents tacit acknowledgment of a lack of control for the safety of others or oneself. The grieving person confronts the "new reality" of living with the loss of a loved one and also adjusting to a new sense of life's insecurity. A grieving person tends to characterize the world as a source of pain, suffering, and/or despair. Such experiences extend beyond one's momentary eruptions, as grief is a long-term disposition, as are feeling homesick, distressed, enthusiastic, and sorry for oneself.

Relations with Local Community Members

Most IDPs interviewed held positive feelings about their relations with the local community, due in part to the generosity exhibited by local community members in the early stages of camp life. The donation of essential materials to the displaced persons fostered a feeling of trust that extends to this day.

Other IDPs found little comfort in their proximity to the community, as they contrasted the comfortable life they enjoyed in the valley to their current plight. In the valley, residents presumably took pride in their community, enjoying the respect from their neighbors, who included Muslims. Before their exile, the IDPs enjoyed good relations with Muslims, even developing a sense of brotherly love for them. Yet, after their exile, the interactions with local community members are severely strained by cultural barriers. "Our culture cannot be found here," so there is little communication between the groups, laments a male teacher in his thirties. According to a 55-year-old female and resident of the Rohini camp, "my Muslim neighbors in the Valley were like brothers. It is not the same here. Life was good there. We don't mingle much [with our current neighbors]." Another IDP attributes his poor health and constant tension to the fractured relations with community members. The local community is, presumably, "materialistic," which prevents integration between the two groups.

Yet, these IDPs cannot return safely to their traditional homeland, as one IDP—a male teacher living in Srinagar's Veesu camp—laments:

> I was being threatened when I left. It is not the same here, the customs are not same, and our ways are different. Our culture cannot be found here. Our language is not the same as theirs. Our elders have difficulty with the language. I was a Kashmiri Pandit in 1980; now I am a Migrant. My children do not know my language. I am not at peace here. Our NGOs were not united; our voices did not reach the top. Conditions are not safe enough to take my family back; my kids will be forced to go to Islamic school and not get the useful education needed for their future.

This IDP has not overcome the identity-based trauma of exile. He is alienated from his former sense of self and simultaneously incapable of finding peace with the members of the local community. Alienated from community life, these IDPs cannot find peace in their new homes. Suffering from the stigma of a migrant identity and failing to find elements of their culture in the local community, some IDPs live a life in limbo, neither here nor there, as if between two worlds. They are living a life between social worlds, neither living there, in the valley, nor fully here, in the camp.

For their part, some local community members cast the IDPs as "problem people," as misplaced intruders in "our" community. Because "they" cannot blend into our culture, "they" are living apart from "us." And because "they" cannot cooperate, "they" are inherently dangerous to "our" way of life. With their misbehavior, character flaws, and failure to accept the local customs, the IDPs represent a malignancy to our way of life.

One community leader living in Delhi expressed deep concern about the social boundary divisions between the community and the IDPs:

> We were happy when [the IDPs] came here. They are loving people, we cooperated, but they did not understand our language. The government compensated them well for their losses, all kinds of policies were made for them, and they got food, rations, money, and oil. We tried to involve them in our community programs, but they did not invite us; they did not make an effort to integrate, so we kept distance. We have two societies in our community. They live here but maintain their own lifestyle. But with their coming, our children started improving in schools.

Notice the identity and difference between these separate communities, with the IDPs not understanding "our" language, not inviting "us" to their social programs, and not blending into the community. One community member, who is a businessman in Rohini, expressed strong disapproval of the IDPs:

We don't like it that they left their own native hometowns. They only ask
for help and are not cooperative. Our society took them in in sympathy;
we helped them. They don't contribute to our ways. They are still thinking
of themselves as Kashmiri and not Delhi residents. They could not mix up,
and don't invite locals to their festivals, they are unable to mingle and are
selfish. Policies have made them dependent, so now they don't work. They
get accommodation at zero cost. They misuse policies; some people have
got two apartments, one in Jammu and one in Delhi. Some sit at home.

While "we" expressed sympathy for their plight and showed compassion
through distributions of material goods, "they" responded to our generosity
by being uncooperative, selfish, and lazy. While "we" provided humanitarian
relief to their life-threatening conditions, "they" continue to demand excessive resources from the government.

The humiliation that the IDPs experience goes to the core of their self-
identity. More a hurt from an accusation of a negative character trait, humiliation is experienced as an enforced injury to the self that is perceived as an affront
to one's value, worth, status, or power. Humiliation is an emotion of self-
attention, where one self-consciously monitors an affront or a challenge to one's
life (Miller, 1993). A humiliated person is demeaned in the eyes of others,
accused of having transgressed expected norms. A humiliated person suffers from
an injury to one's existence, sucking one into a downward spiral of disconnec-
tion, depression, isolation, and self-loathing, sweeping over the horizon with a
fear and foreboding about the future (Lindner, Hartling, & Spalthoff, 2011).
Underlying a humiliating experience is a process of generating images of oneself
and others—my image of you, my image of your image of me, my image of your
image of my image of you, and so on (Sluzki, 2013). With humiliation, my image
of your image of me comes with a judgment of my diminished worth, status, significance, or value. Yet, the humiliated person recognizes the unfairness of the
disapproval, realizing that someone else is morally responsible for an injustice,
and hoping to reverse the moral arrow, as it were, to aim directly at the accusers.
In so doing, the subject's good standing is preserved, while the need for a corrective measure, such as retaliation, is considered (Sluzki, 2013, p. 73).

A Sense of the Future

The IDPs held diverse views about the desire to return to the valley.
For some, the conditions in the valley remain perilous. Yet, the desire to
return is strong, motivated in part by the despair over their life in the camp.
One IDP grandfather in Delhi's Dwarka camp expressed this desire graphically
by declaring that "It is better to die [from a] gun than to come here." With dis-
dain for his current life, the future looked bleak for this camp resident. Other
IDPs were resigned to camp life, recognizing a sense of stability, security, and
comfort that compares favorably to their life in Kashmir before the outbreak
of violence in 1989. Claiming that their life in Kashmir ended years ago,

one IDP—a doctor serving Delhi's main community—declared that she would never go back because "I have rehabilitated myself." Another camp resident, a daughter of parents displaced from the valley and now a librarian in Delhi's Kashmiri community, declared that displacement represents a blessing in disguise, since the services and support acquired in the camps surpass what was available in the valley. A male IDP, shopkeeper in his fifties living in Delhi's migrant market, rejoiced over his new life, declaring that "Here we live like a bird [with] freedom." Another IDP claimed that a vast majority of residents in his camp, over 90 percent, do not want to return.

But a majority of IDPs interviewed expressed ambivalence about the desire to return. To live and die on "my earth," as one IDP put it, is juxtaposed against the dangers associated with such a return. One IDP parent in Delhi's Rohini camp ponders over his fate:

> I left [the valley] on January 20th, 1989; there was mass exodus, and they announced on speaker "either join us or go." We arranged for a car, locked up our jewelry and left. Our Muslim neighbors were very good, we had no issue. The Pandit community was literate; the Muslims depended on us for education and medical services. When we came here, the camps were maxed out; we stayed at the temple for eight days. We were sent from camp to camp to find a place. They were good to us. When we came to Delhi, we sustained ourselves, we were educated. I was born in Kashmir, why would I not want to go back? But my kids don't know the culture and the language, they have now learned English, they are in the dark about my homeland. I want to go back, there is my earth, but there is danger and no freedom.

The hope to return to the valley is contrasted against the aspiration for a good life for their children.

Some IDPs frame their ambivalence by stipulating preconditions for their return. For one camp resident, return is possible only if the Muslim insurgents are driven away and peace returns to the valley. Another IDP, who directs a Kashmiri-based NGO in Delhi's main community, declared that before he returns, his people must have a separate homeland, the government must create a blueprint for essential services, and life in Kashmir could return to normal. Yet, these stipulated preconditions for return are clearly unrealistic, given the current social and political dynamics regarding Kashmir. As a result, this IDP is tacitly resigning himself to his new life, accepting, if begrudgingly, the challenges and opportunities of camp life.

Assessment of Government Services

From the officials' perspective, the government responded to the IDPs' crisis from a sense of humanitarian concern. One policy-maker expressed his sentiments as follows:

Their displacement was a terrible trauma; it was ethnic cleansing by separatists in a disconnected community. Their total community was uprooted. It divided the families. The central government advised the state to set up opportunities for the families, but the state government did not follow up. The government provided education, salary protection, cash relief, and housing for families. The government's goal is to make them comfortable within limitations till they return to Valley with dignity when they are ready. The arrival of IDPs created competition among locals, but there is more cultural synthesis and learning needed on both sides. The government is providing good return packages for the families.

This government official recounts the policies of providing services that are intended to continue until the IDPs return to their home in Kashmir. But relations between the IDPs and government officials have grown acrimonious in recent years. Many officials declared that the government's mission was limited to humanitarian relief only, intended to sustain the IDPs temporarily in anticipation of their return to Kashmir. Yet, the services have been extended and expanded beyond the original mandate to meet elemental needs. As one official of the Delhi government declared:

There was helplessness amongst the families; we provided relief. IDP policies are meant to be temporary. We provided them relief on the condition that when they start earning more than Rs 5,000, the relief will stop. But the relief has continued for the last 22 years. They are our guests, we are looking after them, and we don't ask them about their income. We simply carry out policies.

Some officials expressed resentment that the IDPs have exploited the government's generosity by accruing benefits that they would never enjoy from life in the valley. Some IDPs are accused of mercenary motives, publicly pleading for life-saving services while privately seeking to exploit the government's generosity. According to one official of the Delhi government, IDPs are manipulating the government by lying about their true motive for leaving Kashmir and fabricating claims about the current dangers in the valley. This official accuses the IDPs of being freeloaders:

Kashmiri Pandits were not displaced but became migrants of their own volition to secure a better future. It is a sad motivation; they will have to go back. People want to move when they see better prospects. The people want more and more; they are not satisfied. We support them in many ways. They demand many things; we give them what we think is genuine. These people have their own groups; their groups are not united and pose bottlenecks in policies. The policy goal is a humanitarian outcome to reduce their pain until they go back. The national policy is not intended for permanency; they will have to go back. They choose to stay here as

Table 15.1 IDPs' Ambivalence Toward Government Officials

Positive Assessment of a Government Policy	Negative Assessment of a Government Policy
"The government built schools and a temple right outside the camp."	But "my child is too young to benefit." (mother of a youth)
"The living accommodations are free or subsidized."	But the government "failed to provide monetary compensation to my husband." (family member living in the Krishna camp)
"The government official provided beneficial services."	"But the delays were excessive."
"My husband's salary was protected as he worked for the government before displacement."	"But we only have this [one] room."
"The housing is subsidized."	"But it is situated in a community hall with a temporary partition, which is pathetic." (family member in the Krishna market)
"The school's admission is free, and we get financial compensation."	"But the housing is like animal-living." (family member in the Delhi community)
"The government gave us shops to provide for our livelihood."	"We still lack ownership of the shop, which is vital for this medical practice." (currently practicing medicine in Delhi's Yusuf Sarai district)
"The government was credited with providing education and needed jobs."	"But there are no medical facilities." (currently practicing medicine in Yusuf Sarai)

they will lose provisions. I don't think people want to return; security is their prime concern, and the government believes it is safe, but they have the misperception that it is not. The families feel they are better placed here than they were in valley. Locals treated them well, so they have prospered and stayed or else would have gone back.

Again, the us-them duality is cast in terms of the government's virtues and the IDPs' vices.

With such a collective accusation of deceit, the official is tacitly deflecting criticism from the IDPs and releasing himself and his colleagues from apparent failure in providing adequate services to the IDPs. The majority of IDPs interviewed showed ambivalence to the government efforts (Rajput, 2012). Examples of such ambivalence are presented in Table 15.1 (Rajput, 2012). While recognizing the government's hand in offering a vital service, the IDPs chastised government officials for their short-sighted policies or for their flawed implementation in the camps. While expressing gratitude for the benefits they have received—food rations, education for their children, housing for their family, a shop to sell goods, and financial compensation—the IDPs castigated the government for many failings. One IDP shopkeeper in the migrant market of Delhi complained bitterly about the policies: "Not everyone has benefitted from government policy. After 22 years, I am still in the dark: no education, no medical facility; people helped themselves. Policy did not reach the main public, so how can I assess the policies?"

IDPs cast officials as helpful but stingy, giving with one hand what they take with the other, meeting some needs but not others. Neither imprisoned nor completely free, the IDPs became dependency captives, vulnerable to a wider range of dangers, and reliant on the generosity of others for their survival, at least in the initial phases of exile. Such dependency fosters bitterness and at times hostility toward the government officials. Underpinning this ambivalence over policies is the accusation of government corruption. The IDPs accused the officials of neglecting to consult with them on critical policy issues. Moreover, the testimony of IDPs suggests that perhaps the primary motivation for such policies is careerism and not a commitment to humanitarian relief. As one IDP protested, the government officials try to influence the IDPs in supporting their reelection, but "We are not a vote bank."

III. CONCLUSION

Among the major causal processes impacting the IDPs of Kashmir, we give special attention to the rupture of their moral life. The moral life of a community is driven by shared notions about the ideal path for achieving moral goals, for moving "forward" toward the goals, and avoiding the "false path." In general, one's moral plane comprises the mental apparatus for determining what is morally good and bad, right and wrong, and just and unjust in themselves and others. With such an apparatus, one assesses how one should and should not behave, interact, and associate with others. The trauma that the IDPs experienced directly impacted their normative stance in relation to many others. The moral life of IDPs are awash in humiliations, beginning with the forced exile from their ancestral homeland, continuing through their search for safety, and repeated in their struggles to meet elementary needs for themselves and loved ones. As migrants, they are viewed as socially misplaced, deviants in relation to the "natural" order of society, and as temporary people. The degradation of oneself in the eyes of others is cast as unfair, unjust, or inaccurate. The IDPs seek redress for the injustice of being stigmatized by their immigrant status and for the self-loathing that often comes with such stigmatization. The IDPs' indignation at being targeted by others is interlinked with the hope of restoring one's honor and of receiving the esteem of others, as they had enjoyed in the past. Such hope rests on a sense that they rightfully deserve respect and esteem from the community members.

REFERENCES

Coulter, J. (1986). Affect and Social Context: Emotion Definition as a Social Task. In *The Social Construction of Emotions*, edited by R. Harré. Oxford, pp. 120–134. UK: Blackwell Press.

Gill, K. (2003). *The Kashmiri Pandits: An Ethnic Cleansing the World Forgot.* Accessed March 17, 2012. http://www.satp.org/satporgtp/kpsgill/2003/chapter9.htm

Goffman, E. (1968). *Asylums.* Harmondsworth, UK: Penguin Press.

Gurr, R. (1968). "Psychological Factors in Civil Violence." *World Politics* 20 (2), 245–278.

Gurr, R. (1970). *Why Men Rebel.* Princeton, NJ: Princeton University Press.

Harré, R., & F. M. Moghaddam. (2003). *The Self and Others: Positioning Individuals and Groups in Personal, Political, and Cultural Contexts.* Westport, CT: Praeger.

Harré, R., & L. van Langenhove. (1999). *Positioning Theory: Moral Contexts of Intentional Action.* Oxford; Malden, MA: Blackwell.

Hatfield, E., J. Cacioppo, & R. Rapson. (1994). *Emotional Contagion: Studies in Emotional and Social Interaction.* Cambridge, UK: Cambridge University Press.

Lewin, K. (1951). *Field Theory in Social Science.* New York: Harper.

Lindner, E., L. Hartling, & U. Spalthoff. (2011). "Human Dignity and Humiliation Studies: A Global Network Advancing Dignity through Dialogue." *Policy Futures in Education* 9 (3), 66–73.

Malkki, L. (1995). "Refugees and Exile: From 'Refugee Studies' to the National Order of Things." *Annual Review of Anthropology* 24, 495–523.

Miller, W. E., (1993). *Humiliation: and Other Essays on Honor, Social Discomfort, and Violence.* Ithaca, NY: Cornell University Press.

Nussbaum, M. (2011). *The Upheavals of Thought: The Intelligence of Emotions.* Cambridge, UK: Cambridge University Press.

Rai, M. (2011). "Kashmir: The Pandit Question." Al Jazeera speaks to author Mridu Rai about how the minority Hindu community fits into the Kashmir dispute. Reader comment. Accessed January 2012. http://www.aljazeera.com/indepth/spotlight/kashmirtheforgottenconflict/2011/07/2011724204546645823.html

Rajput, S. (2012). Displacement of the Kashmiri Pandits: Dynamics of Policies and Perspectives of Policymakers, Host Communities and the Internally Displaced Persons (IDPs). PhD diss., School for Conflict Analysis and Resolution, George Mason University.

Rothbart, D., & K. Korostelina. (2011). *Why They Die: Civilian Devastation in Violent Conflict.* Ann Arbor: The University of Michigan Press.

Sekhawat, S. (2009). "Conflict Induced Displacement: The Pandits of Kashmir." *Conflict Trends* 4, 31–37.

Sluzki, C. (2013). Humiliation, Shame and Associated Social Emotions: A Systemic Approach and a Guide for Its Transformation. In *Shame and*

Humiliation, edited by C. Bigliana, R. Moguillansky, & C. Sluzki. London, pp. 57–101. UK: Karnac Books.

Taylor, C. (1989). *Sources of the Self*. Cambridge, MA: Harvard University Press.

UNHCR. (2013). Accessed November 24, 2013. http://www.unhcr.org.uk/about-us/key-facts-and-figures.html

Volkan, V. D. (1997). *Bloodlines: From Ethnic Pride to Ethnic Terrorism* (1st ed.). New York: Farrar, Straus and Giroux.

Williams, B. (1985). *Ethics and the Limits of Philosophy*. Cambridge, MA: Harvard University Press.

EDITORS' COMMENTARY

With their attempts to find the "why" of protracted violent conflict among identity groups, such analysts routinely resort to various notions of causality. In their studies of specific conflicts, researchers invoke ideas about causal processes, mechanisms, factors, or systems that are responsible for producing such violence. Such notions are inextricably linked to attempts to explain why such conflicts occur, how they evolve, and what the opportunities for their possible resolution are. The dynamics of relations among those engaged, or engulfed, in violence rest on different kinds of causal processes. Attempts to reduce such processes to a single form, such as human-oriented causality, are bound to fail.

Rothbart and Rajput illustrate the centrality of causal notions by setting out the working assumptions of those who engage in conflict research. The conflicts are complex, deeply rooted in social and political systems, and spreading far beyond the arenas of actual conflict. The most important causal factors are the *moral emotions* of the various partiers to the conflict, particularly the exiles and others excluded from "the national centers of power, prestige, and promise." Interestingly, Rothbart and Rajput emphasize that the deprivations that fuel "moral emotions" are relative, that is, as seen in relation to the characteristics of the lives of others. This sense of humiliation and frustration leads to a reaction, according to a well-known psychological principle that links frustration with aggressive reaction. This is proposed as a causal mechanism driven by contradictory emotions of hope and despair that produces the necessary conditions for violent conflict to break out. This is the locus of moral emotions, which are "a social-psychological force with intensity and direction." Moral emotions involve biological responses such as anxiety, assessments of a situation in relation to local norms, and a tendency to spread through a population as to highlight issues of rights and duties in relation to situations within the surrounding social order. How does a moral emotion serve as a causal factor, and what sort of causal factor? It is too long lasting to be a trigger, but is too immediate to be a background condition. It must be the core of a causal mechanism. But what sort of mechanism would be so activated? Rothbart and Rajput suggest that the mechanism of conflict is the process of storytelling—stories shared and driven forward by the local shared moral emotions.

Of course, the lives of many participants in violent conflicts are filled with moral emotions. One such group includes those noncombatants who are engulfed in the brutality of war and so suffer from its effects. Rothbart and Rajput illustrate the centrality of moral emotions to the initiation and sustaining of conflict, in the case of those who were exiled from their homes in Kashmir in 1989. This conflict, Rothbart and Rajput argue, is a fragment of a global crisis brought about by the massive numbers of people who have been forcibly exiled from their homes but who remain internally displaced within their own national borders. Following the UN analysis of the causation of this phenomenon, there seem to be "three primary contexts for causing such displacement: natural disasters, infrastructure development projects, and violent conflict": each of these can cause displacement of large portions of the population. What sort of causation is this? In a study based on interviews with such displaced people, Rothbart and Rajput identify several psychological causes for the traumatization of displaced people beyond the mere fact of their displacements. The most important seems to have despair at the insolubility of the problems thrown up by their situation. In cases like this, the causal mechanism is the making of inferences, the conclusion of which is a belief that the situation is dire. Rothbart and Rajput also found a different effect of the reassigning processes of such people—their ambivalence as to whether they wanted to return to their home territory. This makes final and formal causation, to do with meaning systems, and goals, far more relevant to the analysis.

16

This Causes Conflict! On the Risks of Establishing Causalities through Conflict Analysis and the Consequences of Implementing Those Logics in Conflict Resolution Strategies

Tobias Greiff and Jacquie L. Greiff

Resolving conflict—although it remains unclear whether such a practice is, in reality, entirely possible—necessitates an understanding of conflict as a phenomenon to begin with. With this in mind, it is hardly surprising that conflict resolution strategies and their theoretical roots are often grounded in one of a fairly limited number of causal logics. Theoreticians such as Susan Woodward (2007) have recently problematized this focus on "root causes" of conflict, suggesting that focuses on assumed historical roots can blur present realities and possibly even initiate or further conflict. This chapter draws inspiration from these debates and seeks to explore another angle: asking how perceived causal logics, introduced in large part by international actors, influence local conflict situations. What are the unseen consequences of the almost ingrained focus, within the conflict resolution field, on understandable causes?

Before moving into current debates within this field, we will briefly explore its historical development and seek to understand some of the origins of the causal logic under question. Following this, we will highlight how these theoretical standpoints have influenced practical approaches to conflict resolution, carrying this underlying logic into the realm of real-world engagement. Using the case of Bosnia-Herzegovina, we will briefly explore one example of the effects of these strategies and some of their unintended consequences. Finally, we will conclude that while understanding the causes of conflict can certainly be a useful tool in some situations, it has become too much of a singular focus of late, to the detriment of the field and its practice. We advocate for a multiperspective, open-minded approach moving forward, recognizing that the complexity of most conflict settings requires a break in linearity and paradigmatic thinking.

Within this, we wish to make clear that we do not, in fact, seek to abolish all focus on causalities in conflict analysis and resolution strategies. Rather, we side with the growing number of scholars calling for the promotion of ethno-relativism: in this case challenging the prominence of leading causalities and causal logics in many conflict situations and providing more space for alternative and locally derived interpretations.

I. THE DEVELOPMENT OF CAUSAL THINKING

In the years following both World War I and II, we witnessed a rise in academics and practitioners seeking knowledge that would help in understanding and preventing such levels of violence in the future. It was during this time that the field of international relations began to take shape and, in some ways alongside it, the beginning of what would become the field of conflict resolution or conflict analysis. Thinkers categorized as "idealists" sought to create institutions and policies that could control, or even eradicate, war and conflict in the future. Many believed that it was only our own ignorance of human and international relations that led to conflict and that with deeper understanding deeper control would naturally follow (Dunne, Kurki, & Smith, 2007). "Realists" such as Morgenthau challenged such thinking, accusing idealist thinkers of focusing on glorified visions of the world as they wanted to see it, not as it truly was. Morgenthau noted instead that if human behavior could be fully understood or predicted, it would not be through a figurative laboratory experiment, with controlled factors and an understandable pattern, but rather through preexisting biological certainties (Morgenthau, 1946). Nevertheless, Kenneth Boulding, after helping to form the *Journal of Conflict Resolution* in 1957, became perhaps one of the first to suggest that conflicts could indeed be predicted and understood, even if not in their entirety. He used the metaphor of weather forecasting: while meteorologists may never be able to predict with absolute certainty the hour when a storm might start, they are still able to recognize the factors that lead to, for example, either hurricane winds or sunny skies. Boulding envisioned conflict analysts being able to accomplish something similar: understand the causes of conflict, recognize the signs, and predict when and where it might occur (Kerman, 1974, cited in Ramsbotham, Woodhouse, & Miall, 2005).

Following close on this, in the 1960s, while the behaviorist revolution was calling for a focus within the social sciences on hard and observable data as is the case with the hard sciences (Dunne et al., 2007), Johan Galtung, while working in Oslo, put forward the idea of the peace researcher as a "social physician," a figurative doctor able to heal the disease that is conflict and war, and supported by a growing body of scientifically sound knowledge (Lawler, 1997). Perhaps influenced by Kuhn's *Structure of Scientific*

Revolutions (1962), which suggested that scientific advancement occurred only during moments in which one paradigm dominates the field, voices such as Hedley Bull, who argued that such a rigorous focus merely on data collected didn't allow space for interpretation and questions of conceptual understanding, were slowly being phased out (Dunne et al., 2007).

Around the same time as Galtung was working in Oslo, a strong voice out of London, John Burton, put forward the claim that conflict is a part of human relationships and can be understood, as well as mediated, through basic human needs. Unmet recognition, security, and identity needs, Burton argued, will inevitably lead to conflict, and meeting these same needs for the actors on both sides, can, in turn, resolve conflict (Burton, 1990). The authors accept that this is a simplification of Burton's vast body of work, but present it in this way to highlight the causal logic that remains the backbone of this theory, still so influential in the field today: unmet needs *cause* conflict; met needs *resolve* conflict.

Moving further forward, into the 1970s and 1980s, while multiple ideological and theoretical paradigms were vying for dominance within the increasingly popular field of international relations, and with much of the world still reeling from the Vietnam War, a few new paradigms for understanding and addressing conflict began to rise to dominance. With their 1981 publication, *Getting to Yes*, Fischer and Ury concretized conflict resolution and problem-solving approaches of the time: focused on "win-win" and "mutual gain" situations, rather than a dominance of one side over another (Fischer & Ury, 1981). Further seeking to understand conflict in order to properly address it, Paul Wehr introduced the concept of conflict mapping, touting it as "a first step in intervening to manage a particular conflict. It gives both the intervener and the conflict parties a clearer understanding of the origins, nature, dynamics and possibilities for resolution of the conflict" (Wehr, 1979, p. 18). Finally, systems theorist Anatol Rapoport (1986) introduced the idea that social systems have "default values," which actors within these systems understand as unchangeable. It is only through helping conflict actors to realize that these "immutable" values can be changed, Rapoport argued, that we are able to convert from systems of conflict to systems of cooperation.

The end of the Cold War and the collapse of the Soviet Union, along with its many ensuing conflicts in the early 1990s, also marked in some ways the final great turn in conflict resolution theorizing. In 1990, Edward Azar introduced the concept of protracted social conflict, defining it as "the prolonged and often violent, struggle by communal groups for such basic needs as security, recognition and acceptance, fair access to political institutions and economic participation" (Azar, 1991, p. 93). Azar noted that the causes of protracted social conflicts lie within states (rather than between them) and highlighted a series of variables that he believed to be preconditions for an escalation of violence in such settings. While we can certainly witness here a transformation from focusing on conflicts *between* states to those *within* states, the underlying causal logic remains unbroken—in fact, Azar's theories draw heavily on Burton's former concepts of deprivation of basic human needs as a direct and predictable cause of conflict and violence.

Also at the beginning of this decade, a new concept known as conflict provention began to take root. "Conflict provention," Burton and Dukes (1990) explain, "means deducing from an adequate explanation of the phenomenon of conflict, including its human dimensions, not merely the conditions that create an environment of conflict, and the structural changes required to remove it, but more importantly, the promotion of conditions that create cooperative relationships" (p. 2). In other words, provention means understanding the causes of conflict and working to eliminate these before conflicts can take root.

With the rise of civil conflicts during the 1990s and early 2000s, debates abounded around the root causes of this contention. Many speculated about ancient hatred between ethnic groups, while Lake and Rothchild (1996) suggested instead that ethnic conflicts in the post–Cold War era might not be caused by historical grievances at all, but rather by "collective fears of the future" (p. 41). Following this logic, Zartman (2000) distinguished between "creed," "greed," and "need" conflicts, suggesting that one of these three factors was behind most of the ethnic conflicts taking place at this time. "More than anything else," he speculated, "it is the uncertainty following the passing of the old order that allows conflict to break out with such abandon at the end of the millennium" (Zartman, 1997, p. 6). The early 2000s also saw the rise of the greed versus grievance debate (Berdal & Malone, 2000), with conflict analysts arguing over whether civil conflicts were more directly caused by grievances such as unmet needs or pure greed such as a desire for wealth, land, or resources. Paul Collier (2001) famously claimed that the data indicate that major armed conflicts are caused only by greed and that grievance is not a compelling enough driver (although he has problematized this claim further in some of his more recent work).

While this is a simplified trajectory of the field, in the interest of brevity, it nonetheless serves to highlight the main theme on which the authors of this chapter wish to elaborate: while there have been significant theoretical and practical developments over the last half century or so of conflict resolution thinking, the underlying logic driving many, if not most, of these theories has remained the same: simply put—if we can understand what causes conflict, we can find a way to solve it. How we ought to be seeking this understanding, and what we ought to be seeing as possible drivers in our figurative database of causes, has changed many times, but these are merely aesthetic changes, new coats of paint on the same structure.

Before we move to the next section, it is also important to note that while this is an incredibly brief narration of the development of thought in this field, there remains a very large body of knowledge (both practical and theoretical) that lies outside of this trajectory altogether. Much of the theoretical work outside of the Western world, with a few token exceptions, has not made it into the mainstream literature, and thus has very little voice in these debates.

Likewise, the learning derived from practical engagement is often seen as of lower value, within the academy, than that provided by theoreticians and more academically driven researchers. Perhaps because the field is intrinsically so practically bent, this distinction is slightly less stark in the literature of conflict resolution, but it nevertheless still holds true. The interaction between practice and theory in this field will be considered further in the next section.

II. CAUSAL LOGIC'S INFLUENCE ON PRACTICAL ENGAGEMENT

In this section, we will examine some of the consequences of the causal logic highlighted above when it is applied to practical conflict resolution strategies. As could be inferred from the prominence of causal thinking in the theories previously outlined, this pattern of understanding has been translated into many approaches to resolving conflict and violence. As Reimann states, "Usually, the interpretation of theory evident in the field of conflict management is limited to some sort of explanation of observable or personal experience, viewed in terms of causal logic with ensuing policy recommendations" (Reimann, 2004, p. 14).

The prevalence of this logic can be seen, for example, in Hugh Miall's *Conflict Transformation* handbook (2004), in which he suggests that "one can identify five different levels at which contemporary conflicts are caused: the global, regional, societal, conflict party and individual/elite" (p. 7). He goes on to present a chart that demonstrates a possible conflict cause at each of these levels, using the case of Rwanda, and then suggests a corresponding conflict preventer, something that could be used to mitigate this cause and thus, this is the logic, solve or prevent the conflict.

Lederach, in his *Building Peace*, reminds his readers that "those who are concerned with systemic perspectives underlying the crisis tend to pursue a structural analysis of the root causes of the conflict," in order to "analyze and explain the broader systemic factors that must be taken into account." In fact, root causes is the first factor of consideration he mentions in his integrated framework for working toward peace (Lederach, 1997, p. 79).

In his strategy book for *Preventing Violent Conflicts*, Lund states, "whether or not a dispute becomes violent or is prevented may be determined as much by the weight of certain basic 'givens' as by whether or not anyone has done anything to prevent it. The stronger such systemic causal factors are, the more likely it is that a conflict will escalate and the less likely that intervention can prevent it. The weaker these factors are, the less likely conflict will erupt. A flaw of many firsthand accounts . . . is that they tend to exaggerate the impact of human action and thus claim credit for results actually brought about by causal factors that are more or less beyond a third party's control" (Lund, 1996, p. 84).

While Lund's work deals with conflict prevention more than resolution, it is worth noting here both for his prominence in the field and for the transferability of these views from conflict prevention practice into conflict resolution practice. Conflicts, he suggests, have specific causes. If the causes are strong, violence will erupt; if they are weak, violence may not erupt. Importantly, while it is imperative that conflict preventors (and we extrapolate also resolvers) learn about these causes as a tool to preventing (or resolving) conflict, they are "beyond a third party's control."

Many other engagement strategies exist with logics that can be traced back to this same essential understanding, not all of which will be mentioned here, in the interest of space. However, we will draw attention to one final reference for its applicability to later sections: that of Gordan Alport's contact hypothesis. Put simply, Alport's idea is that group prejudice will be reduced when members of contending groups are brought in to frequent and intimate contact with each other (Alport, 1979). A popular understanding of Alport's ideas, and arguably one that he held himself, is thus that prejudice between groups causes conflict, and therefore a reduction of this prejudice, through frequent and intimate group contact, will help to reduce this. (This idea therefore ties in with many of the others mentioned from this time, concerning "ancient hatreds" and "ethnic rivalries" as significant causal factors for group conflicts.)

The above references are presented as only a few examples of what the authors see as a prevailing theme in the field: that the causal logic of conflict theory has taken root in the practice of conflict resolution and that resolution strategies are often designed around an understanding of a conflict's root causes. We do not suggest that this approach is entirely wrong or that it doesn't have substantial merit in certain situations. We also don't contend that it has not previously been questioned (see Susan Woodward, 2007, for the most well-known criticism). Rather, we propose that this focus on causal logic holds perhaps too much prominence and runs the consequent risk of making conflict resolvers blind to other dynamics and potential resolution strategies not based on the removal or reconciliation of perceived historical causes. In the next section, we will turn to a consideration of the case of Bosnia-Herzegovina to explore these claims in one practical example.

III. CAUSAL LOGICS IN ACTION: THE CASE OF BOSNIA-HERZEGOVINA

The conflict in Bosnia-Herzegovina and ensuing resolution and peace-building practices provide an ideal example of the phenomenon we have so far introduced. In this section, we will trace the effects of causal logics on two resolution strategies in Bosnia: the first concerning reconstruction in the divided city of Mostar and the second concerning education reform. In each of these examples, we will illustrate the presence of causal logics, how these understandings were applied to resolution practices, and to what effect.

We will not provide a history of the Bosnian conflict in this chapter; those interested may find many dozens of accounts available in other sources.

Rather, we will begin this exploration by noting a few popular views of the conflict causes and dynamics, which will serve to illustrate and inform later resolution efforts. As the Nederlands Instituut voor Oorlogsdocumentatie highlights well in their analysis of "Western Perceptions and Balkan Realities," the predominant Western view of the Bosnian conflict was characterized by understandings of the region propagated by authors such as Rebecca West, Robert Kaplan, and Lord Owen (Naarden, 2002). These works speak of the Balkans as an area characterized by "ancient hatreds" (West and Kaplan, cited in Holbrooke, 1999), "cultures of violence," and "divided communities" (Owen, cited in Naarden, 2002). In addition, George Kennan's *The Other Balkan Wars* had a significant influence on the analysis of the recent conflict, based on his analyses of previous Balkan wars, and his assertion that "nationalism in the Balkans drew on deeper traits of character inherited, presumably, from a distant tribal past ... and so it remains today" (Kennan, cited in Naarden, 2002).

As Richard Holbrooke notes in his book *To End a War*, both President Clinton and former American ambassador to Yugoslavia, Lawrence Eagleburger (later secretary of state), among others, were deeply influenced by views such as those expressed above (Holbrooke, 1999). It is thus that the narratives surrounding the Bosnian war were colored by language of ancient hatreds, tribal feuds, and perpetual ethnic division. These were understood as both the causes of violence (with the argument that Tito's Yugoslavia had suppressed these divisions and with the dissolution of Yugoslavia they were again coming to a head) and cautionary warnings about the uselessness of outside intervention.

After the eventual UN and NATO interventions, and Holbrooke's mediated Dayton Peace Agreement in 1995, these viewpoints of the Balkan society again became very important in the conceptualization of resolution and rebuilding strategies, as conceived and implemented by international actors. As illustrated in the previous section, the familiar application of causal logics to practical measures was very clear: at a basic level, most practical interventions in Bosnia, especially in the early years, can be boiled down to a common understanding that ethnic tensions had been significant causal factors in inciting violence, and therefore that the road toward future peace would be found in reconciling these tensions and bridging formerly divided groups.

It should be noted here that there is often a distinction raised between arguments that cite ethnic hatreds as the cause of violence and those that favor the influence of corrupt elites. The authors see both of these arguments as drawn on the same logic at their fundamental level, as one cannot argue that elites incited ethnic groups against one another without contending with some level of existing division between these groups. We certainly agree that the second version offers perhaps a more nuanced view of dynamics on the ground, but for our purposes, the core logic of both arguments demonstrates the same fundamental understanding highlighted above: ethnic tensions played a significant role in causing the violence, and therefore, reconciliation between these groups must be found in order to lead to peace.

To explore these ideas and questions further, the next two subsections will consider examples of conflict resolution strategies in the Bosnian case, first looking at the reconstruction of the Old Bridge in Mostar and then turning to some of the experiences of reform within the education system. Both of these examples are selected because of the strong international involvement in the initiatives, and thus their ability to illustrate the effects of causal logic outlined above in practice.

Reconstruction in Mostar: The Story of a Bridge

Many in the conflict resolution field should be familiar with the image of the Old Bridge in Mostar, a southern Bosnian city with a split population of Bosniaks and Croats, because it has been selected as the cover image of several textbooks in this field in recent years (for the most common example, see Ramsbotham et al., 2005).

During the war, the city of Mostar was the site of some of the heaviest fighting between Croat (HVO) forces and the Bosnian army (Bosniak Muslim forces). Through large-scale shelling, as well as ongoing fighting in the streets, most of the city's infrastructure was either destroyed or severely damaged. With the cessation of violence in this area in 1994, and the Washington, D.C., accords on March 18 of that year, which created the Muslim-Croat federation, the city of Mostar was viewed by the international community as the key to maintaining peace between the Bosniak and Croat peoples and, therefore, keeping the federation together.

Thus, as infrastructure reconstruction plans were laid out in the years after the war, the international community sought not to merely rebuild what was lacking, but to use the process of reconstruction as a symbol for reconciliation. Although all of the city's bridges were destroyed (Mostar as a city straddles the Neretva River and bridges are a central aspect of its infrastructure), the reconstruction of the Stari Most, or Old Bridge, a central feature of Mostar's old city and a feature of its Ottoman heritage, was selected as the ideal site for a major reconciliation campaign.

As Dr. Loannis Armakolas, of the CRIC Research Project (Cultural Heritage and the Reconstruction of Identities after Conflict), explains:

> The destruction of the Old Bridge of Mostar was quickly interpreted internationally as an attack on Bosnian multiethnicity. This view also influenced the way that the post-war reconstruction went. For example various alternatives that were proposed as solutions for the Old Bridge, like for example to keep the ruins of the Old Bridge as a reminder of human destructiveness, or to construct an entirely new and modern bridge, or to build a memorial, were all outright rejected. Instead the solution that was selected was the construction of a replica of the Old Bridge, and through this new Old Bridge the international community sought to promote its political project in Bosnia and that political

project was the internationally-driven post-conflict state building and reconciliation attempts in the country. The Old Bridge was supposed to symbolically reconnect the divided sectors of the city, and bring the communities together. (Armakolas, 2012)

Dr. Armakolas highlights in this excerpt the very direct ties of this reconstruction effort to the logic outlined at the beginning of this section: the international drive toward promoting ethnic reconciliation between the peoples of Bosnia as the road toward peace. As he notes, this intention eclipsed any other suggestions concerning possible options for the Old Bridge symbolically or practically. Indeed, as reconstruction in Mostar continued over several years, the Old Bridge became the key image of the Mostar 2004 plan, symbolizing the core intentions of this initiative, to reunite the Bosniak and Croat members of the city at all costs, as can be seen in an image depicted as a large mural in Mostar's Spanish Square, which shows the two communities slowly moving toward one another and meeting together in the center of the bridge.

In order to maintain and reinforce the intended symbolism of the bridge as a connecting and reconciling factor, the international community designed the reconstruction process in very specific ways. Workers from both sides of the city (a.k.a. both Croats and Bosniaks) were selected and trained in the original masonic arts of the bridge's first construction, and old stones were sought and recovered (Pašić, 2006). In this way, not only the bridge itself was intended to be symbolic, but also the very methods of its reconstruction: reuniting Mostar's residents with each other and with a shared past.

However, because this focus was so very strong, and so often touted, everything about the process of rebuilding that didn't fit with this narrative of unity is remembered by those on the ground today with particular strength. Local Mostar residents remember that many of the local masons were in fact replaced with international experts, and thus the concept that the bridge was to be built equally by the city's residents remained merely that, a concept, never fully realized in practice (Hayden, 2007). Perhaps the greatest example of this duality between intended and actual representations can be seen in the opening ceremony for the reconstructed bridge, in which white lilies were strewn across its surface (Bowen, 1993). The international community intended this as a symbol of peace, the lily being a long-standing Bosnian symbol in itself. However, for locals on the ground, the effect was quite different. During the war the lily became strongly associated as a symbol of the Bosniak side alone (indeed, lilies could be seen painted along the frontlines of Mostar's streets even at the time of the ceremony, as symbolic territorial markers). By selecting this symbol during the ceremony, the international community inadvertently linked the bridge very strongly with one side, rather than presenting it as a symbol of connection between the two. The fact that it had been reconstructed along the same Ottoman design further linked it, in many minds, with the Muslim community. Today, as Dr. Armakolas explains, "in the largely Croat West Mostar, the image of the Old Bridge is virtually nonexistent. In contrast, in largely Bosniak East Mostar, the image of the Old Bridge is present virtually everywhere." In contrast to this, "the Old Bridge before the war was the city's landmark"; he explains, "it was not politicized, nor was it associated to visions of communal multiethnictiy, interethnic unity, or even ideas of reconciliation" (Armakolas, 2012). In attempting to bring these new symbolic meanings to the bridge, the international community may inadvertently have created further divisions, rather than healing those previously existing.

This example serves to demonstrate many issues with the Mostar reconstruction process. In some ways, it can be argued that the ideas of the international interveners were founded on good intentions, even if they were poorly carried out due to incomplete understandings of local dynamics. However, this is arguably always a risk when intervening in an outside situation and serves as a cautionary tale against attempting to enmesh oneself in an unfamiliar symbolic realm. Beyond this, however, and of particular relevance to the arguments put forth by the authors of this chapter, is the fact that this example demonstrates many of the dangers of a singular mindset toward reconstruction and reconciliation processes. International interveners in this situation were so focused on the narrative of reconciliation they sought to produce, seeing this as the only way toward peace in the city (based on the causal logics that saw separation as the road to conflict), that the entire process was largely blind to actual dynamics and realities within the communities on the ground.

As noted earlier, many contending proposals for dealing with the Old Bridge (making it into a memorial, keeping it in a destructed state, constructing a new bridge), several of which were actually proposed by local actors, were outright rejected by the international community because they did not fit with the prevailing logic in which these individuals were working. Such a singular focus is problematic in any situation, and in this case arguably served to further the very tensions it set out to cure.

Before we move on, in the final section, to suggestions of how to avoid these pitfalls created by the focus on singular causal logics, one additional Bosnian case study will be raised for comparison, that of interventions in the postconflict education system.

Segregation and Integration: The Story of Education

We wish to clarify at the outset that the process of postconflict education reform in Bosnia is far too large to cover in these few pages; thus, we make no attempt at a comprehensive overview here. Rather, we will present several key examples, within this framework, that are relevant to the arguments of this piece.

If there is one realm in which the international community staged substantial interventions, beyond that of reconstruction and politics, it could arguably be that of education. Beginning with physical reconstruction efforts, and expanding into reforms of policies and practices, one estimate suggests that more than $227 million in international funding found its way into the Bosnian education system just between the years 1996 and 2003 (Nelles, 2006). We will not deal with physical reconstruction in this section, but rather with the curricular and policy reforms of the education system itself, most of which were founded on the same logic highlighted earlier: ethnic tensions caused the violence; reconciliation between ethnic groups will lead to peace.

As Torsti (2009) explains, "during the first years of the war, the schools were divided according to the military positions and frontlines so that the army in control of the area regulated the curriculum used" (p. 67). For the most part, the existence of individual curricula along ethnic lines continued after the Dayton Peace Agreement, and it is this practice that the international community fought hardest against in their reforms, citing it as a means of segregation in which future generations would be likely to be raised on islands of hate, thus perpetuating conflict lines and potentially leading to future violence.

In contrast to this view, it is important to note that there were several moves from authorities within Bosnia to allow the separated curricula to continue. In 1997, in fact, the Federal Minister of Education proposed that the three individual curricula for Bosniak, Serb, and Croat children be officially recognized and that separate classes and institutions for each of these groups be institutionally supported and regulated. However, there was such a strong backlash against this idea from the international community that it was never realized (Kolouh-Westin, 2002).

Instead, the Office of the High Representative, the international authoritative body put into place by the Dayton Accords with the responsibility of overseeing the peace process, created the Sarajevo Education Working Group in 1998, and delivered to this body a mandate of developing a new education program within the year. This new program was expected to accommodate the "needs of children of different ethnic and religious groups in a non-discriminatory manner" as well as "foster democracy and ethnic tolerance, and the removal of all textbooks that 'contribute[d] to ethnic hatred and intolerance'" (Spaulding, 1998). Spaulding also notes, however, that of the appointed international representatives on this committee, "none would appear to be recognized experts on educational policy, planning, reform and development" (p. 10). As could be expected, this mandate was far too much for one group to accomplish within a year, and reform processes along these goals, spearheaded by the international community, continued to be pushed forward for the next decade.

Nearly all of these movements were based on the same understanding, as expressed in a UNDP report of 2003, that "the latest war 'produced' . . . the fragmentation of the education system across entity and cantonal jurisdiction, national divisions into three separate curricula, segregation of pupils . . . and even fostering ethnic and religious enmity among students" (UNDP, 2003, p. 78).

However, as the international community, and most particularly the Organization for Security and Cooperation in Europe (OSCE) after 2002, pushed more strongly for reform and integration of ethnic groups within the system, they met with strong resistance from many locals on the ground. A prevailing narrative expressed by groups in favor of maintaining a separated system was the concept of their own right to recognition based on their ethnic identity. Indeed, the Dayton Peace Agreement officially recognized three constituent peoples, of equal status, within the Bosnian state: Bosniaks, Serbs, and Croats, each with their own recognized, national language (Bosnian, Serbian, and Croatian, respectively). Why, when the peace process had granted them the right to their individual identities, representatives from these groups asked, were international reformers demanding that they compromise these once more in favor of a shared identity reminiscent of the suppression they had felt under the Yugoslav system?

These questions of identity symbolized, in the minds of many in Bosnia, the very thing for which they had fought for the last three years, and for which many had given their lives. In describing the complication of the three languages in particular, Azra Hromadžić explains:

> For most Croats, the "mixed" Serbo-Croat language symbolizes the legacy of Serb hegemony in the former Yugoslavia. Croat language policy since 1991 thus attempted to keep the language "pure," cleansed of orientalisms and other linguistic impurities, such as the words labeled as "Serb." The Croat language, in this framework, was elevated to the throne of Croat peoplehood and its very existence as *narod* (a people). The former principal of the Mostar Gymnasium explains:
> The problem [of integration] becomes obvious when we talk about language. Our local languages are similar in some ways, but they are mostly different. And *narod* without language is not *narod* at all. Which language would students listen to at school? Parents fear that the Croat language will be destroyed . . . This is bigger than politics; it is about society and about culture. (Hromadžić, 2008, p. 556)

As this quote illustrates, there was a fundamental misunderstanding between the international community and many local populations in terms of the effects of integration and segregation within the education system. The international actors, for the most part acting along the same causal logic we have traced through this entire section, understood that segregation of the groups would lead to further violence, as it had done in the past, and that integration was the only valid solution to bring about peace. However, local opinions, such as that quoted above, illustrate a second view, in which separation is not understood as a means of conflicting with other groups, but rather of enjoying the right to an independent identity as a people. In this mindset, integration is seen as a road to suppression, and not at all one toward peace. As Hromadžić explains, "for the majority of people, especially the Croats and the Serbs in B&H, integration is understood as either the return to the prewar Yugoslav ethnic relations or as an assimilation into a larger, dominant group and a related loss of ethno-cultural identity. Both are seen as dangerous to the survival of the ethnically defined communities" (p. 554).

This is merely a glimpse into a few of the very complex dynamics surrounding postconflict education reform efforts in Bosnia, struggles that continue strongly to this day. The authors do not intend these examples to suggest a point of view in favor of either integration or segregation within the system, merely to highlight a few of the prevailing viewpoints on either side, and how the presence of the causal logic guiding the international community in this realm as in all things has served to make many blind to some of the deeper complexities on the ground.

IV. CONCLUDING THOUGHTS: TOWARD A BROADER FRAMEWORK

We have provided, in these pages, several examples within the Bosnian case study that illustrate some of the pitfalls of causal logics in conflict resolution practice. However, we do not intend to suggest that these logics have no validity or role to play in such practices, nor do we advocate that they be abolished entirely. Rather, we began this exploration by highlighting the prevalence, verging on full domination, of causal frameworks in conflict resolution theory, research, and practice, and it is this phenomenon that we seek to argue against.

What we can see through the theoretical development recounted in the earlier sections, and the practical examples provided in the later, is the strong presence of this one dominant, predominantly Western, thought pattern in the last decades. The authors suggest that if this pattern of thinking is to continue, we risk becoming blind to the truly complex web of dynamics governing conflict as a phenomenon in our world as well as conflict research and theory. In this regard, we thus present a deviation and disagreement from Kuhn, arguing that it is not in moments of convergence around a single paradigm that social science will move forward, but rather when multiple, divergent paradigms are considered together. We need to make space in conflict theorizing to think outside of causal logics, as well as outside of the box of dominant Western theorizing. We need to consider alternative perceptions, less-dominant Eastern and Southern theories, and most of all, we advocate for attention to the realities on the ground in each, unique situation. We suggest that the examples presented here from the Bosnian case advocate for a focus, in conflict resolution practice, on the realities of the "here and now," rather than a focus on perceived realities from the past, many of which may no longer be relevant. Peace may not be the opposite of conflict, and it may not be brought about by reversing set understandings of prior causes and consequences.

REFERENCES

Alport, G. W. (1979). *The Nature of Prejudice.* New York: Perseus Books Publishing, LLC.

Armakolas, L. (2012, March 27). *MOSTAR: Heritage Reconstruction in a Divided City* [video file]. Retrieved from https://www.youtube.com/watch?v=T1Cz6UzwDrg

Azar, E. (1991). The Analysis and Management of Protracted Social Conflict. In Volkan, J. D., Montville, J. V., & Julies, D. A., eds. *The Psychodynamics of International Relationships, Vol. II.* (pp. 93–120). Lexington: Lexington Books.

Berdal, M., & Malone, D., eds. (2000). *Greed and Grievance: Economic Agendas in Civil Wars.* Boulder: Lynne Rienner.

Bowen, J. (1993) (prod.). *Unfinished Business: War in Mostar.* Documentary, BBC.

Burton, J. W. (1990). *Conflict Resolution and Prevention.* New York: St. Martin's Press.

Burton, J. W., & Dukes, P., eds. (1990). *Conflict: Readings in Management and Resolution.* London: Macmillan.

Collier, P. (2001). Economic Causes of Civil Conflict and their Implications for Policy. In Crocker, C. A., Hampson, F. O., & Aall, P., eds. *Managing Global Chaos.* (pp. 143–162). Washington, DC: US Institute of Peace.

Dunne, T., Kurki, M., & Smith, S., eds. (2007). *Theories of International Relations: Discipline and Diversity.* Oxford: Oxford University Press.

Fischer, R., & Ury, W. (1981). *Getting to Yes: Negotiating Agreement without Giving In.* London: Penguin Group.

Hayden, R. M. (2007). Moral Vision and Impaired Insight: The Imagining of Other Peoples' Communities in Bosnia. *Current Anthropology,* 48(2), 105–131.

Holbrooke, R. (1999). *To End a War.* New York: Random House.

Hromadžić, A. (2008). Discourses of Integration and Practices of Reunification at the Mostar Gymnasium, Bosnia and Herzegovina. *Comparative Education Review,* 52(4), 541–563.

Kolouh-Westin, L. (2002). *Democracy and Education in Bosnia-Herzegovina and FR Yugoslavia.* Stockholm: Institute of International Education.

Kuhn, T. S. (1962). *The Structure of Scientific Revolutions.* Chicago: University of Chicago Press.

Lake, D., & Rothchild, D. (1996). Containing Fear: The Origins and Management of Ethnic Conflict. *International Security,* 21(2), 41–75.

Lawler, P. (1995). *A Question of Values: Johan Galtung's Peace Research.* Boulder and London: Lynne Rienner Publishers.

Lederach, J. P. (1997). *Building Peace: Sustainable Reconciliation in Divided Societies.* Washington, DC: United States Institute of Peace Press.

Lund, M. S. (1996). *Preventing Violent Conflicts: A Strategy for Preventive Diplomacy.* Washington, DC: United States Institute of Peace Press.

Miall, H. (2004). *Conflict Transformation: A Multi-Dimensional Task.* Berghof Handbook. Accessed August 2014. [http://kar.kent.ac.uk/289/ 1/miall _handbook.pdf]

Morgenthau, H. (1946). *Scientific Man vs. Power Politics.* Chicago: University of Chicago Press.

Naarden, B. (2002). *Srebrenica: A 'safe' area, Appendix V: Western Perceptions and Balkan Realities.* Amsterdam: Nederlands Instituut voor Oorlogsdocumentatie.

Nelles, W. (2006). Bosnian Education for Security and Peacebuilding. *International Peacekeeping,* 13(2), 229–241.

Pašić, A. (2006). *The Old Bridge (Stari Most) in Mostar.* Unpublished.

Ramsbotham, O., Woodhouse, T., & Miall, H., eds. (2005). *Contemporary Conflict Resolution: The Prevention, Management and Transformation of Deadly Conflicts, Second Edition.* Cambridge: Polity Press.

Rapoport, A. (1986). *General System Theory: Essential Concepts and Applications.* Tunbridge Wells: Abacus.

Reimann, C. (2004). *Assessing the State of the Art in Conflict Transformation.* Berghof Handbook. Accessed August 2014. [http://www.berghof-handbook.net/documents/publications/reimann_handbook.pdf]

Spaulding, S. (1998). *An Assessment of Educational Renewal and Reform in Bosnia and Herzegovina.* Pittsburgh, PA: University of Pittsburgh School of Education.

Torsti, P. (2009). Segregated Education and Texts: A Challenge to Peace in Bosnia and Herzegovina. *International Journal of World Peace,* 26(2), 65–82.

United Nations Development Program (UNDP). (2003). Bosnia and Herzegovina Human Development Report/Millennium Development Goals 2003. Bosnia and Herzegovina.

Wehr, P. (1979). *Conflict Regulation.* Boulder: Westview Press.

Woodward, S. L. (2007). Do the Root Causes of Civil War Matter? On Using Knowledge to Improve Peacebuilding Operations. *Journal of Intervention and Statebuilding,* 1(2), 143–170.

Zartman, W. (1997). Toward the Resolution of International Conflicts. In Zartman, W. & Rasmussen, J. L., eds. *Peacemaking in International Conflict: Methods and Techniques.* (pp. 3–22). Washington, DC: United States Institute of Peace Press.

Zartman, W. (2000). Mediating Conflicts of Need, Greed and Creed. *Orbis,* 24(2), 255–266.

EDITORS' COMMENTARY

In this survey of the causal hypotheses that have played a role in the development of conflict resolution strategies, Tobias and Jacquie Greiff survey a number of quite detailed and specific causal hypotheses as to why conflicts arise and why they are so often intractable or irresolvable. Scholars who have promoted several proposals for constructing causal hypotheses have set out these proposals as generic theoretical structures that are applicable everywhere that conflict has emerged. Tobias and Jacquie Greiff, on the contrary, argue for a kind of "ethno-relativism." By this, they mean attention to local conditions and local histories to find the roots of specific conflicts rather than by the application of generic causal logics.

All this effort to come up with plausible causal hypotheses is driven by the belief among conflict analysts that if we can understand the causes of conflict, we can recognize the signs of growing tension. Thus, we will be equipped to predict when and where it might occur and act to defuse the situation.

A popular principle for guiding research has been proposed by John Burton: unmet needs *cause* conflict; met needs *resolve* conflict. Spelled out, this comes down to struggles by "communal groups for such basic needs as security, recognition and acceptance, [and] fair access to political institutions and economic participation." Burton's basic causal proposal is simply that deprivation of basic human needs is a direct and predictable cause of conflict and, ultimately, of violence. This viewpoint bids us to look back in time for the root causes of conflicts.

Tobias and Jacquie Greiff note that an alternative forward-looking pattern of explanation highlights the differences between "creed-," "greed-," and "need-"type conflicts. These are three independent factors, any one of which or, perhaps, any combination of which, is behind ethnic conflicts of the present and recent past, suggesting that one of these three factors was behind most of the ethnic conflicts taking place at this time. In conditions of uncertainty, such as the breakdown of federal super states, these factors become significant. But are civil conflicts more directly caused by grievances sparked by failure to meet certain needs, or are they prompted by greed for things such as wealth or prestige?

Causal thinking seems to be the underlying logic of much of conflict resolution thinking in the recent past. As Tobias and Jacquie Greiff put it, "the underlying logic" is simple: "if we can understand what causes conflict, we can find a way to solve it."

Turning to conflict prevention more than resolution, Tobias and Jacquie Greiff remark that causal explanations of conflict can be strong (i.e., promote violence), or weak, and thereby be unlikely to turn into a violent confrontation. What happens in either case may be beyond anybody's power to manage or control.

Finally, Tobias and Jacquie Greiff note the distinction between citing ethnic hatreds as the cause of violence and the influence of corrupt elites. The core logic of both proposals is based on the hypothesis that ethnic tensions in such conflicts as those in Bosnia-Herzegovina were the basic driving force, so the road to peace would require reconciliation between ethnic groups.

Which of the basic patterns of causality is displayed in these examples? It is surely not exceptionless concomitance between events. Nor is it directly the action of human agents. Tobias and Jacquie Greiff present us with attributes of groups of people as the causal factors and the locus of effects. This level of analysis is one removed from the real world of real people doing real things.

Psychologically, we need to draw on social psychology, particularly the idea of social representations, to bridge the gap between a belief system common to a group of people and the motivations of a solitary sniper picking off random members of a different ethnic group.

Implicit in the layout of Tobias and Jacquie Greiff's discussion is the distinction between acting in ways that are explicable by conditions in the past and acting so as to realize certain conditions in the future. This is the age-old distinction between efficient cause and final cause, and between mechanistic causation and teleology. Philosophers have long ago rejected the idea that it is the future events that draw the past actions toward them in favor of the idea that there are present representations of possible future events. These are among the normal causal factors that, according to some standard analysis of causality, produce the drive to realize them. That drive is always a contemporary pattern of acts in the present.

17

Causality in the Study of Collective Action and Political Behavior

Winnifred R. Louis, Stephen T. La Macchia, Catherine E. Amiot, Emma F. Thomas, Leda M. Blackwood, Kenneth I. Mavor, and Alexander K. Saeri

We are grateful to the editors for this stimulating opportunity to reflect on the nature of causality in our field, focusing on the social psychology of collective action and political behavior. Harré and Moghaddam in their introductory chapter of this volume identify a number of dimensions along which causality may be mapped, and we shall follow their agenda as we tour the terrain. We shall begin with a short overview of the study of collective action. On the assumption that our readers may come to this chapter in isolation from the rest of the book, we shall then revisit the key conceptualizations introduced by Harré and Moghaddam, and consider models of collective action and political behavior under the headings of historical causal models (Aristotelean and Humean), and then turn to modern causal models ("What statistical models tell us" and "Gaps and omissions"). We finish with an extended consideration of agency at the group level and concluding thoughts.

I. A SHORT HISTORY OF THE STUDY OF COLLECTIVE ACTION

"Collective action" can be understood as any coordinated action by groups of humans, and thus in principle could encompass all social behavior from mating to sports and theater to politics. Our focus is necessarily more narrow, and thus we consider collective action as it has been studied in social psychology: as actions by group members on behalf of groups (e.g., Louis, 2009). More particularly, we are interested in collective action as political behavior designed to influence groups' status, power, and identities. Below, we summarize a century of collective action research in four pages (see also Klandermans, 1997, 2007;

van Stekelenburg, Anikina, Pouw, Petrovic, & Nederlof, 2013), for the purposes of our later discussion and analysis.

From Dysfunction to Function

The psychological study of collective action and political behavior can be traced to Lasswell, whose core works from the 1930s to 1950s examined how individuals' anxieties and mental illnesses influence politics (e.g., Lasswell, 1930). A concern with collective action as a reflection of pathology and dysfunction was reinforced by a wave of refugees from Nazi-era Europe to the United States after World War II. Looking back on the social turmoil of the Great Depression in the 1930s, and of war and fascism in the 1940s, it is perhaps unsurprising that theories of collective action as dysfunction flourished in that era. Most prominently, Adorno, Frenkel-Brunswik, Levinson, and Sanford (1950) proposed that individual pathology—childhood dysfunction arising from harsh, punitive parenting—might give rise to social pathology in the form of right-wing authoritarianism by producing individuals who were submissive to authority, punitive to deviance, and hidebound in their understanding of social morality (see also Altemeyer, 1981). Within social psychology, classics such as *When Prophecy Fails* (Festinger, Riecken, & Schachter, 1956) traced the roots of religious collective action to self-delusion and cognitive dissonance. Building on key works by Lazarsfeld, Berelson, and Gaudet (1944) and Campbell, Converse, Miller, and Stokes (1960), Converse (1964) put forward a theory of political behavior that proposed that mass political action is based on fickle and ignorant mass public opinion.

A shift away from pathology occurred in the 1950s, however, when the study of discontent and grievances emerged as a core concern. In this tradition, protest was seen as arising from symbolic interactions among aggrieved people (e.g., Blumer, 1951)—that is, interactions in which actors work together to create a shared social reality. In a similar vein, the "behavioral revolution" in political science (e.g., Lane, 1965; Lasswell, 1950) analyzed motivating reasons for participation in politics, including the desire for power, wealth, well-being, skill, enlightenment, affection, rectitude, and respect. While these explanations differed in their emphasis on symbolic rewards and costs relative to material ones, together they marked a significant departure from the earlier era in focusing on function rather than dysfunction.

But Is It Rational?

The 1960s presented a paradox for grievance models: in a period of increasing prosperity, there was more protest, not less. To address this paradox, in sociology, structural functionalism proposed that protest occurs when rapid social change introduces strains that authorities do not address speedily enough (e.g., Smelser, 1962). In psychology, relative deprivation theory introduced the idea that protest arises when people perceive a gap between their actual status and the status that they expect (Davies, 1962; Gurr, 1970; Runciman, 1966). Both of these approaches agree that collective action seeks concrete social change, even if there is a subjective aspect to appraisal of the change needed in relative deprivation models. In contrast, during this time, other scholars sought to differentiate instrumental collective action (seeking change) from more expressive social movements (e.g., Gusfield, 1963; Searles & Williams 1962). Expressive social movements were seen as ends unto themselves, and participation in expressive collective action (e.g., "black power" or "gay pride" marches) was seen as satisfying psychological needs. Although such action could still be politically subversive (e.g., Handler, 1992), movements for "identity politics" for women and for sexual or ethnic minorities were thought to be motivated by the desire to affirm group identities and connect publicly with other members for support, not just to jostle for status with advantaged groups.

During the 1970s, recognition of the expressive and symbolic functions of protest became marginalized within sociology and gave way to a renewed emphasis on factors outside the head. Starting from the premise that grievances and strains are constant and omnipresent, resource mobilization theory (McCarthy & Zald, 1977) saw collective action as arising when groups perceived that material and social resources presented an opportunity to act. This approach (see also Freeman, 1975; Gamson, 1975; McAdam, 1982; Oberschall, 1973; Tilly, 1978; Zald & McCarthy, 1987) emphasized rational decision-making by collective actors. Collective action was seen as both facilitated by access to resources (such as knowledge, money, media/information, and support from allies or elites) and opportunistic in nature, seeking to acquire further resources for the constituents of the movement and for the social movement organizers themselves.

A dominant theme across the disciplines during this time was rejection of earlier scholars who saw collective action as irrational (e.g., Hoffer, 1951; Le Bon, 1895). In political science, Olson (1965) argued that collective action is rational because it provides individual benefits such as fame and glory. Because of the low marginal benefit for the group of any one person's action and the opportunity for group members to free ride, benefits to the collective were ruled out as a source of motivation. In contrast, resource mobilization theory proposed that groups pursue opportunities when they can. The correspondence between structural factors such as political systems that increase (dictatorships) or decrease (democracy) the costs of participation and prevalence of collective action were cited as further support for this perspective (Carey, 2006; Crelinsten, 2002, 2014; Tilly, 1978).

Groups Matter

In the 1980s, Klandermans (1984) put forward a model of collective action that brought social psychology back into the field. According to the model, participation in collective action was a function of not just perceived individual benefits but also perceived group-based goals and beliefs about the attainability of those goals. This model, in turn, inspired Simon and Klandermans's (2001) formulation of dual paths to collective action, rational choice (instrumental), and identity-based (expressive). In political science, Ostrom (e.g., 1990, 1998) and others also pursued the analysis of collective goals from a rational actor perspective that sought to overcome the short-term focus and individualism of early rational-choice work.

Within social psychology, opposition to irrationalist models in the late 1970s and 1980s had also led to the flowering of new theories about identity, especially social identity theory (Tajfel & Turner, 1979) and self-categorization theory (Turner et al., 1987, 1994). These models were applied to collective action and intergroup behavior by researchers engaged with understanding crowd behavior (e.g., Reicher, 1984; Reicher, Spears, & Postmes, 1995), activists (Kelly, 1993; Kelly & Kelly, 1994), social dilemmas (Brewer & Kramer, 1986; Tyler & Degoey, 1995), discrimination (e.g., Lalonde & Silverman, 1994; Wright, Taylor, & Moghaddam, 1990), and relative deprivation (e.g., Grant & Brown, 1995; Kawakami & Dion, 1993, 1995; Mummendey, Kessler, Klink, & Mielke, 1999; Walker & Mann, 1987). While the projects were diverse, a core element of social identity research was to communicate the conviction that social or collective identity was at the heart of collective action. This was a European group-level theoretical perspective developed in response to the North American individualism that had dominated theory until that point (Taylor & Brown, 1979).

In the 2000s, new thinkers have considered the association between social identity, grievances, effectiveness, emotions, and the interplay among these factors. The role of emotion became more widely acknowledged (Mackie & Smith, 2002), and there have been a variety of causal models put forward: emotion (e.g., anger) as a predictor of collective action (e.g., van Zomeren, Postmes, & Spears, 2008; van Zomeren, Spears, Fischer, & Leach, 2004); emotion as intertwined "encapsulation" of social identity, norms, emotion, and effectiveness (e.g., Thomas, McGarty, & Mavor, 2009) or as "embeddedness" within social networks (Klandermans, Van der Toorn, & Van Stekelenburg, 2008); and emotion as an outcome of collective action participation, feeding forward into future intentions (Becker, Tausch, & Wagner, 2011; Tausch & Becker, 2013). The role of third parties identified in Simon and Klandermans (2001) also served to inspire other thinkers (e.g., Saab, Tausch, Spears, & Cheung, 2014; Saeri, Iyer, & Louis, in press; Subašić, Reynolds, & Turner, 2008; Thomas & Louis, 2014).

In the 2010s, perhaps the most notable new theme to emerge is the renewed emphasis on morality as a predictor of collective action. Originally mainly in the work of Skitka, Bauman, and Sargis (2005); Leach, Ellemers, and Barreto (2007), and Van Zomeren, Postmes, Spears, and Bettache (2011), morality is now very widely studied (e.g., Ginges, Atran, Sachdeva, & Medin, 2011; Zaal, Laar, Ståhl, Ellemers, & Derks, 2011). Increasing engagement with radical forms of collective action is also a feature of early twenty-first-century scholarship, which is unsurprising given the rise of new protest and terror movements during this time period (e.g., Becker, Tausch, Spears, & Christ, 2011; Sweetman, Leach, Spears, Pratto, & Saab, 2013; Tausch et al., 2011; Thomas & Louis, 2014; Thomas, McGarty, & Louis, 2014; Zaal et al., 2011).

II. HISTORICAL MODELS OF CAUSALITY AND THE STUDY OF COLLECTIVE ACTION

We certainly recognize that our historical overview has been partial and selective, and that a great deal of relevant and important detail has been omitted. However, we hope that within the narrow range of the research that we have reviewed, the reader has been able to discern some interesting historical differences both within and between disciplines. We shall present our own analysis of the spectrum of causal models in this research after engaging with historical Aristotelian and Humean models of causality in the following sections.

Aristotelian Causality

Harré and Moghaddam (this volume) begin their review of causality, as most scholars do, with Aristotle. The Greek philosopher (384–322 BCE) established the foundation on which the present book (like so much else of scientific inquiry) rests. In Aristotle's work, he proposed that four types of causes could be interrogated by scholars. The most consistent with the English-language modern usage is the *efficient cause*: that which initiates a process of change, for example, a person who advises someone to undertake a certain course of action, or a person who knocks over a domino, causing a chain to fall. There are also, according to Aristotle, three other types of causes simultaneously at work. The *final cause* is the ultimate purpose of something, such as offering "health" as the purpose for exercise, or curiosity as the reason the person knocked over the domino. The *material cause* is that which constitutes something: for example, the bronze out of which a statue has been made; the plastic of a domino. This meaning does not semantically define "a cause" in the English language any more, but we retain the idea of "constitution" (or constituting). Even less aligned to a modern English understanding of causality but also retained in the idea of constitution is Aristotle's idea of a *formal cause*, which is when the definition of something entails it having certain attributes, or when certain attributes define a construct as having a property or function. For example, the shape of the human body causes a statue of a human to have that form, or a domino tile has two squares of 1–6 dots each, by definition. This is also sometimes called whole-part causation—the form of the whole causes the parts.

So what are the Aristotelian causes of collective action? Efficient causes would include grievances, structural strain, resources mobilized, identities made salient, anger experienced, and other proximal variables. These are the independent variables in empirical research: the variables proposed to cause collective intentions. Bacon (1605) suggested that only material causes and efficient causes were appropriately studied by scientists: the aspects of nature visible to science were proposed to be *matter* and *motion*, in contrast to metaphysical or philosophical inquiries into final or formal causes. Harré and Moghaddam (this volume) comment that psychology follows the rest of empiricism in focusing primarily on efficient causes, and we agree that this observation can also fairly be applied to research into collective action. The study of immediately precipitating factors—whether grievances, social identities, or emotions—defines the social psychology of collective action in large part.

The other Aristotelian causes of collective action are arguably rarely addressed in the mainstream scholarly literature (as we elaborate below). A final cause might be defined as social change by one researcher and actor, or defending the status quo by another; final causes could also include the perpetuation of genes or a group's ideological mission, depending again on the framing of the actors and the researchers. Implicit but differing presumptions concerning the final causes associated with collective action may explain why researchers have disproportionately focused on left-wing and political movements, neglecting right-wing and religious ones (see Louis, 2009; Sweetman et al., 2013; cf. Klandermans & Mayer, 2006). Material causes of collective action might include human bodies, human social networks, or human social identities, depending on the discipline and researcher (an idea that we revisit later). And again, depending on the disciplinary area, the study of collective action may formally cause the study of political institutions, nation-states, parties, and leaders (political science), or of mental representations of groups of humans, identities, and norms, motivating intentions within individuals (psychology). Within any one discipline, the judgment as to whether nations, institutions, groups, individuals, identities, or genes (Dawkins, 1976) have agency is often presumed and rarely explicated. We return to this point below.

It seems to us that while efficient causes are taken for granted as the proper study of empirical social psychological approaches, the study of the other three types of causes has come to be seen as a more theoretical or philosophical enterprise. These latter topics, and thus the alternative causal models, are more likely to be explored in "theory papers" whose authors and models may not be received as credible without an accompanying foundation of empirical papers demonstrating efficient causality. "Theory papers" are also segregated into particular types of outlets, such as special issues of journals (e.g., van Zomeren & Iyer, 2009), virtual special issues (e.g., Becker, 2012), special sections (e.g., Blackwood, Livingstone, & Leach, 2013), review journals (e.g., Louis, Mavor, La Macchia, & Amiot, 2014; van Zomeren, 2013), or edited books, such as this one. These manuscripts can be prestigious and have high impact (e.g., Thomas et al., 2009; van Zomeren, Leach, & Spears, 2012), but again, it appears to us that the legitimacy to provide accounts of formal, material, or final causality is primarily awarded to those who have already proven their abilities by providing accounts of efficient causes. Thus, when we consider the map of causality established by Aristotle, the study in psychology of collective action has remained primarily in the *efficient* quadrant, with tentacles of research exploring the other quadrants.

Humean Causality

Along with the focus on Aristotelean efficient (immediate) causes, European science has historically adopted a rigid temporal ordering of cause and effect. According to Harré and Moghaddam (this volume, p. x), in Western causal models, "A cause of 'something' precedes or is simultaneous with the effect of 'something' in Newtonian time"— a rule established by Hume (1739). Hume proposed that human understanding of causality is subjective, resting upon induction from observed associations. These associations are interpreted based on heuristics such that causes are contiguous in space and time with their effects, the cause always precedes the effect and produces that effect, and the same effect always arises from the same cause (cited in Harré & Moghaddam, this volume, p. x). As Harré and Moghaddam note, causes are abstracted from a broad range of candidates, and it is the researcher's own preoccupations and interests that determine the particular subset that will be considered. Similarly, any one cause almost always generates a broad set of effects, with only a subset identified in any one research agenda.

Hume's argument that causes are *perceived by humans who infer or theorize patterns* seems self-evident to psychologists; for example, it forms the basis for attribution research (e.g., Graham & Folkes, 2014). In the context of collective action, the argument that "What we single out as 'the cause' is almost always interest relative" (Harré & Moghaddam, this volume, p. x) also seems self-evidently true to us. The short history of the study of collective action (see previous section) allows us to examine consistency in the interests of scholars (e.g., for psychologists, variables are disproportionately inside the head; attitudes, feelings, and beliefs are of enduring interest) as well as diversity and change (sociologists study institutions or networks; psychologists pursue waxing and waning interests in psychopathology, or group norms and identities).

Hume's contention that we use heuristics about *temporal precedence*, which posits that causes are proposed to precede effects, also appears to us to have been taken up without much debate by researchers in the psychology of collective action. Of course, collective action often has as its final cause (in the Aristotelean sense) a vision of a better future to be approached, or a worse future to be avoided. But as a rule, in social psychological models, the beliefs, emotions, and actions that have shaped the individual *in the past and present* are presented as motivating that person's *future* intentions and actions. Thus, past collective action cannot be predicted from current beliefs (cf. Blackwood & Louis, 2012), and current beliefs predict future collective action or intentions (e.g., van Zomeren et al., 2008). This heuristic of a linear temporal sequence leads to a chronic neglect of feedback loops, as we argue below.

Regarding Hume's focus on determinism, such that a particular cause is held *always* to imply a particular effect, the relevance to the contemporary scholarship of collective action is more murky. Two scholars of collective action may share independent variables (presumptive causes) while differing substantively in their dependent measures (presumptive effects), or vice versa. We take the underlying philosophical point, however, to be that in Humean determinism, scholars should believe a causal relationship to exist—for example, if A is present, B must follow—inevitably and necessarily. We would say that most modern scholars reject this view and that most have adopted probabilistic models rather than determinist models, particularly when predicting the future. For example, in multiple regression, statistically significant associations between cause and effect may be identified despite the variance accounted for ($R2$) being far less than 100 percent. In modern statistical models, suppression, mediation, and moderation all qualify our understanding of direct causality.

III. MODERN MODELS OF CAUSALITY AND THE STUDY OF COLLECTIVE ACTION

What New Statistical Models Tell Us

Beyond the specific variables that are identified in collective action research, the models of analysis may be interrogated in terms of the understanding that they propose of causal relationships. In current mainstream social psychology, that analysis generally implies quantitative research methods, which rest on a number of assumptions and in particular on the assumption that collective actions are best studied as observed, shared realities that can be quantified (cf. Livingstone, 2013). In addition, common quantitative methods typically assume that variables are distributed normally or have symmetric error. We have critiqued these assumptions elsewhere on the grounds that most forms of political collective action are, in fact, rare or asymmetrically endorsed (see Louis, Mavor, & Terry, 2003). However, for the purposes of this chapter, we would like to highlight that in the last 50 years, important new models have been introduced of multivariate statistics: statistics integrating the impact of multiple causes and effects. Reviewing these new models allows us to see a scholarly shift toward a collective understanding of causality as determined by multiple factors that are interacting and interrelated, and which are contingent and probabilistic rather than certain and deterministic.

For example, the Humean causal model described above proposes a simple, direct relationship in which a single cause (an independent variable, "A") leads to a single effect (a dependent variable, "B"). For example, anger at unfair treatment of their group (A) may cause a person to take collective action (B). In modern multivariate statistics, however, considerably more complex relationships are theorized and tested. In addition to anger (A), variables such as perceived effectiveness of collective action (C) and group norms for responding to disadvantage (D) may each account for some, but not all, of the variance in collective action behavior (the dependent variable, B; e.g., van Zomeren et al., 2008). Other variance in B could be proposed to be accounted for by chance or by unmeasured factors.

In addition, in a theoretical model that includes multiple causes of the same effect, any one independent variable's relationship with the dependent measure might be partitioned—that is, considered to include distinct components. Some components of the relationship between cause and effect may be unique to the particular pair (e.g., cause A and effect B) and some components may overlap (being shared between the A-B relationship and the C-B and D-B relationships). For example, a part of the association between anger and action might be statistically distinct, and another part of the association might be overlapping with or related to a second cause, such as a social norm of collective action within one's group. To restate, modern statistics differentiate an independent causal relationship, in which the association between the cause and the effect is statistically unrelated to the association between the cause and other causes, or between those other causes and the effect, from causal relationships that depend on other variables. This approach recognizes that sometimes the association between one cause and an effect is in fact shared with, or contingent on, other variables, which is an important conceptual advance on Humean simplicity.

Moreover, modern statistical models allow for various *types* of interrelated causes to be described and tested. For example, analysis of a statistical interaction between causes (which is also sometimes called moderation analysis) can identify when a causal relationship between A and B changes depending on a third variable, C. For example, A might lead to B if C1 is present, but if C2 occurs, the association between A and B might be eliminated. In collective action, anger might lead to political collective action if there is a perceived norm of support for the collective action in one's group, for example, but if there is no norm of support, anger might not lead to action. Recognition of the possibility of statistical interactions or moderation in contemporary theoretical models requires that researchers reject the Humean prescription that A must always and only lead to B to be a valid cause-effect relationship.

Similarly, new studies of suppression and mediation have allowed scholars to identify indirect causality and chains of causality, which are not engaged by either Aristotle or Hume. In mediation, a distal cause, A, leads to a mediator, M, which leads to a dependent variable, B. For example, perceived injustice might be a distal cause identified (A), which leads to anger (a mediator, M), which leads to collective action (a dependent variable, B). Thus, A (injustice) *indirectly causes* B (collective action) via M (increased anger). This model departs from pure consideration of the efficient cause in Aristotelian causality because the mediator, M, is both an outcome of A and a cause of B: a three-variable causal chain has been identified. It also departs from Humean simplicity in proposing that three variables can be a causal chain, beyond two-variable associations.

Even more complex, but interesting, is the case of suppression, another statistical relationship that can be tested in contemporary studies of collective action (e.g., Thomas & Louis, 2014). In suppression, a distal cause, A, is found to trigger two opposing processes, which simultaneously affect a dependent variable, B. The distal cause, A, might lead to the suppressor variable, S, which increases the dependent variable, B (A indirectly increases B via S), yet at the same time that same distal cause, A, also decreases B via another process: A decreases B as well as increasing it! For example, a death in the family may lead to increased stress, which leads to increased conflict, but at the same time, a death in the family may reduce conflict, by causing people to support each other and affirm their relationships. Thus, a suppression model of death and conflict implies that death both increases and decreases conflict, a causal model that Hume would have presumably rejected. In collective action, in turn, low social power might increase collective action by heightening perceived grievances, with grievances associated with more collective action, at the same time as low social power decreases collective action by increasing perceived vulnerability to reprisals, with vulnerability to reprisals associated with lower collective action. The two processes may appear to cancel each other out, so that it looks as though power is unrelated to action. However, our distal cause, low power, is, in fact, both increasing and decreasing our distal effect, collective action, at the same time—and even though the two effects work in opposition, modern statistics allows for both to be tested. Suppression analyses are not for the statistically faint of heart,[1] but add a powerful new level of causal modeling. Not only do they introduce complex causal chains with multiple variables, but they also allow an apparent null relationship to be unpacked to reveal significant opposing effects.

Finally, modern statistical models identify that the impact of causes vary in effect size, rather than simply being present, or absent that, our tests of the cause-effect relationships vary in power, and our measures of the variables vary in reliability and validity. All of these propositions—effect size, power, reliability, validity—qualify the simplicity of Humean causal modeling whereby causes are proposed to always and inevitably lead to effects.

---

[1]To be testable empirically, at least one of the intervening variables must be identified and measured (the suppressor). Even so, spurious suppression relationships can sometimes arise (Mavor, Louis, & Laythe, 2009, Mavor et al., 2011). Using particular multivariate statistical models implies recognition of the possibility of those causal relationships, which is valuable. But of course, in any given data, inferring causality depends on choices not only of statistical analyses but previously of methods and measurement, and of theory or conceptualization. For the statistical analyses to lead to the right judgment of causality, we have to have thought of the right variables to measure or manipulate, and we have to have measured or operationalized them in the right way. It is a tricky but fun process.

Current Causal Models and Collective Action: Gaps and Oversights

Despite the predominance of quantitative methods in the analysis of collective action, with their implicit presumption of shared, objective, quantifiable causes and effects, many scholars would agree that causality is constructed and that the construction of causality about social disadvantage, collective action, and government reactions is a significant project of political elites and media actors (e.g., Cooper, 1992). Thus, the prevalence of quantitative methods is itself an indicator of significant gaps in the literature, of missing consideration of the agents of collective action research (cf. Livingstone, 2013), and of the positioning or meaning of the collective actions (cf. Louis, 2008). In the historical overview of research above, for example, we have not addressed (nor are we aware of data that address) the changing agents of the study of collective action as this preserve of the straight white male researcher opened to new influxes of women, of Asian or black researchers, and of sexual minorities. Nor have we addressed the stable privileges of collective action researchers (predominantly university-based, European or North American, English-speaking), nor the important distinction between scholars of collective action informed by liberal/democratic/capitalist ideologies versus those informed by Marxism/socialism. Analyzing the construction of the scholarship of collective action in relation to disciplinary and scholarly privilege is an important direction of future analysis (see also van Stekelenburg et al., 2013; Sweetman et al., 2013). Below, we focus on the models rather than the agents of collective action scholarship, and we highlight three critical areas of innovation needed: attention to feedback loops, to systemic influences, and to implicit models of agency.

The Need for Recursive Models

Although we have argued that the above statistical models have broken many of the chains of Humean simplicity, the analyses described continue to reinforce the Humean model of temporal sequence such that causes precede effects and causal relationships are presented as if they ran in one direction only. There is an incredible lack of attention to feedback loops in the psychological study of collective action—an issue raised by many, such as Louis (2009), Wright (2008), and Thomas, Mavor, and McGarty (2012). Studies that have examined the outcomes of collective action quantitatively are comparatively few, and the exploration of non-recursive models that explicitly include feedback mechanisms is an important direction for future research.

In general, European sociological social psychology has been more respectful of and oriented toward historical analyses that incorporate dynamic feedback, including van Stekelenburg and colleagues' (2013) longitudinal analysis of anti-Muslim collective action in a neighborhood, and much of the research by Klandermans (see, e.g., Klandermans, 2007). Within social psychology, the work of Reicher also continues to provide exceptions (e.g., Drury & Reicher, 2000, 2005, 2009; Reicher & Haslam, 2013) and there is an exciting flurry of attention to historical dynamism recently (e.g., Becker et al., 2011; Blackwood & Louis, 2012; Sani et al., 2007; Tausch & Becker, 2013; van Zomeren et al., 2012). Within research methods, increasing familiarity with longitudinal analyses, cross-lagged correlations, and latent growth curves may also gradually allow for quantitative causal models that embrace historical change and the outcomes of collective action, as well as simultaneously accounting for its antecedents.

The Neglected Influence of Systemic Forces

Social psychology is sometimes defined as the study of how the thoughts, feelings, and actions of humans affect the thoughts, feelings, and actions of other humans (e.g., Myers et al., 2014). Such a formal definition invites a neglect of systemic or macro-factors that in theory are addressed by sociology or political science. The growing popularity of political psychology has allowed consideration of how political systems shape individuals' attitudes and behavior (Almond & Verba, 1963; Verba, 1978), how bidirectional influence from individual to political system is exerted (e.g., Hermann, Preston, Korany, & Shaw, 2001), and how dynamic interdependencies form between protest actions and authorities' reactions, or vice versa (Carey, 2006; Crelinsten, 2002, 2014). Yet, the impact of systemic forces, and the interplay within a group in consideration of internal hierarchies, rivalries, bureaucracies, factions, wealth, and institutions, are also largely neglected in the social psychology of collective action (cf. Sani, 2005, 2008).

Are Humans Agents? The Need for Explicit Consideration of Agency

Considering the appropriate window for causal analysis, Harré and Moghaddam write (this volume, p. x):

> Causal chains in nature regress indefinitely. This is made manageable in the special sciences by local decisions as to the salience of one or a few among a myriad of antecedent conditions. Is human agency an exception to this pattern? In the midst of the myriad conditions surrounding some sequence of events in the human world do we not find a human decision as the starting point of such a sequence and a human actor as the source of the causal efficacy that brings about the effect in question? Put otherwise, "The buck stops here!," or, as Wittgenstein (1953, §217) remarked, "[t]his is simply what I do!"

For Harré and Moghaddam, there is a debate between behaviorists and cognitivists about the importance of human agency. Behaviorists such as Skinner (1969: "The real question is not whether machines think but whether men do") see external stimuli as leading to behavior. For example, external threat might be modeled as leading to collective action directly. In contrast, cognitivists put thinking agents as intermediaries who act on perceptions to achieve goals. Summarizing this distinction, Harré and Moghaddam write (p. x):

> Behaviorists and neo-behaviorists try to give an account of human behavior in terms of Humean correlations between types of stimuli and types of responses.... But one group of cognitivists (see Harré & Moghaddam, 2012) think of the sequences of events, states, and social relationships and so on that come about in the course of human interactions as the products of the actions of people as active agents following rules, carrying through projects according to certain standards of achievement and so on. The conceptual requirements for an explanation include "agent, task, and schema."

The key issues are thus: (1) whether individuals' subjective appraisals of a situation are appropriately considered as causal variables, in contrast to positioning the external stimuli as the "true" causes; and (2) whether individuals in some sense choose to act, versus responding relatively automatically to internal or external stimuli. We certainly are firmly in the camp of the cognitivists and believe that research has shown the importance of subjective cognitive appraisals of external events for human action (e.g., Blascovich & Tomaka, 1996). Yet, we also are aware that recent research has questioned the primacy of cognitions and consciousness in human decision-making and that within the individual, there is the perennial argument of how thoughts, emotions, attitudes, and behavior should be ordered causally (Quintelier & Deth, 2014).

Agents within the Self?

As we have discussed above, in the context of the different theorized roles of cognition, emotion, and intention as antecedents, outcomes, or encapsulated by group identities, there is a tendency for different scholars to put forward different implicit models of agency within the self without explicitly contrasting them or empirically testing them (see also Louis, 2008; Louis et al., 2014). For some researchers, the capacity to be an independent causal agent is an attribute of the individual human as a whole person. For others, separate cognitive and emotional forces within the skull are independent actors. Different social identities might have meaningful agency; even smaller units—thoughts, emotions, instincts, beliefs—might be at play as agents within the self. Yet if, for example, there is an implicit model whereby thoughts lead to emotions that lead to intentions, then are thoughts separable from emotions, and from intentions? Do thoughts and emotions temporally precede intentions, in the brain? Some research suggests the boundaries between these constructs, and the temporal sequence in which they are modeled, are both blurred (e.g., Oosterwijk et al., 2012). The implicit theory that an individual's intentions lead to collective action behavior also underpins the vast majority of social-psychological research on collective action, yet other research calls into question this association as well as the direction of causality between intentions and behavior (e.g., Sheeran, 2002).

Another assumption that is rarely made explicit by collective action scholars is that there is a coherent choice maker acting on thoughts, feelings, and intentions or, alternatively, that there is just a "sum of the parts" mechanistic delivery system (Louis, 2008). Our own approach is influenced by Baumeister's (2008) observations on free will, which eschews absolutes but points out that some actions are freer than others. Thus, some of our individual behavior is more stimulus bound (e.g., the reflex to yawn when tired, or when others yawn, or when yawning is made salient) and other behaviors are more acutely experienced as chosen (e.g., whether to join the army) and that external factors (e.g., conscription, wealth) can moderate the degree of agency that individuals experience. More broadly, we agree with Baumeister (2008) that it is also a levels-of-analysis issue: if our behavior and our thoughts are free and causal, this is an emergent freedom not reducible to the nonfree movement of neurotransmitters and action potentials, or epigenetic triggers and protein emissions, at lower levels of analysis. Similarly, at higher levels of analysis, the experience of conscious choice is arguably within unconscious bounds and influenced by unconscious (macro-)forces such as class, wealth, culture, and history. Making explicit assumptions about agency, both within the self and outside of it, is an important direction for future cognitivist research. But there is another important direction needed for causal models in collective action: consideration of the agency of groups.

IV. WHO IS THE ACTOR IN COLLECTIVE ACTION?

To many psychologists as well as laypeople, it seems self-evident that only individuals have agency, and that is why we study collective action by asking individuals about their intentions to act. However, we would argue that a moment's thought will call into question the tight lens on individual members: groups act collectively; groups revolt, riot, attack, liberate, repress, and strategize. Just as free will for the individual has a levels-of-analysis issue, with the possibility of internal causation (e.g., thoughts may sometimes lead to emotions; emotions may bias thoughts; and external factors may generate both), so too groups have levels-of-analysis issues that involve but transcend individuals' agency. That is, groups influence individuals, reactively and proactively. The interaction of two individuals is more than the sum of their individuality: they form a dynamic system that calls out emergent qualities both complementarily (e.g., speaker/listener turn-taking) and communally (e.g., coupledom). So too, groups are more than individual group members: they structure individuals relationally (e.g., leader-follower) and define them jointly (e.g., with group identities and norms). These processes may precede individuals' decisions and shape them by social influence, as well as evoking individuals' qualities of resistance, leadership, innovation, and so on (e.g., Louis, 2009).

This dynamic of emergent collective agency is rarely explicated or empirically addressed in psychology (cf. e.g., Haslam, Reicher, & Platow, 2013). However, in political science, Oliver (e.g., 1980, 1993) has distinguished models of collective action based on groups as actors from other models. Collective action, as the aggregated outcome of individuals' choices, are the outcome of the dynamics of individuals' choices where not all group members have the same interest. We hope that this complexity will increasingly be acknowledged in social psychology, particularly as new statistical models such as multilevel modeling and hierarchical linear modeling facilitate explicit analyses of the impact of individuals on group-level decisions and vice versa.

In social psychology, to identify one key theory that has obvious multilevel properties, Reicher and Haslam's theorizing about the *entrepreneurship of identity* draws attention to how leaders can be seen as competing not only with each other to win the right to lead but also with followers to be seen as representing them and the group's interests (Haslam, Reicher, & Platow, 2013; Reicher & Haslam, 2013). In this approach, the group is not reducible to its members. By defining itself through the constellation of members' actions and other groups, a group calls upon leaders who reflect it. Groups have affordances and these affordances elicit the leaders, which can fill the vacuum and generate action.

To elaborate on this point, collective action often implies that groups act collectively—that is, they act together. In an individualistic approach, individuals may choose to act together in response to an individualistic appraisal of a shared situation; the affordances of the shared situation generate collective action, yet agency is experienced at the individual level (e.g., van Zomeren et al., 2008). However, we propose that group members differ in how pressured or autonomous they feel about their collective action (Amiot, Sansfaçon, & Louis, 2012, 2013, 2014). Moreover, there is a temporal and interactive dynamic whereby individuals' perceptions and subjectivities are shaped by normative forces, and by intragroup discussion, consensualization, and social influence that create a group-level emergent process (e.g., Thomas & McGarty, 2009; Thomas et al., 2014). Considered differently, there is a need for collective action because of an affordance in the situation or environment, so the group acts. A leader arises not so much because of individual choices, in this approach, but because of collective attributes: s/he was latent in the group; s/he was elicited by the situation—which individual emerges as leader is uncertain, but that someone would emerge is certain, given the situation. The group thus coalesces behind the beliefs that can make sense of the constraining social situation, and chooses the tactics that orient to the threat that needs to be addressed; while each individual experiences himself or herself as having had choice within the situation, there is a level of analysis at which the actions of the collective individuals were determined by the context of their group, as well as by the dynamics of individuals and subgroups within the group. Each individual Christian may choose to attend church on Sunday, and each American voter to vote in November, yet on a different level, those actions are determined by group membership. In voting, for example, the opportunity for choice depends on group membership (citizenship), and the nature of the choice (to vote or not to vote, partisanship) is in turn shaped by social factors such as class and race.

Following the lead of Baumeister (2008) on individuals' free will, however, we propose that for collective action, in addition to making the point that levels of analysis define the location of agency differently, it is also important to make the point that some collective actions are more versus less agentic. A group's collective agency might depend on a variety of historical and situational factors, including the group's structure, its resources, the frequency and norms with which group members meet and coordinate, and the pressure of its environment. There is already a line of research that shows that some groups are perceived to be more homogenous agents than others (entitativity research; e.g., Brewer, Hong, & Li, 2004) and, as such, are expected to exert more control over the environment (Fritsche, Jonas, & Kessler, 2011; Fritsche et al., 2013). In sociology, to pursue the "levels of analysis" issue further, the idea of collective agency has been put forward as an emergent property of group interactions that may involve even higher-order agents, such as political climate (Gerhards & Rucht, 1992), the influence of corporate sectors (e.g., London & Williams, 1988), or even ecosystems (e.g., Lockie, 2004).

But more broadly, different disciplines have tended to focus on different groups of actors in the collective action chain—such as protest groups (e.g., psychology), social movements (e.g., sociology), or political parties (e.g., political psychology). Across those levels of analysis, in turn, lie other dimensions on which actors can be grouped and their group's agency examined: gender, age, rural/urban community, class, race, language, environment, and religion. The interrelationships of individual and collective agencies are thus complicated by the intersecting nature of group identities and the multiple levels at which the relationships can be mapped. Each level of analysis and dimension tends to have its own segregated publication outlets, and particular conventions and citation patterns that do not typically inter-cite (as elaborated below).

Explicit consideration of the nature and location of collective agency is a vital future direction for the scholarship of collective action. For example, in the review by van Stekelenburg et al. (2013), efficacy has been identified as a major causal factor in the social psychology of collective action since the 1970s. Yet, arguably the use of the same label by a variety of scholars and disciplines has obscured important differences in causal models concerning the location of agency concerning who or what is empowered. Efficacy may be an individual's internal appraisal of their group's power (van Zomeren et al., 2008), as distinct from effectiveness perceptions for a target's behavior (Louis, 2012), or for material resources in the world and political opportunities in a sociopolitical sphere (Klandermans, 1984). Alternatively, efficacy may be an emergent property of group interactions and experiences in other models (e.g., Blackwood & Louis, 2012; Blee, 2013; Drury & Reicher, 2000, 2005, 2009; Quintelier & Deth, 2014; Thomas et al., 2012, 2014). These questions cannot be articulated unless the location of agency is explicitly proposed and interrogated.

V. CONCLUDING THOUGHTS: REALITY DEPENDS ON THE JOURNAL

The hidden promulgation of causal models of collective action is affected by the promulgation of outlets for publication: new journals (and the subdisciplines they support) are constantly forming (Moghaddam, 1997), in part to promote particular causal models perceived to be neglected elsewhere. To pick out only a few, the *Journal of Social and Political Psychology* (2014; founded in 2013) reports in its aims that it seeks "to counterbalance the current overreliance on the hypothetico-deductive model of science, quantitative methodology, and individualistic explanations by also publishing work following alternative traditions" (2014). *Peace and Conflict: The Journal of Peace Psychology* (founded in 1995) offers an interdisciplinary outlet friendly to quantitative and qualitative approaches, focusing on social harmony as the dimension for collective action research. The journal *Political Psychology* (2014; founded in 1978) announces itself to be "dedicated to the analysis of the interrelationships between psychological and political processes." More than 80 outlets are listed for peace and conflict studies by the Peace and Justice Studies Association (2014). It is clear that feedback loops operate whereby individuals and groups seeking to promote particular causal models and levels of analysis found journals, and the presence of these journals that publish particular causal models and levels of analysis allows the careers of individuals who espouse those approaches to flourish and to influence others.

It is difficult to consider mainstream collective action when in some ways it is not mainstream: for example, there is no journal of collective action (a notable omission in an era of increasing outlet specialization). Moreover, we approach collective action from the perspective of social psychologists, which is arguably non-mainstream within collective action scholarship (cf. van Stekelenburg et al., 2013).[2]

Within the current social psychological scholarship of collective action, perhaps the most highly cited model is the Social Identity Model of Collective Action (SIMCA; van Zomeren et al., 2008), which can be considered as pursuing efficient causality as preferred by Bacon: intentions to engage in collective action (a dependent measure) are predicted by anger, efficacy, and, in recent models, moral conviction (mediators), which, in turn, arise from social identification (a distal cause). Both causes and effects are usually measured at one point in time, with intentions to engage in collective action

[2]Google Scholar, in October 2014, generated no social psychological articles among the first 10 listed for collective action; 9 were political science and 1 was sociological.

in the future introducing the temporal sequence preferred by Hume. The model includes mediation of identification by anger, efficacy, and moral convictions, however, which deviates from Humean associations. All of the variables are measured at the individual level, and within the individual's head, typically via self-report questionnaires. Analyses predict individual differences in responses. Beyond the individual level of measurement and analysis, there is a theoretical backstory whereby individuals are considered as group members (they are sampled from within particular groups), and the content of the social identity and the form of the collective action are defined by the groups' norms (nonnormative forms of collective action and groups that do not support collective action are omitted; see also Louis et al., 2003). Causality is typically thought to flow one way, from identity to emotions and appraisals (awarded joint priority) to intentions. Reverse causality from intentions to beliefs is not typically modeled, although in the dynamic extension of the SIMCA model, feedback loops from collective action to identification and efficacy, anger, and moral convictions are now also explored (van Zomeren et al., 2012; see also Tausch & Becker, 2013; Thomas et al., 2011).

From the flow of the chapter thus far, it is clear how much is missing. In general, these within-group individual-level analyses are missing accounts of group processes (e.g., intragroup positioning, roles, and leadership); the temporal sequences are ahistorical and neglect feedback loops; the multiple-group world and the mutually intersecting nature of multiple group identities are neglected (only one social identity and dimension of collective action is typically considered at a time); and the role of leadership and norm contestation within and between groups is rarely elaborated. Of course, any one model addresses only one piece in the puzzle. Arguably, other models within social psychology, as well as other disciplines such as political science, sociology, economics, history, and social movement studies, jointly address different levels of analysis. Yet, as our analysis above anticipates, we look forward to a future in which analyses of meaning and history are integrated into the study of collective action, and where multiple identities, norms, groups, and levels of analysis are jointly considered. Our causal model of scholarly change leads us to hope that this chapter takes a step for the field in this direction.

REFERENCES

Adorno, T. W., Frenkel-Brunswik, E., Levinson, D. J., & Sanford, R. N. (1950). *The authoritarian personality*. New York: Harper & Row.

Almond, G.A., & Verba, S. (1963). *The civic culture: Political attitudes and democracy in five nations*. Princeton, NJ: Princeton University Press.

Altemeyer, B. (1981). *Right-wing authoritarianism*. Winnipeg, Canada: University of Manitoba Press.

Amiot, C. E., Sansfaçon, S., & Louis, W. R. (2014). How normative and social identification processes predict self-determination to engage in derogatory behaviours against outgroup hockey fans. *European Journal of Social Psychology, 44(3)*, 216–320. doi: 10.1002/ejsp.2006

Amiot, C. E., Sansfaçon, S., & Louis, W. R. (2013). Investigating the motivations underlying harmful social behaviors and the motivational nature of social norms. *Journal of Applied Social Psychology, 43*, 2146–2157. doi: 10.1111/jasp.12167

Amiot, C. E., Sansfaçon, S., Louis, W. R., & Yelle, M. (2012). Can intergroup behaviors be emitted out of self-determined reasons?: Testing the role of group norms and behavioral congruence in the internalisation of discrimination and parity behaviors. *Personality and Social Psychology Bulletin, 38(1)*, 63–76. doi: 10.1177/0146167211429804

Bacon, F. (2012/1605). *The advancement of learning*. Modern English edition. London: Random House.

Baumeister, R. F. (2008). Free will in scientific psychology. *Perspectives on Psychological Science, 3(1)*, 14–19.

Becker, J. C. (2012). Virtual special issue on theory and research on collective action in the European Journal of Social Psychology. *European Journal of Social Psychology, 42(1)*, 19–23. doi: http://dx.doi.org.ezproxy.library.uq .edu.au/10.1177/0146167211407076

Becker, J. C., Tausch, N., Spears, R., & Christ, O. (2011). Committed dis (s) idents: Participation in radical collective action fosters disidentification with the broader in-group but enhances political identification. *Personality and Social Psychology Bulletin, 37(8)*, 1104–1116.

Becker, J. C., Tausch, N., & Wagner, U. (2011). Emotional consequences of collective action participation differentiating self-directed and outgroup-directed emotions. *Personality and Social Psychology Bulletin, 37(12)*, 1587–1598.

Blackwood, L. M., & Louis, W. R. (2012). If it matters for the group then it matters to me: Collective action outcomes for seasoned activists. *British Journal of Social Psychology, 51(1)*, 72–92.

Blackwood, L., Livingstone, A. G., & Leach, C. W. (2013). Regarding societal change. *Journal of Social and Political Psychology, 1(1)*, 105–111.

Blascovich, J., & Tomaka, J. (1996). The biopsychosocial model of arousal regulation. In M. P. Zanna (Ed.), *Advances in experimental social psychology, vol. 29* (pp. 1–51). New York: Academic Press.

Blee, K. (2013). How options disappear: Causality and emergence in grassroots activist groups. *American Journal of Sociology, 119(3)*, 655–681.

Blumer, H. (1951). Social movements. In A. M. Lee (Ed.), *New outline of the principles of sociology* (pp. 199–220). New York, NY: Barnes & Noble.

Brewer, M. B., & Kramer, R. M. (1986). Choice behavior in social dilemmas: Effects of social identity, group size, and decision framing. *Journal of Personality and Social Psychology, 50(3)*, 543.

Brewer, M. B., Hong, Y. Y., & Li, Q. (2004). Dynamic entitativity. The psychology of group perception. In V. Yzerbyt, C. Judd, & O. Corneille (Eds.), *The psychology of group perception: Perceived variability, entitativity, and essentialism* (pp. 25–38). New York: Psychology Press.

Campbell, A., Converse, P. E., Miller, W. E., & Stokes, D. E. (1960). *The American voter*. Oxford, England: John Wiley.

Carey, S. C. (2006). The dynamic relationship between protest and repression. *Political Research Quarterly, 59(1)*, 1–11.

Converse, P. E. (1964). The nature of belief systems in mass publics. In D. E. Apter (Ed.), *Ideology and discontent* (pp. 206–226). New York: The Free Press of Glencoe.

Cooper, A. H. (2002). Media framing and social movement mobilization: German peace protest against INF missiles, the Gulf War, and NATO peace enforcement in Bosnia. *European Journal of Political Research, 41(1)*, 37–80.

Crelinsten, R. D. (2002). Analysing terrorism and counter-terrorism: A communication model. *Terrorism and Political Violence, 14(2)*, 77–122. doi: 10.1080/714005618

Crelinsten, R. (2014). Perspectives on counterterrorism: From stovepipes to a comprehensive approach. *Perspectives on Terrorism, 8(1)*.

Davies, J. (1962). Toward a theory of revolution. *American Sociological Review, 27*, 5–19. doi:10.2307/2089714

Dawkins, R. (1976). *The selfish gene*. New York City: Oxford University Press. ISBN 0-19-286092-5

Drury, J., & Reicher, S. (2000). Collective action and psychological change: The emergence of new social identities. *British Journal of Social Psychology, 39(4)*, 579–604. doi: 10.1348/014466600164642

Drury, J., & Reicher, S. (2005). Explaining enduring empowerment: A comparative study of collective action and psychological outcomes. *European Journal of Social Psychology, 35(1)*, 35–58.

Drury, J., & Reicher, S. (2009). Collective psychological empowerment as a model of social change: Researching crowds and power. *Journal of Social Issues, 65(4)*, 707–725.

Festinger, L., Riecken, H. W., & Schachter, S. (1956). *When prophecy fails: A social and psychological study of a modern group that predicted the destruction of the world*. University of Minnesota Press. ISBN 1-59147-727-1. Reissued 2008 by Pinter & Martin with a foreword by Elliot Aronson, ISBN 978-1-905177-19-6

Freeman, J. (1975). *The politics of women's liberation*. New York: David McKay.

Fritsche, I., Jonas, E., Ablasser, C., Beyer, M., Kuban, J., Manger, A.-M., & Schultz, M. (2013). The power of we: Evidence for group-based control. *Journal of Experimental Social Psychology, 49(1)*, 19–32. doi: 10.1016/j.jesp.2012.07.014

Fritsche, I., Jonas, E., & Kessler, T. (2011). Collective reactions to threat: Implications for intergroup conflict and for solving societal crises. *Social Issues and Policy Review, 5(1)*, 101–136. doi: 10.1111/j.1751-2409.2011.01027.x

Gamson, W. A. (1975). *The strategy of social protest*. Homewood, IL: Dorsey Press.

Gerhards, J., & Rucht, D. (1992). Mesomobilization: Organizing and framing in two protest campaigns in West Germany. *American Journal of Sociology* 98, 555–596.

Ginges, J., Atran, S., Sachdeva, S., & Medin, D. (2011). Psychology out of the laboratory: The challenge of violent extremism. *American Psychologist*, 66(6), 507.

Graham, S., & Folkes, V. S. (Eds.). (2014). *Attribution theory: Applications to achievement, mental health, and interpersonal conflict*. London: Psychology Press.

Grant, P. R., & Brown, R. (1995). From ethnocentrism to collective protest: Responses to relative deprivation and threats to social identity. *Social Psychology Quarterly, 58(3)*, 195–212. doi: http://dx.doi.org.ezproxy.library.uq.edu.au/10.2307/2787042

Gurr, T. (1970). *Why men rebel*. Princeton, NJ: Princeton University Press.

Gusfield, J. R. (1963). *Symbolic crusade*. Urbana-Champaign: University of Illinois Press.

Handler, J. F. (1992). Postmodernism, protest, and the new social movements. *Law & Sociology Review, 26(4)*, 697–731. doi: 10.2307/3053811

Haslam, S. A., Reicher, S. D., & Platow, M. J. (2013). *The new psychology of leadership: Identity, influence and power*. London: Psychology Press.

Hermann, M. G., Preston, T., Korany, B., & Shaw, T. M. (2001). Who leads matters: The effects of powerful individuals. *International Studies Review, 3(2)*, 83–131.

Hoffer, E. (1951). *The true believer: Thoughts on the nature of mass movements*. Harper Perennial Modern Classics. ISBN 978-0-060-50591-2

Hume, D. (1978/1739). *A treatise of human nature*. Modern English edition. Oxford, England: Oxford University Press.

Journal of Social and Political Psychology. (2014). Focus and scope. Downloaded May 6 2014 from http://jspp.psychopen.eu/about/editorialPolicies#focusAndScope

Kawakami, K., & Dion, K. L. (1993). The impact of salient self-identities on relative deprivation and action intentions. *European Journal of Social Psychology, 23(5)*, 525–540.

Kawakami, K., & Dion, K. L. (1995). Social Identity and affect as determinants of collective action; Toward an integration of relative deprivation and social identity theories. *Theory & Psychology, 5(4)*, 551–577.

Kelly, C. (1993). Group identification, intergroup perceptions and collective action. *European Review of Social Psychology, 4(1)*, 59–83.

Kelly, C., & Kelly, J. (1994). Who gets involved in collective action? Social psychological determinants of individual participation in trade unions. *Human Relations, 47(1)*, 63–88.

Klandermans, B. (1984). Mobilization and participation: Social-psychological expansions of resource mobilization theory. *American Sociological Review, 49(5)*, 583–600. doi:10.2307/2095417

Klandermans, B. (1997). *The social psychology of protest.* Oxford, UK: Blackwell Publishers.

Klandermans, B. (2007). The demand and supply of participation: Social-psychological correlates of participation in social movements. In D. A. Snow, S. A. Soule, & H. Kriesi (Eds.), *The Blackwell companion to social movements.* Oxford, UK: Blackwell Publishing Ltd. doi: 10.1002/9780470999103

Klandermans, B., & Mayer, N. (2006). *Extreme right activists in Europe: Through the magnifying glass.* London: Psychology Press.

Klandermans, B., Van der Toorn, J., & Van Stekelenburg, J. V. (2008). Embeddedness and identity: How immigrants turn grievances into action. *American Sociological Review, 73(6),* 992–1012. doi:10.1177/000312240 807300606

Lalonde, R. N., & Silverman, R. A. (1994). Behavioral preferences in response to social injustice: The effects of group permeability and social identity salience. *Journal of Personality and Social Psychology, 66(1),* 78–85.

Lane, R. E. (1965). The politics of consensus in an age of affluence. *American Political Science Review, 59(04),* 874–895. doi: 10.2307/1953211

Lasswell, H. D. (1930). *Psychopathology and politics.* Chicago, IL: University of Chicago Press.

Lasswell, H. D. (1950). *Power and society: A framework for political inquiry.* Piscataway, NJ: Transaction Publishers.

Lazarsfeld, P. F., Berelson, B., & Gaudet, H. (1944). *The people's choice: How the voter makes up his mind in a presidential campaign.* New York: Columbia University Press.

Le Bon, G. (1895). [Psychologie des foules.] *Psychology of crowds.* English modern edition 2009. Sparkling Books.

Leach, C. W., Ellemers, N., & Barreto, M. (2007). Group virtue: The importance of morality (vs. competence and sociability) in the positive evaluation of in-groups. *Journal of Personality and Social Psychology, 93(2),* 234–249.

Livingstone, A. G. (2013). Why the psychology of collective action requires qualitative transformation as well as quantitative change. *Contemporary Social Science: Journal of the Academy of Social Sciences, 9,* 121–134.

Lockie, S. (2004). Collective agency, non-human causality and environmental social movements: A case study of the Australian 'Landcare Movement.' *Journal of Sociology, 40(1),* 41–57.

London, B., & Williams, B. A. (1988). Multinational corporate penetration, protest, and basic needs provision in non-core nations: A cross-national analysis. *Social Forces, 66(3),* 747–773.

Louis, W. R. (2008). Intergroup positioning and power. In F. M. Moghaddam, R. Harré, & N. Lee (Eds.), *Global conflict resolution through positioning analysis* (pp. 21–39). New York: Springer.

Louis, W. R. (2009). Collective action – and then what? *Journal of Social Issues, 65(4),* 727–748. doi: 10.1111/j.1540-4560.2009.01623.x

Louis, W. R. (2012). Collective efficacy. In D. J. Christie (Ed.), *Encyclopedia of peace psychology.* Hoboken, NJ: Wiley-Blackwell.

Louis, W. R., Mavor, K. I., La Macchia, S. T., & Amiot, C. E. (2014). Social justice and psychology: What is, and what should be. In M. Arken & J. Yen (Eds.), *Justice and psychology*, special issue of the *Journal of Theoretical and Philosophical Psychology, 34(1)*, 14–27. doi: 10.1037/a0033033

Louis, W. R., Mavor, K. I., & Terry, D. J. (2003). Reflections on the statistical analysis of personality and norms in war, peace, and prejudice: Are deviant minorities the problem? *Analyses of Social Issues and Public Policy, 3(1)*, 189–198. doi:10.1111/j.1530-2415.2003.00025.x

Mackie, D. M., & Smith, E. R. (Eds.). (2002). *From prejudice to intergroup emotions: Differentiated reactions to social groups.* New York, NY: Psychology Press.

Mavor, K. I., Macleod, C. J., Boal, M. J., & Louis, W. R. (2009). Right-wing authoritarianism, fundamentalism and prejudice revisited: Removing suppression and statistical artefact?*Personality & Individual Differences, 46(5–6)*, 592–597. doi:10.1016/j.paid.2008.12.016

Mavor, K. I., Louis, W. R., & Laythe, B. (2011). Religion, prejudice, and authoritarianism: Is RWA a boon or bane to the psychology of religion? *Journal for the Scientific Study of Religion, 50(1)*, 22–43. doi: 10.1111/j.1468-5906.2010.01550.x

McAdam, D. (1982). *Political process and the development of Black insurgency 1930–1970.* Chicago, IL: University of Chicago Press.

McCarthy, J. D., & Zald, M. N. (1977). Resource mobilization and social movements: A partial theory. *American Journal of Sociology, 82(6)*, 1212–1241. doi: 10.2307/2777934

Moghaddam, F. M. (1997). *The specialized society: The plight of the individual in an age of individualism.* Westport, CT: Praeger.

Mummendey, A., Kessler, T., Klink, A., & Mielke, R. (1999). Strategies to cope with negative social identity: Predictions by social identity theory and relative deprivation theory. *Journal of Personality and Social Psychology, 76(2)*, 229–245. doi:10.1037/0022-3514.76.2.229

Myers, D., Haslam, N., Louis, W. R., Allen, F., Denson, T., Karantzas, G., Passmore, N., & Zinkiewicz, L. (2014). *Social psychology.* Sydney: McGraw Hill. ISBN: 1743070454

Oberschall, A. (1973). *Social conflict and social movements.* Englewood Cliffs, NJ: Prentice Hall.

Oliver, P. E. (1980). Rewards and punishments as selective incentives for collective action: Theoretical investigations. *American Journal of Sociology, 85*, 1356–1375.

Oliver, P. E. (1993). Formal models of collective action. *Annual Review of Sociology, 19(1)*, 271–300.

Olson, M. (1965/1971). *The logic of collective action: Public goods and the theory of groups.* Boston: Harvard University Press.

Oosterwijk, S., Lindquist, K. A., Anderson, E., Dautoff, R., Moriguchi, Y., & Barrett, L. F. (2012). States of mind: Emotions, body feelings, and thoughts share distributed neural networks. *NeuroImage, 62(3)*, 2110–2128.

Ostrom, E. (1998). A behavioral approach to the rational choice theory of collective action: Presidential address, American Political Science Association, 1997. *American Political Science Review, 1*, 1–22.

Ostrom, E. (1990). *Governing the commons: The evolution of institutions for collective action.* Cambridge: Cambridge University Press.

Peace and Justice Studies Association. (2014). Journals in peace studies and conflict resolution. Downloaded 6 May 2014 from http://www.peace justicestudies.org/resources/journals.php

Polletta, F. (2009). *It was like a fever: Storytelling in protest and politics.* Chicago, IL: University of Chicago Press.

Political Psychology. (2014). *Aims and scope.* Downloaded 6 May 2014 from http://onlinelibrary.wiley.com/journal/10.1111/(ISSN)1467-9221/ homepage/ProductInformation.html

Quintelier, E., & Deth, J. W. (2014). Supporting democracy: Political participation and political attitudes. Exploring causality using panel data. *Political Studies, 62(S1)*, 153–171. doi: 10.1111/1467-9248.12097

Reicher, S. D. (1984). The St. Pauls' riot: An explanation of the limits of crowd action in terms of a social identity model. *European Journal of Social Psychology, 14(1)*, 1–21. doi: 10.1002/ejsp.2420140102

Reicher, S., & Haslam, S. A. (2013). Towards a 'Science of Movement': Identity, authority and influence in the production of social stability and social change. *Journal of Social and Political Psychology, 1(1)*, 112–131.

Reicher, S. D., Spears, R., & Postmes, T. (1995). A social identity model of deindividuation phenomena. *European Review of Social Psychology, 6(1)*, 161–198.

Runciman, W. G. (1966). *Relative deprivation and social justice.* London, UK: Routledge.

Saab, R., Tausch, N., Spears, R., & Cheung, W. Y. (2014). Acting in solidarity: Testing an extended dual pathway model of collective action by bystander group members. *British Journal of Social Psychology, 54(3)*, 539-560.

Saeri, A. K., Iyer, A., & Louis, W. R. (in press). Right-wing authoritarianism and social dominance orientation predict outsiders' responses to external group conflict: Implications for identification, anger, and collective action. *Analyses of Social Issues and Public Policy.* doi: 10.1111/asap.12081.

Sani, F., Bowe, M., Herrera, M., Manna, C., Cossa, T., Miao, X., & Zhou, Y. (2007). Perceived collective continuity: Seeing groups as entities that move through time. *European Journal of Social Psychology, 37(6)*, 1118–1134.

Sani, F. (2005). When subgroups secede: Extending and refining the social psychological model of schism in groups. *Personality and Social Psychology Bulletin, 31(8)*, 1074–1086.

Sani, F. (2008). Schism in groups: A social psychological account. *Social and Personality Psychology Compass, 2(2)*, 718–732.

Searles, R., & Williams, J. A., Jr. (1962). Negro college students' participation in sit-ins. *Social Forces, 40(3)*, 215–220. doi: 10.2307/2573631

Sheeran, P. (2002). Intention-behavior relations: A conceptual and empirical review. *European Review of Social Psychology, 12*, 1–36.

Simon, B., & Klandermans, B. (2001). Towards a social psychological analysis of politicized collective identity: Conceptualization, antecedents, and consequences. *The American Psychologist, 56(4)*, 319–331. doi:10.1037/0003-066X.56.4.319

Skinner, B. F. (1969). *Contingencies of reinforcement: A theoretical analysis.* New York: Appleton-Century-Crofts.

Skitka, L. J., Bauman, C. W., & Sargis, E. G. (2005). Moral conviction: Another contributor to attitude strength or something more? *Journal of Personality and Social Psychology, 88(6)*, 895–917.

Smelser, N. J. (1962). *Theory of collective behavior.* New York, NY: Free Press.

Subašić, E., Reynolds, K. J., & Turner, J. C. (2008). The political solidarity model of social change: Dynamics of self-categorization in intergroup power relations. *Personality and Social Psychology Review, 12*, 330–352. doi: 10.1177/1088868308323223

Sweetman, J., Leach, C. W., Spears, R., Pratto, F., & Saab, R. (2013). "I have a dream": A typology of social change goals. *Journal of Social and Political Psychology, 1(1)*, 293–320.

Tajfel, H., & Turner, J. C. (1979). An integrative theory of intergroup conflict. In S. Worchel & W. G. Austin (Eds.), *The social psychology of intergroup relations* (pp. 33–47). Chicago, IL: Nelson-Hall Publishers.

Tausch, N., & Becker, J. C. (2013). Emotional reactions to success and failure of collective action as predictors of future action intentions: A longitudinal investigation in the context of student protests in Germany. *British Journal of Social Psychology, 52(3)*, 525–542.

Tausch, N., Becker, J. C., Spears, R., Christ, O., Saab, R., Singh, P., & Siddiqui, R. N. (2011). Explaining radical group behavior: Developing emotion and efficacy routes to normative and nonnormative collective action. *Journal of Personality and Social Psychology, 101(1)*, 129.

Taylor, D. M., & Brown, R. J. (1979). Towards a more social social psychology? *British Journal of Social and Clinical Psychology, 18*, 173–180. doi:10.1111/j.2044-8260.1979.tb00322.x

Thomas, E. F., & Louis, W. R. (2014). When will collective action be effective? Violent and non-violent protests differentially influence perceptions of legitimacy and efficacy among sympathizers. *Personality and Social Psychology Bulletin, 40(2)*, 263–276. doi: 10.1177/0146167213510525

Thomas, E. F., & McGarty, C. (2009). The role of efficacy and moral outrage norms in creating the potential for international development activism through group-based interaction. *British Journal of Social Psychology, 48*, 115–134.

Thomas, E. F., McGarty, C., & Louis, W. R. (2014). Social interaction and psychological pathways to political extremism. *European Journal of Social Psychology, 44(1)*, 15–22. doi: 10.1002/ejsp.1988

Thomas, E. F., McGarty, C., & Mavor, K. I. (2009). Aligning identities, emotions, and beliefs to create commitment to sustainable social and political action. *Personality and Social Psychology Review, 13(3)*, 194–218. doi: 10.1177/1088868309341563

Thomas, E. F., Mavor, K. I., & McGarty, C. (2012). Social identities facilitate and encapsulate action-relevant constructs: A test of the social identity model of collective action. *Group Processes and Intergroup Relations, 15*, 75–88. doi:10.1177/1368430211413619

Tilly, C. (1978). *From mobilization to revolution.* Reading, MA: Addison-Wesley.

Turner, J. C., Hogg, M. A., Oakes, P. J., Reicher, S. D., & Wetherell, M. S. (1987). *Rediscovering the social group: A self-categorization theory.* Oxford, UK: Blackwell.

Turner, J. C., Oakes, P. J., Haslam, S. A., & McGarty, C. (1994). Self and collective: Cognition and social context. *Personality and Social Psychology Bulletin, 20*, 454–454.

Tyler, T. R., & Degoey, P. (1995). Collective restraint in social dilemmas: Procedural justice and social identification effects on support for authorities. *Journal of Personality and Social Psychology, 69(3)*, 482.

Van Stekelenburg, J. V., Anikina, N., Pouw, W. J. T. L., Petrovic, I., & Nederlof, N. (2013). From correlation to causation: The cruciality of a collectivity in the context of collective action. *Journal of Social and Political Psychology, 1(1)*, 161–187. http://dx.doi.org/10.5964/jspp.v1i1.38

Van Zomeren, M. (2013). Four core social-psychological motivations to undertake collective action. *Social and Personality Psychology Compass, 7(6)*, 378–388.

Van Zomeren, M., & Iyer, A. (2009). Introduction to the social and psychological dynamics of collective action. *Journal of Social Issues, 65(4)*, 645–660.

Van Zomeren, M., Leach, C. W., & Spears, R. (2012). Protesters as "Passionate Economists": A dynamic dual pathway model of approach coping with collective disadvantage. *Personality and Social Psychology Review, 16(2)*, 180–199.

Van Zomeren, M., Postmes, T., & Spears, R. (2008). Toward an integrative social identity model of collective action: A quantitative research synthesis of three socio-psychological perspectives. *Psychological Bulletin, 134*, 504–535. doi:10.1037/0033-2909.134.4.504

Van Zomeren, M., Postmes, T., Spears, R., & Bettache, K. (2011). Can moral convictions motivate the advantaged to challenge social inequality? Extending the social identity model of collective action. *Group Processes & Intergroup Relations, 14(5)*, 735–753. doi: 10.1177/1368430210395637

Van Zomeren, M., Spears, R., Fischer, A. H., & Leach, C. W. (2004). Put your money where your mouth is! Explaining collective action tendencies through group-based anger and group efficacy. *Journal of Personality and Social Psychology, 87(5)*, 649–664. doi:10.1037/0022-3514.87.5.649

Verba, S. (1978). *Participation and political equality: A seven-nation comparison.* Chicago, IL: University of Chicago Press.

Walker, L., & Mann, L. (1987). Unemployment, relative deprivation, and social protest. *Personality and Social Psychology Bulletin, 13,* 275–283. doi:10.1177/0146167287132012

Wright, S. C., Taylor, D. M., & Moghaddam, F. M. (1990). Responding to membership in a disadvantaged group: From acceptance to collective protest. *Journal of Personality and Social Psychology, 58,* 994–1003.

Wright, S. C. (2008). Strategic collective action: Social psychology and social change. In *Blackwell handbook of social psychology: Intergroup processes* (pp. 409–430). Oxford, UK: Blackwell.

Zaal, M. P., Laar, C. V., Ståhl, T., Ellemers, N., & Derks, B. (2011). By any means necessary: The effects of regulatory focus and moral conviction on hostile and benevolent forms of collective action. *British Journal of Social Psychology, 50(4),* 670–689.

Zald, M. N., & McCarthy, J. D. (1987). *Social movements in an organizational society: Collected essays.* New Brunswick, NJ: Transaction Books.

EDITORS' COMMENTARY

The discussion by Louis, La Macchia, Amiot, Thomas, Blackwood, Mavor, and Saeri on causality in collective action and political behavior reveals a number of themes, as well as some confusion in how psychologists have addressed collective action. The authors first pick up on the theme of collective action as reflecting pathology and dysfunction, which is part of the general distrust of crowds and collectives evident in the writings of Le Bon (1897) and other nineteenth- and early-twentieth-century authors. The "madness of crowds" was a theme for these early writers, and this approach very much influenced Freud in his discussions of collective behavior and irrationality (see Taylor & Moghaddam, 1994). Irrationality, as a cause of collective action and political behavior, is a dominant theme in this tradition. In this instance, "irrationality" has the classical Freudian meaning of the collective being causally influenced by factors that have been repressed into the unconscious.

It would be convenient if the theme of irrationality neatly cut across another theme identified by the authors: the distinction between material and psychological causes in collective action and political behavior. It would be highly convenient if we could identify material causes as rational and psychological causes as irrational, or at least categorize all material causes as irrational. But this simple classification quickly falls apart, particularly in political behavior. For example, consider the materialist accounts of collective behavior embodied in classical Marxist theory, or Realistic Conflict Theory, or Resource Mobilization Theory, or even sociobiology. They all assume some level of irrational causation. For example, Marxist theory assumes that the working class is suffering from false consciousness, which prevents them from recognizing their true group membership and interests. Realistic Conflict Theory similarly assumes that group members are driven to like or dislike, be peaceful or violent, toward others without recognizing the causes of their behavior. Resource Mobilization Theory assumes that the causes of how people feel, their level of deprivation or satisfaction for example, is the material resources mobilized by elites who control resources. Sociobiology assumes that genetic factors cause people to behave in certain ways toward others based on genetic similarity and dissimilarity, without them recognizing the causal role of genes. Thus, in all these material accounts, irrationality plays a major role in collective behavior.

As Louis et al. point out, the issue of agency becomes more complicated when considering the collective. Of course, in practical terms, not all group members have the same level of influence, and in many groups it is the agency of leaders that matters most. This is particularly so in dictatorships such as Russia, Iran, North Korea, and China. However, the situation is not necessarily very different in societies labeled as "democratic." For example, consider how the members of certain families, including the Bush and Clinton families, have influenced political decision making in the United States in the early twenty-first century. It would be naïve to assume that collective agency in American politics is really about all of American society, when key decisions are made by elites. In this situation, "causation" in political behavior concerns the factors that influence elite leadership.

REFERENCES

Le Bon, G. (1897). *The crowd: A study of the popular mind.* London: T. Fisher Unwin.

Taylor, D. M., & Moghaddam, F. M. (1994). *Theories of intergroup relations: International social psychological perspectives*, (2nd ed.). Westport, CT: Praeger.

18

Assumed Causes of Collective Excellence

Kelly Comolli and Fathali M. Moghaddam

Psychologists have had a historic interest in measuring and trying to discover the causes of excellence, where an individual or group achieves outstanding performance. An enormous international testing industry has evolved, with thousands of different psychological tests for measuring intelligence, creativity, resilience, leadership, and other such characteristics. The pioneering work in this area began in the nineteenth century with Francis Galton (1822–1911), and continued in the early twentieth century through the efforts of Alfred Binet (1857–1911) who helped develop the first modern intelligence tests, focused on higher-order comprehension and analytical thinking. The testing industry gained impetus during World War I and II, when millions of recruits were assessed using intelligence tests. In the twenty-first century, tests such as the ACT, SAT, GRE, GMAT, MCAT, and LSAT are integral to the education system, and are highly influential internationally.

A peculiar feature of these standard tests is that they almost exclusively assess individual performance (for some exceptions, see Nijstad, 2009; Woolley, Chabris, Pentland, Hashmi, & Malone, 2010). This is peculiar because in everyday life most performances involve groups, not isolated individuals. For example, medical doctors work in teams, but an aspiring doctor must first achieve "excellence as an isolated individual" on the SAT, the MCAT, and the USMLE, on the path to becoming a practicing medical physician. If successful on these individual tests, this doctor becomes a member of a healthcare team, but her ability to perform in a team setting has never been officially tested or honed. While individual performance is tested by MCAT and many other specially designed tests, the ability to work in groups is assessed in a far more informal and haphazard way through interviews and subjective reports of social interactions. The history of testing reveals this lack of assessment of groups, as well as individuals in groups.

The scant research that does exist on performance in groups depicts individual performance as declining in group settings, because of *social loafing*, where individuals put less effort into tasks when they work in groups, and the *bystander affect*, where the presence of others makes it less likely that individuals will help others (see Moghaddam, 2005). A long tradition of research on conformity, from Muzafer Sherif in the 1930s, to Solomon Asch in the 1950s, to Serge Moscovici in the 1960s, to twenty-first-century researchers (see Moghaddam, 2013), highlights how group pressure leads individuals to conform to arbitrary and incorrect norms. In a similar way, Irving Janis (1971) put the spotlight on how even highly intelligent individuals in collectives make costly mistaken decisions through *groupthink*, where concurrence seeking dominates and leads to a shutdown of critical thinking and mistaken group decisions, such as decisions leading to the 2003 invasion of Iraq by U.S.- and U.K.-led forces.[1] Thus, the psychological literature warns that groups tend to cause a decline in the performance of individuals.

This is concerning because society relies heavily, and sometimes exclusively, on group performance in many important areas. For example, in the medical field, patients have to trust the performance of healthcare teams for their very lives. In the athletic world, owners, managers, and coaches believe that forming the right team can enhance overall performance. With this high reliance comes a natural desire for excellent performance. But what results in excellence in-group performance? What is it that makes people recognize particular groups as superior, to recommend one hospital over all the others or place bets on one team to win the FIFA World Cup and not another? Given that psychological research has not focused on the "causes" of excellence in group, we decided to caste a wider net.

EXCELLENCE IN TEAMS

We found the following variables to be causal factors leading to healthcare team excellence:

1. a leader who is present as "team champion" (passionate advocate for the team);
2. the ability to obtain resources;
3. shared mutual respect among group members;
4. a grouping of the appropriate size;
5. there is a continuous focus on quality improvement;
6. an awareness of the situation with respect to task priorities;
7. team members recognize their mutual interdependence;
8. roles and rules are well understood;
9. all members feel free to speak up;
10. team members make assertions and demands appropriately;
11. debriefing takes place regularly to re-evaluate team performance, and team processes and outcomes are assessed using appropriate measures;

---

[1]See Sunstein (2014), for a discussion of tactics for overcoming groupthink.

12. team members follow rules;
13. there is openness to innovation in the team.

Through a similar literature search, a set of key variables were uncovered as assumed causal factors underlying sports team excellence. A number of the assumed causes were found to be specific to sports teams. For example, in the sports literature, we found that the positive benefits of some competition between team members, and a balance between attention to individual needs (such as "star" performers) and attention to team needs, were given higher importance than in healthcare teams. However, we also identified four "superordinate" assumed causes of excellence in both healthcare teams and sports teams, and we labeled these: leadership, communication, cohesion, and clear roles.

I. CAUSAL FACTORS IN TEAM EXCELLENCE VERSUS INDIVIDUAL EXCELLENCE

A key difference in perspectives emerges when we consider assumed causal factors in team excellence compared to assumed causal factors in individual excellence. The vast literature on individual performance has been dominated by dispositional characteristics, such as personality traits, emotions, and intelligence, as reflected by IQ. This focus on the isolated person is in line with the laboratory tradition in psychological research, involving the testing of individuals in isolation—a tradition that cannot possibly result in attention being given to relationships between people, or the idea that humans in interaction are, in many important ways, different from isolated individuals. Performance in teams leads to outcomes that are foundationally different from, and greater than, performance by isolated individuals—reminding us of the Gestalt motto, *the whole is more than the sum of its parts.*

Of course, some psychologists have recognized and studied persons in interaction, rather than in isolation. The great Russian psychologist Lev Vygotsky (1896–1934) highlights how performance through social interactions becomes different from and often superior to performance by isolated individuals. The contributions of the four causal factors identified as common to both medical teams and sports teams comes about through social interactions and build on collective characteristics such as "teamwork" and "team cohesion" rather than changes at the dispositional level within isolated individuals. For example, increased "team cohesion" can only come about when team members interact, influence one another, and take on new characteristics that could only come about through collective processes.

Leadership

Leadership is directly correlated with team performance (Weinberg & Gould, 2007). The results of having excellent leadership include player satisfaction, cohesion, and increased motivation (Hackman & Johnson, 2013; Weiss & Friedrichs, 1986). Successful leaders change communication style to suit particular players (Lavallee, Kremer, Moran, & Williams, 2004). STEEPS is a system that increases teamwork for the purpose of increasing patient safety and is based on the approach that individual competence is not enough for achieving a high level of team effectiveness (Deering, Johnston, & Colacchio, 2011). Leadership involves the ability to both interact with individuals and to organize and direct events and the actions of the team, while making sure everyone understands their role and the overall goal. The necessity of leadership for collective excellence on sports teams is illustrated by thousands of case studies of team performance (Rinehart, 2010).

Communication

Effective communication is a key factor in determining team success in healthcare and sports teams (Klein, DiazGranados, Salas, Burke, Lyons, 2009; Mitchell et. al., 2010; Shortell et al., 2004; Weinberg & Gould, 2007). Teams need procedures in place for members to openly converse, share ideas, and check in on other parts of the team. Honesty was also emphasized as directly relating to improvement in this area, including fostering trust and increased performance. Effective communication also requires transparency about goals, judgments, doubts, and errors.

Case studies of healthcare teams underline the vital importance of communications. For example, the MD Anderson Cancer Center was the focus of a case study, which highlighted what effective communication looks like in practice. MD Anderson's use of technology is one area that sets it above others. Patients and healthcare teams alike use the my MD Anderson Web portal to search medical records and correspond with other team members without having to actually set up an appointment or wait for a response. MD Anderson has seen patient satisfaction rise with the implementation of this Web portal because there is easy, uninterrupted, smooth, and transparent communication for entire teams and patients, which allows for better patient care.

Studies of healthcare teams show that 70 percent of inadvertent patient harm, including cases of patient death, is due to communication failure (Deering et al., 2011; Leonard, Graham, & Bonacum, 2004). Creating an environment where all team members feel they can input their concerns, specifically on the safety of a patient, is one remedy for this problem. Methods have been developed to help create such environments. "SBAR," which stands for: situation, background, assessment, recommendation, is one of a number of models now used to improve communications when a patient is introduced to a healthcare team. Debriefing on what went well, what did not, and what can be improved next time has been shown to be a key in a large learning curve in surgery (Pisano, Bohmer, & Edmondson, 2001).

Cohesiveness

Cohesion is an intangible team spirit and bond between people as they strive toward one goal. Task cohesion refers to how well a team works together, while social cohesion is how much a team enjoys one another. Increasing the cohesion of a team, in general, leads to better performance and success (Carron, Spink, & Prapavessis 1997). Social bonding has been shown to increase performance in healthcare teams (Hansen, 1999) as well as sports teams (Moran, 2004).

Case studies of excellent team performance reveal that rituals and the development of a "team culture" is a major factor. For example, in *Men of Kent: Ten Boys, a Fast Boat, and the Coach Who Made Them Champions*, the author describes the experience of crew team members being transformed from individuals into a "band of brothers" (Rinehart, 2010, p. 96). Their prerace rituals included jumping up and down like microwavable popcorn before races and wearing unique hats. Similarly, a case study of the excellent Credit Valley Hospital (CVH), Ontario, Canada, revealed rituals and debriefing followed by all hospital teams at the same time each day (Bendaly & Bendaly, 2012).

Clear Accepted Roles

A role is the mandatory and expected attitude and actions assigned to a person with a certain position on a team. When a team defines roles clearly and they are in turn accepted, the probability that the team will perform at a high level increases (Weinberg & Gould, 2007). All the team members know when it is their turn to act and can synchronize their movements with ease. On the other hand, when people are unsure of their roles, this leads to anxiety and uncertainty about when to act, in turn, which leads to poor performance (Eys, Carron, Beauchamp, & Bray, 2003).

Studies in both healthcare (Mitchell et. al 2010) and sport (Lazenby, 2014) underline the importance of clear roles in teams. The complexity of activities in healthcare teams makes clear roles imperative (Deering et al., 2011). For example, a single team can involve the obstetrical staff providers (obstetricians/family medicine/midwives), the pediatrics anesthesia resident, resident specialists who participate on labor and delivery, the nursing staff, operating room technicians/assistants, administrative support personnel (front desk and reception), and pathology (blood bank personnel for hemorrhage protocols). In a study of 40 healthcare teams serving patients with chronic illness, clear roles were reported to be a key factor for success (Shortell et. al., 2004).

Case studies of successful sports teams have also underlined the importance of clear roles (Williams & Crothers, 2011). Successful coaches, such as Roy Williams, the current head coach of the University of North Carolina's men's basketball team, have discussed the need for clear roles (Williams & Crothers, 2011). Michael Jordan, a member of one of the best teams in NBA history, understood that each player on a team must have a clearly understood and executed role in order to achieve excellence together at the highest level (Lazenby, 2014). On the Chicago Bulls championship roster in 1996, there were a variety of players with different abilities. Michael Jordan and Scottie Pippen were the vocal leaders on and off the court. Steve Kerr was the shooter, while

Dennis Rodman was the key rebounder. Capping off the starting five was Ron Harper, who took the role of defensive specialist. Harper would guard the best player on the opposing team night in and night out, not only because he was great at defense, but also because this gave the offensive leaders, like Jordan and Pippen, an opportunity to put more of their effort and focus on scoring. Each of these individuals knew their role and was able to execute a championship because of it.

II. CONCLUDING COMMENT

Despite the central importance of behavior in teams, psychological research has almost exclusively focused on assessing individual performance. The historic debates in psychology have been about the causal role of genetic and environmental factors in intelligence, personality, creativity, and other (assumed) dispositional characteristics. The scant research on individuals in in-group settings has depicted the collective as causing a decline in individual performance. This contrasts with real-life experiences in healthcare and sports teams, where leadership, communication, cohesion, and clear roles have been seen as causal factors determining excellent team performance. Team excellence is seen to arise from such collective features as "cohesion," "team spirit," and "teamwork," all characteristics that can only arise through collective processes. To put it in Vugotskian terms, we need to look at social processes between people and not just what happens within individuals in order to explain excellence in team performance.

REFERENCES

Bendaly, L. & Bendaly, N. (2012). *Improving healthcare team performance: The 7 requirements for excellence in patient care.* Canada: Wiley & Sons.

Carron, A. V., Spink, K. S. & Prapavessis, H. (1997). Team building and cohesiveness in the sport and exercise setting: Use on indirect intervention. *Journal of Applied Sport Psychology, 9*, 61–72.

Deering, S., Johnston, L.C., & Colacchio K. (2011). Multidisciplinary teamwork and communication training. *Semin Perinatol, 35(2)*, 89–96.

Eys, M. A., Carron, A.V., Beauchamp, M.R., & Bray, S.R. (2003). Role Ambiguity in Sport Teams. *Kinesiology and Physical Education Faculty Publications*, 25(4), 534–550.

Hackman, M. Z., & Johnson, C. E. (2013). *Leadership: A communications perspective.* 6th ed. Long Grove, IL: Waveland Press.

Hansen, A. (1999). *A matter of opinion.* London: Patridge.

Janis, I. L. (1971). Groupthink. *Psychology Today, 5(6)*, 43–46.

Klein, C., DiazGranados, D., & Salas, E., Burke S.C., Lyons, R., & Goodwin G. (2009). "Does Team Building Work?" Small Group Research: Sage Publications.

Lavallee, D, Kremer, J., Moran, A.P., & Williams, M. (2004). *Sports Psychology: Contemporary Themes*. Palgrave MacMillan: New York.

Lazenby, R. (2014). *Michael Jordan: The Life*. New York: Hachette Boot Group.

Leonard, M., Graham, S., & Bonacum, D. (2004). The Human Factor: The Critical Importance of Effective Teamwork and Communication in Providing Safe Care. *Quality and Safety in Health Care*, 13, 85–90.

Mitchell, P., Wynia, M., Golden, R., McNellis, B., Okun, S., Webb, E.C., Rohrbach, V., & Von Kohorn, I. (2012). Core Principles& Values of Effective Team-Based Health Care *Institute of Medicine of the National Academies*.

Moghaddam, F. M. (2005). Great ideas in psychology. Oxford: Oneworld.

Moghaddam, F. M. (2013). *The psychology of dictatorship*. Washington D.C.: American Psychological Association Press.

Moran, A. (2004). *Sport and Exercise Psychology: A Critical Introduction*. New York: Routledge.

Nijstad, B. A. (2009). *Group performance*. New York: Psychology Press.

Pisano, G.P., Bohmer R.M.J. & Edmondson, A.C. (2001). Organizational Differences in Rates of Learning: Evidence from the Adoption of Minimally Invasive Cardiac Surgery. *Journal of Management Science*, 47(5), 752–768.

Rinehart, R. (2010). *Men of Kent: Ten Boys, a Fast Boat, and the Coach Who Made Them Champions*. Guilford, Connecticut: Lyons Press.

Shortell, S. M., Marsteller, J. A., Lin, M., Pearson, M. L., Wu, S.; Mendel, P., Cretin, S.; & Rosen, M. (2004). The Role of Perceived Team Effectiveness in Improving Chronic Illness Care. *Medical Care*, 42(11), 1040–1048.

Weinberg, R.S. & Gould D. (2007). *Foundations of Sports and Exercise Psychology*. Champaign, IL: Human Kinetics.

Weiss, M.R., & Friedrichs, W.D. (1986). The Influence of Leader Behaviors, Coach Attributes, and Institutional Variables on Performance and Satisfaction of Collegiate Basketball Teams. *Journal of Sports Psychology*, 8, 332–346.

Williams, R., Crothers, T. (2011). Hard Work: A Life on and Off the Court. New York: Workman Publishing.

Woolley, A. W., Chabris, C. F., Pentland, A., Hashmi, N., & Malone, T. W. (2010). Evidence for a Collective Intelligence Factor in Performance of Human Groups. *Science*, 330, 686–688.

EDITORS' COMMENTARY

What "causes" collective excellence? This thorny question is taken up by Comolli and Moghaddam, who begin by criticizing traditional psychology for focusing almost exclusively on individual excellence. The question addressed in traditional psychology is, "What causes individual excellence?"

The answer given by researchers is part of the ongoing and often heated debate between those who emphasize the role of heredity and those who give priority to the environment. This overwhelming emphasis on causation behind individual performance is misplaced in a number of ways. In this commentary, we limit our concern with the nature of the assumed causes.

In traditional research, the assumption is that excellence is caused by some characteristic, such as IQ, within the person. Both when IQ is assumed to be shaped mainly by inherited factors, and when it is assumed to arise mainly out of environmental factors, measures of IQ are supposed to indicate a fixed dispositional feature of the individual. In the history of intelligence testing, there have been different ideas about the specific stage of development in which IQ becomes fixed. For example, the highly influential British psychologist Sir Cyril Burt believed IQ becomes fixed at the age of 11. Burt's ideas, later shown to be incorrect (Hearnshaw, 1974), influenced the British school system to adopt the 11+ test used to place children at the age of 11 into three different streams, intended to separate children who would go to university from those who would receive technical training. Such a perspective on the "causes of excellent," as fixed and contained within the individual, is not at all useful when searching for explanations of group excellence.

The characteristics of groups that Comolli and Moghaddam identify as being associated with excellence are all concerned with social relationships and the social features of collective life, rather than being fixed and contained within individuals. These characteristics include leadership, communications, cohesiveness, and clear and accepted roles. All of these characteristics are flexible rather than fixed, and related to the meaning systems constructed as part of collective life. The medical teams and sports teams Comolli and Moghaddam discuss, all assume that they can alter leadership, communications, cohesiveness, clear and accepted roles, as well as all the other features of their teams assumed to influence excellence in performance. Thus, rather than seeing the causes of excellence as fixed, as in traditional IQ research for example, those who are actually involved in the everyday performance of groups work on the assumption that they are able to influence the causes of collective excellence.

REFERENCE

Hearnshaw, L. S. (1974). *Cyril Burt, Psychologist*. London: Hodder and Stoughton.

Part Six

....

Causal Concepts and Legal Proceedings

19

Cause and Consequence in the Law

William C. Bryson

Causation is a concept of central importance in the law. Questions of causation have engaged lawyers and judges for centuries. Yet despite the amount of attention the issue of causation has received, it continues to be a source of controversy. As a leading treatise said regarding the issue of causation in legal cases based on claims of negligence: "There is perhaps nothing in the entire field of law which has called forth more disagreement, or upon which the opinions are in such a welter of confusion. Nor, despite the manifold attempts which have been made to clarify the subject, is there any general agreement as to the best approach."[1]

Unlike in some other fields, controversies in the law are not principally the products of academic debates among scholars, but arise instead from decisions by courts in resolving disputes among parties to lawsuits. In the so-called common law countries—mainly the United States, the United Kingdom, and present and former Commonwealth countries—the courts have law-making authority. That is, their decisions, and the opinions that accompany and explain those decisions, have precedential force that guides the outcome of subsequent cases. Legal academics frequently comment on those decisions, often critically, and seek to shape the development of future court decisions through their analysis. That dynamic has been very active in the case of the ongoing discourse among judges and scholars about the role of causation in Anglo-American law.[2]

---

[1] W. Page Keeton and W. L. Prosser, *Prosser and Keeton on the Law of Torts* 263 (5th ed. 1984).

[2] In the United States, the interaction between courts and academics is promoted by the activities of the American Law Institute, an organization of scholars, judges, and private practitioners. The institute publishes Restatements of the Law in various fields that attempt to present comprehensive accounts of what the state of the law is in each field and suggest where changes may be occurring or may be expected.

The issue of legal causation typically surfaces when a person has been harmed and has asked the courts to make a determination of legal liability for that harm. Of course, in many instances the law imposes liability when no actual harm has occurred. In criminal cases, for example, the law prohibits and punishes particular conduct even if the conduct has caused no harm, as in the case of offenses ranging from attempted murder to speeding. In some civil (i.e., noncriminal) cases as well, the law imposes liability even in the absence of any clear harm, as in cases of trespass onto land and unlawful threats. Most civil cases, however, involve a claim that one party has been harmed, that a second party has caused the harm, and that the second party must compensate the first party for his loss. It is in cases of that type, which can be found in every field of law, that lawyers and judges grapple with issues of causation and the consequences that flow from findings of causation.

The way the law addresses the issue of causation has some parallels with the treatment of causation in other fields, but it differs in significant ways as well. In particular, issues of social policy, moral culpability, and the shared community sense of fairness frequently affect the way in which the law views causation and the consequences of finding that one actor's conduct has "caused" injury to another. That is because in many respects the law endeavors to reflect commonly shared moral sensibilities. If legal doctrine or the results of legal disputes wander too far from what the community regards as just outcomes, the law loses credibility with the persons it is intended to serve. For that reason, regardless of what philosophical or scientific concepts of causation might seem to dictate, the law frequently resists holding an individual liable for harm suffered by a victim if the common sense of fairness would dictate that the individual should not be held responsible for the harm. Such legal decisions that seek to reflect community values regarding rights and responsibilities are sometimes referred to as responding to the "corrective justice" purposes of the law.

In addition, the law frequently responds to extraneous social concerns that shape the way the courts treat questions of causation. Extending liability too far down a causal chain can be regarded as socially undesirable in that it may expose persons to unlimited risks of liability that will make them unwilling to engage in socially desirable conduct. An example of such a policy-driven application of the principles of causation is the rule, adopted in many places, that bars firefighters from suing homeowners for negligence when the firefighters are injured in a fire. The rationale behind that rule is that, since most fires are the product of negligence, a rule allowing firefighters to sue homeowners for negligence when injured fighting a fire would discourage homeowners from summoning firefighters to put out a fire, which in turn could lead to the fire spreading more broadly throughout the community.[3]

---

[3] A recent case applying that doctrine is *Cole v. Hubanks*, 681 N.W.2d 147 (Wis, 2004).

I. CAUSATION IN THE LAW OF TORTS: NEGLIGENCE

Questions of causation abound in the law of torts, the field of law that deals with civil wrongs committed by one person against another, such as injuries resulting from negligent conduct, inherently dangerous products, and intentionally inflicted harms. In a tort case, the injured party (referred to as the plaintiff) seeks to recover damages from the party claimed to be responsible for the injury (referred to as the defendant). To do so, the plaintiff typically has to prove that the defendant engaged in some form of wrongful conduct and that the wrongful conduct caused the plaintiff's injury or loss. When the claimed wrongful conduct is negligence, the traditional test for liability requires the plaintiff to prove that (1) the defendant had a duty to conform to a certain standard of conduct for the protection of others against unreasonable risks, (2) the defendant breached that duty by failing to conform to that standard, (3) there was a sufficient causal connection between the conduct and the plaintiff's injury, and (4) as a result of the defendant's actions, the plaintiff suffered a quantifiable loss, such as medical expenses, loss of employment, or pain and suffering.[4]

Although the traditional proof requirements for negligence refer to only one causal factor, courts and commentators have increasingly come to recognize that the requirement to prove a causal connection has two quite different components. First, the plaintiff must prove causation, sometimes referred to as "factual causation" or "actual causation." Second, the plaintiff must prove what the law commonly refers to as "proximate cause."[5] The U.S. Supreme Court recently provided a succinct summary of the conventional description of those two terms and the relationship between them, as follows (with citations and quotation marks omitted):

> As a general matter, to say one event proximately caused another is a way of making two separate but related assertions. First, it means the former event caused the latter. This is known as actual cause or cause in fact. The concept of actual cause is not a metaphysical one but an ordinary, matter-of-fact inquiry into the existence of a causal relation as laypeople would view it.
>
> Every event has many causes, however, and only some of them are proximate, as the law uses that term. So to say that one event was a proximate cause of another means that it was not just any cause, but

---

[4] That traditional statement of the elements of a negligence claim is set forth in many legal treatises and cases, such as William L. Prosser, *Handbook of the Law of Torts* 143 (4th ed. 1971).

[5] In a recent treatise, for example, the four elements recited by Professor William Prosser in the 1971 edition of his *Handbook of the Law of Torts* are restated as five. The "causal connection" element is divided into requirements that "the defendant's conduct in fact caused harm to the plaintiff," and that "the defendant's conduct . . . was also a proximate cause" of the harm. Dan B. Dobbs, *The Law of Torts* 269 (2000).

one with a sufficient connection to the result. The idea of proximate cause, as distinct from actual cause or cause in fact, defies easy summary. It is a flexible concept that generally refers to the basic requirement that there must be some direct relation between the injury asserted and the injurious conduct alleged. A requirement of proximate cause thus serves, *inter alia*, to preclude liability in situations where the causal link between conduct and result is so attenuated that the consequence is more aptly described as mere fortuity.[6]

Because issues of causation play a central role in tort cases based on negligence, and because the treatment of issues of causation in negligence law is generally representative of the way causation is treated in other legal fields, this chapter will focus on the role of causation in negligence cases.

II. ACTUAL CAUSE OR CAUSATION IN FACT

The requirement that a plaintiff demonstrates that the defendant's conduct or omission caused the plaintiff's injury has long been a part of negligence law. That is because tort law is designed, in large measure, to serve "corrective justice" purposes: "to right wrongs, i.e., to restore the moral balance between injurer and injured" (Robertson, 2004, pp. 116–117). As a leading torts scholar of his time put it, it is "too clear for argument" that a defendant should never be held liable to a plaintiff for loss where it appears that his wrong did not contribute to it, and no policy or moral consideration can be strong enough to warrant the imposition of liability in such a case" (Carpenter, 1935, pp. 941–947).[7]

In one respect, the inquiry into actual causation is simpler in law than in other disciplines. In law, the court ordinarily asks not "What are the causes of X event?" but a much narrower question: "Did a particular act or omission by actor A cause a particular injury to actor B?" The causation issue is narrowly focused in that manner because the issue of causation arises in the context of a lawsuit in which one party claims that another party caused him harm. The lawsuit typically identifies a single act or omission by the defendant that is alleged to have caused the injury or loss to the plaintiff; other factors that might be claimed to be causal contributors are often regarded as simply background conditions. Moreover, the law requires not just that the defendant's conduct cause the harm at issue, but that the wrongful aspect of the defendant's conduct cause the harm.[8] This focus on a single act or omission, and only on the negligent aspect of that act or omission, allows judges and juries to focus on the effect of the defendant's negligence, and not to have to

---

[6]The Supreme Court opinion is *Paroline v. United States*, 134 S. Ct. 1710 (2014).
[7]Charles E. Carpenter, *Concurrent Causation* 83 U. Pa. L. Rev. 941, 947 (1935).
[8]This point is discussed in Richard W. Wright, *Causation in Tort Law*, 73 Cal. L. Rev. 1735, 1759 (1985).

make judgments about the effect of multiple other conditions that may have had some causal relationship to the plaintiff's injury.

The most commonly employed test for finding factual causation in negligence cases is the "but-for" or "sine qua non" test, which has been characterized as "a familiar part of our legal tradition."[9] Under that test, if an injury would not have occurred "but for" the wrongful conduct that is at issue, the wrongful conduct is said not to be a "cause" of the injury. Put more precisely, under the but-for test negligent conduct is not regarded as a cause of harm if the plaintiff would have sustained the harm even if the defendant had not been negligent. The choice of the but-for test has been explained by saying that it "seems to be the best the law can do in its effort to offer an approximate expression of an accepted popular attitude toward responsibility."[10]

Despite the widespread acceptance and intuitive appeal of the but-for test, its application presents certain difficulties, largely stemming from the fact that it requires a hypothetical inquiry into how things would have been if the wrongful conduct that is alleged to be the cause of the injury had been different. Besides the inherent difficulty of drawing conclusions as to what would have happened if circumstances had been different, the hypothetical scenario can be challenging to apply in some instances. It requires a judge or jury to make the even more exacting determination whether the harm in question would have occurred if the wrongful conduct were changed just enough to make it no longer wrongful.

For example, suppose a child darts out between two parked cars and a speeding driver hits the child. If the child's representatives bring a lawsuit charging the driver with negligence because he was speeding, the but-for test for factual causation would ask whether the driver would have hit the child if he had been driving at the speed limit and exercising reasonable caution, not whether he could have avoided the child if he had been driving well below the speed limit and had been exercising extraordinary care. Importantly, in limiting the but-for test to the minimum change in the facts necessary to eliminate the alleged wrongful conduct, the judge or jury must disregard considerations that would come to the mind of the philosopher or scientist, such as the observation that if the driver had not been speeding, he would not have arrived at the place where the child ran into the street until the child had safely returned to the sidewalk.[11] In a lawsuit alleging the tort of negligence, the burden of proof to show that the injury was caused by the alleged negligent conduct falls on the plaintiff, the party who is seeking compensation. That means the plaintiff will lose the case unless the judge or jury is persuaded that it is more likely than not that the plaintiff's injury was caused by the defendant's negligence.

---

[9]*Paroline v. United States*, 134 S. Ct. at 1722.

[10]Wex S. Malone, *Ruminations on Cause-in-Fact*, 9 Stan. L. Rev. 60, 66 (1960).

[11]See Fowler V. Harper, Fleming James, Jr. & Oscar S. Gray, *The Law of Torts* § 20.5, at 165 (2nd ed. 1986).

The but-for test of causation, in conjunction with the imposition of the burden of proof on the plaintiff, ordinarily produces results that comport with common moral sensibilities and the basic sense of justice. It ordinarily seems just that if person A is going to ask a court to make person B pay for the harm done to him, A should be required to prove that B caused the harm; that is, A must prove that but for B's conduct the harm would not have occurred. There are important exceptions to that general rule, however. In those instances, the but-for test, in combination with imposing the burden of proof on the plaintiff, produces results that seem plainly wrong or at least dubious. The courts have responded to those cases by modifying the governing principles of causation in order to reach results that are more in line with widely shared instincts of fairness. Those special cases fall into several discrete categories.

The first category consists of tort cases involving "multiple sufficient causes." In those cases, two or more actors engage in conduct that is individually sufficient to produce an injury, and the plaintiff seeks to hold one or both of them liable for the harm. A classic example of this type of case is the following: two careless campers, acting independently, fail to extinguish their campfires in a dry forest, resulting in a large fire that destroys the plaintiff's house on the edge of the forest. Suppose the facts show that the negligent act of either one of the campers would have caused the fire that destroyed the plaintiff's house. In that event, the but-for test produces a perverse result. Each camper can point out that his negligent act was not the but-for cause of the injury, because the loss of the plaintiff's house would have occurred even absence his negligence, due to the negligent act of the other camper.[12]

That argument has the air of a parlor trick, and courts have consistently found ways to avoid having to say that neither of the defendants is liable. The most straightforward manner to deal with such cases is to recognize that the but-for test, while useful in many settings, has its limits, one of which is the "multiple sufficient causes" category of cases such as the "two campfires" case. As one treatise put it, "the 'but for' rule serves to explain the greater number of cases, but there is one type of situation in which it fails. If two causes concur to bring about an event, and either one of them, operating alone, would have been sufficient to cause the identical result, some other test is needed."[13] Abandoning the but-for test in that group of cases enables the court to conclude that both defendants are liable for the destruction of the plaintiff's house, since each defendant has engaged in conduct that most persons would regard as sufficient to have "caused" the loss.

---

[12]The case on which this example is based is *Corey v. Havener*, 182 Mass. 250, 65 N.E. 69 (1902).

[13]Keeton and Prosser, supra note 1, §41, at 266-67; see also *Restatement (Third) of Torts*, § 27, comment e (2010). ("Multiple sufficient causes are also factual causes because we recognize them as such in our common understanding of causation, even if the but-for standard does not.")

Courts have generally reached that conclusion by ruling that in cases involving multiple sufficient causes, the "but-for" test should be supplanted by the "substantial cause" test, which allows the plaintiff to prevail by showing that the defendant's act was a "substantial cause" of the loss. As one court put it, the "substantial factor" test is used "[w]hen two causes concur to bring about an event, and either cause, operating alone, would have brought about the event absent the other cause."[14]

The use of the "substantial factor" exception to the but-for test has been criticized by academics as unprincipled on the ground that it is not based on reason, but simply substitutes a new verbal formula for the but-for test to allow recovery in a particular setting in which the but-for test produces results that feel unjust. Another criticism of the "substantial factor" test, particularly when it has been extended beyond the narrow confines of the "multiple sufficient cause" cases, is that the term "substantial" gives judges and juries almost no guidance. Juries that are instructed using language such as "substantial cause" are left with little direction and may sometimes conclude that a cause is not a "substantial" cause of the loss because the loss would have occurred anyway, which is precisely the result that the substitute terminology was intended to avoid. While those criticisms are fair, the advantages of the "substantial cause" test—that it is easy to articulate and that it responds to the common sense of justice, at least in "multiple sufficient cause" cases—have been regarded as sufficient justification that the test has been widely accepted in that context.[15]

In a second category of cases, the imposition of the burden of proof on the plaintiff can defeat the plaintiff's claim when the commonly shared sense of justice would demand that the plaintiff be afforded a remedy. A classic example of such a case is one in which two hunters negligently fire their guns in the same direction at the same time and one of the bullets hits and injures the plaintiff. Both hunters were equally negligent in firing in the direction of the plaintiff, but there was no way to determine which hunter's bullet struck the plaintiff.[16] In that type of case, the courts have found it unacceptable to apply the but-for test, combined with imposing the burden of proof on the plaintiff, with the result an innocent plaintiff could not obtain relief from

---

[14]The quotation is from *Magee v. Coats*, 598 So. 2d 531, 536 (La. App. 1992).

[15]In the Second Restatement of Torts, the American Law Institute endorsed the "substantial factor" test as applied to "multiple sufficient cause" cases. See *Restatement (Second) of Torts* § 232(2) (1979). In the Third Restatement of Torts, the institute reversed position, favoring instead to deal with multiple sufficient cause cases by adopting a special definition of causation, which provides that if multiple acts occur, each of which would have been a factual cause of the harm in question, in the absence of the other act or acts, "each act is regarded as a factual cause of the harm." *Restatement (Third) of Torts*, supra note 14, § 27.

[16]The case with these facts is *Summers v. Tice*, 33 Cal. 2d 80, 199 P.2d 1 (1948), decided by the California Supreme Court. The California court decided that in this kind of case the burden of proof should be shifted to the defendant to prove that his bullet was not the one that injured the plaintiff.

either defendant, even though both were clearly negligent. Finding exoneration of both defendants in cases such as the two-hunter case to be unpalatable, the courts have found ways to impose liability on both defendants. If the hunters were hunting together, the court can treat the hunters as having engaged in concerted action in which each hunter's act is imputable to the other. In that way, both are deemed to have caused the injury and both are liable to the victim.

Another way that courts have achieved the same objective is to rule that in such cases the burden of proof should be shifted to the defendants, so that one or the other defendant can avoid liability only if that defendant can show that the bullet that struck the plaintiff was not his. That was the course followed by the court in the actual case involving the two negligent hunters. In most such cases, it is difficult if not impossible to determine which actor was causally responsible for the injury. Therefore, shifting the burden of proof will effectively decide the case, leaving both defendants subject to liability. Although that result is difficult to square with conventional views of but-for causation,[17] it accords with the common-sense view that because each defendant has engaged in negligent conduct that may well have injured the plaintiff, it is fair to subject both defendants to liability, at least unless one or the other can show that his individual conduct did not cause the loss. While that solution seems equitable for a case such as the two-hunter case involving a small number of defendants, it has been criticized as unfair to the defendants if the number of defendants is very large and the likelihood that any particular defendant actually caused the plaintiff's harm is very small.[18]

A variant of the "multiple sufficient cause" scenario is the set of cases in which the defendant has engaged in negligent conduct that would be sufficient to cause the plaintiff's loss, but other causal factors intervene and render the defendant's conduct de minimis. An example of that sort of case is one in which a negligently constructed dam is destroyed by an unforeseeably severe flood that would have destroyed even a properly constructed dam.[19] Typically, courts regard such a de minimis contribution to the ultimate injury to be insufficient to establish factual causation, even if the contribution, standing alone, would have caused the injury. The courts reach that conclusion, which appeals to the common sense of fairness, by once again having recourse to the principle that the act or omission in question must be a

---

[17]It has been suggested, with some force, that the shifting burden of proof can be justified on the ground that "each defendant, by his negligent shot, created the doubt about causation or despoiled the evidence that otherwise would have been available to the plaintiff so that as a matter of policy, the defendants, rather than the plaintiff, should bear the loss." Dobbs, 2000, supra note 3, p. 427.
[18]The court in Senn v. Merrell-Dow Pharmaceuticals, Inc., 751 P.2d 215, 222 (Ore. 1988), made that point.
[19]That example is taken from Restatement (Third) of Torts, supra note 14, § 27, comment i (2010).

"substantial" cause of the harm, this time using the "substantial factor" test to limit the defendant's liability rather than to extend it.[20]

A third group of cases that have proved problematical for the but-for test are those in which the defendant's negligent act and some innocent factor concur to result in injury to the plaintiff, and either factor, acting alone, would have been sufficient to produce the injury. The introduction of an innocent cause as one of the multiple sufficient causes has given courts more difficulty in concluding that the culpable actor should be held liable. The argument in favor of liability is that the fortuity of some other innocent cause should not absolve the negligent defendant whose conduct was fully sufficient to cause the plaintiff's harm. The contrary argument is that the plaintiff is no worse off because of the defendant's act, since the innocent factor would have caused the plaintiff's injury anyway.

Most courts have held defendants liable for the loss in this situation, just as they would if the independent cause had been another culpable actor.[21] Some commentators, however, have pointed out an anomaly in the law with respect to such cases, as illustrated by this example: Suppose the defendant negligently allowed his dam to release a flood onto a neighbor's property that destroyed the neighbor's house. If a hurricane came through the following day that would have destroyed the neighbor's house, the defendant is clearly liable to the plaintiff for damages, but the plaintiff's damages would be limited to the loss of the use of the house for the one day between the flood and the hurricane. On the other hand, if the hurricane occurs before the flood, the defendant would not be liable for any part of the damages suffered by the plaintiff homeowner, based on the well-settled legal principle that if a harm precedes the wrongful act in question, the wrongful act cannot be regarded as the cause of the harm. Yet, under the approach used by most courts, if the impact of the hurricane and the effect of the defendant's negligent construction of the dam occurred simultaneously, the defendant would be liable for the full value of the plaintiff's house, a result that is hard to square with the outcome in the case in which the hurricane comes through the day after the flood and the defendant is liable for only nominal damages.[22] That is one of the logical discontinuities in the law that occasionally plague courts as they attempt to meld logical principles of causation with common sensibilities about the proper allocation of responsibility. Fortunately, the case of simultaneous impacts of

---

[20]*Restatement (Third) of Torts*, supra note 14, § 27, comment I.

[21]The case most often cited for this principle is *Anderson v. Minneapolis, St. Paul & Sault Ste. Marie Railroad Co.*, 146 Minn. 430, 179 N.W. 45 (1920). The case is discussed in Prosser, *supra* note 3, at 240 n.26.

[22]This anomaly is discussed by Professor Robertson, who favors finding the defendant liable in such cases, see David W. Robertson, *Causation in the Restatement (Third) of Torts: Three Arguable Mistakes*, 44 Wake Forest L. Rev. 1007, 1025–28 (2009), and by Professor Green, who takes the opposing position, see Michael D. Green, *The Intersection of Factual Causation and Damages*, 55 DePaul L. Rev. 671, 688 (2006).

negligent and innocent causes rarely arises outside of law professors' hypothetical cases, so the anomaly is not one that has significant practical effect.

Another set of cases that has posed difficulties for the application of the but-for test is the "increased risk of loss" cases. Suppose that a surgeon operates on a patient in an effort to save the patient's badly injured leg. The operation is a risky one that has only a 30 percent chance of success. However, the surgeon bungles the operation in a way that reduces the chance of a successful outcome to essentially zero. Does the patient have a case against the surgeon for malpractice? Strict application of the but-for test would suggest not, since even absent the doctor's negligence, the patient would probably have lost his leg, and the surgeon therefore cannot be said to have "caused" the loss of the leg under normal but-for principles. Yet common notions of justice would suggest that the patient has been wronged. While courts for many years applied the but-for test to deny recovery in such cases, more recently courts have held that the patient suffered an injury because of the surgeon's negligence—the injury being the loss of a 30 percent chance of saving his leg. While the fact that a competent surgery would have given the patient only a modest chance of saving his leg will likely reduce any damages award that the patient will receive, courts have held that the patient is nonetheless entitled to some form of compensation for the loss of even a small chance for a successful outcome.[23]

Finally, courts have encountered especially challenging causal questions when the alleged negligence has consisted of an omission rather than an affirmative act, such as the failure to take a precaution or the failure to warn purchasers of a risk associated with the use of a product. In that setting, the hypothetical and counterfactual nature of the but-for inquiry is even more difficult than in the case of affirmative acts. In order to determine whether a negligent omission caused the plaintiff's injury, a court applying the but-for test has to hypothesize not just what would have happened in the absence of a negligent act, which is difficult enough, but must determine what would have happened if the negligent omission had not occurred and some other, undefined, nonnegligent act had occurred in place of the omission. That is an even more difficult inquiry, since it invites speculation as to what the action might have been that would have taken the place of the omission, and what effect such hypothetical action might have had on the plaintiff.[24]

---

[23]This theory of liability has been the subject of academic discussion by various scholars and has been adopted by a few courts, mainly in medical malpractice cases, although most courts have been reluctant to employ the "reduction of chance" approach. For a discussion of the theory and those cases that have adopted or rejected it, see Robertson, *The Common Sense of Cause in Fact*, 75 Tex. L. Rev. 1765, 1784–86 (1997). This is likely to be an area of continuing debate and change in tort law.

[24]See David A. Fischer, *Causation in Fact in Omission Cases*, 1992 Utah L. Rev. 1335, 1336–37.

Cases involving two or more omissions have proved especially challenging. Consider a case in which an automobile rental company negligently rents a car with defective brakes, but the driver negligently fails to apply the brakes to avoid hitting a pedestrian. In that case, is the car rental company or the driver (or both) liable to the pedestrian? The rental company can argue that, because the driver did not apply the brakes, the accident would have occurred regardless of the company's negligence. The driver can argue that, because the brakes would not have worked if he had applied them, the accident would have occurred regardless of his negligence. In the actual case with those facts, the court ruled that the rental car company was not liable (the driver was not a party to the lawsuit).[25] Although some courts have followed that lead, others have analogized the "two omissions" situation to cases of "multiple sufficient cause" for affirmative acts and have held the negligent defendant liable even though that defendant's omission was not a but-for cause of the injury.[26]

Because intuition suggests that the driver and the rental company should not both be exonerated simply because of each party's negligence, some scholars have suggested that each should be held liable on the ground that the negligence of each deprived the plaintiff of a right of recovery against the other. That is, absent the faulty brakes, the driver's negligent failure to apply the brakes would clearly make the driver liable to the pedestrian; and, absent the driver's negligence, the faulty brakes would clearly make the rental car company liable. By depriving the plaintiff of a right of recovery for his injuries, each defendant would be held liable for that tort, regardless of whether either could be held liable under the strict application of the but-for test.[27]

Another fact pattern that has arisen in a number of cases is the following: a manufacturer of a drug or other product fails to provide an adequate warning regarding its use, but the user fails to read the warning, and the user suffers harm from the product. In that situation, the inadequate warning is not a but-for cause of the resulting harm, because even if the warning had been adequate, the user's failure to read it would have led to the same outcome. Most courts have found that the inadequate warning was not a cause of the harm, either on the ground that it was not a but-for cause of the injury or on

---

[25]The case on which this example is based is *Saunders System Birmingham Co. v. Adams*, 217 Ala. 621, 117 So. 72 (Ala. 1928).
[26]See, for example, *Basko v. Sterling Drug Co.*, 416 F.2d 417 (2d Cir. 1969), and *Kitchen Krafters, Inc. v. Eastside Bank of Mont.*, 242 Mont. 155, 789 P.2d 567 (1990).
[27]The "destruction of a personal injury lawsuit" theory of liability is discussed by Professor Robertson in Robertson, supra note 24, at 1787–89. This theory has not been frequently employed by the courts, although it was used by the House of Lords in *Baker v. Willoughby*, 107 App. Cas. 467 (1969), in imposing full liability against both a negligent driver who injured the plaintiff's leg and a robber who subsequently shot the leg, necessitating its amputation. This is another area of potential flux in tort law.

the ground that the user's failure to read the warning was an intervening cause that negated the effect of the inadequate warning.

Commentators have criticized both of those rationales, arguing that the courts appear not to have recognized that the omission cases are analogous to the "multiple sufficient cause" cases and should be decided the same way.[28] Nonetheless, there is no clear analytical path to the right result. In fact, one commentator expressed the view that multiple sufficient cause cases involving omissions "cannot be resolved adequately by the application of strictly mechanical tests," but instead raise questions that are best viewed as a matter of policy or "resolved on the basis of human intuition about causation that are not reflected in the mechanical tests" (Fischer, 1992, supra note 25, pp. 1359–60). In attempting to give a reasoned basis for that intuition, some have suggested that the temporal sequence of omissions can explain the court decisions, with the omission that is closest in time to the harm being deemed the cause of the harm. Applying that approach to the case of the rented automobile with defective brakes would require the conclusion that the driver's failure to apply the brakes can be viewed as the sole cause of the accident, because the driver's failure to apply the brakes meant that the defective brakes never came into play, but remained just a looming hazard that, as it happened, had no real-world impact.

The same point applies to the cases involving inadequate warning labels in which the user of the product failed to read the warning label at all. As one commentator summarized the court decisions on this issue, "If the plaintiff failed to read the content-inadequate warning, it is frequently difficult to see how a more adequate warning would have made any difference" (Dobbs, 2000, supra note 5, p. 1017).

The situation is more complicated when a negligent omission is paired with a second, innocent cause. An example of such a case is the following: a pilot for a small airplane charter company negligently fails to check the plane's fuel level (which is dangerously low) before taking off. The plane, however, encounters a freak storm shortly after take-off that causes the plane to crash before the fuel is exhausted. In that situation, even though the pilot's negligence in not checking the fuel level would have been sufficient to cause the plane to run out of fuel and crash before it reached its destination, the innocent factor—the storm—intervened and caused the airplane to crash at an earlier point in time. In that case, courts have typically held that the charter company's negligence, which ultimately played no actual role in the destruction of the plane, was not a cause of the accident for which the charter company should be held liable.

Finally, courts are disinclined to find the defendant liable when the plaintiff himself is responsible for one of the omissions, as opposed to a case in which two potential defendants are responsible for omissions and a third-

---

[28]See, for example, Fischer, supra note 25.

party plaintiff is injured. For example, in an inadequate warning case in which the plaintiff is the one who failed to read the warning label on the product, the corrective justice purpose of tort law is not served by holding the negligent product manufacturer liable, when the plaintiff's action would have resulted in his own injury no matter how sufficient the warning on the product label.

III. CRITICISMS OF THE BUT-FOR TEST FOR ACTUAL CAUSATION

While generally agreeing with the fundamental soundness of the but-for test for actual causation, legal scholars have frequently criticized the application of that test in certain classes of cases. Some, most notably law professor Richard W. Wright, have favored a refinement of the but-for approach to causation known as the "NESS" test. NESS stands for "necessary element of a sufficient set." Under the NESS test, an act or omission is regarded as having caused a result if, and only if, the act or omission was necessary to the sufficiency of a set of actual, existing antecedent conditions sufficient for the occurrence of the result (Wright, 1985, supra note 9).[29]

In many cases, the NESS test functions in the same manner as the but-for test. That is, in the ordinary case, the NESS test establishes that the defendant's negligence caused the plaintiff's injury if the negligent aspect of the defendant's conduct was necessary to the result. But in cases in which the but-for test poses difficulties, such as multiple-sufficient-cause cases, the NESS test establishes causation because the defendant's negligence is one of a set of existing conditions that are sufficient to have caused the injury and is a necessary element of that set.

Consider, for example, the case discussed earlier in which two campers independently set campfires, each of which is sufficient to have caused the forest fire that destroys the plaintiff's house. Under the but-for test, each camper could claim that his contribution was not necessary to cause the loss of the house, since absent one of the campfires, the other campfire would still have produced the forest fire. Under the NESS test, however, both campers would be liable. That is because the set of conditions sufficient to cause the destruction of the plaintiff's house can be defined as the first camper's negligent act plus all the other conditions necessary to produce the fire, such as wind, dry weather, and fuel, but omitting the second camper's negligent act. The first camper's negligence would thus be a necessary element of a sufficient set of conditions to cause the loss. By parallel analysis, the second camper's negligence can also be viewed as a necessary element of a sufficient set of conditions, where those conditions are defined as the second camper's negligent act, plus all of the other conditions necessary to produce the fire, but not

---

[29] As Professor Wright acknowledges, the NESS test has its origin in the groundbreaking work by Hart and Honorè, H. L. A. Hart and Tony Honorè, *Causation in the Law* (1961). Professor Wright's work has elaborated upon, and in some respects departs from, the original and more rudimentary description of the test by Hart and Honorè.

including the first camper's negligent act. In that manner, the NESS test solves the problem that the but-for test leaves unresolved—it points to a logically consistent way to apply a but-for type analysis but find liability for each actor in the "multiple sufficient cause" scenario.

In other situations as well, the NESS test establishes causation where the simple but-for test fails to do so, even when the case for finding causation seems intuitively powerful. Besides establishing liability for both defendants in "multiple sufficient cause" cases such as the two-campers case, the NESS test would establish liability, for example, in a case in which the defendant stole the plaintiff's purse, but sought to avoid responsibility by proving that if the defendant had not stolen the purse, another actor would subsequently have done so. Under the but-for test, that argument would prevail, because the harm would have occurred even if the defendant had not acted. Under the NESS test, however, the defendant would be liable because the defendant's act was a necessary element of the set of actual conditions that was sufficient for the harm to occur. On the other hand, to use an example offered by Professor Wright, if a third party shot and killed the victim just as the victim was about to drink a cup of tea that the defendant had poisoned, the defendant would not be liable under the NESS test. While it is true in that the act of poisoning the cup would be a necessary condition in a set of conditions leading to the victim's death, the conditions associated with the poisoning would not be sufficient to cause the victim's death. That is because one of the conditions—that the victim be alive when the poison took effect—would not be an actual, existing condition, since the victim was already dead by the time he would have drunk the poison (Wright, 1985, supra note 9, pp. 1794–95). That result accords with the general sense that liability should not flow from an event that could have had adverse effects if it had happened, but in fact never occurred.

Notwithstanding its strengths, the NESS test has several weaknesses. First, it arguably goes too far in making defendants liable for only minor contributions to the causal nexus. In the case in which the negligently constructed dam was destroyed by a storm of unprecedented strength that would have destroyed the dam even if it had been properly constructed, the negligent builder would be liable under the NESS test, because his negligence would have been a necessary element of a set of conditions sufficient to destroy the dam, if those conditions were defined as all the conditions in place other than the unprecedented storm. Even in cases in which the defendant's negligent act would not be sufficient, standing alone, to cause the injury in question, the NESS test would make the defendant liable if a set of conditions could be selected that would make the defendant's conduct necessary to the loss. For example, if 100 companies discharged pollutants into a river, and the contamination of downstream property would have occurred (and been equally severe) even if there were as few as 10 polluters, the NESS test would say that each one of the 100 polluters caused the contamination because each one would be a necessary element of a sufficient set containing nine other polluters. In fact, in a case in which multiple negligent actors contribute to an outcome that harms the plaintiff, one defendant's contribution could even be considerably less than that of the others, but that defendant would still be held liable under the NESS test as long as his conduct, when hypothetically combined with the actions of certain of the other actors, would have been just sufficient to cause the harm. Such results would represent a significant expansion in the concept of factual causation beyond what the courts typically recognize. Applied in that fashion, the NESS test would also be in tension with the commonly held sense that acts that contributed only minimally to a particular harm, and were not in fact necessary to the harm that resulted, should not be regarded as causes of the harm in question.[30]

Second, in addition to producing a significant broadening of the concept of causation as typically applied by courts, the NESS test has been criticized for failing to deal effectively with negligence claims based on omissions, rather than affirmative acts. In the case involving the rental car with defective brakes, for example, proponents of the NESS test would hold the negligent driver (who did not apply the defective brakes) liable to the victim, but not the negligent rental car company (which rented the car without repairing the brakes). The explanation for why, under the NESS test, the first omission would not lead to liability but the second would is that the driver's failure to apply the brakes is a necessary element of a set of conditions sufficient to cause the injury, as long as the rental car company's failure to repair the brakes is omitted from that set of conditions (Wright, 1985, supra note 9, p. 1801). But as has been pointed out, omitting the failure to repair the brakes is equivalent to treating the rental car company as having actually repaired the brakes, which it manifestly did not do. It is only if one assumes the brakes have been repaired that the failure to apply them becomes a cause of the harm under the NESS test. Therefore, rather than looking to conditions that actually exist, as the NESS test purports to do when constructing sets of sufficient conditions, in the case of omissions the NESS test appears to rely on a condition that does not exist at all (Fischer, 1992, supra note 25, pp. 1357–60).

Finally, the NESS test has a pragmatic weakness: It adds a layer of complexity to the but-for test that would be likely to prove difficult for lay juries to readily comprehend and apply. Therefore, whatever its value as a logical improvement over the but-for test, the NESS test is not suitable for application by judges and juries in the courtroom. Here, as is true in other areas of the law, it is preferable to sacrifice elegance in favor of simplicity. For most

---

[30]The Third Restatement of Torts endorses the NESS test in the commentary to section 27, which deals with "multiple sufficient cause" cases. See *Restatement (Third) of Torts*, supra note 14, § 27, comments f and i. However, the Restatement provides an escape valve for cases involving conduct having a *de minimis* impact. In a separate section, the Restatement provides that when a defendant's negligent conduct constitutes only a trivial contribution to a causal set that is a factual cause of harm, the harm is not considered to be within the scope of the defendant's liability. *Restatement (Third) of Torts*, supra note 14, § 36.

cases, the but-for test is therefore the solution that is most suitable, and the one the courts are likely to continue to apply. For exceptional cases involving problems that the but-for test does not handle well, judges who are alert to the limitations of the test can adjust the test as necessary to present the causation issue to the jury in terms the jurors can readily understand. In those cases, courts can use alternative approaches, such as the substantial factor test, with appropriate instructions to the jury, avoiding the complexity of the formulation of the NESS test, but nonetheless achieving much the same result. That is the approach the courts have used, and it is the one that, from a pragmatic point of view, is the most sensible.

In sum, although the NESS test may provide a more precise articulation of the standard for causation in some cases, the unembellished but-for test is much simpler to apply and in most cases is responsive to common sensibilities about causation. Of course, the but-for test requires judges to be sensitive to its limitations, but properly applied, that test, together with its exceptions, offers the best chance for ensuring rational decision-making on issues of factual causation in negligence cases.

IV. PROXIMATE CAUSE

As noted earlier, the law does not impose tort liability on a defendant merely upon proof that the defendant's negligent act or omission was the cause in fact of the plaintiff's injury. A second requirement is that the act or omission must have been the "proximate cause" of the loss.

The purpose of the requirement of proximate cause is to impose limits on the scope of the defendant's liability for harms caused by the defendant's negligent conduct. It makes intuitive sense that the law should not automatically impose responsibility on any defendant who can be said to have caused injury. If causation alone were sufficient to give rise to liability, there would be no end to the possible liability of persons for even minor acts of negligence, and liability would be imposed far beyond what the generally shared sense of justice would support.

Consider the following example: Suppose I negligently leave an outside faucet running and the water floods my neighbor's basement. Suppose further that my neighbor was intending to purchase a lottery ticket that afternoon and had intended to purchase a ticket with a number corresponding to his daughter's social security number. But because he was racing to minimize the water damage to his basement, my neighbor was unable to get to the store to purchase the ticket. Sure enough, the winning lottery number corresponded to his daughter's social security number, and he would have won $10 million if he had been able to buy the lottery ticket that he intended to buy. My negligence was not only a but-for cause of the damage to my neighbor's basement, but also a but-for cause of his losing the $10 million he would have won in the lottery. Nonetheless, under the law it is clear that I would be liable for the damage to the basement, but not for the $10 million in lost lottery winnings.

The law has long struggled with the question of how to explain to my unhappy neighbor that he can recover from me for the damage to his basement but not for his lost lottery winnings. The explanation that has traditionally been given is that my negligence was the "proximate cause" of the damage to the basement, but not the "proximate cause" of his loss of the $10 million in lottery winnings. But what does that mean to my neighbor? Defining the rationale and scope of the "proximate cause" limitation on liability for negligence has been a long and difficult process that is still in progress and still provokes disagreement among courts and scholars.

To begin with, it is easy to see that the decision that I am not liable for the lost lottery winnings does not turn on the factual question of causation: my conduct was clearly an important factual cause of the loss. Instead, the issue of liability presents a policy question divorced from the factual issue of causation itself. A judge or jury addressing that question is forced to assess whether the defendant's conduct, even though it may be a but-for cause of the plaintiff's injury, has a sufficiently important relationship to that injury that the defendant should be held legally responsible for the plaintiff's loss (Prosser, 1971, supra note 4, p. 244).

The doctrine of proximate cause is one of ancient vintage. Since the period in legal history even before the development of the tort of negligence, courts have ruled that injuries caused by a defendant do not necessarily lead to liability, and the doctrine of proximate cause has been the principal vehicle used to address that limit on liability. For that reason, it has come to be widely recognized that proximate cause, despite its name, is not about causation, but involves the distinctly policy-based determination as to the appropriate scope of responsibility.

The term "proximate cause" is traceable to Lord Chancellor Bacon's 1630 maxim that the law looks to the near cause ("causa proxima" in Bacon's Latin version of the maxim), not the remote one. He added, with prescience as to the problem inherent in relying on actual causation alone: "It were infinite for the law to judge the cause of causes, and their impulsion of one another; therefore it contenteth itself with the immediate cause, and judgeth of acts by that, without looking to any further degree" (Prosser, 1988, supra note 4, p. 244).

By the nineteenth century, when courts began to develop the doctrinal grounds for the modern tort of negligence, they applied the principle of proximate cause essentially as set out by Bacon, by requiring that the defendant's action be a "direct" cause of the plaintiff's loss (Addison, 1860, pp. 4–5). That articulation led to rigid analysis and rulings that were often unfavorable to plaintiffs. For example, in one famous nineteenth-century case, the defendant negligently failed to make timely delivery of certain goods to the plaintiff, and a flood destroyed the goods while they were in a warehouse waiting to be picked up. The court concluded that the flood, not the defendant's negligence, was the direct cause of the loss, and it therefore ruled that the plaintiff had not established the proximate cause needed to find the defendant liable for the loss, even though the defendant's delay was the reason the goods were still in the warehouse when they were destroyed.

The concept of "directness" still remains a part of many formulations of the concept of proximate cause. In fact, the quotation above from the Supreme Court's description of the test for proximate cause referred to the "direct relation between the injury asserted and the injurious conduct alleged." However, over time the difficulty of distinguishing between "direct" and "indirect" causes and the unduly restrictive effect of the "direct cause" definition of proximate cause, have become apparent. As a result, courts have increasingly turned to other verbal formulations in an effort to capture the notion that liability for tortious conduct should extend to some, but not all, consequences of the negligent party's conduct.

A number of other formulations have been used in an effort to capture the concept of a limitation on the scope of a defendant's liability for harm causally traceable to his acts. Courts have variously defined "proximate cause" to mean the "dominant and efficient cause," the "responsible, active, operative, and continuing cause," the "immediate cause," the "cause which in natural and continuous sequence, unbroken by any efficient intervening cause, produced the result complained of," the "natural and probable cause" and the "cause which naturally or foreseeably leads to the result," or the "nearest or next cause."[31] None of those formulations provides a ready answer for the question that is asked. The problem, in essence, is that they all constitute efforts to capture, in a verbal formula, a matter of judgment that must be exercised in each case: whether the relationship between the negligence of the defendant and the injury suffered by the plaintiff is close enough that the law should hold the defendant accountable for the plaintiff's loss. Nonetheless, because courts need to use language that is readily understandable to a lay audience when they instruct juries as to how to determine whether the proximate cause requirement is satisfied, giving up the search for an appropriate verbal formula to capture the underlying policy decision is not an option.

Over time, most courts have come to treat proximate cause as turning on reasonable foreseeability. That is, the courts have ruled (and have instructed juries) that the scope of liability should extend only to risks that were reasonably foreseeable at the time of the negligent act. If the defendant reasonably could or should have foreseen the kind of event that ultimately caused the plaintiff's loss, the defendant's negligence would be deemed the proximate cause of the loss.[32] Under that approach, a negligent defendant is liable for all the kinds of harms that were reasonably foreseeable risks associated with

---

[31]See Keeton and Prosser, supra note 1, at 272–79.
[32]English judges began employing such an approach in the mid-nineteenth century, and American courts and commentators increasingly turned to that approach shortly thereafter. See Patrick J. Kelley, *Proximate Cause in Negligence Law: History, Theory, and the Present Darkness* 69 Wash. U.L.Q. 49, 75–81 (1991).

his negligent conduct, and he is liable to the class of persons he foreseeably put at risk by that conduct (Dobbs, 2000, supra note 5, p. 444).

The requirement of foreseeability dictates that if a second person or a new force unforeseeably intervenes to trigger the plaintiff's injury after the defendant's act is complete, responsibility for the injury falls on the second actor, not on the defendant. In that situation, the second actor's unforeseeable conduct is typically characterized as a "superseding cause" of the injury (Dobbs, 2000, supra note 5, p. 444).

Inherent in the foreseeability requirement are three weaknesses or sources of confusion. First, there is a risk of confusion between the use of foreseeability in determining when a defendant has been negligent and the use of foreseeability in determining whether the defendant's negligence was a proximate cause of the injury suffered by the plaintiff. The two types of foreseeability play different roles in the analysis, but they are sometimes conflated. Foreseeability is relevant in determining whether an act is negligent at all, because negligence requires a showing that the defendant should have foreseen that his conduct could cause harm of some sort; foreseeability is relevant in determining proximate cause because proximate cause requires a showing that the defendant should have foreseen the kind of harm that resulted and whether the plaintiff was in the class of persons that might suffer that harm (Dobbs, 2000, supra note 5, p. 448).

Second, it is not always easy to determine whether a particular eventuality should be considered foreseeable. Nearly everything can be regarded as foreseeable if foreseeability includes anticipating not only events that are likely to occur, but also events that can be imagined, but for which the possibility of occurrence is extremely remote. The courts, however, have declined invitations to regard highly unusual circumstances as foreseeable. Use of the formulation "reasonable foreseeability," with an emphasis on reasonableness, is designed to mitigate this problem, and while that test may lack much in the way of specificity, it helps to foreclose extreme arguments that nearly every eventuality is foreseeable at some minimal level of probability.

Third, whether a particular outcome is regarded as foreseeable or not can depend on the specificity with which the foreseen event is described. For example, suppose an adult hands a loaded rifle to a five-year-old child, and the child drops the rifle on her younger brother's leg, breaking his foot. If one asks whether it is foreseeable that giving a loaded rifle to a five-year-old child will result in injury to herself or others, the answer is plainly yes. But if one asks whether it is foreseeable that the child will drop the rifle on another child, breaking that child's foot, the answer is probably no. The courts have addressed that problem by holding defendants liable if the harm suffered was of the same general kind as the harm the defendant should have reasonably foreseen and the plaintiff who was injured was in the same general class of people who were put at risk by the defendant's negligence (Dobbs, 2000, supra note 5, p. 454).

The U.S. Supreme Court made that point clear more than a century ago in a case in which a horse-cart driver negligently took his horse-cart and passengers across a rail line when there was too little time before the arrival of a train at the road crossing. Just as the horse-cart began to cross the rails, it was delayed by the negligent lowering of gates by the gatekeeper. There ensued a collision between the train and the horse-cart in which one of the passengers on the horse-cart was injured. When the passenger sued the owners of the horse-cart, the owners defended on the ground that the horse-cart driver could not have foreseen that the gatekeeper would negligently lower the gates at the wrong time. The Supreme Court rejected that argument, pointing out that it was immaterial that the driver of the horse-cart "had no ground to expect the particular negligent act of lowering the gates, and the consequent obstruction to his passage across the steam-car tracks"; it was enough that it was foreseeable that any delay in getting the horse-cart across the tracks could result in an accident. The Court wrote: "It was not necessary that the driver should foresee the very thing itself which did cause the delay. The material thing for him to foresee was the possibility of a delay from any cause, and this he ought naturally to think of."[33]

In accordance with the approach in the horse-cart case, courts have usually defined the objective of the foreseeability inquiry in fairly general terms. Nonetheless, there is necessarily a degree of vagueness in courts' characterization of the specificity of the harm that should have been foreseen. As a consequence, different results are sometimes reached in factually similar cases.

Notwithstanding those difficulties, the foreseeability test has emerged as the governing standard and is applied broadly by courts in addressing issues of proximate cause. There is, however, one issue in the law of negligence that is not subject to principles of foreseeability. That issue relates to the extent of harm caused by a particular negligent act. While foreseeability governs the question whether a defendant is liable for his conduct, in that he is subject to liability if he could reasonably foresee the general nature of the harm that his conduct might give rise to, foreseeability does not apply to the extent of the resulting harm, at least when the harm takes the form of personal injury to the plaintiff. If a skateboarder negligently knocks down a young man, who cuts his knee on the sidewalk, the skateboarder is liable even if, wholly unpredictably as far as the skateboarder is concerned, the victim turns out to be hemophilic and bleeds to death. Commentators have recognized that there is tension between this rule and the rule that liability is limited to harms that are foreseeable, but the prevailing view has been that countervailing policies, such as the likelihood that the injured party is wholly without fault, counsel against limiting the injured party's recovery based on the lack of foreseeability regarding the extent of the harm the injured party would likely suffer from the defendant's wrongful conduct.[34]

---

[33]*Washington & G.R. Co. v. Hickey*, 166 U.S. 521, 527 (1897).
[34] *Restatement (Third) of Torts*, supra note 14, p. 510–11.

Although the foreseeability requirement for finding probable cause is generally understandable by lay juries and thus provides an effective way convey to juries how they should think about limitations on the scope of defendants' liability, there are several categories of cases that present special difficulties in applying the proximate cause test, even when its application is based on foreseeability.

First, there is the class of cases in which the defendant's negligence risks one type of harm, but an entirely different type of harm results. In such cases, modern courts typically ask whether the defendant should have reasonably foreseen the type of injury that occurred. If not, the defendant will not be liable, even if the defendant's act clearly qualifies as a cause of the injury.

A pair of cases decided by English courts illustrates how this principle has developed over time. In the first, known as the *Polemis* case, a stevedore servicing a ship placed planks across a hatchway, one of which was dislodged by a sling being used for loading. The sling knocked the plank into the ship's hold, where it ignited a fire that destroyed the ship. The Court of Appeal of England and Wales noted that the risk of some harm coming to person or property from the plank falling through the hatch was readily foreseeable, even though it was not foreseeable that the wooden plank would ignite a fire. Nonetheless, the Court of Appeal held the defendant liable for all harms directly caused by the negligent action, including unforeseeable harms.[35]

Some years later, the Privy Council of the House of Lords disapproved the *Polemis* decision in a case known as *The Wagon Mound*. In that case, a ship that was docked in Sydney harbor negligently released some oil into the water. Because it was known that oil under those circumstances is not especially flammable, the risk that was foreseeably created by the ship operators' negligence was that the oil would foul equipment in the harbor, not that it would cause a fire. However, because of a confluence of unusual circumstances, the oil did catch fire, and the fire damaged the plaintiff's facility at the harbor. Notwithstanding that the ship operators' negligence was plainly a cause of the fire, the Privy Council ruled that the risk of fire was not the particular risk that was created by the ship operators' negligence. Applying the foreseeability rule, the Privy Council ruled that because the fire was not a foreseeable consequence of the ship operators' negligence, their negligence was not the proximate cause of the destruction of the plaintiffs' facility.[36] The approach taken by the Privy Council in *The Wagon Mound*, rather than the approach taken by the Court of Appeal in the *Polemis* case, is now clearly the predominant approach used by Anglo-American courts.

A second category of cases involves injuries to "unforeseeable plaintiffs," that is, plaintiffs other than those who would be expected to be at risk as a result of the defendant's negligence. The most famous American case involving an unforeseeable plaintiff is the New York Court of Appeals' decision in Palsgraf

---

[35]*In re Polemis & Furness, Withy & Co., Ltd.*, [1921] 3 K.B. 560.
[36]*The Wagon Mound (No. 1)*, [1961] 1 All E.R. 404 (P.C.).

against the Long Island Railroad.[37] Virtually all first-year American law students study the case, and even though the case is nearly 100 years old now, it is still instructive regarding the way courts have attempted to deal with restrictions on liability to unforeseeable plaintiffs. The case involved the unfortunate Ms. Palsgraf who, having no ambitions to becoming a leading figure in the history of American law, was standing on a platform of the Long Island Railroad in New York one morning, waiting for a train. While she was waiting, a different train began to leave the station, at which point two men ran along the platform attempting to jump aboard the train. One of the men successfully boarded the train, but the second, who was carrying a package, was having more difficulty. A guard on the train reached out to help the man onto the train, and a second guard, on the platform, pushed him from behind. At that point, the man dropped his package. The packaged, it turned out, contained fireworks, and when the package hit the tracks, it exploded. The shock of the explosion caused a scale at the other end of the platform to fall. The scale, as it happens, fell on Ms. Palsgraf and injured her. She sued the Long Island Railroad based on the negligence of its guards in trying to aid the two men to board a moving train.

Notwithstanding the negligence of the guards and the railroad's responsibility for the guards' conduct, the court ruled that Ms. Palsgraf could not recover damages from the railroad. The court viewed the problem in the case as turning on the scope of the railroad's duty to Ms. Palsgraf, which in turn depended on the reasonable foreseeability of the harm that she suffered. Because the court discerned nothing in the facts of the case "to suggest to the most cautious mind that the parcel wrapped in newspaper would spread wreckage throughout the station,"[38] the court ruled that the railroad was not liable for the conductor's negligence. Although the court found that the railroad owed no duty of care to Ms. Palsgraf under the circumstances, and thus did not reach the issue of proximate cause, the court's reliance on the unforeseeability of Ms. Palsgraf as a potential victim of the railroad employees' negligent actions is consistent with the approach commonly followed by modern courts in such cases under the rubric of proximate cause.

The courts have identified a third category of cases, known as "intervening cause" cases, that have posed difficulties for courts applying the foreseeability test. The intervening cause cases are those in which the defendant creates a risk of harm, but a second actor or force intervenes after the first actor's conduct and directly injures the plaintiff. In the past, such cases were frequently identified as presenting a discrete proximate cause issue. Intervening causes that were regarded as sufficiently independent of the defendant's original negligence would be termed "superseding causes" and would relieve the defendant of liability for his negligence. The law regarding when intervening acts were sufficiently independent to be termed superseding became complex; arbitrary

---

[37]*Palsgraf v. Long Island Railroad Co.*, 248 N.Y. 339, 162 N.E. 99 (N.Y. 1928).
[38]The Official New York Report of Cases, case 248, p. 345; see also unofficial report of cases from New York and other northeastern states, case 162 (2d), p. 100.

distinctions were drawn among categories of cases in ways that were not particularly responsive to the underlying policy objectives of the doctrine of proximate cause. For example, at one time courts regarded all criminal conduct as a superseding force. Under that rule, if hotel-cleaning personnel negligently left my room door open after cleaning the room while I was away, and a thief stole my property from the room, the theft of my property by a third party would relieve the hotel of liability. That would be so even though the risk of theft was exactly the reason that leaving my room door open was negligent in the first place. Modern courts have discarded hard-and-fast rules in this area (although they frequently employ the "intervening/superseding cause" nomenclature). The modern view is that principles of foreseeability apply in the same manner to intervening cause cases as to proximate cause issues in general. As viewed by modern courts, this category of cases is therefore really just a subset of the general category of proximate cause cases based on foreseeability.

The courts in such cases ordinarily ask whether the intervening force superseded the original action or otherwise displaced it. The way the courts typically look at that issue is, again, through the lens of foreseeability. That is, they ask whether the intervening cause was foreseeable to the defendant when he acted. Suppose that while I am carelessly riding my motorcycle I run into a pedestrian, who falls to the ground and is temporarily dazed. Suppose further that while the pedestrian is in her dazed state, a thief, seizing the opportunity, grabs her purse, which contains a precious diamond ring. I am clearly liable for any injury that the pedestrian may have suffered in the fall. But am I liable for the loss of the diamond ring? Courts dealing with such cases normally say that intervening criminal activity is not foreseeable and therefore my negligence was not a proximate cause of the loss of the ring. However, the analysis could be different if, for example, the area in which I was riding my motorcycle was a high-crime area where it would be reasonably foreseeable that if I knocked a pedestrian down (clearly a foreseeable risk of my negligent driving) a thief might take advantage of the pedestrian's temporary disability and steal her property.

V. CRITIQUES OF THE DOCTRINE OF PROXIMATE CAUSE

Because neither the term "proximate" nor the term "cause" accurately describes the function of the proximate cause requirement, legal academics have long favored jettisoning the term "proximate cause" in favor of a different term, such as "legal cause." They have also urged courts to distinguish clearly between actual causation, a factual issue, and legal cause, a legal issue that turns on policy-based judgments as to proper limits on liability. Although many courts continue to use the term "proximate cause," courts have increasingly come to recognize and apply the distinction between actual causation and legal cause (or proximate cause), as urged by academic critics.

Some commentators have also argued that legal cause (or proximate cause) should be defined by reference to the risks associated with the negligent actor's conduct, rather than being defined by the reasonable foreseeability of harm. The third Restatement of Torts recommends the following standard for legal cause: "An actor's liability is limited to those harms that result from the risks that made the actor's conduct tortious."[39]

Under the "risk rule" approach, the court would find the defendant liable if the court concluded that the plaintiff's loss was caused by the defendant's negligent act and that the risk of the particular harm suffered by the plaintiff was one of the reasons that the defendant's conduct was regarded as negligent. In the example of the flooded basement, described above, a court using the risk rule would conclude that (1) my act of leaving the water running caused both the flooding of my neighbor's basement and his loss of a lottery jackpot, but (2) while the risk of flooding a nearby basement was one of the risks that made my action wrongful, the risk of the loss of lottery winnings was not.

As explained in one leading treatise, the risk rule "serves the purpose of avoiding what might be unjustified, and potentially enormous, liability by confining liability's scope to the reasons for holding the actor liable in the first place."[40] That treatise recommends that under the risk rule, the jury should be told that, "[I]n deciding whether the plaintiff's harm is within the scope of liability, it should go back to the reasons for finding the defendant engaged in negligent or other tortious conduct. If the harms risked by that tortious conduct include the general sort of harm suffered by the plaintiff, the defendant is subject to liability for the plaintiff's harm."[41]

The rationale underlying the risk rule is the following: When I go about my affairs, I have a duty to others to act with reasonable care and therefore avoid exposing them to unreasonable risks. But that duty is not boundless. When driving, for example, I have a duty to other drivers and pedestrians to operate my automobile with reasonable care so as to avoid hitting other vehicles and like adverse consequences. As noted earlier, the duty extends to losses that I might not have anticipated. Thus, for example, if I carelessly rear-end a car in front of me that is stopped at a red light, I am liable for the resulting damage, whether the car is a $3,000 used Fiat or a $300,000 Ferrari. But what if the sound of the collision startles a violinist in a house a quarter of mile away who is playing a Stradivarius violin worth $3,000,000, and causes the violinist to drop the violin? Would I be liable to the owner of the Stradivarius? Courts would likely say, "no."

But why? The reason, according to those who favor the risk rule, is that when driving my car, I undertake a responsibility to other drivers, pedestrians, and property owners in the immediate vicinity to drive with reasonable care, and a failure to do so creates the risk of certain harms to others. Those risks are the reason that the law treats my conduct as negligent. The justification for considering my conduct to be negligent does not, however, include risks

---

[39]*Restatement (Third) of Torts*, 1998, supra note 14, § 29.
[40]*Restatement (Third) of Torts*, 1998, supra note 14, p. 496.
[41]*Restatement (Third) of Torts*, 1998, supra note 14, § 29.

of harm that would not be expected to result from my conduct. To put it another way, the risk of loss to the unfortunate violinist is not a risk that made my conduct negligent. Those who advocate the foreseeability rule, on the other hand, would conclude that the risk of damage to another car is a foreseeable consequence of my careless driving, but that the risk that my conduct would cause someone to drop a violin blocks away was not reasonably foreseeable.

As even the advocates of the risk rule acknowledge, the risk rule and the foreseeability approach produce similar outcomes in most cases. The argument made by advocates of the risk rule is that it provides "a more refined analytical standard than a foreseeability standard"[42] and is more forthright in recognizing that the scope of a defendant's liability is a policy decision based on how broadly society wishes to cast the net of responsibility for actions that cause injury. They argue that the test of proximate cause based on foreseeability substitutes an exercise in hindsight with respect to a specific case for what should be a more general judgment regarding the proper scope of individual's duty to others. Those who favor use of the foreseeability-based proximate cause test view the fact-specific nature of the foreseeability inquiry as one of its strengths. By focusing the attention of the jury on the specific facts of a particular case, its advocates say, the proximate cause doctrine allows the jury to apply the common sense of justice more accurately to the case before it.

Notwithstanding the problems with the foreseeability test, its strength is that it is readily understandable and reasonably easy to apply. The "risk rule," on the other hand, can present more difficulties to those called upon to apply it. In fact, it is likely that a judge or jury trying to decide whether a particular risk was among those that made the defendant's conduct negligent would ask whether a reasonable person would have foreseen the possible harm that in fact ensued. If so, the two approaches would effectively merge, at least in application if not in theory. Given that the two approaches are likely to produce similar results and even similar analytical paths for those applying them, ease of application provides a strong argument in favor of the simpler "foreseeability" rule.

The law is far from a pure science, and while it aspires to be logical, law is not the product of pure logic. While consistency, predictability, and analytic soundness are important in the law, as in other fields, other values have their claim on legal doctrines as well. As discussed above, a legal system for assessing liability for harms resulting from wrongful conduct must respond to the community's sense of fundamental justice. Otherwise, the legal system will lose credibility with those it purports to serve. At the same time, the legal system, which relies on lay jurors as well as busy lawyers and judges, is best served by rules that are straightforward enough for lay jurors, lawyers, and judges to apply with relative ease. In the field of tort liability for negligent conduct,

---

[42]*Restatement (Third) of Torts*, 1998, supra note 14, p. 499.

those interests favor the use of the but-for test for actual causation (with exceptions for certain cases, such as cases involving multiple sufficient causes), and the use of the foreseeability test for legal (or proximate) cause. While academics can fairly complain that those tests lack the precision and elegance of certain alternative approaches, the but-for and foreseeability tests have simplicity of application and commonsense appeal on their sides. For that reason, it is not surprising that those tests, despite their flaws, have emerged as the principal guideposts that the courts employ as they pursue the elusive goal of defining causation and linking it to liability in cases involving the law of negligence.

REFERENCES

Addison, C. G. (1860). *Wrongs and their remedies: Being a treatise on the law of torts*. London: V. and R. Stevens and Sons.

American Law Institute. (2010). *Restatement of the law third, torts: Liability for physical and emotional harm*. St. Paul, MN: American Law Institute Pub.

Carpenter, C. E. (1935). Concurrent causation. *University of Pennsylvania Law Review*, 83(8), 941–952.

Dobbs, D. B. (2000). *The law of torts*. St. Paul, MN: West Group.

Fischer, D. A. (1992). Causation in fact in omission cases. *Utah Law Review*, 1992(4), 1335.

Malone, W. S. (1956). Ruminations on cause-in-fact. *Stanford Law Review*, 9(1), 60–99.

Prosser, W. L. 1898 (1971). *Handbook of the law of torts*. St. Paul, MN: West Pub. Co.

Robertson, D. W. 1937 (2004). *Cases and materials on torts*. St. Paul, MN: Thomson/West.

Wright, R. W. (1985). Actual causation vs. probabilistic linkage: The bane of economic analysis. *The Journal of Legal Studies*, 14(2), 435–456. doi:10.1086/467780

EDITORS' COMMENTARY

Lay opinion would surely link the role of the concept of causation in the law with questions of responsibility. This is in line with a normative approach in psychology, where some measure of intentionality and conscious decision making is assumed (Harré & Moghaddam, 2012). A person as agent is responsible for certain speeches and actions and these act upon other people, their thoughts and decisions, their places in society, and even on the material world in which they live, sometimes blaming them, sometimes bringing about a greater good. This lay analysis is supported by Bryson when he explains that, "the issue of legal causation typically surfaces when a person has been harmed and has asked the courts to make a determination of legal liability for that harm." This seems to suppose there is a chain that leads, link by link, back to a human being or a corporate body with the rights and duties of a human being, which is presented as the agent from which the causal sequence flows to the actual or possible harm done to a person or legal person like a bank. Bryson remarks that, "the law imposes liability when no actual or clearly established harm has occurred," for example, in cases of speeding or trespassing.

Legal decisions implying attributions of causality to an agent differ from decisions about what caused what in physics, chemistry, or biology because of the close tie between being the "cause of" and being "morally responsible for." Extenuating circumstances intervene in many cases between the proof of causal responsibility and the kind of moral responsibility that requires redress or punishment.

A notion that is part of everyday causal thinking, namely proximate cause, has been a matter of considerable discussion and refinement in the law. To say one event proximately caused another is a way of making two separate but related assertions. First, it means the former event caused the latter. This is known as actual cause or cause in fact. The law recognizes an event or agent as the proximate cause of a certain occurrence; it is not only a necessary but a sufficient cause of the event at issue. As Bryson remarks, the idea of proximal cause is used to underline a direct relation between the causal agent and the troublesome consequence. A person may have had an input to a causal chain with many links and branches that led to an undesirable consequence at so many removes that, as Bryson puts it, responsibility is attenuated.

In order to apply the concept of negligence, a different kind of causal concept from those familiar to us in the natural sciences, in accordance with how it is understood in legal contexts, one must attend to a pattern of several propositions, some of which are factual and others are hypothetical. The concept of "negligence" seems to be causal in that we say things like "It was due to (because of) the negligence of the doctor that the patient developed a more severe illness." This "due to" fits comfortably in the sentence. A person is negligent when bringing about or performing (and that is a causal concept) a certain act that causes harm to someone. The actor does not intend to harm the victim but the person who did the harmful act could have done something else that did not cause harm. This is a hypothesis and its acceptance in a particular case could require very diverse items of evidence, such as character assessments, issues about attention by the actor to what is going on and so on. So, here we have the two-step causation we have noted elsewhere—the person as agent brings about a certain potent state of affairs, which brings about the event, state, or even thing in question.

Bryson calls this whole genre of simple causal patterns "but-for" analyses. When called in defense of a defendant, lawyers try to specify what the "actual cause" of something is. They do not search for additional material or consider psychological studies—they adopt, rather, the "but-for" device. If an injury would not have occurred "but for" the wrongful conduct that is at issue, the wrongful conduct is said not to be a "cause" of the injury. Put more precisely, under the but-for test negligent conduct is not regarded as a cause of harm if the plaintiff would have sustained the harm even if the defendant had not been negligent. Bryson confesses that the choice of the but-for test has been explained by saying that it "seems to be the best the law can do in its effort to offer an approximate expression of an accepted popular attitude toward responsibility."

Bryson's comprehensive survey of arguments for assigning responsibility based on causes includes some cases that have been much discussed among philosophers. Multiple sufficient causes create problems of assigning responsibility. Prime casual efficacy, in cases where two chains of causal influences converge simultaneously on a certain situation, brings about a change. Bryson seems to suggest that the courts are not consistent in how they deal with such cases. The hard question would be to try to decide between both or neither as agents in the case.

The other case that Bryson presents is also familiar to philosophers. A certain causal influence is in the process of impinging on a certain situation, but before it can do so, a different influence preempts it in affecting the target. The first person with murder in his heart was preempted in his attack by the successful assault of the second assassin. In this case, the first killer would have succeeded in committing murder but for the advent of the second villain. Bryson notes that the courts have required the defendant to show that the lethal bullet did not emerge from his gun. This is, of course, a forensic question to which there is, in principle, a definite empirical answer. However, this leaves the deeper question of morality ambiguous. The court may relieve him of responsibility if the bullet had not come from his gun but the Christian doctrine is clear: murder in one's heart is also a grievous sin.

Philosophers, as is clear from the comprehensive survey in Chapters 1, 2, and 3, do not have a simple, universally applicable repertoire of causal concepts. As Bryson remarks, "a legal system for assessing liability for harms resulting from wrongful conduct must respond to the community's sense of fundamental justice." The rules for the use of causal concepts in the assignment of responsibility are easiest to manage and apply when the "but-for" test for actual causation is used. But for deterring what is to be taken as a proximal cause in these cases, the foreseeability test for proximate cause seems to be workable. "It is not surprising," says Bryson, "that those tests, despite their flaws, have emerged as the principal guideposts that the courts employ as they pursue the elusive goal of defining causation and linking it to liability in cases involving the law of negligence."

REFERENCE

Harré, R., & Moghaddam, F. M. (eds.) (2012). *Psychology for the third millennium*. Thousand Oaks, CA: Sage.

20

No Bad Deed Goes Unrewarded: Cause, Consequence, and Deviance in Emerging Technological Regimes

Rodrigo Nieto-Gómez

Le secret des grandes fortunes sans cause apparente est un crime oublié, parce qu'il a été proprement fait.[1]
— Le Père Goriot (1835), Honoré de Balzac

There is an implicit causal claim made by governments when creating regulatory regimes for emerging technologies (i.e., those technologies still in development and not yet widely adopted). The claim is simple, but not trivial: it is claimed that usage regulation is enacted to cause good user behavior and that good regulatory regimes are enforced to cause good market practices. The same claim implies that those good behaviors are known in advance and must be encouraged and preserved by regulatory regimes, and that deviant behaviors (those opposed to those practices) must be discouraged and punished.

In other words, when a governmental entity provides the "dos and don'ts" about how to use a particular emerging technology, it is implying that it knows what good behavior will look like, and that regulatory regimes (the cause) will provoke predictable positive behaviors in the usage and manufacturing of technologies (the consequence).

Most of the literature on the "theories of regulation" explores the topic of the causal origins of regulation from the vantage point of monopolistic or quasi-monopolistic corporations and not from the point of view of the user. It does it in order to understand either if the regulation is created as an element of "public interest" to deal with market failures or if regulation mostly results from the capacity of utilities or big corporations to "capture" the regulatory entities that oversee their operations (Priest, 1993).

---

[1]."The secret of great fortunes without apparent cause is a crime forgotten, for it was properly done."

On the one hand, the "public interest" theory considers regulatory intervention as a way to balance the imperfections of the market (like the formation of monopolies or price fixing); it is the scaffold to the causality claim that this chapter analyzes. On the other hand, the "regulatory capture" theory emphasizes that "as a rule, regulation is acquired by the industry and is designed and operated primarily for its benefit" (Stigler, 1971). This hijacking of the regulation by the industry is what today we call regulatory capture (e.g., a utility using its influence over the regulatory entity to keep its geographic monopoly).

Nevertheless, the "public interest" versus "regulatory capture" debate is less concerned about how user behavior relates to these regulatory regimes and mostly omits to discuss how innovation triggers the creation of new technologies and markets. Therefore, the evolving nature of user behaviors vis-à-vis technological innovations is not given a central role in this literature.

A second lens to observe the emergence of regulatory regimes explores the complex interaction between intellectual property as a kind of regulation and innovation. Authors like Larry Lessig or Tim Wu (2010) observe how dominant actors use regulatory regimes for their advantage. For Lessig, for example, regulatory authorities have a choice: They can "give power to network owners to regulate innovation, or . . . remove power to regulate" (Lessig, 2001) In his view, when the rules give power to the network owners to regulate innovation (e.g., removing net neutrality protections for the Internet, empowering established Internet Service Providers), the consequence is a decrease in innovation capacities.

This lens is particularly concerned with the consequences of copyright and intellectual property laws with respect to the capacity of newcomers to innovate. Do patents and copyright still cause inventors, artists, and entrepreneurs to create, or are they tools employed by monopolists to corner a market?

On one side of this debate we have the example of the famous "letter to hobbyists" that Bill Gates, founder of Microsoft, wrote in 1976 to members of the Homebrew Computer Club who were copying his software without authorization: " One thing you do [by stealing software] is prevent good software from being written. Who can afford professional work for nothing? . . . Most directly, the thing you do is theft" (Gates, 1976).

On the other hand, others like David Noble have argued that "patents petrified the process of science, and the frozen fragments of genius became weapons in the armories of science-based industry" (Noble, 1978, p. 111). The whole open source (Coleman, 2013) and the Creative Commons License (Creative Commons, 2011) movements are an operationalization of this side of the argument to provide an alternative to traditional copyright regulation.

Nevertheless, none of these analytical frameworks is particularly interested in the causality claim introduced at the beginning of this chapter with respect to the user: Governmental actors claim that usage regulation is enacted to cause good user behavior of emerging technologies, thus presuming that good user behavior can be known in advance and enforced. Therefore, the regime encourages behaviors deemed "good" and punishes those labeled as "bad."

I. INNOVATION'S RED FLAGS

The "public benefit" causality claim is implied in every legislative process because legislators and regulators will always assert to be working for the good of their constituencies (even dictators with de facto authority to create norms will make that claim). However, in the case of norms that surround emerging technologies, the causality claim is of a peculiar nature because emerging technologies are by definition those whose adoption and usage is not yet widespread, and therefore the social changes that their usage will bring (or has the potential of bringing) are not yet known.

The main target of the regulatory claim studied in this chapter is not the regulatory or the corporate entities (albeit both are important). Instead, at the center of this causality relation we find the user, as it is his or her behavior that governments want to modify when regulating usage of an emerging technology.

If the technology is emerging, it means that it is still in development and not yet widely adopted. How is it then possible for governments to affirm they know what good and bad behaviors will look like, once and if society adopts the technology? Furthermore, as usage is an important component of what I will call here the "complex-creative system" that produces social and technological innovation in nonlinear ways, by encouraging some behaviors and punishing others, regulatory regimes intervene in systems they do not fully understand, triggering unintended consequences. The complex nature of this system means that consequence does not follow linearly its causes.

For example, traffic codes that govern the behavior of drivers are justified by those with authority to create them as a necessity to cause good driving practices. Equally, the laws and regulations that govern car production are framed as a cause of good manufacturing practices. While today this specific regulatory regime (including usage norms) is quite mature, at the beginning of the twentieth century the automobile was an emerging technology and the regime did not exist. Usage regulation created licensing requirements for motorists, speed limits, traffic signs with meanings that had to be codified and memorized, and many other rules that today we follow and consider to be an intrinsic part of the "driving experience."

This regime also gave authority to police officers to enforce those laws, and punish users who abandon the accepted standards (i.e., those who act deviantly), imposing fines or even imprisonment for the worst of those deviances. The implications for the user are clear: using a technology deviantly (in this case, an automobile) may cause her to lose her freedom because the regulatory regime that governs its usage imposes a "right" way and discourages a "wrong" way of using it.

Continuing the example, regulatory regimes also impose manufacturing rules to the car industry to mandate design and engineering choices to be incorporated into their products (e.g., seat belts to increase safety or catalytic converters to curb pollutant emissions) and to refrain from incorporating some others. If a car design deviates from these rules, it will not be considered "street legal" and as a consequence, it will not be granted a registration to use public roads.

Every time a regulation imposes usage and industrial rules for technologies, the regulatory body is claiming that it knows how the technology should be adopted and when usage and production should be punished; for example, speeding can get you a traffic ticket, driving under the influence of alcohol can get you imprisoned, and car manufacturers that do not follow the Environmental Protection Agency's (EPA) fuel emission standards will not be able to sell their cars or can be fined large amounts of money.

The problem with this causality assumption is that, in the case of emerging technologies, this "knowledge" is in reality a prediction because the impact of the new technology is yet unknown. For example, when cars were an emerging technology, regulators claimed to be concerned about the danger of combustion engines exploding. On the other hand, they were not concerned about traffic jams, the aggregated climatological impact of millions of combustion engines, or the way non-laminated glass breaks during an accident, all examples of real problems of this technology that were completely ignored by those first regulatory forecasts.

Instead, in the nineteenth century, some of the first norms for self-propelled vehicles were heavily influenced by "the horse-drawn transportation interests" (Flink, 1990, p. 2). and imposed draconian regulations to this emerging technology to deal with the perceived threat of explosion. Known collectively in the United States and the United Kingdom under the name of Red Flag Laws, in the United Kingdom, the Red Flag Act "limited the speed of road locomotives to 2 mph in towns and 4 mph on the open highway and required that an attendant walk sixty yards ahead carrying a red flag by day and a red lantern by night" (Flink, 1990, p. 2).

In reality, these laws obstructed on purpose the capabilities of the new technology, protecting as a consequence the established business model of the horse carriage industry in an archetypical case study of regulatory capture. In other words, the regulatory process served as a way to delay the entry into the market of a "disruptive" innovation"; that is, a technology that disrupts the established value proposition of the market (Christensen, 2011).

Car manufacturers had to fight against these Red Flag Laws in order to be able to conquer the market controlled by the horse carriage manufacturers. By pursuing multiple strategies to modify the regulatory regime, the nascent automobile industry and early adopters behaved deviantly, sometimes acting at the edge of the law, and in some cases breaking it on purpose.

At the end, we know what happened: The technological virtues of the combustion engine displaced the horse as the preferred land-based transportation technology, despite the lobbying effort of the horse carriage industry, and thus becoming the new dominant paradigm. Car manufacturers ceased to be deviant actors and became the new protectors of status quo, actively lobbying legislative authorities to shape a regulatory regime that is beneficial to their business practices. While they have not always been successful at halting regulatory changes they do not want (e.g., the introduction of fuel efficiency standards or seatbelts), the auto manufacturers and the auto dealers are today a powerful force to be reckoned with, vis-à-vis the regulation that shapes motorists' behaviors.

The significance of this example for the original causality claim we are discussing in this chapter is clear. Red Flag Laws were not the cause of good user behavior, despite governmental claims. Instead, the consequences of Red Flag Laws were to limit the users from experimenting and learning about the new technology unless they were ready to break the law (and many did break the law), to try to halt the capacity of the nascent industry to disrupt the horse carriage business market. Regulators in the nineteenth century failed to forecast the shape that the transportation complex-creative system would acquire, but that did not stop them from trying to regulate the emerging technology.

As demonstrated by this example, disruptive innovation follows an episodic pattern not unlike the one identified by Thomas Kuhn to describe the structure of scientific revolutions: Periods of incremental improvement (known in innovation theory as incremental innovation) are punctuated by dramatic changes in the paradigm brought by revolutionary behavior (known as disruptive innovation). The defenders of the established paradigm will then oppose this transition, until the new paradigm becomes the dominant one. As Kuhn identified:

> Almost always the men who achieve these fundamental inventions of a new paradigm have been either very young or very new to the field whose paradigm they change. And perhaps that point need not have been made explicit, for obviously these are the men who, being little committed by prior practice to the traditional rules of normal science, are particularly likely to see that those rules no longer define a playable game and to conceive another set that can replace them. (Kuhn, 1996, p. 90)

Emerging technologies are also almost always brought to market by young startups that have no commitment (no sunk cost) to the established rules. Nevertheless, one important difference between scientific revolutions and technology disruptions is that, while those young scientists that challenge established paradigms have to fight mainly at the cognitive level of scientific minds, technological revolutions need not only to change mental paradigms (translated into consumer behaviors) but also to confront adverse regulatory regimes. In simple terms: to be successful, they often have to fight (or break) the law, to get it changed. The implications of these situations are counterintuitive because in those cases, breaking the law causes an improvement in social conditions.

Therefore, the common claim (common among regulators, at least) that there is a linear causality relation between regulation enacted by governments and good user behavior of emerging technologies is misleading, or at least incomplete. This is why I am expanding in this chapter the regulatory capture argument to include usage as another target of this act of institutional corruption and user-driven innovation as another collateral victim.

The collective memory attributes to Balzac the dictum "behind every great fortune there is a great crime."[2] Given the fact that many of the most successful technological changes have resulted from an explicit transgression to established business practices and the laws surrounding them, the French novelist known for his morally complex characters was probably right.

II. THE COMPLEX-CREATIVE SYSTEM

It is not the objective of this chapter to discuss the meaning or desirability of technological progress. Nevertheless, to talk about the importance of innovation-friendly regimes, I consider important to briefly answer the Luddite question: why should regulatory regimes be positively predisposed toward technological innovation?

The answer is survival. Even if we succeed in becoming better stewards of the Earth (probably through technological progress itself, in the form of green technologies), as long as we remain a single planet species, the latest we will go extinct is the day Earth becomes uninhabitable. According to current estimates, that will take place in between 1.75 to 3.25 billion years as "we are roughly 70% of the way through the HZ [habitable zone] lifetime of our planet" (Rushby, Claire, Osborn, & Watson, 2013, pp. 833–849) and civilization (at least the kind we know today, under our current level of technological progress) would be heavily disrupted by rising temperatures and solar activity even before those dates.

Therefore, the only known alternative to technological progress to create a sustainable multiplanetary civilization is humanity's extinction. As such, innovation is the only process available to humankind to increase its odds of survival.

Ending poverty and unnecessary suffering and increasing the health and life spans of all humans while providing a better environment to all living beings are also goals that can only be achieved through technological progress.

We may become extinct because of technological irresponsibility (e.g., nuclear Armageddon) but we will become extinct for sure if innovation does not continue. Because of these very long-term reasons, I consider a survival necessity for regulatory regimes to be innovation-friendly.

As discussed in the previous section, governmental agents claim a causal linearity between regulation and positive outcomes every time they regulate an emerging technology. This claim could be stated like this, in the voice of a regulator: If good rules are put in place (e.g., the Red Flag Laws),

---

[2.]In reality, the closest one can get to identifying this idea in Balzac's work is in the sentence used as the epigraph of this chapter.

predictable good behavior by users and entrepreneurs will follow (e.g., early warning to other people that a horseless carriage is nearby). A complementary argument is implicitly made: breaking usage rules is always bad behavior and breaking regulatory regimes is bad. That is why usage punishments are put in place.

These causal assumptions are not particularly interested in the future innovation capacities of users and entrepreneurs, and they largely consider the technology as a fixed value at the time of the enactment of the regulation. For example, because regulators were so concerned about regulating the "horseless" nature of the horseless carriages, they were unable to see the potential social consequences (good and bad) of the automobile.

But innovation occurs in the context of a "complex-creative system" where creative and adoption paths cannot be rigorously predicted. In this complex-creative system, present technologies are the cause of future social changes that cannot be foreseen because (like other complex adaptive systems) the causality relations propelled by innovation are nonlinear. The system organizes around a series of rules, but because of the great number of interlocked interactions among its components, it is impossible to know in advance the consequences of each change in the system. Moreover, the linkages among those interlocked agents are dynamic because they change with every interaction, so the system "rewires itself" all the time.

A simple example demonstrates these properties of the complex-creative system: If an actor could forecast with precision the nonlinear dynamics behind the trajectory of technological innovation and user desires, that knowledge could be put into practice by investing in the companies that depend on the state of particular technologies behind a particular stock. Nevertheless, we all have been warned when investing in the stock market that "past performance is no guarantee of future results" and this is why most portfolios hedge the risk by diversifying. This diversification is an admission that without a time machine, we cannot know with certainty which companies backed by which technologies will be high performers because the complex-creative system is nonlinear.

What I am naming here the complex-creative system is the mechanism behind each and every innovation that shapes our technologically dependent civilization. From the adoption of the wheel to the deployment of NASA's Curiosity robotic rover exploring Mars in 2014 (that uses six wheels), complex creativity emerges across time and ages as a result of the nonlinear interactions between creative agents and users (intellect), objects (building blocks), and rules (those rules include regulation, but also social conventions and the human condition; for example, ambition is also a systemic rule).

Even if the rules that caused prehistoric humans to master fire are different to those that motivated entrepreneurs to invent the computer mouse, both groups of innovators were responding to the contextual rules of the complex-creative system, using their intellect and modifying their environment with building blocks. The process is directly associated to what Brian Arthur calls combinatorial evolution of technology:

Stated in a few words this would work as follows. Early technologies form using existing primitive technologies as components. These new technologies in time become possible components—building blocks—for the construction of further new technologies. Some of these in turn go on to become possible building blocks for the creation of yet newer technologies. In this way, slowly over time, many technologies form from an initial few, and more complex ones form using simpler ones as components. The overall collection of technologies bootstraps itself upward from the few to the many and from the simple to the complex. We can say that technology creates itself out of itself. (Arthur, 2009, pp. 21–24)

Each new technology becomes a building block for other new technologies to emerge, but plotting that trajectory can only be done in hindsight. The pre-historic humans who mastered fire were in no position to know that their innovation would cause sociotechnical changes that can be directly traced to most technologies we use in the twenty-first century.

Despite this uncertainty between causes and effects in the innovation process, regimes that regulate emerging technologies claim that they can create rules for emerging technologies to cause "good" adoption paths and punish "bad" adoption paths, even if it is impossible to anticipate what good behavior will look like when the technology is adopted.

III. DEVIANT INNOVATION

Up to this point, this chapter has discussed how regulatory regimes claim to be able to cause good usage and manufacturing practices for emerging technologies, punishing users and entrepreneurs who deviate from those practices, often for the benefit of existing incumbents. It has also demonstrated how the complex-creative system follows nonlinear routes that cannot be predicted and therefore make it very difficult to forecast the social consequences that a technology will bring once it is widely adopted.

Evidently, there is a fundamental tension between the two premises: If governmental actors often make mistakes and regulate in ways that are not beneficial, but technological progress continues in spite of that, there has to be a social process that solves this causality paradox.

The solution to this regulation/innovation dilemma can be found in a process that I will call deviant innovation. Fundamentally, deviant innovation takes place when innovators do not play by the rules.

This "not playing by the rules" has been studied in Science, Technology, and Society (STS) studies under the name of technological appropriation. I will define it here following the conventions of the field, as the process in which the users of technologies "appropriate" the technologies by using and modifying them in ways the designer of the technology did not anticipate. Silvia Lindtner,

Ken Anderson, and Paul Dourish (2012) frame it as a cultural process that "refers to the ways that people adapt and 'make technology their own.'"

Users will "reinvent these products and rethink these knowledge systems, often in ways that embody critique, resistance or outright revolt" (Eglash, 2004, pp. vii–xxi) and implies a fracture in the assumed linear causality between design, technology, regulation, and usage.

Appropriation also represents a transference of power from the formal designers to the users. As such, the process of appropriation blurs the line between users and innovators, as the former become the later when they appropriate the technology in unanticipated ways.

Examples of appropriation are abundant, and they are strictly intertwined with the process of combinatorial evolution of technology previously described. Using a shoe to drive a nail, making a baby incubator in the developing world out of car parts (Lite, 2008), or employing a 300-euro drone toy as a tool of political protest (TorrentFreak, 2013) are all examples of technological appropriation. The shoe designer did not conceive his/her creation as a hammer, the engineers of Toyota never anticipated that their autoparts would be used as a medical tool, and the engineers of Parrot Inc. did not design Drone 1.0 to be used in a political rally in Germany as a symbol of privacy concerns.

Once a technology is "released into the wild," it is impossible to forecast how users will appropriate it. This is why the causality claim that regulatory regimes make when trying to forecast how emerging technologies will be adopted by society is fundamentally fallacious. While the cause of social changes may be known (an emerging technology) its consequences (social change) are unpredictable as the technology becomes a new building block in the complex-creative system.

In fact, for technological progress to take place, entrepreneurs must appropriate existing building blocks to create their new tools in ways the original designers did not anticipate. The inventors of the wheel did not anticipate that Henry Ford would use it in his model T, and the inventors of the sonar did not anticipate that Mercedes Benz and Tesla Motors would use it as part of their assisted driving technologies. Causality is nonlinear, but because the linear pretension of regulation to try (and fail) to forecast emerging behaviors, quite often those unanticipated user behaviors become explicitly rebellious against usage norms.

Appropriation is a kind of technological deviance, as entrepreneurs who create a new value proposition need to depart from acceptable and predictable standards and rules. Nevertheless, as technology regimes enforce standards and often criminalize conducts outside the behaviors that regulators anticipated for a given technology, the innovator will have to confront the regulatory regime.

Eduardo Calvillo and I classified the process of appropriation into three different categories (Gámez & Nieto-Gómez, 2011, p. 210):

1. *Simple appropriation:* It occurs when a user appropriates a technology in an unforeseen way, encouraged by the designer in order to improve the user experience. Every app developer who discovers new uses for the sensors in an iPhone appropriates the technology in ways that Apple did not foresee. For example, a series of apps emerged in 2011 to take advantage of the high-definition cameras in smartphones to measure the heart rate.[3] While nobody anticipated that smartphones could be used in this way, the appropriation became so popular that Apple integrated the feature in its Apple watch.
2. *Subverted appropriation:* Users engage in subverted appropriation when they rebel against the designer's intentions. For example, the most popular Internet browser extension in 2014, Adblock, removes (most of) the advertisements found in Web sites for a cleaner experience. The act deprives the Webmaster from the revenue s/he expected to make from advertising, but it is not an illegal practice.
3. *Illicit appropriation:* Illicit appropriation takes place when the user appropriates the technology in a way that is forbidden by the law. Breaking the encryption systems of DVDs to distribute them through peer-to-peer (P2P) networks or adapting a Nokia phone as a remote detonator for Improvised Explosive Devices (IED) are examples of illicit appropriation.

The contradiction arises because this categorization of appropriation is far from being morally dichotomic, given that simple appropriation and illicit appropriation are not antithetical choices. If they were, it would be very simple for the regulator to just regulate in favor of simple appropriation and enact punishments against the illicit appropriation of technology.

In reality, as this chapter will demonstrate in the following case studies, illicit appropriation can cause deviant innovations that are building blocks for future technologies that end up being morally accepted by the community, forcing a regulatory change. On the other hand, the simple appropriation of a technology considered uncontroversial may have unintended second- or third-degree consequences when a deviant innovator recombines it in a new way.

As long as rules are created to encourage some behaviors and punish others, creators involved in the process of appropriation will necessarily incur in deviant practices. This deviant behavior will be particularly significant in the context of emerging technologies, as regulatory regimes that may have been sufficient under the previous conditions may now be unprepared to deal with the potential for social changes that an emerging technology brings, once widely adopted.

When Mohr analyzed why Merton classifies gangsters and juvenile delinquents as innovators, he concluded that: "The delinquent is an innovator,

---

[3.]Cardiio is one of the most popular apps that appropriated the camera, popularizing this feature: http://www.cardiio.com/

according to Merton, in that he has accepted the cultural goal of individual material success but rejected socially accepted means, and adopted a non-accepted means, of attaining the objective" (Mohr, 1969, pp. 111–126).

In reality, though, most innovators, including CEOs of Fortune 500 corporations, behave in the same deviant way Merton describes gangsters. Deviant innovators also reject accepted means and quite often follow non-accepted means to attain the objective of material success. They do so by appropriating technologies to do things that have not been done before, encouraging usage in ways that the regulation did not foresee and, therefore, challenging the causality claim between good usage and regulations made by governments. From the point of view of technological innovation, deviance can be a cause of progress. Maybe not a crime (not all the time), but behind most fortunes there is a great deviance.

The following two case studies of technological transitions illustrate this nonlinear causality relation between deviance and technological progress.

Napster

In 1999, Napster went online creating a platform for people to exchange music files (mostly in MP3 format) through the use of Peer-to-Peer (P2P) networking technology. "Peer-to-Peer (P2P) is a way of structuring distributed applications such that the individual nodes have symmetric roles. Rather than being divided into clients and servers each with distinct roles, in P2P applications a node may act as both a client and a server" (Reynolds & Vahdat, 2013).

While Napster did not invent P2P, it was the first widely adopted technology based on this model, and its release consolidated P2P as an alternative to client-server models. The choice behind the network architecture of Napster was an act of deviance because of two important characteristics: "A peer-to-peer service generally uses bandwidth, storage, and/or CPU time provided by users of the service. Further, a robust peer-to-peer service should be decentralized enough that no administrator can disable the system" (Reynolds & Vahdat, 2013, pp. 485–496, 485).

The fact that P2P uses the hardware and bandwidth of the users decreases network costs for the provider of the service, creating an opportunity for small actors to enter markets that in a client-server model would be too expensive for them.

More importantly, the decentralized architecture of P2P means that the system cannot be easily "turned off." This was important, because Napster presented a direct challenge to copyright regulation.

The dawn of the MP3 age initiated a revolution in music distribution. While the data compression characteristics of the popular format made it possible for people to start exchanging music files online, it wasn't until P2P networking that this capacity became widely available.

For more than a decade (and well after the demise of Napster in 2001), the music industry fought the appropriation of digital technologies by users to try to save the physical CD album as the primary means of music distribution.

Notice-and-takedowns litigation was the main tool the music industry employed to fight against this technological deviance, but the industry went as far as suing individual users for hundreds of thousands of dollars for reparations and damages.

> The publicity over these and other cases triggered public questioning of the industry's motives and business model, and escalated growing discontent from its customer base. The loss of goodwill brought about the direct litigation campaign might have been acceptable collateral damage had it been effective, but it did not bring about any reduction in the amount of file sharing. Indeed, despite the unprecedented number of lawsuits, . . . P2P infringement actually appeared to increase over the relevant period. In late 2008 the music industry abruptly announced an abandonment of its mass litigation strategy against end users. (Giblin, 2011, p. 3)

Napster was shutdown in 2001. While file exchanges within the network were peer to peer, the system depended on central servers for its catalogue databases, and those servers could be turned off.

After Napster went dark, other P2P networks (e.g., Gnutella or Torrent) took its place. The act of deviance Napster represented challenged a business model that was, in the digital age, socially unacceptable despite the wishes of the dominant players in the market, and the efforts of the regulatory entities that sided with them.

The claim that the regulatory regime from predigital times was the cause of positive user behaviors in the emerging digital era was challenged by the millions of users that made Napster a popular music distribution platform, despite the legal ramifications of those actions. A network of users appropriated digital technologies created by the music industry in ways unforeseen by its designers (the compact disc was developed by Philips and Sony and its release is the triggering event of the digital revolution), to challenge the regulatory regime governing information technologies.

Later, the complex-creative system absorbed P2P technologies making them mainstream, legal and desirable. For example, anybody who has placed a phone call through Skype has used a P2P technology ("P2P communications," 2012). The multibillion-dollar technology of Voice over IP, an unintended consequence of P2P, in its turn, disrupted long-distance markets, giving us the social connectivity we have and cherish today.

Spotify, the popular (and 100% legal) music service, used a hybrid P2P architecture until 2014 (TorrentFreak, 2014) and MP3 files accounted for most of the music sales in the same year. Apple's iTunes, and not a legacy music company, is the main actor in the market. Also, millions of artists shared their compositions for free in Soundcloud and YouTube, in what is probably the most interesting of all the consequences triggered by Napster.

Napster's deviance was the genesis of many new legal markets that have modified social conventions and forced changes in business practices and regulatory environments.

Behind the fortune of Skype, Apple, and Spotify, there are many great crimes. Those crimes challenged regulatory regimes that protected incumbent business practices in music distribution. People did go to prison or paid hefty fines for these transgressions, but what used to be unthinkable (dirt cheap digital access to music) is now the status quo.

Regulatory regimes of information technology were not the cause of good usage practices. Instead, deviance caused changes in those regimes and disruptive innovation took place despite those regulations.

Uber

Taxis are one of the oldest "legacy" technologies in urban transportation. The first records of vehicles for hire can be traced to the 1640s in Paris and by 1654 it is possible to identify in the United Kingdom the first "Ordinances for the Regulation of Hackney Coachmen" to dictate usage and service rules (Mundy & Nelson, 2010, p. 1). This ordinance predates the combustion engine, so the first Hackneys (or "Hacks") were horse carriages.

A "fare-registering apparatus" (what we would call today a taximeter) was patented in 1892 by Friedrich Wilhelm Gustav Bruhn who is regarded as the father of the tool that gave us the final sociotechnical component of the traditional taxi industry (Bruhn, 1892). The taximeter is so essential to the "taxi experience" that it also gave us the etymology for naming the industry.

The main creative agents (the intellect) involved in the complex-creative system include the management of taxi companies, cab drivers themselves, the employees of dispatch centers, and the teams of car manufacturing companies. Other smaller actors participate too: employees of smaller companies design and sell the taximeter, the communication radio equipment, and credit card representatives provide mobile credit card terminals. Also, aftermarket entrepreneurs provide customization options to outfit a taxi (i.e., dividing walls, televisions, etc.).

The car and its aftermarket equipment plus the communication tools in the taxis and in the dispatch centers form the building blocks of this complex-creative system.

Finally, city ordinances and regulation create the rules that have shaped the taxi experience since its inception.

It is not hard to follow the evolution of taxi regulations. In the seventeenth century, the British government passed the Ordinances for the Regulation of Hackney Coachmen to deal with what were, according to those with regulatory power, the undesirable usage practices of this emerging technology. This first regulation dealt in particular with what the British government deemed the key problem of this technology: the inconvenience provoked by the rising number of service providers within the city of London.

This ordinance instructed that "the number of persons keeping Hackney-coaches and Hackney horses for Coaches, within the City of London, Westminster and six miles about the late lines of communication, do not exceed at one time two hundred; nor the Hackney-coaches to be used by them, three hundred; nor their Hackney Horses for Coaches do not exceed the number of six hundred" (Firth & Rait, 1654).

It also named (by name!) the first 13 individuals allowed to keep Hackney-coaches, and Hackney-Coach-horses, formalizing a regulatory monopoly.

Lastly, the ordinance gave authority to the Court of Aldermen to impose "Rules, Directions, and Bye-laws, for and concerning the distribution of Coaches amongst the said Coach-men, their places of Standing, their Rates for Carriages, Penalties for disobedience by them."

From the text of this original legislation, it is clear that the central objective was to create artificial scarcity where market forces were creating abundance.

Other rules emerged around the taxi industry, most claiming to be put in place to cause good user experience. For example, London's Hackney drivers (the iconic black cabs) have to be able to approve a very demanding series of tests designed to "demonstrate that [they] are able to take passengers to their destination by the shortest possible route. To do this [they] must first learn the 'Knowledge of London' and then pass a series of examinations" (Mayor of London, 2012).

Because of its difficulty, the Knowledge (always with capital K), as this test is known, has limited the capacity of individuals to become cab drivers in London, making taxis scarce.

While no other city in the world has rules as draconian as London's taxi ordinances, most cities do regulate taxis in one way or another, giving them a monopolistic access to a market rendered artificially scarce by imposing elevated regulatory barriers to entry in the name of safety concerns. In most cities in the United States, taxis have a level of regulation comparable to that of a utility, and they enjoy a relation with their regulatory entities (including the capacity to capture them) similar to the ones utilities have.

There is abundant literature to demonstrate that a liberalization of the taxi markets would have an increase in the quality of service offered to the user. Those benefits include:

- "Lower fares, as more service providers compete in the market.
- Lower operating costs, due to competitive incentives.
- Improved service quality, as competition encourages taxi drivers to provide friendly reliable service and clean vehicles, and to avoid taking advantage of passenger ignorance. With competition reputation becomes more important.
- Innovations such as shared-ride markets and special services for the disabled, creating market niches where none had existed.
- Increasing demand for taxi services, as prices fall and quality improves" (Moore & Balaker, 2006, p. 112).

In 2010, the company UberCab (today, Uber) launched its mobile apps for the IOS (iPhone) and Android systems.

These apps appropriated mobile technologies in a way that improved the vehicle-for-hire user experience by making it possible to request a ride with one click, using the GPS included in many smartphones. The app removed all the uncertainty associated with hauling a taxi, and introduced a trust network into the system that includes user reviews for drivers, real-time tracking of the ride, and other key enhancements like direct payment, removing the need (and the risk) of using a credit card or cash to complete the transaction.

While the first Uber services were oriented to the limousine market, the concept rapidly evolved and other competitors emerged (e.g., Lyft). The appropriation of Internet technologies to upgrade the vehicle-for-hire market was so radical, that it became a category in itself, under the umbrella term of car-sharing, and part of the bigger concept of the "sharing economy" or, maybe more appropriately, "P2P economy." Private individuals can now register to participate in the network, and offer their services as a driver for hire. Uber provides the insurance and acts as a trusted third party in the transaction.

The system created abundance where the regulation had created scarcity, and given the high rate of adoption of new users, (Tiku, 2013) it is fair to affirm that the market reacted positively to this innovation that challenged the regulatory monopoly of the legacy taxi industry, without a degradation of the quality of the service (quite the opposite) or a decrease in safety. In fact, the trusted third party model that Uber offers has increased the safety of taxi services in emerging markets.

These facts alone should be enough to cast a doubt about the causality claim contained in taxi regulations: An important portion of the user base has voted with their smartphones, and they do not think that taxi regulations are the cause of enhanced user experience. While not a true zero sum game (Uber users may still use taxis, and taxi companies may deploy their own apps) this rapid adoption of the new technology against the regulation-dependent incumbent model demonstrates that it is hard to claim that legacy regulation in the vehicle-for-hire industry causes better user experience.

Uber has been confronted by contemporary versions of Red Flag Laws. For example, in Paris, a change in regulation forced Uber drivers to wait 15 minutes before allowing a passenger to board the car (AFP, 2013). This rule degraded the user experience in the name of protecting the legacy monopoly.

Like Napster, Uber management understood that behind their innovation was a great deviance, but unlike Napster, Uber knew that there are ways to oppose the law and survive. Justin Kintz, Uber's policy director for the Americas, admitted in an interview in June 2014 that "In 128 of our cities, we've got regulatory issues in about 128 of our cities" (Hume, 2014). Uber has built a budget and a team to lobby at the scale of city politics (GrowthHackers, 2013) and selected David Plouffe who managed the successful campaign of President Obama in 2008 as its Senior Vice President of Policy and Strategy (Isaac, 2014) to fight local and city regulatory commissions.

The legality of the business model of this multibillion-dollar corporation is controversial because of the shape of the regulatory environment surrounding the technologies it appropriated. User desires, on the other hand, are clear.

IV. CONCLUSION: CAUSES AND CONSEQUENCES

Governmental regulatory entities claim that regulatory regimes for technologies cause good people to do good things and that breaking the law is bad behavior.

In reality, good consequences come from deviant causes all the time in the technological complex-creative system. Technology regimes are notoriously bad at forecasting positive second-degree consequences of emerging technologies, and when the value proposition of a market changes because an emerging technology is widely adopted, creative deviance is used as a mechanism to change the regulatory regime. Entrepreneurial actors in those cases engage in a kind of causal bargaining between the present and the future, deciding that a future good justifies a present deviance.

Every technological appropriation is an act of rebellion, and some of those rebel acts are also illegal. Nevertheless, those acts of rebellion often cause positive social transformations that later become a new status quo and cause changes in regulatory regimes. The crime comes first, the benefits later.

While this chapter has placed the emphasis on the changes brought to the complex-creative system by emerging technologies, the innovations that improve the world do not have to happen only at the level of changes in the building blocks.

Rosa Parks got into a General Motors bus in December 1955. The bus was a 1948 TDH-3610 for 36 passengers with a diesel engine and hydraulic transmission (GM, The Henry Ford, 2010) (the tool or building block). Rosa Parks was a user of the very established technology that was the public transportation system of Montgomery, Alabama. The creative agents were the managers of the system, the drivers, and all the people involved in making the technology perform its task. Many rules converged to give shape to this public transportation system, including the laws of segregation, or Jim Crow laws. Rosa Parks decided to challenge the rules of the system using the technology in a deviant way: "When a white man entered the bus, the driver (following the standard practice of segregation) insisted that all four blacks sitting just behind the white section give up their seats so that the man could sit there. Mrs. Parks, who was an active member of the local NAACP, quietly refused to give up her seat" (The Henry Ford, 2008).

In this case, it was not an entrepreneur who challenged the rules of the complex-creative system through the appropriation of a new technology, but a user acting deviantly against the regulatory regime that established how the technology should be used.

Acts of civil disobedience, like that of Rosa Parks when using a transportation technology, have successfully forced changes in social norms and regulatory regimes. It is not my intention to compare her heroic action to fight against the unfair segregation laws to the for-profit interests of Uber, even if the copyright reform movement behind both Napster and the overarching P2P economy has its own civil liberties struggles. When Larry Lessig, professor of law and leadership at Harvard Law School, wrote about the suicide of copyright activist Aaron Swartz, he defined his acts of civil disobedience as a "moral obligation" (Lessig, 2013).

Technological deviance is a kind of civil disobedience through appropriation (sometimes with a for-profit objective) to subvert regulatory regimes. The more important consequences of emerging technologies often come in the form of changes in social behaviors once the users appropriate them. Those deviant innovations often trigger changes in the law, making great fortunes in the process.

REFERENCES

AFP. (2013, December 28). Taxis: Les VTC devront bien patienter quinze minutes. Retrieved from http://www.liberation.fr/economie/2013/12/28/taxis-les-vtc-devront-bien-patienter-quinze-minutes_969443

Arthur, W. B. (2009). *The nature of technology: What it is and how it evolves.* New York: Free Press.

Bruhn, F. (1892). Patent US485529—Apparatus for vehicles. Retrieved from http://www.google.com/patents/US485529

Cardiio, Inc. (2015). Cardiio: Your heart rate monitor, reinvented. Retrieved from http://www.cardiio.com/

Christensen, C. M. (2011). *The innovator's dilemma: The revolutionary book that will change the way you do business.* New York: Harper Business.

Coleman, E. Gabriella. *Coding freedom: The ethics and aesthetics of hacking.* Princeton University Press, 2013.

Creative Commons. (2011). "About." Retrieved on October 13, 2014, from https://creativecommons.org/about

Eglash, R. (2004). Appropriating technology: An introduction. *Appropriating technology: Vernacular science and social power.* University of Minnesota Press.

Firth, C. H., & Rait R. S. (eds.) (1654, June). An ordinance for the regulation of Hackney-Coachmen in London and the places adjacent. Retrieved from http://www.british-history.ac.uk/report.aspx?compid=56562

Flink, J. J. (1990). *The automobile age.* Cambridge, MA: MIT Press.

Gámez, E. H. C., & Nieto-Gómez, R. (2011). The case of "Illicit appropriation" in the use of technology. *Technology for facilitating humanity and combating social deviations: Interdisciplinary perspectives.* Hershey, PA: IGI Global.

Gates, B. (1976, February 3). An open letter to hobbyists. Retrieved from http://www.digibarn.com/collections/newsletters/homebrew/V2_01/index.html

Giblin, R. (2011). *Code wars: 10 years of P2P software litigation.* Cheltenham, UK: Edward Elgar Publishing.

GM, the Henry Ford. (2010). Bus specifications. Retrieved from https://www.thehenryford.org/exhibits/rosaparks/specifications.asp

GrowthHackers. (2013). What's fueling Uber's growth engine? Retrieved from https://growthhackers.com/companies/uber/

Henry Ford, The. (2008). Rosa Parks bus—The story behind the bus. Retrieved from https://www.thehenryford.org/exhibits/rosaparks/story.asp

Hume, E. (2014, June 12). Uber's rapid growth pits innovation against existing laws. Retrieved from http://www.npr.org/sections/alltechconsidered/2014/06/12/321008384/ubers-rapid-growth-pits-innovation-against-existing-laws

Isaac, M. (2014, August 19). Uber picks David Plouffe to wage regulatory fight. Retrieved from http://www.nytimes.com/2014/08/20/technology/uber-picks-a-political-insider-to-wage-its-regulatory-battles.html?_r=0

Kuhn, T. S. (1996). *The structure of scientific revolutions.* Chicago, IL: University of Chicago Press.

Lessig, L. (2001, December 19) Innovation, Regulation, and the Internet. Retrieved from http://prospect.org/article/innovation-regulation-and-internet

Lessig, L. (2013, December 22). Why they mattered: Aaron Swartz (1986–2013). Retrieved from http://www.politico.com/magazine/story/2013/12/aaron-swartz-obituary-101418.html#.VWIkgs6gT8E

Lindtner, S., Anderson, K., & Dourish, P. (2012). Cultural appropriation: Information technologies as sites of transnational imagination. In *Proceedings of the ACM 2012 conference on Computer Supported Cooperative Work.* ACM.

Lite, J., & Scientific American. (2008, December 16). Baby's hot wheels: An incubator made of car parts. Retrieved from http://www.scientificamerican.com/blog/post/babys-hot-wheels-an-incubator-made-2008-12-16/?id=babys-hot-wheels-an-incubator-made-2008-12-16

Mayor of London. (n.d.). The "knowledge of London" examination system. *The "Knowledge of London."* Available at: https://tfl.gov.uk/info-for/taxis-and-private-hire/become-a-taxi-licensee/learn-the-knowledge-of-london

Mohr, L. B. (1969). Determinants of innovation in organizations. *The American Political Science Review, 63*(1), 111–126. doi:10.2307/1954288

Moore, A. T., & Balaker, T. (2006). Do economists reach a conclusion on taxi deregulation? *Econ Journal Watch, 3*(1), 109–132.

Mundy, R., & Nelson, J. (2010). *Taxi!: urban economies and the social and transport impacts of the taxicab.* Burlington, VA: Ashgate Publishing.

Noble, D. F. (1978). America by design: Science, technology, and the rise of corporate capitalism. *Science, Technology & Human Values, 3*(1), 111. doi:10.1177/016224397800300158

Priest, G. L. (1993). The origins of utility regulation and the "Theories of Regulation" debate. *The Journal of Law and Economics, 36*(S1), 289–323. doi:10.1086/467276

Reynolds, P., & Vahdat, A. (2013). Peer-to-peer keyword search: A retrospective. *Middleware 2013 Lecture Notes in Computer Science, 485*–496. doi:10.1007/978-3-642-45065-5_25

Rushby, A. J., Claire, M. W., Osborn, H., & Watson, A. J. (2013). Habitable zone lifetimes of exoplanets around main sequence stars. *Astrobiology*, 13(9), 833–849. doi:10.1089/ast.2012.0938

Stigler, G. J. (1971). The Theory of Economic Regulation. *The Bell Journal of Economics and Management Science*, 2(1), 3-21. doi:10.2307/3003160

Tiku, N. (2013, April 12). Leaked: Uber's internal revenue and ride request numbers. Retrieved from http://valleywag.gawker.com/leaked-ubers-internal-revenue-and-ride-request-number-1475924182

TorrentFreak. (2013, September 17). Pirate party crashes spy drone in front of German chancellor Angela Merkel. Retrieved from http://torrentfreak.com/pirate-party-crashes-spy-drone-in-front-of-german-chancellor-angela-merkel-130917/

TorrentFreak. (2014, April 16). Spotify starts shutting down its massive P2P network. Retrieved from https://torrentfreak.com/spotify-starts-shutting-down-its-massive-p2p-network-140416/

Wu, T. (2010). The master switch: The rise and fall of information empires. New York: Alfred A. Knopf.

EDITORS' COMMENTARY

Governments have always faced the challenge of how to influence the behavior of their citizens. In most instances, governments follow the basics of a behaviorist model: they reward citizens for behavior they want to encourage, and punish citizens for behavior they want to prevent. The general assumption has been that punishment causes behavior to stop and rewards cause behavior to continue. Obviously, this is a simplistic assumption based on a limited idea of causality, usually efficient causation is the only focus. We can see that a far more complex approach is needed by considering the example of the penal system. The relationship between crime and punishment is complex: the level of crime tends to be related to complex economic, cultural, and other factors, with punishment being only one factor among many.

Nieto-Gómez has considered cause and effect in a far more complex situation: when governments attempt to regulate behavior regarding emerging technologies. The tools adopted by governments to regulate emerging technologies are the same ones used to regulate behavior in other domains, consisting of rewards and punishments. Even when well-established technologies are the targets of regulations, the relationship between rewards, punishments, and behavior regarding the technology is seldom straightforward. As Nieto-Gómez points out, with emerging technologies, the number of unknown and unpredictable factors dramatically increases.

With emerging technologies, the government has to become even more involved in the task of predicting both the use of new technologies and future behavior. This becomes a highly challenging and, at times, an impossible task, because of the tremendously fast pace of technological innovations in the twenty-first century. For example, Facebook, Twitter, Snapchat, Yik Yak, and many other such innovations were not predicted a few decades ago, and it is impossible to predict what new innovations will arise in another few decades. This means that the use of such new technologies, such as the use of Twitter for "e-Swarming," is very difficult to regulate. As Nieto-Gómez points out, it is easy for governments to make elementary mistakes when attempting to causally shape behavior in these rapidly changing domains.

Inevitably, social scientists have stepped forward to offer advice about how governments can more effectively shape behavior. Books such as *Nudge* (Thaler & Sunstein, 2009) and *Blink* (Gladwell, 2007) explore implicit cognitive processes, suggesting how governments can subtly move people in one direction or another "for their own good," without people being conscious of the government influence. The general assumption seems to be that people are influenced by the environment anyway, so why should government programs intentionally move them toward "desired goals." The last time this kind of social science–based "social engineering" argument was put forward was by B. F. Skinner and other behaviorists, through books such as *Beyond Freedom and Dignity* (1971). There was a loud and violent reaction to the behaviorists and the idea of government "shaping" human behavior. No such reaction has been evident to the twenty-first-century social engineering proposals—a sign of political change.

REFERENCES

Gladwell, M. (2007). *Blink: The power of thinking without thinking*. New York: Back Bay Books.
Skinner, B. F. (1971). *Beyond freedom and dignity*. New York: Knopf.
Thaler, R. H., & Sunstein, C. R. (2009). *Nudge: Improving decisions about health, wealth and happiness*. New York: Penguin.

Part Seven

....

Causal Concepts and Theological and Poetry Studies

21

Theological Studies

Margaret M. Yee

The question of causality raises broad and profound questions for theological studies. There is good reason. A quick search of the history of ideas easily explains why.

For theological studies, the belief that we are created and have a divine creator is fundamental to monotheism (Ward, 1996). It was not until the rise of modern science that belief in divine creation began to be challenged radically. Prior to this period the concept of divine creation had remained unquestioned. Changes in thought of paradigmatic proportions, however, first came about with the Copernican Revolution. As will be seen, highly complex challenges to *divine causation* developed as a consequence.

This chapter will seek to present in broad brushstrokes the overall dilemmas that have confronted theological studies since the rise of modern science. Basic causes and their consequences will be identified. It will be argued that ultimately the primary concern was with the principles of knowing for *all* inquiry, including theology. Ongoing struggles to settle this issue particularly with regard to *divine causation* will be assessed in the light of current research in theology as well as the sciences.

I. AN IMPORTANT BACKDROP: THE RISE OF MODERN SCIENCE AND ITS COMPLEXITIES

In 1543, Nicolaus Copernicus published his book *De Revolutionibus Orbium Coelestium* (1965). Prior to this time, the geocentric more static model of the heavens by Ptolemy (c.100–170 CE), which had described Earth as stationary at the center of the universe, had prevailed for 1,400 years. In sharp contrast, a heliocentric model was introduced by Copernicus. He proposed that the Sun was at the center of the Solar System, the heavenly bodies rotating around the Sun, and Earth rotating daily on its axis. Tycho Brahe (1546–1601), through extensive observations, further advanced and refined Copernicus's thought. After Brahe's unexpected death, his work was developed by his assistant Johannes Kepler. Kepler's publications from 1596 through to 1619 proved revolutionary in support of Copernicus's heliocentric model of the cosmos.

It was in this period also that Galileo Galilei, through the design of his own telescope, made observations of Venus, which resulted in leading astronomers converting to various heliocentric models. Gone was the former more static Ptolemaic view of the universe. Even more important was Galileo's effective application of mathematics and experimentation in scientific exploration. By the middle of the seventeenth century change in scientific outlook and research method had become widely accepted. In particular, Isaac Newton's book *Philosophiae Naturalis Principia Mathematica,* first published in 1687, formally expressed his law of universal gravitation along with his three laws of motion.

The above thumbnail sketch of the rise of modern science portrays key aspects of the Copernicus-Galileo-Newton scientific revolution that brought a major shift in the history of ideas. The impact of the change affected all areas of study in the seventeenth century. The predominant Ptolemaic geocentric model of the universe, which had been developed from a view held from ancient time by thinkers such as the notable Greek philosopher Aristotle (BCE 394–BCE 322), was no longer acceptable. Not only was there a change in how the universe was viewed. A new research method, combining observation and experimentation, also challenged research methods in other disciplines, including theology.

As will be discussed more fully below, theology, in the twelfth century, had unfortunately become aligned with the more static concepts of *motion* and *rest* in Aristotelian thought. It therefore needed to come to terms with all these changes of paradigmatic proportion.

II. IMPACT OF PARADIGM CHANGES: METHODOLOGICAL ISSUES

Thomas Kuhn's well-discussed reflections in *The Structure of Scientific Revolutions* (1970) has alerted us to the many complexities involved when a paradigm change occurs. Issues relating to one's method of approach and the credibility of one's claims to have knowledge of the world are called into question.

Paradigmatic changes carry in their sway a threefold impact, raising questions that are: (i) *metaphysical* (concerned with one's worldview); (ii) *epistemological* (concerned with the credibility of the knowledge gained), and (iii) *methodological* (concerned with how one acquires trustworthy knowledge). Unless these fundamental and closely related issues are recognized and tackled, conflicts in each of these areas will prove problematic and difficult to resolve.

Of prime importance to this chapter on *Questioning Causality—Theological Studies* is an analysis of how the paradigmatic change of the scientific revolution not only brought challenges to previous unquestioned views of reality and the search to know for theology, but also caused immense hostility between science and religion. These reactive responses led to deep social and intellectual barriers, preventing communication and dialogue.

There was also the additional problem of theology's claim to knowledge of the world and divine causation through *Inspiration* and *Revelation*. In the light of new empirical research methods in the sciences, could claims of *Inspiration* and *Revelation* still be justified as acceptable ways for acquiring knowledge of a divine creator and creation itself? For theology, these methodological complexities, which needed unravelling and addressing, were not recognized at the time. As a consequence, deep methodological differences between theology and the sciences arose and remained unresolved.

III. CONFLICTS IN SCIENCE AND RELIGION: CAUSES AND CONSEQUENCES

Galileo's Disputes with the Catholic Church

At the rise of modern science, one of these dilemmas was brought to the fore by Galileo's disputes with the Catholic Church. As precise methodological differences were not easily identified, prolonged impassioned struggles to overcome contentious difficulties followed. These resulted ultimately in Galileo's excommunication from the church. The problem was twofold. The changed heliocentric and active thought-world in the sciences challenged the geocentric and more static worldview of earlier Aristotelian natural philosophy, expounded by Ptolemy. In turn, since theology had become closely aligned with the more static thought-world of Aristotelian natural philosophy, it was inevitable that theological disputes would arise as well.

In the twelfth century, Christian Doctrine, with its claims to *Inspiration and Revelation*, had been presented within the contextual framework of Aristotelian natural philosophy by Thomas Aquinas. His scholarly writings, *Summa Contra Gentiles* (1975) and the monolithic *Summa Theologica* (1990), had sought to convey Christian teaching within the framework of the thought of his day. Once challenges to the more static concepts of *motion* and *rest* in Aristotelian thought resulted from the rise and advances of modern science, and the changed scientific thought-world was not distinguished from an envisaged challenge to the authority of Christian Doctrine itself, serious conflict resulted.

Major research undertaken on the topic "The Validity of Theology as an Academic Discipline in the Light of the History and Philosophy of Science with Special Reference to Relevant Aspects of the Thought of Austin Farrer" (Yee, 1987) critically assessed these impregnable difficulties, especially with regard to Galileo's controversy with the Catholic Church. The investigation indicated, among other things, that differences between theology and modern science are in essence methodological rather than doctrinal.

In hindsight it is possible to see that because the actual causes of the dilemmas were not properly identified or carefully analyzed at the time, the residual effects of the great disagreement between Galileo and the Catholic Church smoldered on for some 350 years. It was not until 1992, when Pope John Paul II officially apologized, acknowledging the mistaken interpretation of the scriptures at the time by theologians, that dialogue between theology and the sciences concerning the nature of the universe became more amenable. Vitriolic partisanship and unhelpful, emotional passions had prevented proper understanding of the issues at stake for well over three centuries (Cowell, 1992).

Nor does the story of the conflicts between science and religion end here.

Charles Darwin and "The Species Question"

After the traumas with Galileo in the seventeenth century, in the nineteenth century an even more catastrophic challenge to theological studies arose with the publication in 1859 of Charles Darwin's book *On the Origin of Species by Means of Natural Selection*. The change in paradigm was formidable, constituting in essence a direct threat to Christian Doctrine. The long-established belief that the universe was in fact the work of a divine creator came under severe questioning. One of the unforgettable incidents was the acrimonious debate in 1860 of the Bishop of Oxford, Samuel Wilberforce, with Thomas Huxley in the Oxford University Museum. Again, passionate and vitriolic resistance, on this occasion to natural selection, prevented a proper understanding of the actual causes of the conflicts. The masked problems remained unaddressed.

Darwin had argued that existing species had evolved from a common ancestry, had survived the struggle for existence, and now existed in their present form as a result of natural selection, not design. Obvious gaps in his meticulously kept record of observed species were explained by Darwin as the nonsurvival of a large number of variations. Adaptation had enabled survival. His view challenged the long-established theological position that each species was created in its present form for a purposive end. If Darwin's argument concerning common ancestry were true, then belief in man's elevated and unique place in creation was indeed under threat (Yee, 1987, p. 47).

Historically, long wrangles over Darwin's espousal of natural selection and his "species question" ensued. Theologians, unable to produce contrary evidence to Darwin's findings, resorted to rhetorical argument, pouring scorn and abuse on natural selection and the species question. Their efforts, however, were only to be further thwarted later by advances in genetic and embryological studies. As support for the theory of evolution continued to develop, mutual antagonism escalated from the ferocity of the conflicts. A sharp separation and compartmentalization of science from religion followed, and the gap has widened globally since.

Contrary to the popular view that the Church's conflicts with Galileo and Darwin were instances in which the Church's doctrines per se were at odds with the findings of science, critical analysis can reveal the actual deep-seated nature of the problems. The two distinctly separate philosophical outlooks that emerged were not only over a difference in worldview (metaphysical) but also over the ways that knowledge can be acquired critically and empirically (epistemological) and the method of approach to be used to acquire knowledge (methodology). Observation, mathematics, and experimentation had enabled the sciences to advance scientific knowledge. The major question was whether methods of enquiry being applied in all other disciplines, theology included, could be shown to be comparable.

IV. DISCLOSURES FROM THE HISTORY AND PHILOSOPHY OF SCIENCE

Since this period, residual effects of scientific advances in empirical research coupled with advances in evolutionary theory have required the attention of *all* disciplines, not least humanities, philosophy, and theology. Space does not permit tracking the many routes of enquiry, some more productive than others, which have been undertaken.

Pursuits have covered a broad spectrum of methodological questions across the disciplines in an attempt to come to terms with serious research in a science-oriented world. The writings in particular of A. C. Crombie in *Medieval and Early Modern Science* (1959, Vols. I and II), W. Whewell's *History of the Inductive Sciences* (1837, vol. 1), and in more recent times Mary Hesse's *Revolutions and Reconstructions in the Philosophy of Science* (1980) along with J. Hedley Brooke's *Science and Religion* (1991) provide invaluable discussions of the long struggles for disciplines to come to terms with meeting the demands of scientific enquiry over the years. Current debates in the social sciences over "qualitative" versus "quantitative" methods of study, and discussions in clinical medicine in search of improved principles of practice in health and safety to prevent misdiagnosis are just two examples of continuing methodological concerns.

Promisingly, in the twentieth and now the twenty-first century, critical studies have enabled researchers to unearth and refine underlying methodological issues across the disciplines to establish the origins (i.e., *the causation*) of ourselves and our world. In actuality the overall methodological concern at heart has been with principles of knowing: *How can we know, how can we know that we know, and how can we know that we don't know?*

V. PRINCIPLES OF KNOWING: SCIENCE, HUMANITIES, AND THEOLOGY

My own earlier enquiry into the validity of theology, referred to above, sought to pinpoint what these principles of knowing might be. I began first by investigating the principles employed when great scientific discoveries have been made in the world. The next step considered whether these principles were also applicable to the arts disciplines, including theology.

A central inescapable principle was identified (Yee, 1987, chs. 3–6, pp. 246–249). The application of *both* empirical (sensory) *and* critical (cognitive) thought in close interrelation was specifically pinpointed as the means by which scientists were enabled to avoid error and establish the facts of a case as best as possible. Interestingly, my research also showed that this central principle of applying *both* empirical (sensory, practical) *and* critical (cognitive, rational) thought together was already being used in certain areas by the humanities and in historical and philosophical theology. These examples made clear that the principles of empirical enquiry adopted by the sciences were in fact applicable to disciplines in the arts faculties as well (Yee, 1987, chs. 7–9).

On closer analysis, my research also indicated the importance of recognizing that scientific principles, which are generally described by most as "*empirical*" or "*scientific,*" are more properly described as "*empirico-cognitive.*" The reasons are as follows.

Since the rise of modern science, empirical methods of approach have been successful where cognitive thought has been tested by empirical means and vice versa. This primary action, which brings theory and practice into close interrelation, enables enquiry to harness and establish the credibility of our understanding of ourselves and the world around us. The action is indispensable regardless of whether the enquiry is in the humanities or the sciences. Without these crosschecks, one's research will be vulnerable to error, errors that the constraints and crosschecks of an "empirico-cognitive" approach would otherwise have quickly exposed (Yee, 1988).

Hence, given that the age-old academic question of *the nature of human beings and the question of their ultimate origin* is rearing its ugly head once again, it should be clear that research into the question of *causation* will need to comply with the demands of scientific and critical enquiry if the search is to prove successful.

Returning then to the main question in this chapter, and in the light of "empirico-cognitive" principles of knowing, what can be made of claims such as *divine causation*? Is the long-held belief that the origin of creation can be attributed to divine activity rather than chance, necessity, and natural selection sustainable?

Here is the nub of the issue: *Is causation best explained by divine action as theologians claim or by nature itself as nonbelieving scientists maintain?*

It will now become obvious why such a prolonged prologue to this chapter on *questioning causality—theological studies* has been thought essential.

Without this backdrop it would be difficult to appreciate how intolerable dilemmas between theology and the sciences arose, and proved irresolvable. It also partly explains why a residual separation still remains between the arts and the sciences. Only when such difficulties are understood in their contextual background, and seen as belonging to deeper methodological differences, will the passions and impasse created by past misunderstandings be possible to dismantle and traverse.

In the remainder of this article, a critical analysis of current questions for theological studies with regard to *divine causation* will be pursued. Application of the "empirico-cognitive" principles enunciated above, with direct reference to the thought of a renowned Oxford philosopher and theologian, Austin Marsden Farrer (1904–1968), will be undertaken. It was Farrer's writings that stirred my own thinking originally. Most importantly, it will be argued that Farrer's personal metaphysics has opened a way through the difficulties that have bogged down relations between theology and the sciences for centuries.

Farrer's innovative approach, presented in his Bampton Lectures and published in *The Glass of Vision*, began by examining *divine activity* within the context of *the human imagination*:

> The subject of these lectures is the form of divine truth in the human mind: ... Our intention is not to make truth as narrow as the Church which professes it, but as high as the God who proclaims it. (Farrer, 1948, p. 1)

His shift of focus to *the human imagination*, its functions and capacities (Farrer, 1948, chs. 2–4), was purposeful. He had spotted that curiosity was one of the prime functions of the human imagination, which inspired the human mind to think, search, and explore. In actuality he had placed his finger on the very pulse of the search to know, namely the workings of the human mind and of human consciousness. He argued that it was by this means that researchers of whatever ilk were motivated to conduct enquiry. He held, therefore, that this was true of research not only in the arts and the sciences, but in theological enquiry as well.

Farrer realized that once theological enquiry was freed from emotional traumas, it would be possible to undertake critical and scientific analysis (Farrer, 1948, p. 20–22). Hence, first and foremost, he set about examining the capacities and functions of *the human imagination*. His initial endeavor was to determine how the human mind explores reality. He perceived that this critical method could enable him to settle complex questions as to whether the ultimate origin of the universe was attributable to divine causation or natural causes. Nevertheless, he acknowledged that the exploration of causation, divine or natural, was far from straightforward.

At the close of this chapter, I shall argue that there are sound reasons for holding that the answer to the question of the *origin of the universe* may ultimately prove to be one of the greatest surprises for theologians and scientists alike.

VI. DIVINE CAUSATION

Our immediate task is to tackle the tenability of theology's claim of *divine causation*, a belief that Christian Doctrine has maintained was acquired by *Inspiration and Revelation*. Many questions arise as a consequence of such a claim: Is theology able to meet the demands of science in claiming knowledge of God, not least the belief that we have a Divine Creator and a world attributable to a Divine Hand? Are its claims reconcilable with the findings emanating from the sciences? Are these two bodies of learning compatible or incompatible? Would some form of *dialogue* between theology and the sciences prove mutually enlightening toward resolving the question of causation?

Extraordinarily, these very questions were ones taken up in a most poignant manner by Austin Farrer. At his untimely death in 1968 he was Warden of Keble College, University of Oxford. His thinking was well ahead of his times. In the following discussion it will be seen that his reflections not only offered an illuminative approach for underpinning theological studies philosophically in a scientific world, but also suggested innovative moves toward a philosophy of *all* knowledge.

From 1948 to1967, in his published works on philosophical theology, Farrer presented and developed *five distinctive moves* for establishing his innovative stance. Ultimately, they are the inchoate building blocks of a lively *philosophy of action*, which he argued was capable of conversing with evolutionary theory and the findings of modern science. The *five moves* were sequential, and may be quickly summarized as follows:

1. Most important of all was his primary move to investigate the function of the *human imagination*. In this way, he brought new insight into the capacities and powers of exploration of the human mind. This shift in worldview to what he called "a bigger view of the world" would enable conversation between the sciences and theology (Farrer, 1948, p. ix; 1966, p. 15).

2. In addition, he insisted that *theory* and *practical* experience, the *cognitive* and *empirical* aspects of human thought, were two sides of the one coin. Unity of both was paramount in order to perceive reality correctly. He represented reality in terms of a "cone" in which all aspects were integral to the whole (Farrer, 1948, pp. 22–27).

3. Thereafter, by drawing together the power of reflective thought and the mind's dynamic capacity to symbolize, analyze, create, image, and explore, he held that the *human imagination,* through "movements of thought" (Farrer, 1948, pp. 6–7, 76–77, ch. 4), was cognitively capable of discovering new horizons and perceiving new patterns along with dynamically active relations, lively connections, and rich insights of ourselves and the world around us. Farrer's independence of mind and thought should not be underrated. We shall see the impact of this step in his defence of claims of *Inspiration* and *Revelation* (Farrer, 1948, chs. 2–3).

4. Nor, for him, should the testing of our sensory experience by critical means be ignored, even by theologians. For Farrer, both the cognitive and sensory aspects of human experience were integral to the advances and demands of modern science. It was just as important for theology to meet these crosschecks (Farrer, 1948, chs 4–5).

5. Lastly, Farrer held that criteria of judgment needed to be established in theology as in the sciences. In this way, evidences "for" as well as evidences "against" situations could be properly assessed. For Farrer, this was an inescapable requirement of theology in a science-oriented world (Farrer, 1966, p. 10).

The following fuller discussion of his published works will help indicate how these *five distinctive moves* enabled him to unlock the tightly barred gate to theology in an increasingly science-oriented world. The result was the mapping of an illuminative and rational path forward for theology.

VII. THEOLOGICAL STUDIES: A WAY FORWARD

Initially, Farrer sought to rid theological thought of its static concepts of *motion* and *rest* adopted in the twelfth century when theology was aligned closely with Aristotelian Natural Philosophy. As mentioned above, the realization of how this could be achieved was published in his second book, *The Glass of Vision* in 1948, in which he undertook a deep consideration of the *human imagination*. Here we find a significant change in worldview from his earlier thinking in his first book, *Finite & Infinite*, published in 1943. The change is acknowledged by him in the new preface to the second edition of *Finite & Infinite* in 1959:

> *Eighteen to sixteen years ago I sat down and wrote this book, because I was possessed by the Thomist vision, and could not think it false. The core of the doctrine must somehow be sound, only it must be freed from the period trash in which it was embedded; it must be rescued from dependence on the breath-taking naivety of old linguistic realism.* (Farrer, 1959, p. ix)

The significance of this change in his thinking was paramount. Farrer effectively shifted the exposition of Christian Doctrine away from the premodern scientific and more static Ptolemaic worldview incumbent within Aristotelian natural philosophy to the lively and active thought-world of modern science and modern theology. He achieved this by expounding the traditional concepts of Christian Doctrine within the context of the lively and active functions of *the human imagination*. It is at this point that we are presented with the *first of his five groundbreaking moves*.

Whereas the idea of God in Aristotelian thought had been understood as *Actus Purus* or "Absolute Being," Farrer now argued for a more dynamic and active understanding of the Analogy of Being. For him, the nexus of the divine and the human, what he perceived as "the causal joint" of divine agency with human agency, required explanation if divine creation and the existence of a divine creator were to be properly accounted for. A "voluntary" personal metaphysics, incorporating expressions of dynamic *action* and *activity* of the human mind and the human agent, was considered conducive to the task (Conti, 1995, chs. 5–6). As a consequence, *Divine Being* came to be expressed by him as *agency acting* and *being as becoming*.

By focusing on the function and processes of *the human imagination* as a *first move*, Farrer presented his first step to *a new philosophy of action*, which he would develop and expound throughout his life.

The change was radical; the impact on theologizing profound. A marked shift that was *metaphysical*, involving a worldview that was personal and dynamic; *epistemological*, dealing with knowledge of God; and *methodological*, concerned with rational research principles, had begun. His dynamic concepts of *action* and *activity* developed in the context of his "voluntary" personal metaphysics were fundamental to his expositions of life and reality. Study of their *potentiality* would be pursued to achieve a better understanding of ourselves and our world.

Emphasis on the *human imagination* also opened up a more *inclusive* view of reality, enabling him to make his *second move*. An inclusive, expansive horizon made possible an investigation into whether creation was by *divine causation* or not. For Farrer, an *exclusive*, limited, and bounded view of reality, which, by sheer definition, excluded theological thought, was unacceptable. He argued that serious academic research, not least in the sciences, needed to address all possible issues. On the grounds of *inclusiveness* and wholeness of approach, his *second move* was in place (Farrer, 1948, chs. 2–3; 1966, ch. 2).

Next he established his *third* move. Here he tackled theology's claims of *inspiration* and *revelation*.

Through an analysis of the symbolic cognitive functions of the human imagination, Farrer was able to provide a rational defence for theological *inspiration* and *revelation*. He argued that lively images, related to significant events, develop cognitively. These form great and dominant images, capable of conveying profound, spiritual truths. Further development of these images on reflection as well as in lived practical belief ensured the continuation of depths of spiritual experience and faith (Farrer, 1948, chs. 3–5).

The apprehension of "great and dominant images" (Farrer, 1948, ch. 3) through the mind's capacity for "movements of thought" ((Farrer, 1948, chs. 3–5; 1963, pp. 93–96) revealed an understanding of their source, divine agency. Also, the relation of divine and human agency is accounted for rationally through the role and function of images. Their symbolic and metaphorical forms are capable of portraying different levels of signification at one and the same time ((Farrer, 1948, pp. 3, 33).

In particular, it was through the symbolic, dynamic, and vital activity of the *human imagination* that knowledge of the noncontradictory activity of the finite and infinite, and the human and divine aspects of the life and actions of Jesus, was acquired. The "movements of thought" of the *human imagination* were the process by which inspiration, revelation, and knowledge of human and divine things were acquired cognitively.

By mapping how inspiration and revelation were functions of higher-order thinking, and distinguishing these from weird and irrational thinking

(Farrer, 1948, pp. 16–28), Farrer was able to articulate aspects of higher thought, which are enabled by the *human imagination*. Consequently, he established a far more *holistic* view of reality in which a *multidimensional* understanding was embedded. His descriptions of the dynamic capacity of the *images* of the *human imagination* explained the means cognitively by which divine things are understood, developed, and communicated. His *third move* was "done and dusted."

Nevertheless, the question of *divine causation*, whilst rationally credible, required empirical grounding. This led to his development of his *fourth* and *fifth moves*.

One thing for Farrer was obvious. The "creationist" arguments in defence of theology, which rejected any consideration of the findings of evolutionary theory, were unacceptable. These did not meet the critical demands of scientific enquiry. On the other hand, theological apologetics that to a greater or lesser degree liberalized the claims of traditional theology were equally unacceptable.

The possibility of overcoming these dilemmas and advancing some form of *dialogue* between theology and the sciences was taken in hand by Farrer in 1966 with the publication of *A Science of God?* The task of the theologian, he argued, was not to "ape" the sciences but rigorously to apply the critical principles required for *all* academic enquiry. Whereas scientific enquiry was concerned with observation, experimentation, and measurement, the method of approach in theology required that comparable demands of critical thought should also be applied to its investigations. Thus, relevant documentary sources all required careful analysis, be these literary-historical, sociopolitical, physical, biological, psychological, or personal (Farrer, 1948, p. 78.). What was inescapable was "a scientific spirit" that took seriously the evidential force of the findings of critical enquiry (Farrer, 1966, chs. 1–2, 6).

Having described himself as *a practical man*, concerned to bring *thinking* and *practice* together, in his *fourth move*, Farrer insisted that the close interrelation of the *practical* aspects of life and faith with *theoretical* aspects was basic to enquiry if error was to be avoided. Thus the checks and constraints of empirical enquiry were as vital as the checks and constraints of cognitive enquiry. A failure to check assumptions and presuppositions in one's theological apprehensions, perceptions, or insights for their empirical justifiability was as unacceptable as a failure to check their logical consistency and cognitive credibility.

At this point, it is imperative to note that Farrer's innovative approach involved a marked departure from conventional procedures adopted in rational enquiry. Reliance on either a strictly *cognitive* or a strictly *empirical* approach to enquiry was unacceptable. Because of his own pragmatic outlook, which held thinking and practice together, Farrer was already committed to the critical demands of scientific enquiry, which I have described as "empirico-cognitive" (Farrer, 1966; Yee, 2011, p. 37).

Hence, using "empirico-cognitive" principles, Farrer tackled the question of whether evolutionary theory could be related to divine creation in a manner that was both rational and scientifically critical (Farrer, 1966, ch. 3 [(I)–4 [II]).

A close study of his works indicates that a set of *higher-order principles* was being mapped out in his writings. In this way ungrounded, unfounded, erroneous claims could be exposed. At the same time, the highest critical stringency would be achieved by adhering to the application of *both* empirical and cognitive checks and constraints in close interrelation. As a consequence, investigators would be enabled to explore different levels and different aspects of causation, whether in the sciences or in the arts faculties, particularly theology, using methods appropriate to each task.

From this viewpoint, he maintained that divine activity in creation, supportive of life, was concerned with a different aspect of causal activity to the ones engaging a physicist or a chemist (Farrer, 1948, pp. 6–7; 1966, ch. 3). Understood in this way, divine creation was not in fact in conflict with evolutionary theory. On a multidimensional and inclusive frontier, God and mature were reconcilable (Farrer, 1966, ch. 5). Thus we find him saying:

> If I am challenged to say in one sentence why there are what men call natural disasters, I shall say this: It is because God makes the world make itself; or rather, since the world is not a single being, he makes the multitude of created forces make the world, in the process of making or being themselves. It is this principle of divine action that gives the world such endless vitality, such vital variety in every part. (Farrer, 1966, p. 90)

By this means Farrer believed that his *fourth move* had been rationally defended: the locked gate, it would seem, could be unlocked.

Nevertheless, theological claims were by no means "guaranteed" by sheer conviction based on rational argument alone. Critical testing of such cognitive, rational claims was still essential—his position is unquestionably "empirico-cognitive." Facts of a case could only be properly established by *evidence*. Here we find him making his *fifth move*.

[1]His answer to the question of whether an empirical theology is possible was "Yes" and "No." The reason for this circumspect reply was to highlight that the methods of approach in theology and sciences were necessarily different because of their subject matter. What was, however, common and essential to apply in both areas of enquiry were the *higher principles* designated by him for cross-checking cognitive with empirical claims and vice versa, the very essence of modern scientific enquiry (Farrer, 1966, chs. 1, 6).

On these grounds, rational arguments in theology, as in the sciences, would ultimately only be possible to establish in the light of "evidence for" and "evidence against" any claims held. By applying this *fifth and last move* and testing

---

[1]A full analysis of Farrer's defence of the relation of divine and natural causes may be found in my article "Austin Farrer's Science of God" (op. cit.).

the evidential force of data, erroneous claims could be exposed, and the facts of a case established as best possible.

Farrer's *five distinctive moves* enabled him to achieve his twofold target for theological studies, namely: (i) to meet the demands of modern scientific investigation, and (ii) to provide a significantly rational argument for *divine causation* without compromising the demands of traditional theology. In essence, his *five moves* form the inchoate building blocks for *his new philosophy of action*.

VIII. THEOLOGICAL STUDIES IN A SCIENCE-WORLD

In 1967, in his last publication, *Faith and Speculation*, Farrer's commendation of a new philosophical approach for underpinning theology's claims of *divine causation* in a science-world was explicitly delineated. However, he insisted that there was still one *very definite difference* that needed to be reiterated between his *new philosophy of action* and the then-current *process theology*.

Instead of aligning with the process philosophy of Alfred Whitehead adopted by modern process theologians as Charles Hartshorne and others had done, Farrer expounded a highly illuminative pathway of greater significance for theology. Contrary to process theology, which was committed philosophically to an *immanent* view of God, Farrer maintained that there was no reason to renege on traditional theology's far more comprehensive *transcendent* and *immanent* view of God. Since the human imagination used by *all* disciplines was capable of traversing open, unlimited, and unbounded horizons, compatibility with scientific thought was in no way impaired by this broader worldview. A departure from traditional theology was therefore both unnecessary and unwarranted (Farrer, 1967, p. 170).

At journey's end, Farrer held that a strict choice between *divine causation* and *natural causation* need not be so firmly demarcated; a conciliatory stance was possible.

The following citations from contemporary scholarship since would seem to suggest that Farrer's innovative defence of the compatibility of *divine causation* and *causality in the natural world* is an explanation that should not be indiscriminately excluded from current thought.

IX. CONVERGENT FINDINGS AND OTHER PARALLELS: CURRENT RESEARCH

Proposals by Anthony Kenny in *Faith and Reason* in 1983 stressed the need of meeting empirical demands if a rational defence for theological claims were to be achieved. Despite a healthy agnosticism, Kenny, known earlier by Farrer, made clear the inescapability of these critical requirements for theological enquiry. His concern, however, was whether theology could meet such a demand. Interestingly, in one of his most recent publications, *What I Believe* (2006), Kenny has proposed that mind is a *capacity* and not a substance, and

it is not to be confused with body that is a physical substance. Holistic considerations of human agency are raised by such thinking. My own questions
are these. Given Kenny's stance, where might one place spiritual things?
Are these integral to mind, or are they of a higher order, yet related to mind
and body? The implications of such are very important when considering
causal relations.

One is also reminded of Rom Harré's earlier thoughts in *Causal Powers—A
Theory of Natural Necessity* (1975) published with E. H. Madden. Their chapter on the rebuttal of the central pillars of the Humean theory (Harré &
Madden, 1975, ch. 3), followed by their argument for the importance of
"causal powers" (Harré & Madden, 1975, ch. 5) and "potentialities," (Harré
& Madden, 1975, ch. 9) do seem to fit happily with the particular concepts
of activity and action depicted by Farrer. It will be seen that their "fleshing
out" of their notion of "causal powers" aligns their understanding unmistak-
ably with the form of activity so vital to scientific considerations to which
Farrer also adhered. In addition, Harré's description of his Realms 1, 2, and 3
beings, in his much later publication of *Varieties of Realism* (1986, chs. 2–3),
provides us with valuable distinctions whereby spiritual things may well be
classed as Realm 3 beings. Realm 3 beings will not be available to direct detection, they include such "beings" as quantum states, naked singularities, social
structure, and Freudian complexes (Harré, 1986, p. 73). To these, theological
concepts such as Trinity, Incarnation, and Resurrection, though not cited by
Harré, could, I believe, be added (Yee, 1987, pp. 246–280).

Turning to ongoing research in philosophy of religion, invaluable contemporary studies of *causal relations* have been pursued by a breadth of scholars
concerned with a more holistic understanding of creation similar to Farrer's.
One thinks of the earlier "cumulative argument" presented by Basil Mitchell
in his book *The Justification of Religious Belief* (1973). This concept was developed significantly by Caroline Franks Davis, one of Mitchell's former students,
in her most worthwhile publication *The Evidential Force of Religious Experience*
(1989, chs. 4, 9). Her discussions of different religious experiences and the
critical assessment of these are particularly helpful (Davis, 1989, chs. 1–2).
In addition, it is essential to mention the robust discussion found in Janet
Martin Soskice's publication of *Metaphor and Religious Language* (1985).
The vital importance of Soskice's research has made clear that the very nature
of the lively relations of thought and language is better understood in terms of
interanimation theory rather than Max Black's *interactive theory* (Soskice, 1985,
pp. 38–43). She indicates how metaphor is an "intercourse of thoughts" by
which networks of associations in thought operate, linking up with models
in complex cognitive processing (Soskice, 1985, pp. 43–51).

Lively traversing of specific areas of essential enquiry have developed for us
a vital picture of aspects of Farrer's dynamic understanding of divine/human
action, commended in his *new philosophy of action*.

We may also note present wider, commonly cited ongoing research in children's cognition by experimental psychologist Olivera Petrovich of nonnatural

causality in children and adults, indicating nature's cognitive capacities for "thinking outside the box" (Petrovich, 1997, pp. 8, 151–165). Preschoolers, in attributing the primary origin of natural kinds to God, rather than people are not inherently *artificialist* as Piaget claimed. Of great significance also has been the testing of my "empirico-cognitive" principles in clinical medicine by Peter Collett, Senior Specialist, Department of Respiratory Medicine, Liverpool Hospital, Sydney, N.S.W., Australia, and his research team. Findings from trial-runs for improving the accuracy and timeliness of diagnosis for oxygen treatment in patients with chronic obstructive pulmonary disease (COPD) and acute breathlessness, presented concurrently at the International Forum on Quality and Safety in Healthcare Paris in 2014 and the Adelaide Scientific Meeting of the Thoracic Society of Australia and New Zealand, have been positive and promising (Kashif et al., 2014). One hope is that with further testing an improved clinical support tool may ultimately be achieved for treating other serious causal conditions in emergency such as clots or sepsis, in which there are so many unknowns which can be life threatening. Examples such as these continue to confirm the efficacy of "empirico-cognitive" principles as the principles of *all* knowing for exploring *causality* in human life and our world, whatever the discipline.

The current exciting detection at CERN of the Higgs Boson and ongoing research, confirming the ever-widening horizons of our world, dubbed "Particle Fever," provide another example of the many unknowns increasingly becoming known. What might future explorations unleash?

Farrer's *new philosophy of action* in support of *divine causation* would appear to fit well with critical findings emerging in both the arts and the science faculties currently. A more advanced methodological approach, akin to that presented by Fathali Moghaddam for "omniculturalism" (Moghaddam, 2012, pp. 304–330), would seem to be the "order of the day." A multidisciplinary, critical, and inclusive enquiry that could ensure a broader, all-encompassing, and holistic understanding of human commonalities could prove most enlightening in a global world.

X. CLOSING REFLECTIONS

In what has become a scamper through the history of ideas over several centuries, I have sought to highlight exceptional endeavors to come to terms with overwhelming changes occasioned by the rise of modern science.

I am reminded of the wonderful work of Chinese brushstroke painters, whose skills I greatly admire. The brushstroke image of a tiger, advancing, is unmistakable. By analogy, we may ask whether my summary brushstrokes in defence of *divine causation* have been successful. Have my readers sensed "a live tiger" advancing?

Since Farrer's *new philosophy of action*, based on "empirico-cognitive" principles, has been able to forge a promising pathway forward for theological studies, *divine causation* remains a lively possibility. Could it be, as Farrer has argued, that, given the compatibility of *divine causation* and *evolutionary theory*, the more likely outcome of future enquiries in theology and the sciences may disclose a *God of Nature* rather than a necessary choice between *God* and *Nature?* Thereby hangs a tale!

EDITORS' COMMENTARY

In her survey of the long-running disputes between theology and the emerging sciences, Margaret Yee identifies the core issue in the claim that a divine agency brought the physical universe into being and later populated a certain part of it with organisms, plants, people, and other animals. The explanation of the existence of these two realms of being provided by the sciences is, at first sight, in flat contradiction to one another. If the organic world arose by processes of natural selection, then that world would seem to be natural and not created by a divine agent. Given that a material universe does not lend itself easily to so brusque an answer, if the material universe came to being in an instant—*nihil fit ex nihilo* ("nothing comes from nothing"), as the saying went—that could only by a divine act. Perhaps that moment is the action of a divine agent the primary being of which is not material. We could hold to agent causality for the universe and natural causality, in some form, for the organic world, once brought into being. A well-known nineteenth-century compromise was to imagine that God, or some divine agent, created a world by divine agency that would inexorably develop an organic overlay on its material substratum.

Margaret Yee's way of outflanking this impasse draws on the writings of Austin Farrer. She took from him the key idea that the differences between those who defended divine causation and naturalists of various kinds were not a matter of metaphysics but of epistemology. It seemed that there were two ways of knowing and that, when the scientific way of knowing was applied to the issue of divine causation, the result was a strong negative and divine causation could not be known. Farrer's solution was to point out, that in both ways of knowing, the imagination was involved at the very core. The history of science reveals just as deep a reliance on imagination as does the history of religious thought. In contemporary terms both disciplines rely on models rather than on direct perception. Electrons are no more perceivable than gods. Both are dependent on concepts that have developed through a pattern of metaphor and analogy that is condensed into a working model.

What causal concept is in tune with this radical shift of philosophical perceptive? In neither context does the Humean exceptionalist correlation, as the meaning of a causal claim, make sense. One of the conjuncts is missing. The powers of the gods and the powers of the electromagnetic field are not displayed in themselves but only in the consequences of their exercise. As in many disciplines, the final result of the analysis of typical discourses reveals the underlying assumption that the world of matter and the worlds of human life are both driven by the causal powers of the beings that are the unanalyzable fundamental entities of each world—fields in the world of matter and persons in the world of human cultures.

A key feature of Austin Farrer's point of view is his five principles of knowing and it is from a critical exposition of these that Margaret Yee reaches her conclusion that all knowing must be both acquired and examined in an empirico-cognitive framework. Neither empirical research nor conceptual analysis could generate sustainable knowledge on its own. If divine causation is to find support, it must be analyzed within the empirico-cognitive framework, the way that natural causation has been analyzed. This would tend to make a rapprochement between the divine and the natural more acceptable, by the criticisms of the purely empirical analysis provided by David Hume.

REFERENCES

Aquinas, Thomas, 1225–1274. (1975). *Summa contra gentiles*. Notre Dame, IN: University of Notre Dame Press.

Aquinas, Thomas, Shapcote, L., & Sullivan, D. J. 1. (1990). *The summa theologica*. Chicago: Encyclopaedia Britannica, Inc.

Brooke, Hedley J. (1991). *Science and religion*. Cambridge: University Press.

Conti, C. (1995). *Metaphysical personalism—An analysis of Austin Farrer's theistic metaphysics*. Oxford: Clarendon Press.

Copernicus, N., 1473–1543. (1965). *De revolutionibus orbium coelestium*. New York: Johnson Reprint Corp.

Cowell, A. (1992, October 31). "After 350 years, Vatican says Galileo was right: It moves," in Archives, *The New York Times*.

Crombie, A. C. (1959). *Medieval and early modern science*. Cambridge, MA: Harvard University Press, Vols. I & II, New York: Doubleday Anchor Books.

Darwin, C., & WRLC EBSCO eBooks. (2009). *On the origin of species by means of natural selection*. Waiheke Island: Floating Press.

Davis, C. F. (1989). *The evidential force of religious experience*. Oxford: Clarendon Press.

Farrer, A. M. (1948). *The glass of vision*. Westminster, London: Dacre Press.

Farrer, A. M. (1959). *Finite and infinite*. Westminster, London: Dacre Press.

Farrer, A. M. (1963). "Inspiration: Poetical and divine." IN *Promise and Fulfilment*, ed. F.F. Bruce. Edinburgh: T & T Clark.

Farrer, A. M. (1966). *A science of god?*. London: Bles.

Farrer, A. M. (1967). *Faith and speculation*. New York: New York University Press.

Harré, R., & Madden, E. H. (1975). *Causal powers: A theory of natural necessity*. Totowa, NJ: Rowman & Littlefield.

Harré, R., & Madden, E. H. (1986). *Varieties of realism: A rationale for the natural sciences*. New York; Oxford [Oxfordshire]: Blackwell.

Hesse, M. B. (1980). *Revolutions and reconstructions in the philosophy of science*. Bloomington, IN: Indiana University Press.

Kashif, N. M., Wainwright, C., Tighe, C., Harrington, Z., Taylor, B., & Collett, P. (2014). "Target O2 pathway for oxygen treatment in patients with COPD and acute breathlessness." *Respirology* 19 (Suppl. 2), 118.

Kenny, A. J. P. (1983). *Faith and reason.* New York: Columbia University Press.

Kenny, A. J. P. (2006). *What I believe.* New York; London: Continuum.

Kuhn, T. S. (1970). *The structure of scientific revolutions.* Chicago: University of Chicago Press.

Mitchell, B. (1973). *The justification of religious belief.* New York: Seabury Press.

Moghaddam, F. M. (2012). "The omnicultural imperative." *Culture & Psychology,* 18(3), 304–330. doi:10.1177/1354067X12446230

Newton, Isaac, Sir, 1642–1727. (1687). Philosophiae naturalis principia mathematica. Londini: Jussu Societatis Regiae ac typis Josephi Streater, prostat apud plures bibliopolas.

"Particle fever: The hunt for the Higgs Boson." (2014, October 15). Retrieved from http://www.bbc.co.uk/programmes/b04lcyzy

Petrovich, O. (1997). "Understanding of non-natural causality in children and adults: A case against artificialism," *Psyche en Geloof.*

Soskice, J. M. (1985). *Metaphor and religious language.* Oxford; London; New York: Clarendon Press.

Ward, K., (1938 [1996]). *Religion and creation.* Oxford; New York: Clarendon Press.

Whewell, W., 1794–1866. (1883). *History of the inductive sciences: From the earliest to the present time.* Vol. 1, London: J. W. Parker.

Yee, M. M. (1987 [1988]). "The validity of theology as academic discipline." Copyright Bodleian Library Oxford. Available: http://ora.ox.ac.uk/objects/uuid:2045ddd1-056a-4eb9-830c-cd26f51fbb00

Yee, M. M. (2009). "Divine-human action—Austin Farrer: A contrast with the classical action theories of Maurice Blondel and Edith Stein, and some contemporary thinkers." IN: Praxis. Jahrbuch der Internationalen Maurice Blondel-Forschungsstelle für Religionsphilosophie. Vol II. Klassische Handlungstheorien. Ed. Michael Gerhard, Stephan Grätzel. London, Turnshare Ltd.

Yee, M. M. (2011). "Austin Farrer's science of God" in *Philosophie, Théologie, Littérature–Hommage à Xavier Tilliette, SJ pour ses quatre-vingt-dix ans* (ed.) Miklos Vetö, Louvain-Paris: Peeters.

22

Causality and the Poetry of Witness

Duncan Wu

The poet and critic Carolyn Forché has isolated certain kinds of human experience—war, suffering, struggle—as catalysts for a genre of verse she has called "poetry of witness." Describing the difference between these works and others, she writes: "I realized that the arguments about poetry and politics had been too narrowly defined. Regardless of 'subject matter,' these poems bear the trace of extremity within them, and they are, as such, evidence of what occurred" (Forché, 1993, p. 30). I want to ask in this brief chapter what causes someone to become the author of this kind of poetry, and will begin by outlining the career of two such writers.

Eliza Hamilton Dunlop was born in 1796, a year after Keats. Academics might, as a result, be tempted to categorize her as Romantic, and it is true that her early writings betray, in etiolated form, traits of the loco-descriptive manner that characterized verse of the late eighteenth and early nineteenth centuries. But her most interesting work dates from the Victorian era, and it is untypical of other writings in several respects.

Dunlop arrived in Australia shortly before the Myall Creek Massacre, which took place on June 10, 1838, when a gang of 11 white stockmen slaughtered 28 aged men, women, and small children. This was not an isolated incident: between 1838 and 1843 it is estimated over 800 Aborigines were killed in 45 separate incidents across the three pastoral regions of Victoria. Dunlop had the option of ignoring what was going on in the rapidly expanding British colony of Australia but instead became the outraged witness to genocidal policies carried out against indigenous peoples. That outrage manifested itself first in the form of "The Aboriginal Mother," published in a newspaper, *The Australian*, with the subtitle, "From Myall's Creek," on December 14, 1838, four days before some of the murderers were executed. (This was the first and only time in Australian history Europeans were so punished for killing Aborigines.) The poem purports to record the speech of a black woman as she addresses her child whose father has been killed.

Oh hush thee, dear—for weary
And faint I bear thee on—
His name is on thy gentle lips,
My child, my child, he's gone!
Gone o'er the golden fields that lie
Beyond the rolling cloud,
To bring thy people's murder cry
Before the Christian's God.

Yes! o'er the stars that guide us,
He brings my slaughter'd boy:
To shew their God how treacherously
The stranger men destroy;
To tell how hands in friendship pledged
Piled high the fatal pire;
To tell—to tell of the gloomy ridge!
And the stockmen's human fire.

Dunlop took care with her facts, having read reports of the ensuing trial: the stockmen first slaughtered the natives with machetes then piled up the corpses and incinerated them. Her invocation of the Christian God is not designed to vindicate their cold-blooded butchery but to condemn them for having betrayed the religion into which they were born.

Dunlop put her initials, "E.H.D.," to the poem when it appeared in one of the most prominent newspapers in the colony—a brave move in 1838. The place of women in British society was still that of a subordinate species and their status was more marginal still in a male-dominated colony like Australia, where the male–female ratio was 17 to 1. Within the space of six months, the *Sydney Herald* published six separate attacks on her, alleging, inter alia, "that her only knowledge of the aboriginal natives, was acquired by reading the Last of the Mohicans." This is the only instance of which I am aware on which a newspaper devoted so much space to condemnation of a single lyric poem.

Dunlop did not allow herself to be silenced; on the contrary, she responded in kind, writing letters of protest to the newspaper concerned, while publishing more poems that articulated to a white readership the aboriginal perspective—most notably "The Aboriginal Father" and "The Eagle Chief." She also embarked on the longer-term project of preserving aboriginal culture by learning the dialects of those tribes close to her, and transliterating their lyric poems.

Dunlop's poetic career became an act of resistance to a dominant ideology—that of the genocidal interests that conspired to dispossess aborigines of the land they had inhabited for millennia, principally by means of genocide. It would have been easier for her, her husband, and her children, had she abandoned it. But she never relented. In 1848 she would publish the best known of her transliterations of aboriginal songs, beginning "Our home is the gibber-gunyah," its subject the sacredness of aboriginal land, at a moment when native Australians were being shot and poisoned by whites, and mounted police operated as extermination squads in Queensland.[1]

My second example is that of James Orr, who was born in 1770, the same year as Wordsworth. The academic response might, again, be to cast him as Romantic but, as with Dunlop, the facts expose such classifications as thin, unsound, and arbitrary. Orr was a weaver who contributed, on an occasional basis, to one of the newspapers of the United Irishmen, the *Northern Star*. When the '98 uprising came to fruition, he rounded up and led his troops to the mustering ground at Donegore Hill, from where on June 7 they intended to join the Battle of Antrim against the British army. It was not Orr's fault his contingent was too late to make any difference to the outcome (a victory for the occupying army who were already slaughtering their prisoners when Orr's men arrived at the battlefield), nor that his own troops had been deserting since leaving their homes in Ballycarry.

In the event, he and the few left on the battlefield were compelled to flee. At that point, Orr was in acute danger; having raised a force of more than 100 rebels, he was automatically counted as a fifty-pounder—that is to say, information leading to his apprehension would win an informant fifty guineas (a huge sum for the impoverished peasants among whom he lived). He fled immediately to America.

The most important of his writings is *Donegore Hill*, which describes the battle and its aftermath. It is one of the most authentic records of the uprising of the United Irishmen in 1798, with its intimate account of the rebel soldiers, their grieving wives, and the press of battle. In one of its most important sections, it describes the retreat of some of Orr's contingent when confronted by the British army.

> The camp's brak up. Owre braes an' bogs
> The patriots seek teeir sections;
> Arms, ammunition, bread-bags, brogues,
> Lye skailed in a' directions; *scattered*
> Ane half, alas, wad feared to face
> Auld fogies, faps, or women;
> Though strong, untried, they swore in pride,
> "Moilie wad dunch the yeomen,"
> Some wissed-for day.
>
> Come back, ye dastards! Can ye ought
> Expect at your returnin',

---

[1] I have dealt in greater detail with Dunlop in "'A Vehicle of Private Malice': Eliza Hamilton Dunlop and the *Sydney Herald*," *The Review of English Studies* 65 (November 2014): 888–903.

But wives an' weans stripped, cattle hought,
An' cots an' claughin's burnin'? *cottages, hamlets*
Na, haste ye hame; ye ken ye'll 'scape,
'Cause martial worth ye're clear o';
The nine-tailed cat or choakin' rape
Is maistly for some hero
On sic a day. . . .

The leuks o' wheens wha stayed behind *The faces of those who*
Were marked by monie a passion;
By dread to staun, by shame to rin, *stay, run*
By scorn an' consternation;
Wi' spite they curse, wi' grief they pray,
Now move, now pause a bit ay;
" 'Tis mad to gang, 'tis death to stay!" – *to go*
An unco dolefu' ditty *very sad refrain*
On sic a day.

The achievement of this poem is only consolidated by Orr's deft handling of Ulster-Scots dialect, and when I say the poem is "authentic," I refer to such elements as Orr's use of a phrase like "Moilie wad dunch the yeomen," which comes straight from the mouths of his comrades. A "moilie" is a hornless cow—a symbol of the impoverished peasants who supported the republican cause; "dunch" is a verb meaning "to butt." What the men who march so bravely to the battlefield are saying is that, though provided only with improvised pikes, they could defeat the better-equipped yeomanry. It takes us to the heart of the culture, as well as to the men's conflicted psyches, for their words belie the fear that will, within moments, compel them to slink away.

"'Tis mad to gang, 'tis death to stay!" These words have the rhythm and urgency of the spoken word. Something so insignificant as the verb "gang," meaning "to go," commends Orr's decision to write in the language in which he experienced the uprising, and in which he observed its unraveling from the battlefield. If it goes without saying that his use of localized dialect is an act of defiance against the colonial power to which he was opposed, it is equally true that it is a device for reconstructing the psychology of the forces of resistance. Its effectiveness is evident in both Orr's poem and that of Dunlop, and confirms what Forché says about the tendency of poems of witness, "written in conditions of extremity, [to] rely on the immediacies of direct address" (Forché, 1993, p. 33).

Both writers were changed irrevocably by the experiences I have described. In each case it can be argued that the act of bearing witness was formative of their genius. Which raises the problem of causality. What is it that makes a writer into a poet of witness? My approach is to refer to Forché's phrase, "the impress of extremity upon the poetic imagination" (Forché, 1993, p. 30), which lays emphasis on the role played by external circumstance in the shaping of the psyche. In the case of Dunlop or Orr, the remarkable things they witnessed—terrifying as they may have been—were to become inescapable elements of the poetry by which they are remembered.

That in turn raises the question of what traits or habits of mind might predispose a writer to be receptive to such things. A predisposition to resist conformity, perhaps, or at least a refusal to defer to the dominant ideology? And what, in turn, would give rise to that? A situation so obscure or marginal there is no need for fear? But that was hardly true of Dunlop, attacked repeatedly in the Australian press for portraying aborigines as human, or, indeed, of Orr, a man hunted down by the British army and its agents from the moment the 1798 uprising failed. Both had much to lose by writing as they did, yet they proceeded to write, regardless of the risk. In fact, the act of writing was in both cases an act of defiance against forces more powerful than them. In that sense the composition of poetry falls into the category of an illogical act, against the interests of either person—more than that, it had the potential to bring about their destruction. Words like "defiance" or "resistance" hardly do justice to such impulses, which take scant account of the kind of moral courage these poets displayed. It may be that the question of what causes people to behave in that manner is unanswerable.

Writers like Dunlop and Orr are, in a sense, heroes. But heroism can be hard to understand for those who stand outside the act itself; likewise, the factors that prompt an individual to emerge as a poet of witness can be obscure. Both poets emerge from what is now known as the Romantic period, and it is sometimes assumed that to have one's roots in that era comprises, in itself, an explanation as to one's identity and objectives. My argument is pitched against that assumption. If it is true that neither perceived themselves as Romantic, it is even more so that neither regarded themselves as poets. And if that is so, the conventional labels are of little use in explaining who they were and why they acted as they did. Their status as poets of witness affirms the authenticity of their response—and that, at least from a literary point of view, may be the more valuable judgment.

REFERENCES

Forché, C. (1993). *Against forgetting: Twentieth-century poetry of witness.* New York: W.W. Norton.

Orr, J. (1804, 1993). *Donegore hill.* Belfast, Ireland: Fortnight Publications.

Wu, D. (2014). "A vehicle of private malice": Eliza Hamilton Dunlop and *The Sydney Herald. Review of English Studies*, 65(272), 888–903. doi:10.1093/res/hgu034

EDITORS' COMMENTARY

Wu's discussion of the "poetry of witness" (a concept developed in Forché, 1993; Forché & Wu, 2014) intersects with at least two traditions in psychological research. The first tradition is focused on questions such as, "why do people obey and conform in conditions where their obedience and conformity results in serious and even fatal harm to others?" The second tradition explores the question, "what leads to heroism?"

Since the research of Mozafer Sherif in the 1930s, followed up by seminal studies by Solomon Asch, Serge Moscovici, Stanley Milgram, and Philippe Zimbardo, among others, psychological research has highlighted the power of context to lead to conformity and obedience (Moghaddam, 2005, chs. 15–16). The key lesson from the empirical studies has been that under certain conditions, "normal people" could conform and obey to harm others. "You would have done the same, if you had been there" is the usual response from a wide variety of defendants, from the Nazis at the Nuremberg Trials, to Lieutenant William Calley during Vietnam, to Lynndie England and other defendants at the Abu Ghraib torture trials. But a closer examination of results from psychological research shows that not everyone responds to social pressure in the same way; even in the notorious Milgram studies, about one-third of American participants refused to obey (disobedience was even higher among participants in some countries). The question becomes: what is it about some individuals that leads them to refuse to obey?

In terms of personality, we know that those who score low on measures of authoritarianism are also less conformist and obedient. More recent research on cognitive style suggests that those low on "need for closure," and high on "tolerance for ambiguity," are also less likely to conform and obey (see the discussions in Hogg & Blaylock, 2012). In contrast, those higher on "social dominance orientation" are more influenced by authority figures (Umphress, Simmons, Boswell & del Carmen Triana, 2008). In essence, the "poet of witness" is more likely to have a style of behavior that rejects authority figures and is accepting toward minorities, perceives the world as complex, with ambiguous categories and boundaries, and challenges hierarchical structures and the assumption that there is a "natural" order justifying inequalities.

But the two cases discussed by Wu involve heroism, and the question "What leads to heroism?" has received less attention from psychologists. One line of research suggests that the environmental context is the key determinant. Just as, under certain conditions, most people can "do evil," under certain other conditions most people can act in a heroic manner (Zimbardo, Breckenridge, & Moghaddam, 2013). Of course, to become a hero as a "poet of witness," one has first to actually or potentially be a poet.

REFERENCES

Forché, C., & Wu, D. (Eds.) (2014). *Poetry of witness: The tradition in English 1500–2001*. New York: W.W. Norton.

Forché, C. (ed.) (1993). *Against forgetting: Twentieth century poetry of witness*. New York: W. W. Norton.

Hogg, M. A., & Blaylock, D. L. (eds.) (2012). *Extremism and the psychology of uncertainty*. Oxford: Wiley-Blackwell.

Moghaddam, F. M. (2005). *Great ideas in psychology*. Oxford: Oneworld.

Umphress, E. E., Simmons, A. L., Boswell, W. R., & del Carmen Triana, M. (2008). "Managing discrimination in selection: The influence of directives from an authority and social dominance orientation." *Journal of Applied Psychology*, 93, 982–993.

Zimbardo, P. G., Breckenridge, J. N., & Moghaddam, F. M. (2013). "Exclusive" and "inclusive" visions of heroism and democracy. *Current Psychology*, 32, 221–233.

Epilogue

Rom Harré and Fathali M. Moghaddam

Where, how and when could this young countess, who had had a French émigrée for governess, have imbibed from the Russian air she breathed the spirit of that dance? . . . But the spirit and the movement were . . . inimitable, unteachable, Russian . . . Her performance was so perfect, so absolutely perfect, that Anisya Fiodorovna, who had at once handed her the kerchief she needed for the dance, had tears in her eyes, though she laughed as she watched the slender, graceful countess, reared in silks and velvets, in another world than hers, who was yet able to understand all that was in Anisya and in Anisya's father and mother and aunt, and in every Russian man and woman.
                                                                —Tolstoy[1]

In one of the most memorable scenes in *War and Peace*, Tolstoy's (1957) timeless novel, the young countess Natasha is with a hunting party in the Russian countryside. Food and drinks are served, music is played, and the young countess gets an opportunity to dance in a traditional Russian style, more in keeping with the Russian peasants serving them than with the French-speaking aristocracy she had grown up with. Somehow, the young countess is able to perform the traditional Russian dance perfectly, as if all the French culture and aristocratic training she had received was not powerful enough to prevent the Russian soil and Russian air to soak into her and shape her movements. If we wanted to discover the "cause" of Natasha's ability to dance in a distinctly Russian style, where would we begin? Would we have to start with her teenage years, or with her first dance lessons, or with her early childhood, or perhaps her birth? Clearly, whatever choices we made, we would be selecting a particular period of time and a particular set of factors as the source of causes. In the real world, identifying causes necessarily involves selecting a particular time period to look at and, within that time period, selecting a particular set of factors to examine from a far larger potential set of factors.

---

[1] *War and Peace*, 1957/1865–1868, vol. 1, p. 604.

The specialized fields of study represented in this volume adopt different ways of achieving this narrowing down and different accounts of causation within each narrow field of study.

In the preceding 22 chapters our collaborators have offered a variety of discourse modes and highlighted the concepts of causality that have been salient in their different specialized areas of study. In our commentaries we have extracted the core of their illustrations and the kind of causality that has become an integral part of the conceptual resources in such widely diverse studies as theology, law, psychology, epidemiology, and psychiatry. Furthermore, the kinds of causal concepts have been equally diverse.

Philosophical analysts, beginning with Aristotle, have brought to light two main causal notions. Popular since the eighteenth century has been the pattern of exceptionless concomitances—with various devices and ad hoc measures to distinguish causation proper from mere coincidence. The root metaphysics has been built around the concept of "event." On the contrary, since the time of Aristotle and popular in the twenty-first century is the idea of causation as the workings of agents—active beings that bring about the changes those causal concepts have always been introduced to make sense of. These two seemingly irreconcilable concepts of causation are linked through the suggestion that exceptionless regularities are the result of the workings of causal mechanisms, or productive systems that survive the changes in the universe that we put in order as causes and their effects. We have learned to make sense of probabilistic causation as patterns of events in which, however precisely the situation is set up, the same mechanism with the same type of triggering event does not lead inexorably to a fully determined outcome but to a probabilistic distribution of possible outcomes. We have learned how to disentangle multiple causes for a single outcome and to partition causes among a variety of events.

With all this in mind let us look at two very widely found causal discourses—the causes of historical events, such as wars, depressions, and election outcomes, and the causes of the production and style of works of art. In each field there exists a vast literature in which proposals are made and critically examined.

The Great Depression of 1929–1934 has been the subject of numerous analyses and hypotheses as to what brought it about. However, before we can look at the proposals for a causal story, it is necessary to set out some of the components of "the depression" as social and economic *processes*. The collapse of a bank that occurred in a matter of days is more event-like, but the decline of the money supply that is often cited as a feature of the conditions that led to the loss of jobs, and the decline of industrial production and so on, both would have taken place over a matter of years. Given the complexity of the phenomenon, it is not surprising that there should be several contenders for acceptance as "the prime cause" of the phenomenon. Setting aside the absence of wisdom among certain key leaders, such as President Hoover, two claims to have identified the cause of the great depression have been prominent. One proposal, by John Maynard Keynes (1935), suggests that the phenomena that make up the "great depression" were "demand driven"; that is to say, the demand for goods and services declined catastrophically and this led to a loss of jobs, a failure of banks, and so on. The other proposal, by Milton Friedman (1962), identified the driving force of the decline in economic activity in "monetarist" terms. The decline in the money supply led to all the consequential events and processes that constituted the Great Depression.

Schematizing the two proposals, we have a failure of demand, which seems to be, at least partly, a psychological phenomenon, linked to such matters as lack of confidence, saving when you should be spending. On the other hand, we have a shortage of money, which seems to be a "material" feature of the economic system of the time that exists, or appears to exist, independently of the psychological states of the actors.

Turning to our categories of causality, this seems to be similar to the case of the two bullets and the one glass bottle. Either could have broken it but they arrived simultaneously. We cannot say both broke it or that neither broke it. Turning to the moral question, it seems that the ballistics facts drop out, and depending on the rest of the story, we could have each or both responsible for the shattering of the glass, without encountering any paradox.

In the case of the Great Depression, the formula "this rather than that" can be applied if the matter is the assignment of responsibility. Printing money rather than maintaining the stability of prices is something that follows on from someone or some committee making a decision and implementing it. The "demand" story deals in more recondite and ephemeral psychological phenomenon such as "confidence" but with an expanded semantics that takes in a large number of people.

The study of the "Causes of World War I" is on a similarly complex and almost heroic scale (Hewitson, 2014). Bibliographies offer more works with titles that include the word "origins" rather than "causes," but the content is much the same. The assassination of an Archduke in a small city remote from the centers of power, decisions of individual royal rulers, prime ministers, and other small-scale events in contrast to the massing of vast armies and revolutionary movements like the collapse of the Russian Empire are, scale-wise, incommensurable. In the backgrounds there are predisposing conditions, necessary but not sufficient to "cause" a war in any of the senses we covered in the introductory chapters. The rivalry of empires, realized in the attitudes of their rulers, particularly Kaiser Wilhelm and Franz-Joseph of Austro-Hungary, can form part of the long-standing but stable background conditions to local political and military activities. Germany is an emerging and aggressive power, and its citizens, severally and collectively, are full of confidence. Austro-Hungary, the main German ally, is a conglomerate of many, mostly discontented Magyar and Slav states. Britain, France, and Russia make up the alliance opposing the expansionist plans of the Germans. Applying our analytical eye to the situation, we see an initial state of affairs that is a complicated array of many changing and loosely linked phenomena at various levels of abstraction from the lives and thoughts of individual people to something intangible, but nonetheless real, such as the zeitgeist of nations. Like the Great Depression that seemed expressed as a pattern of discrete events but was actually a process lasting several years and the events of World War I, which can be understood as abstractions from a seamless flow of patterns of change in many dimensions. The war involved a transformation and translocation of populations, economic processes of depression and inflation, changes in the boundaries and possessions of empires, and changes in the very mode of government in Germany, Austro-Hungary, and Russia. From stability Europe modulated into chaos and disorder. As Hewitson (2014, p. 1) puts it,

> The question of the war's causes remains a perplexing mixture of consensus, ignorance and contestation. Even the notion that the war could have specific and definable causes or antecedent actions which bright it about, is a matter of dispute. We must take into account the force of arguments of inadvertence. Although protagonists concealed or did not understand their own motives, their actions had … unintended consequences produced by particular sets of circumstances.

In both examples, attempting to describe these processes in the language of cause and effect requires a careful delineation of what "cause" and "effect" are going to mean at these much-expanded scales of action and the myriad of causal sequences on the modest scale that appears in the philosophical literature. The model of the bullet and glass bottle is almost beside the point. Though there was a trigger "event" in both of these cases, the collapse of a bank and the assassination of Archduke Ferdinand by Princip may have played a role in the latter. The procession of cars in the royal visit to Sarajevo was diverted in such a way that Princip, who was waiting at the "wrong" place, had the opportunity to kill the Archduke. This diversion, with respect to all else that went on that day, is a matter of luck or fate. In the language of the general survey in the first three chapters, we have here a case of "but for"—but for the diversion the Archduke, he would have survived. It makes no sense to pick out the diversion as the cause of World War I though it is plainly in hindsight a necessary condition without which the great conflagration might never have occurred. Why not? It is not an agency. But an assassination is not going to disturb the peace of a populous continent unless there exist conditions that give the event (e.g., the bullet and bottle paradox) its power to bring about vast changes on a very different scale in space and time and with very different long-term consequences.

Turning to the distinction between necessary and sufficient conditions, it is important to make clear the context in which causes might be sought. Identifying the simple causal conditions to juxtapose to the subsequent event occurrence may prove too schematic, in that there are a myriad of interacting and predisposing standing conditions, ephemeral events, changes in background material, and social parameters to take into account. Using the phrase "the causes of WWI" can only be an invitation to catalog a vast array of conditions and a multitude of triggering events that, taken together, lead to the conflict, which is itself a complex pattern of phenomena of many different kinds juxtaposing the state of the world at one time against the state of the world at a subsequent time in a local arena. The phrase is a metaphor that invites us to consider the necessary conditions for grand processes and changes to occur and continue to unfold.

REFERENCES

Friedman, M. (1962). *Capitalism and Freedom*. Chicago: Chicago University Press.

Hewitson, M. (2014). *Germany and the Causes of World War 1*. Oxford: Berg.

Hewitson, M. (2014). *History and Causality*. New York: Palgrave Macmillan.

Keynes, J. M. (1935). *The General Theory of Employment, Interest and Money*. Cambridge: Cambridge University Press.

Tolstoy, L. (1957). *War and Peace* (Vols. 1–2; R. Edmonds, Trans.) Harmondsworth, England: Penguin. (Original work published 1865–1868).

Name Index

Wilson, W., 165
Winston, A. S., 62
Winter, N., 107
Wittgenstein, L., 5, 27, 39,
  42, 43, 46
Wolskee, P., 191
Wolters, G., xi
Woodhouse, T., 260, 266
Woodward, S. L., 259, 265
Woodworth, K., 107
Woolley, A. W., 305
Wright, R. W., 318n8, 327–329
Wright, S. C., 280, 287
Wu, D., 387
Wu, S., 308, 309
Wu, T., 344

Wundt, W., 84–85, 99
Wynia, M., 308, 309

Yaffe, K., 224
Yee, M. M., 367, 368, 370, 375, 378,
  380–381
Yelle, M., 291

Zaal, M. P., 280–281
Zald, M. N., 279
Zanger, A., 190
Zarit, S. H., 227
Zartman, W., 262
Zhou, Y., 288
Zimbardo, P. G., 388
Zubieta, J. K., 197, 198

Subject Index

acetylcholine, 222
acquired immunity deficit syndrome
  (AIDS), 9–10
ACT, 305
active placebo, 72
actual causation: criticisms of the but-for
  test for, 327–30
actual cause, 318–27. *See also* causation
  in fact
adult day care centers, 224
*Advancing Scientific Research in
  Education*, 108–9
affordances, 8–9
agentive causality, 43–44
agents: causes as, 5–7; humans as,
  288–89; within the self,
  289–90
aimless wandering, 226, 229–30
Alcoholics Anonymous, 215
alcoholism, 214–15
Alzheimer's disease (AD), 221; adult
  day care centers, 224; aimless
  wandering, 226, 229–30; case
  examples, 224–26, 228–30; in the
  context of long-term care, 226–27;
  delusions and irrational hostility,
  224–26, 228–30; fundamental attribution error, 222; social consequences
  of the fundamental attribution error,
  230–31; understanding "behavioral

problems" through a biomedical lens,
  223–24
American Dental Association, 71
American psychology, 53
analogy: and multifactorial disease, 181
analysis of variance (ANOVA), 83, 97–98
antecedents, 14–16; conjunctive causes
  and singular effects, 15; disjunctive
  causes and singular effects, 15–16;
  singular causes and conjunctive
  effects, 14; singular causes and
  disjunctive effects, 15
anthropological transparencies, 162
Apple, 354–55
appropriation: illicit, 352; simple, 352;
  subverted, 352
Aricept, 222
Aristotelian causality, 281–83
Aristotelian Natural Philosophy, 373
Aristotelian origins, of explanation,
  35–38; efficient cause, 35, 36; final
  cause, 35, 36; material cause, 35, 36.
  See also explanation
"Aristotle on Causality," 37
"Aristotle on Explanatory Discourse
  Formats," 37
attributes: conditionalized, 44–46;
  powers as, 46–47
attribution theory, 67
autism, 206

About the Editors and Contributors

EDITORS

ROM HARRÉ studied chemical engineering and mathematics. His graduate studies at Oxford were under the supervision of J. L. Austin, leading to an interest in the role of language in thought and action. For many years, he was university lecturer in the Philosophy of Science at Oxford, and he is currently Distinguished Research Professor at Georgetown University in Washington, D.C. He has recently been the director of the Centre for Natural and Social Science at the LSE. He continues his interest in chemistry as the president of the International Society for Philosophy of Chemistry.

FATHALI M. MOGHADDAM is a professor of psychology and director of the Interdisciplinary Program in Cognitive Science, Georgetown University. He serves as the editor of *Peace and Conflict: Journal of Peace Psychology* (published by the American Psychological Association). His most recent books are *The Psychology of Dictatorship* (2013) and *The Psychology of Democracy* (2016). Prior to joining Georgetown University, he worked at McGill University and the United Nations. His website: fathalimoghaddam.com

CONTRIBUTORS

CATHERINE E. AMIOT (PhD, Ottawa, 2004) is an associate professor at the Department of Psychology of Université du Québec à Montréal. She researches identities and the self-concept, how norms are internalized and self-determination, and human-animal relations.

JAMES T. BEDNAR is an assistant professor in the Department of Philosophy at Wofford College. Dr. Bednar received his BA from Hanover College and his PhD from Vanderbilt University. He specializes in epistemology and has abiding interests in American pragmatism, modern philosophy, and decision theory.

His current research examines the role of emotions (e.g., fear and hope) and pragmatic factors (e.g., the cost of information) in the conduct of inquiry.

LEDA M. BLACKWOOD (PhD, University of Queensland, 2007) is a lecturer in the School of Psychology at the University of Bath, UK. Her research examines inter- and intragroup processes of social inclusion and exclusion, politicization, leadership, and social movement participation.

ALISSA BLAIR is a postdoctoral researcher at the Wisconsin Center for Education Research at the University of Wisconsin-Madison. She holds a PhD in curriculum and instruction from the University of Wisconsin-Madison with a specialization in English as a second language and bilingual education. Her research focuses on the language and literacy engagement of emergent bilinguals in and out of school, including language development in academic contexts.

JENS BROCKMEIER, a professor at the American University of Paris, has a background in philosophy, psychology, and language studies. His interests are in issues of human identity, mind, and language, which he has examined in a variety of cultural contexts.

WILLIAM C. BRYSON is a judge on the U.S. Court of Appeals for the Federal Circuit, which sits in Washington, D.C. He has served on that court for more than 20 years. Prior to his appointment to the court, he served as the deputy solicitor general of the United States.

KELLY COMOLLI graduated with honors in psychology from Georgetown University and is completing her medical training.

KATE DE MEDEIROS is an associate professor of gerontology at Miami University, Oxford, Ohio. Her research interests include narrative constructions of self in older age, friendships in later life, and the cultural arts in dementia care. Her work has been funded by the National Institutes of Health, the Alzheimer's Association, and the Brookdale Foundation.

RAVEN DUNSTAN studies psychology at Georgetown University. Her research focuses on psychology and justice.

ADRIAN FURNHAM was educated at the London School of Economics, where he obtained a distinction in an MSc Econ., and at Oxford University, where he completed a doctorate (DPhil) in 1981. Previously a lecturer in psychology at Pembroke College, Oxford, he has been a professor of psychology at University College London since 1992.

JACQUIE L. GREIFF is a PhD student in Education Culture and Society at the University of Pennsylvania's Graduate and has held a number of School of Education, and co-director of f-r-e-e, USA (friendship-respect-enrichment-engagement), an international NGO working on community building in central Bosnia-Herzegovina.

TOBIAS GREIFF is a professorial lecturer for international affairs at the Elliott School of International Affairs (The George Washington University), instructor for peace and conflict resolution at the School of Professional & Extended Studies (American University, Washington, D.C.), and a visiting research fellow at the University of Pennsylvania's Political Science Department.

SIR JOHN GRIMLEY EVANS has held a number of distinguished academic positions, including the chair of clinical geratology at Oxford University. He was a founder of the *European Academy of Medicine of Ageing* and editor of *Age and Ageing*.

STEPHEN T. LA MACCHIA is a PhD candidate at the University of Queensland. He researches group processes including how people interact with groups of different size, the social signals sent by claiming minority and majority friendships, and leadership contests.

JAMES T. LAMIELL is a professor of psychology at Georgetown University in Washington, D.C., where he has been a member of the faculty since 1982. He has spent three academic terms as Fulbright scholar at the University of Heidelberg (1990), the University of Leipzig (1998), and the University of Hamburg (2004). In Hamburg, Lamiell was Ernst Cassirer Guest Professor in the Institute for Philosophy.

NAOMI LEE, PhD, is an associate researcher at the Wisconsin Center for Education Research at the University of Wisconsin-Madison. Her research has focused on improving the classroom engagement and academic achievement of English Language Learners in U.S. school contexts. She holds a doctorate in psychology from Georgetown University.

DR. JOHN C. LEFEBVRE is a professor and the chair of the Department of Psychology at Wofford College. He received his BA from McGill University and his PhD from Duke University in clinical psychology. Dr. Lefebvre's research interests focus on the experience of pain in humans, especially the effects of worry on pain and the ability to recall painful experiences.

DAVID W. LIGHTFOOT is a linguist focusing on parameters of language variation. Those parameters define possible variations between languages and the parameters children set in their first few years as they acquire their native linguistic competence. Sometimes children set parameters differently from the way that earlier members of the same speech community did and that enables us to understand language change in new ways.

WINNIFRED R. LOUIS (PhD, McGill, 2001) is an associate professor in the School of Psychology at the University of Queensland. Her research interests focus on the influence of identity and norms on social decision-making.

KENNETH I. MAVOR (PhD, University of Queensland, 2004) is a lecturer in the School of Psychology and Neuroscience at the University of St. Andrews, UK. His research interests revolve around the fluid and complex nature of our personal and social self-categories and identities.

PETER MÜHLHÄUSLER received his university education at Stellenbosch, Reading, UK, and the Australian National University. He lectured at the Technical University of Berlin and at the University of Oxford before becoming Foundation Professor of Linguistics at Adelaide, Emeritus Professor of Linguistics at the University of Adelaide (Australia), and Supernumerary Fellow of Linacre College, Oxford. He is the manager of the Mobile Language Team of the University of Adelaide, an innovative approach to looking after the 40+ endangered Aboriginal languages of South Australia. He has also been actively involved with the revival of the Norf'k language (Norfolk Island—South Pacific) for the last 20 years.

RODRIGO NIETO-GÓMEZ is a research professor at the Center for Homeland Defense and Security (CHDS) and the National Security Affairs (NSA) Department of the Naval Postgraduate School in Monterey, California. His research takes place at the intersection of the accelerating pace of innovation and security, safety and defense policies. In particular, he studies how governments can improve their strategies to respond to the deviant innovation capacities of criminal organizations. He is a Mexican lawyer and holds a master and a PhD from the French Institute of Geopolitics of the University of Paris.

DR. SUDHA G. RAJPUT lives in the Washington, D.C., area and is an adjunct faculty at the School for Conflict Analysis and Resolution, George Mason University. Pursuant to her research in Kashmir, she has developed and teaches a graduate course on Refugee and IDP Issues, focusing on policy framework. Her 31-year career at the World Bank touched on many aspects of international development. Sudha's blog on internal displacement can be found at www. internaldisplacement.info where she tracks and analyzes global issues. Sudha is passionate about international development and enjoys teaching and bringing innovation to traditional pedagogy. Dr. Rajput can be reached at srajput2@ gmu.edu

DANIEL ROTHBART is a professor of conflict analysis and resolution at the School for Conflict Analysis and Resolution, George Mason University. He has published extensively on the topics of identity-based conflicts, ethics and conflict, conflict theory and philosophy, and civilians in war.

STEVEN R. SABAT is a professor of psychology at Georgetown University in Washington, D.C. His interests include the intact social and cognitive abilities of people with Alzheimer's disease in the moderate-to-severe stages as revealed in natural, everyday life settings. He is the author of *The Experience of Alzheimer's Disease: Life through a Tangled Veil* and co-editor of *Dementia: Mind, Meaning, and the Person*.

ALEXANDER K. SAERI is a PhD candidate at the University of Queensland. He researches group inequality and collective action, and in particular how people react to such inequality or conflict when they are structurally and psychologically separate, as bystanders.

PAUL STEINBERG is a psychiatrist in Washington, D.C., the former director of the Georgetown University Counseling and Psychiatric Service. His specializations include adolescent and young adult psychiatry and sports psychiatry. He is the author of the recently released creative nonfiction memoir *A Salamander's Tale: My Story of Regeneration—Surviving 30 Years with Prostate Cancer* (Skyhorse Publishing).

EMMA F. THOMAS (PhD, Australian National University, 2009) is an Australian Research Council research fellow and senior lecturer within the School of Psychology at Murdoch University. She researches how people come together to resist social inequality and injustice.

DUNCAN WU is a professor of English at Georgetown University. He previously held academic positions at the universities of Oxford and Glasgow. He is the author of a seminal study on William Hazlitt (2008) and co-editor, with the poet Carolyn Forché, of *Poetry of Witness: The Tradition in English, 1500–2000* (2013).

DR. MARGARET M. YEE is a senior research fellow at St. Cross College, University of Oxford, UK. She has been a member of the Faculty of Theology. Her main academic interests have been concerned with the *Principles of Knowing: Science, Humanities and Theology*.

Lightning Source UK Ltd.
Milton Keynes UK
UKOW06n2200220216

268909UK00010B/179/P

9 781440 831782